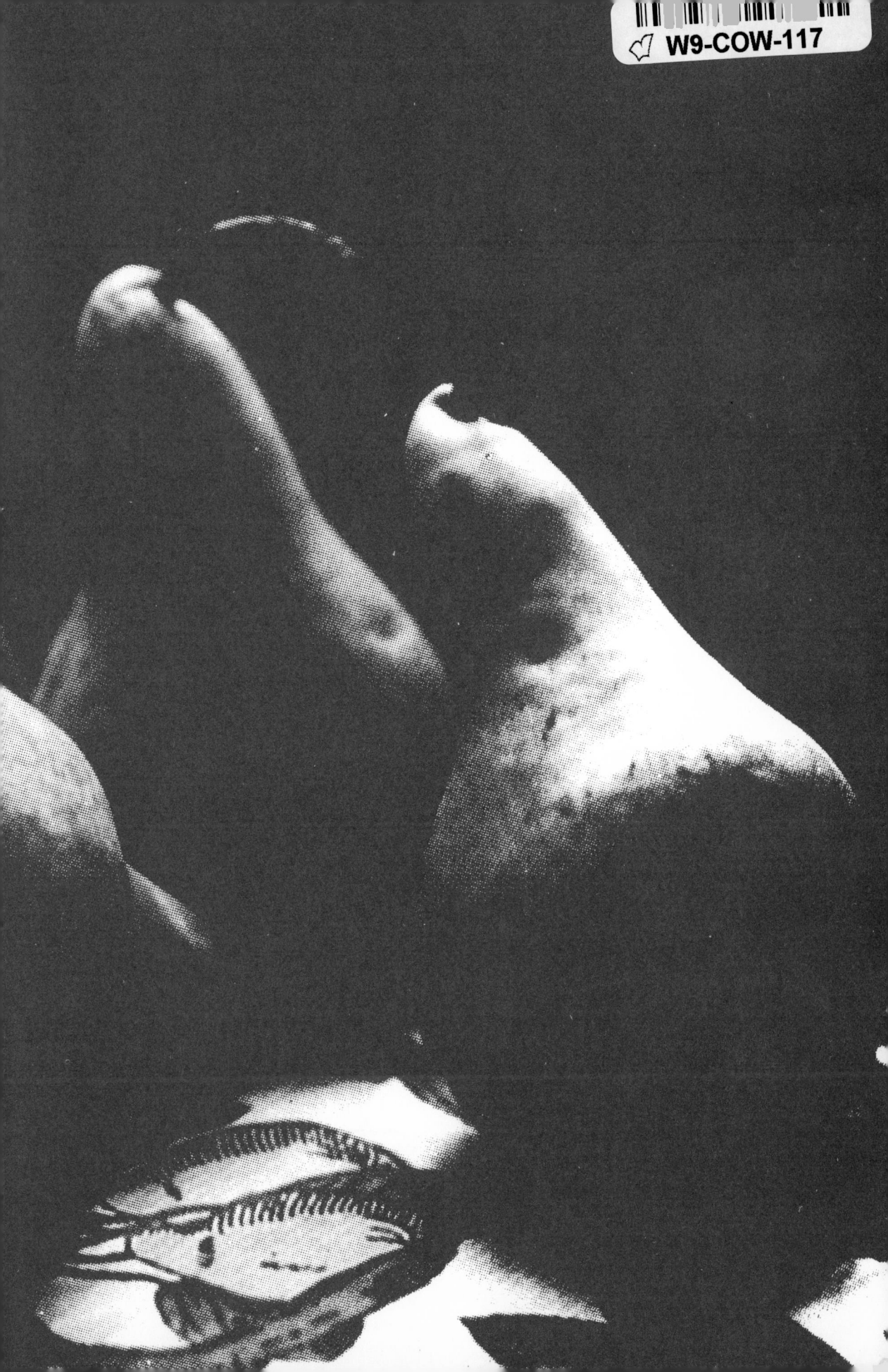

# FRUIT
## FOR THE HOME AND GARDEN

Leslie Johns & Violet Stevenson

Illustrated by Marianne Yamaguchi

**ANGUS & ROBERTSON PUBLISHERS**

*ANGUS & ROBERTSON PUBLISHERS*

*Unit 4, Eden Park, 31 Waterloo Road,*
*North Ryde, NSW, Australia 2113*
*and*
*16 Golden Square, London W1R 4BN, United Kingdom*

*First published as* The Complete Book of Fruit
*by Angus & Robertson Publishers in 1979*
*This edition 1985*

*Copyright © Leslie Johns and Violet Stevenson 1979*

*National Library of Australia*
*Cataloguing-in-publication data.*

*Johns, Leslie.*
  *Fruit for the home and garden.*

  *Previously published as: The complete book of fruit.*
  *Sydney: Angus & Robertson, 1979.*
  *ISBN 0 207 15068 0.*

  *1. Fruit-culture. 2. Cookery (Fruit). 3. Fruit —*
  *Preservation — Amateurs' manuals. I. Stevenson, Violet.*
  *II. Yamaguchi, Marianne. III. Johns, Leslie. The complete*
  *book of fruit. IV. Title. V. Title: The complete book*
  *of fruit.*

*634*

*Typeset in 10pt Plantin*
*Printed in Hong Kong*

# CONTENTS

# Fruit for the Home and Garden

# Index

# INTRODUCTION

Anyone who wishes to do so can grow some kind of fruit. You don't have to have a large garden – in fact it isn't necessary to have a garden at all, for there are many fruits that can be grown in pots and some can be grown indoors. Even the very special fruits – peaches, figs and vines for instance – can be grown in a very small area so long as their roots are properly nurtured. You don't have to live in the heart of the country, either. There are a few streets in the centre of London where you can stand and admire grape vines, often rising from a few bare inches of earth on some lower, heavily paved 'area', up to the second floor or beyond. In summer the vines clothe the bare walls with a thick mantle of green leaves, often framing windows which otherwise look out only on to buildings on the other side of the street and traffic rushing by below. On some evenings, when summer is on the way, you can catch the special perfume of vine blossom. Come the autumn and you can be sure of seeing in some newspaper a photograph of the grape pickers, the proud vintners, and you may be informed of how many litres of wine and kilos of grape jelly or fresh table fruit the town-trapped plant has yielded.

Such urban harvests are not rare, neither are they confined to one country, nor to one kind of fruit. We have driven through Rome and halted inside the maelstrom of hooting and press of manic drivers to enthuse over some stately little persimmon tree almost pressed against a stuccoed town villa, tight inside the railings, the plant bare but for the cherry orange fruits hanging from its branches, waiting for the proper ripening. In little towns in France we have very often admired the way a house wall will be commandeered to give tenancy to a pear, plum, apricot or cherry. In Switzerland, in Basle, we learned how Morello cherries, blossoming on fan-trained branches along the garage wall, could add many square metres to the productive area of a tiny garden. In another city in the same country, and right near the railway line, we walked under an alley of apple and pear trees which had been trained up and over the path leading from the gate to the back door. Almost everywhere around the Mediterranean it seems in retrospect that we have admired the contrasting colours of orange and yellow citrus fruits seen against the blue, blue sky. We have lusted after ripe figs seen through garden gates.

We have wondered how the owners prepared the Indian figs, growing on the giant prickly pears. At the foot of many an old town wall we have stopped to look up at the apricots topping the ancient stones, golden against the light. We have wondered at pomegranates in bloom and fruit at the same time, clothing an arch over a busy road by Orange in Provence. In Albany in Western Australia we have stopped to ask the house owner about her loquat tree loaded with golden fruit and have come away, of course, bearing a little more knowledge and a bag of fruit. In Perth we have envied the owner of a little house who boasted a lemon on one side and an olive on the other, and we've given up counting the number of gardens in which grew all kinds of citrus trees as we passed through town after town. In the Balmain district of Sydney we've delighted in the papaw plant by one doorway and the ribbon-leaved banana trees just down the road from it, shading the windows in the front of the houses, often a few metres from the pavement. We've smelled the passion fruit which grew unasked through the mixed hedge of a friend's garden in another district and applauded the way another friend was clothing an old tree stump with the same fruit vine. We've sampled the peaches growing in a most abandoned manner outside the kitchen window in a busy district. We've reached up for mangoes hanging just above a garden fence in Brisbane. In Ontario we've seen fruit we never thought would survive the snowy winters, and admired a relative's store of grape, peach, apricot, quince and cherry preserves. In America we seem to have seen the lot in one backyard or another and remember most vividly native blueberries, quinces, strawberries and blackberries in Philadelphia and a pineapple in a New York apartment. We've picked up mulberries from the tiny lawn in a Welsh town garden, and sampled cherries in a densely populated area on the fringe of an industrial northern English city. We've tasted alpine strawberries grown in earthenware crocus pots on a tiny patio. And we could go on for ever, but we have proved, we hope, that fruits are not exclusive to farms, plantations and orchards, nor to outsize gardens. We hope also that we have indicated that fruit can be grown in urban and suburban gardens, for this is a main purpose of this book.

There are many people, we know, who would like to grow some special fruit and wonder not only how to set about it but also if it is possible in the first place. Often this is a fruit not commonly seen in the shops, or it may be one which is usually expensive to buy. Sometimes, we suspect, it is to help allay homesickness; there is a longing for some fruit rare in one country but common 'at home'. Most often, though, the fruit is quite rightly seen as an advantage, a means of easing catering problems, boosting the budget and simultaneously being able to enjoy the delicious succulence of freshly picked fruit.

It may help such people to know that many fruits are very easy to grow and that there is a special satisfaction in so doing. Nothing else seems to give quite the same pleasure to the gardener and the whole family alike. Often this pleasure spreads to influence relatives and friends as well. How many times a visit begins or is brought to a happy conclusion with a gift of fresh fruit, perhaps 'the biggest strawberries you've ever seen' or the most delicately flavoured raspberries, the juiciest plums, the sweetest pears, the crispest apples – there appears to exist a definite element of competition in this particular branch of gardening. Or perhaps the gift comes in more compact form – some delicious preserve, a sweetmeat, cake, loaf, ice-cream, usually something impossible to buy in the average store. We cherish the story our neighbour tells us of her apple tree, or rather the fruit from it. The tree grows elsewhere in the village and when its owner died she left instructions in her will that each year the fruit from her special tree should be carried up the hill to her old friend, our neighbour, with whom she had so often shared it in the past. After many years the gift continues to arrive and is much appreciated and enjoyed.

One of the most delightful things is that all this pleasure and profit can be gained from something as simple as one tree, one climber, one row of neat plants or a cluster of bushes. Quite often one is enough. Sometimes space alone demands that this should be so. Not everyone wishes to burden himself with crops of unmanageable proportions. But if space is so tight, why not just one kind of fruit? In today's world every little helps to ease the demand on the world's larder. One kind of fruit can become a yearly treat, even if it is no more than a Morello cherry on the side of the garage. Beyond that, of course, growing more than one kind of fruit means that one's catering

problems are considerably eased, especially if one can spread the produce over most of the months of the year. Large crops need not be a problem. In any urban or suburban area there are ways and means of dealing with them. On occasions when the harvest means dealing with a bumper crop, there are always willing hands ready to help. Gathering fruit appeals more than other gardening chores. Those who might not wish to weed or dig will often willingly stoop to gather strawberries or climb ladders for plums, even help strip blackcurrants or halve peaches for processing. We would urge anyone who can to make room for fruit in the garden, or – should ground space be limited or already occupied – to think of furnishing the walls of the house and other buildings, thereby extending his domain, his interests and his profit. Fruiting plants do not necessarily have to fit into formal rows in a kitchen garden. Those planning new gardens are advised to stay their hands until fruit trees and other plants have been considered. You might as well have an attractive fruiting tree on the lawn or to shade the patio as a flowering shrub that will give you no fruit. The first will look better than the second at harvest time. A family fruit tree on which several varieties are grafted is ideal for the little plot and the small household. You might be better served with a path edging or bed border of alpine strawberries than of some low-growing annual. The first is just as pretty in its own way and you can gather the little fruits for months. You might just as well have a screen of raspberries, blackberries or any of their kind as, say, an unproductive privet or olearia. If you want a few shrubs dotted about, you might as well have a feijoa, a kumquat or a neat orange as anything else, for they are every bit as decorative. If you want a spectacular tree why not grow an elderberry? If you are in a hot climate and looking for shade, why not a mango or a carob? If you have a pathway, why leave the space above it unoccupied? Why not arch it over? So many fruit trees can be trained to go up and over and pruned to remain compact and productive. There are climbers for this purpose also, enough to suit most countries. There is no need for any gardener to be without fruit, and having planted it, there is no cause for him to have anything other than an attractive and interesting garden.

Having grown the fruit, there comes the joy of tasting. Most fruits, fortunately we think, can be eaten raw. Others improve with cooking. Some need another substance to enhance their flavours. Some can be cooked or otherwise processed when they are unripe, a good way of spreading a crop. Some fruits are much richer than others in certain vitamins and minerals and their content may influence those who are making a choice of fruits to grow. Those with few fruits of a special kind may never need to do other than eat them raw, but we believe that those same people will not confine themselves to that fruit alone, but will buy or be given others about which they may wish to know more.

Our advice on growing, therefore, has been complemented by information on the content and on the culinary qualities of the fruits. The recipes have been selected to give as wide a range as possible. Often what serves for one fruit can be used to process a similar kind, peach for apricot and nectarine for plum for example. We hope that these are sufficient, varied and interesting enough to engage the attention of those who shop for particular fruits as well as for those who grow them.

Some of the fruits we have listed are not tremendously important economically, but they do grow in gardens and are the products of familiar plants, shrubs and sometimes trees, and we feel that the gardener might as well use them as let them go to waste. Some of these are included as the result of many letters we have received over the years from worried people who feared the fruits might be poisonous. For this reason some fruits have been included for reassurance as much as anything else.

There must be many fruits grown in certain localities which are not mentioned here but which readers might think would prove ideal for urban and suburban gardens in other localities or countries. While we have included a number of what might be termed 'local' fruits (about which more later), we do feel that others will have to wait until more is known about how they will respond to cultivation. In many cases no research at all has been carried out. On the other hand there are some interesting things going ahead, such as the quandong, the Australian native peach, *Santalum acuminatum*. Since this fruit is now at about the stage of the original crab apple, it is hoped that the day will come when there are cultivars from which we can pick fruit like peaches, rather than the thin-fleshed, large-seeded fruits of today, even though these do make delicious jellies and pies. The flavour of the species certainly justifies the proposed work on the plant.

In order to make this book as useful as possible we have travelled widely and spoken to a great number of scientists and fruit growers. We have consulted books, pamphlets and learned papers seeking answers to our questions and in order to benefit from the latest research and developments. We collected vast amounts of information, much of it applicable only to local conditions. We have had to generalise the particular, to give advice that can be followed by the home gardener in any part of the world. Some of our sources were contradictory: one expert or scientist would say one thing and another would say the opposite; one book would give one spelling of a name and another reference would disagree. We have tried to sort out these anomalies, and where one book has blindly followed the errors in a previous publication we have corrected the mistake at the risk of being thought pedantic ourselves. Where there has been a need for a single, definitive authority, we have accepted that of the Royal Horticultural Society and used their definition, their spelling or their advice.

In certain countries, localities or climates we have found that some fruits grow so easily, so well and above all so quickly, that two things happened. First, these fruits have largely lost their value. Why, ask residents, spend time and effort on special cultivation when without any effort we can get average fruits? And secondly, because of this attitude there have appeared pests and disease attacks so devastating and potentially dangerous that special legislation has had to be enacted to control them and the import of certain fruits over local or state boundaries has had to be prohibited. But this happens only in certain parts of the world, and any plant of more than local danger we have omitted from our list.

Each fruit mentioned in this book is listed first under its popular name, for who but a botanist thinks, for example, of a grape as *Vitis vinifera*? Popular names can be duplicated, so to identify the fruit accurately and internationally the botanical name, in its curious dog-Latin, is then given. (On the very rare occasions that botanical names do seem to be duplicated, it will normally be found that one fruit is a form of the other.) After the botanical name, in most cases there follow a few brief historical notes, a description of the fruit, some information about cultivation (including harvesting and storing if they need some special mention), a description of the plant itself, pointing out any ornamental value it may have, and finally a section on the culinary uses of the fruit.

# CULTIVATION

Before getting on with the details of actual cultivation, we would like to point out here that little mention is made throughout this book of pests and diseases suffered by fruit crops. There are several reasons for this, the main one being that fruit growing conditions vary so widely in different parts of the world that it would be quite impossible to generalise in any way that would be helpful. But a few words about pests and diseases might be useful.

## PESTS AND DISEASES

A pest can be defined as almost any creature which damages plants. Most pests are insects, but snails, mice, rabbits, birds, many other creatures and even children can be called pests on occasion. Pests damage plants and fruit directly and by introducing virus diseases. They can eat foliage and so reduce leaf area. They can damage fruits, roots, kill young shoots, distort leaves. Some pests can increase in numbers at an unbelievable rate.

In order to control garden pests it is first necessary to identify them and then to select the most effective insecticide, vermicide, molluscicide, acaricide, nematicide, ovicide or repellent. It is necessary to decide whether to employ a powder, a liquid or a smoke, a systemic or a nonsystemic, whether to go for immediate knockout or long-term control.

All pesticides are necessarily poisons, which means that they must be treated with respect and stored with care. They should preferably be bought in small quantities so that residual packs or bottles will not hang about in the garden shed to lose labels and so become unidentifiable. They must be kept out of the reach of children and household pets and on no account should any be decanted into soft drink or milk bottles even for the briefest periods. Because they are poisons they should be employed only where really necessary and in as small a quantity and for as brief a period as is compatible with successful control of the pest. Overkill can do more damage than the pest itself. Always follow meticulously the directions on the pack. On fruit and other edible plants always make sure that any pesticide used will be dispersed before the fruit is harvested and consumed.

Pests vary enormously in different parts of the world, in their type, in their virulence, in their sheer quantity and in their importance. Some pests in some parts are so damaging to certain crops that the transport of certain fruits or plants over state lines or from country to country is either prohibited or tightly controlled by legislation and inspection. In other regions pests can be so minor a problem that some gardeners find they can do without any kind of pesticide and still obtain worthwhile crops. It is a fact that a well-grown plant can be expected to some extent to shrug off minor attacks of pests and diseases, much as a strong child will avoid or shake off infections that might cause illness to a less healthy friend or neighbour.

Plant diseases are a somewhat more complex matter than plant pests, largely because most pests can be seen while most diseases cannot. In general terms a plant disease can be defined as any upset in the normal healthy growth of a plant which leads to twisted or abnormal growth, stunting or a slowing of growth or the weakening or death of certain parts of a plant or the entire plant.

Diseases can be parasitic or physiological. Parasitic diseases are occasioned by attack from fungi, bacteria or viruses, spread by insects, by spores floating through the air or by transfer from infected hands, secateurs, pruning knives and other gardening tools. Some parasitic diseases can begin in a small way so that plants appear to be slightly affected in some way but not seriously enough to take action, but they will build up over the weeks, months or even years until they take control and devastate a crop or an area.

Physiological diseases arise through environmental difficulties, an excess or lack of water, light or temperature and a competent gardener will be able to avoid or minimise the effects of most of these except under rare circumstances. Physiological diseases are not infectious, while parasitic diseases can be.

Some plant diseases can be prevented to save them having to be cured when they later appear. The winter spraying of fruit trees with an ovicide will kill eggs which would later have hatched out into insects. Preventive spraying of certain fruits with fungicides can cover the plant with a fine film which destroys the fungus and/or prevents spores developing to float off and attack other plants.

It will be seen from the foregoing that pests and diseases are somewhat complex matters. They vary widely in different parts of the globe and the symptoms of their attack are not always easy to see, to recognise or to define. For these reasons it is not proposed in this book to attempt to describe different fruit pests and different fruit diseases. Both are very much local perils. Their recognition and their treatment should be local matters. Expert advice is obtainable in almost all parts of the world, usually free of charge. Learn as much as you can about your local problems and seek advice early rather than attempt control of a problem you have been unable to recognise. Carefully obey any local laws concerning the growing or treatment of certain fruits and you will be acting both to your own benefit and to that of your neighbourhood as a whole.

## TYPES OF FRUIT AND FRUIT PLANT

There are so many types of fruit and fruit plant that one wonders where to begin. There are soft fruits, tree fruits, cane, top and bush fruits; there are bushes and half bushes, cordons, espaliers, fans, maidens, pillars, spindles, standards and half standards, and then there are melons, which are a form of cucumber, and strawberries which are a vegetable, grapes and the difficult category of rhubarb, which seems to fit in nowhere. The simplest, most intelligible and least gobbledegook definition we have been able to find comes from the Marshall Cavendish *Encyclopedia of Gardening*: 'A fruit is a case containing one or more seeds, usually formed from the ovary and ovule which develop into the fruit wall and seed respectively. Horticulturally fruit means the edible produce of plants. Top fruit grow on trees, e.g. apples, pears, plums, etc., soft fruit on bushes and trailing plants, e.g. currants, gooseberries and strawberries, while stone fruits include cherries, plums, gages, apricots, nectarines and peaches.' Which still leaves us with rhubarb!

Top fruit, soft fruit, stone fruit, then, are easy enough to identify, but who among non-gardeners can explain the difference between a bush and a half bush, a standard and a half standard, and who can say what is a cordon, an espalier, a fan, a maiden, a pyramid, a pillar or a spindle?

Most of these names have been given to top fruits, mainly apples and pears, and they are merely the shape in which the trees can be grown. Shape is a matter of convenience, depending on the space available. Where, for example, bushes might need from 3 m (9 ft) to 5 m (16 ft) between each separate plant, dwarf pyramids might need only 1–1.5 m (3–4½ ft) and cordons 75–90 cm (2½–3 ft). Few trees today, even in commercial orchards, are grown on their natural root stocks. They are all grown on special dwarfing stocks for both ease of handling and treatment and because of earlier fruiting. Only tree fruits are grown on stocks, with one or two exceptions. Soft fruits and cane fruits are grown from suckers, runners, layers or cuttings. A further point to take seriously into consideration is how much fruit is desired of one variety. A cordon tree, for example, is said to produce roughly 1.5–2.5 kg (3–5 lb) of apples, a pyramid 3–4 kg (6–8 lb), a dwarf bush on M9 rootstock 11–13 kg (25–30 lb), and a bush on Malling 2 up to 45 kg (100 lb). Not every family wishes to have large quantities of one variety of fruit; some may prefer to have several cordons or dwarf pyramids of different varieties rather than one or two larger trees all giving the same kind of fruit.

For this last type of gardener there are available in many countries 'family' trees with up to five, usually three, different varieties of one kind of fruit all growing on the same tree, grafted at an early stage and capable of providing that number of different varieties of apple, pear, plum or whatever for the life of the parent tree, so long as simple pruning rules are obeyed.

A bush tree has a trunk of about 90 cm (3 ft) from soil level to lowest branch, while a dwarf or half bush is a bush growing on a dwarfing rootstock with a trunk about 60 cm (2 ft) high. A standard has a trunk about 2 m (6 ft) high and a half standard about 1.5 m (4 ft). A cordon has had its growth pruned to a main stem bearing spurs and short branches from top to bottom, and the stem may be grown upright, oblique or horizontal, usually the second for the purpose of higher yield and space saving. An espalier consists of a main stem with branches in pairs trained at right angles to the stem. A fan-trained tree spreads out from near the base into a fan shape and is employed mainly for peaches, cherries and the like so that they may be trained against a wall or fence. A maiden is a one-year-old tree, a mere whippy single stem ready to be trained to whatever shape is required. A pyramid is similar to a dwarf bush but has its branches pruned rather more vigorously, while a pillar is again similar except that the side branches are now pruned even more rigorously with the intention that they shall last only three seasons and then be replaced. A spindle is again similar to the last two, but here the side branches are not pruned but are looped around and tied to the main stem. Wood which has cropped for from one to three years is constantly replaced, so branches bearing fruit are always young and strong.

These types of tree shape are really for the professional rather than the amateur, for they require considerable attention as well as an almost instinctive awareness of their progress and their needs. They are designed to produce the greatest quantity of quality fruit in the least space with the least expense in time, labour and materials. On the other hand the amateur gardener with fewer trees to tend might very well find a fascination in training one or more of these into one of these formal designs or even into a shape or pattern exclusive to himself.

# FRUIT GROWING IN CITIES

It is just as easy to grow a fruit tree in the city as it is in the country. So long as the climate is suitable and so long as there is sufficient space for the tree it should succeed and give you just as much fresh, tasty fruit as it would if growing in a country orchard. If space is strictly limited so that the backyard consists of nothing more than a small paved area, it is still possible to grow several kinds of fruit in containers and to obtain at least a taste of the real thing.

The urban gardener tends to point to his problems, such as poor, thin, sour soil, lack of light, poor drainage and lack of space as reasons why he does not even attempt to grow any fruit for consumption by his family. But the soil is easily enough improved by the addition of some good humus-making compost, and light can be increased if only by painting surrounding walls or fences with a light colour. The improvement of the soil quality and texture will result in better drainage and, where space is really limited, dwarf varieties of several fruits are available, or it may be possible to grow a fruit such as a grape or a peach or apricot against a wall, which would require only a few square centimetres of space where the stem enters the soil.

To an extent the urban gardener benefits from the conditions about which he complains. The surrounding buildings of his little plot are protection against strong winds and burning sunlight, yet at the same time they absorb warmth during the day and gently release it at night to the soil and the plants of the neighbourhood. This is one reason why city gardens are almost always earlier with their flowers and their crops than comparable gardens in the country.

Space limitations can be overcome to some extent by a judicious choice of what fruit to grow; and with some it is possible to obtain examples grafted on to a dwarfing rootstock that will ensure small, compact trees even when mature. Even greater value can be obtained by growing so-called family trees, mentioned earlier, where several different varieties are grafted on to a single rootstock. Although theoretically many fruits could be grown this way and although theoretically the only limit to the number of different varieties growing on a single tree would be simply the number of branches available, in practice the only family trees normally available from specialist nurserymen are apples and pears in bush form and these usually limit their varietal choice to three. A moment's thought suggests that three varieties of apple and pear are likely to reveal greater differences than, say, three oranges, three plums or three olives. However, nothing can stop the interested and enthusiastic amateur from experimenting with his own trees to see just what he can grow in this manner and how many varieties he can grow on a single tree. The highest recorded number is sixty, which would not really be a reasonable proposition for the average gardener.

To be practical, the urban gardener who grows one or more family trees gains not only, shall we say, three types of apple in the space normally taken by one, but he also obtains better and more apples, for those selected for grafting will all be compatible pollinators. Urban areas can suffer from a dearth of fruit trees, therefore to have suitable pollinators so immediately convenient can be of the greatest assistance.

A family tree requires no special treatment other than ensuring that no one of the three or so varieties dominates the others. As vertical shoots grow more strongly than horizontal, these should be cut away completely if they appear, otherwise the variety to which they belong might take over the whole tree in time.

It is helpful with a family tree to label or otherwise mark the different varieties at their point of origin so that as the tree grows and identification becomes more difficult, it will always be possible to follow a branch down to its graft to discover exactly which variety it is.

## POLLINATION

Pollination is the process of the transference of the male pollen in a flower to the female stigma and it immediately precedes fertilisation. Most plants have both sexes within the same flower and the pollen can be transferred easily enough by the motion of the plant in the wind, without the necessity of insect, bird or even human assistance.

It will be obvious that where a plant fertilises itself repeatedly, this continual inbreeding can lead only to its gradual degeneration. It is particularly important with most fruit that pollen should come from outside. Thus, although some plums, and some apples and pears among other fruits, are self-fertile, better crops will always result if they receive some of the pollen from a local tree of the same fruit which although of another variety blossoms at much the same time. This pollen can be transported on the winds, by insects such as bees, by birds, bats and even by rats and the human hand. When buying fruit trees

for planting always ask about their pollination needs and make sure that sources of pollen will be available.

## ROOTSTOCKS

Most of the smaller and less vigorous fruits are grown on their own roots, for they can be easily controlled. Some of the larger fruit trees might be denied to the urban gardener were it not for the fact that they can be grown on 'dwarfing' roots that will keep the trees small and compact, yet allow the formation of large quantities of fruit. It will be obvious that a small tree, besides fitting comfortably into a small garden, will be easier to tend, to spray, to prune and to pick, for one does not wish to have to use ladders or machinery for these simple procedures.

Apples, pears, plums and many other fruits are grafted or budded on to selected types of their own fruit, often wild. Sometimes they may be grafted on to nearly related species. Pears, for example, tend to make very large trees unless they are grown on a dwarfing stock, in this case usually a quince. There are many of these stocks with varying characteristics which have been developed by research stations throughout the world, and they bring specific qualities of pest- or disease-resistance or heavy yields as well as mere dwarfing capabilities.

Rootstocks are also available which are particularly suited to certain soils or climatic conditions, and a Bramley's Seedling, say, grafted on to the dwarfing rootstock M9, will not necessarily be as suitable in South Africa as it may be in England. So always question your supplier and make sure that the rootstock you are ordering is the right one for your location, your climate and the space available in your plot.

# PROPAGATION

Most of us as children have grown a young lemon tree from a pip, rooted a pineapple top or grown an avocado tree from a stone. Seldom have these young fruit trees been grown on to maturity, and even less frequently have they reached fruiting stage themselves. The reason why seeds or pips are seldom used commercially to propagate fruit trees and bushes is that only infrequently will the plants they produce be identical with the plant from which seed is taken. This is because varietal characteristics are not retained by the seeds and can only be transmitted by vegetative means.

## SEED SOWING

Nevertheless, seed sowing is undoubtedly the most important means of propagating plants and the techniques employed should certainly be examined. A problem so far as the amateur fruit grower is concerned is that if he sows and germinates seed successfully he will certainly obtain many more plants than he will need for the average small garden plot, but we suggest that the means of coping with this problem must lie in the gardener's own hands.

To germinate successfully, seeds need moisture, air and warmth. In some cases all of these can be provided by rain, atmosphere and the sun, and seeds can therefore be sown in the open ground, usually in spring or summer. Everyone at some time has sown seeds, so it is unnecessary to go into great detail except to stress that the soil must be fine and just moist, the seed must be sown thinly and not too deep, the temperature must be sufficiently warm and you must make sure that the seedlings are not allowed to dry out or to bake in too hot a sun once they have appeared.

Some fruit seed must be sown 'in heat' or 'under enclosed conditions', both of which mean that the seeds will not normally germinate unless they are subjected to the exceptionally warm and humid conditions made available by a greenhouse or a special propagating case. Seedlings grown under these conditions will have to be introduced to the outside world gradually if they are not to sustain a lethal shock.

Other seeds, particularly in colder climates, must be frosted to break up their cells before they can germinate. This process is called stratification or vernalisation and it applies mainly to berries. The normal process is to bury the seeds or berries in fine sand and leave them in a safe place (secure against mice and similar predators) in the garden during winter so that the frost can get at them and help the outer cells to disintegrate. In the spring they can be sown in the normal way and they will germinate. Some people have quite successfully resorted to refrigeration to carry out this process. If seeds are not vernalised or stratified, some of them will probably germinate safely enough if sown directly into the soil, but they will take several years and many will be lost by disease or taken by insects or garden pests.

The average urban gardener will generally prefer to buy a fruit tree ready-grown rather than grow one himself, but there are occasions when an example of a certain fruit or variety of fruit is just not obtainable and the only way to get a plant is to grow one yourself from a piece obtained from some known source.

So if we wish to propagate a fruit tree, bush or vine we will have to use a portion of the original plant if we wish to grow one that is identical. The method we choose will depend on the plant as well as on our skills or the facilities available to us, but we will not as a general rule wish to grow as large a number of the plants as we might when propagating more decorative plants for the garden. So the advantages of a unit designed for wholesale propagation will be of little real value. We should use simpler means of growing plants from cuttings or by dividing or layering them. It is when we come to techniques such as budding and grafting that some skill, dexterity and experience are helpful.

## DIVISION

Most gardeners have used this means to increase and rejuvenate certain of their perennial plants in the herbaceous border. They dig up a clump and simply divide it into several portions, the best of which are planted again separately and the poorest of which are discarded. There are not many fruits which can be propagated in this manner, but it is so simple and so foolproof a technique that it should certainly be adopted whenever possible.

# SUCKERS

Some fruits, for example bananas and raspberries, send up young shoots from their underground roots or stems, frequently when the older, fruiting stems are old or exhausted. These new shoots can be used to replace the older stems, either by cutting them away with a portion of root and planting them separately, or more usually by cutting down the older shoot to ground level and allowing it to be replaced by the younger.

# CUTTINGS

Cuttings can be taken from soft, green stem growth, from semi-ripe or from hard stem growth. In some cases, they can also be taken from a single leaf, a bud or from certain roots. Soft green cuttings should be taken in the spring, the lower leaves removed and trimmed just below a joint and then inserted to about a quarter of their length in a moist, sandy soil in a propagating frame where the temperature should be maintained at about 13–15°C (55–60°F). They should be kept moist with a fine spray once or twice a day, yet not so wet that they damp off. When new green growth indicates that roots have been formed, pot up the young plants individually or, if climate permits, plant them out directly into the garden after they have been hardened off, making sure that they receive sufficient moisture, that they are shaded from too strong sunlight and that they are protected from hot or drying winds.

Semi-ripe cuttings are taken in summer, some with a 'heel' of the old wood attached, but most merely trimmed just below a node or joint. They should be planted to about a quarter their depth in a moist and sandy soil mixture in pots or directly into the soil of a propagating bed in a cold frame. These too should be sprayed daily until they show signs of growth, when they can be removed and planted out.

Hardwood cuttings should be taken at the beginning of winter. They should consist of pieces of the current year's growth, roughly as thick as a pencil, about 30 cm (12 in) long, with the cut made just below a bud eye. Rub off all leaves except one or two at the top and insert the cutting in sandy soil about 10–13 cm (4–5 in) deep. They should have some protection from sun and wind and in colder climates will probably benefit from having a cloche placed over them. Roots will have formed on most of these cuttings by the next spring and they can then be dug up and planted where required.

It is frequently helpful, although not always necessary, to use a special chemical aid when taking cuttings like this. Hormone rooting powder or liquid is simple to use and greatly improves the chances of an early 'take' for the cuttings. Simply dip into the preparation the part of the stem to go underground and then plant as normally.

# LAYERING

If the stem of some plants can be placed on or buried in the soil it will frequently produce roots at the point of contact, so that if the stem is severed from the main plant a new one will have been produced. This is the process known as layering, a process essentially simple but limited in effectiveness because the stems of many plants, particularly trees and some shrubs, cannot be induced to bend down to the ground. But several other plants, blackberries for example, admirably fill the required conditions. It is helpful, though not entirely necessary, for the stem to be nicked, cut or have its inner tissues exposed in some way at the point where it is touching or buried in the soil. The blackberry, again, and several other plants, will also root if the tips of their long stems or canes rest on the soil. This is known as tip layering.

When it is impossible to bend a branch or stem down to soil level, it is possible with some plants to alter the technique slightly and carry out a process known as air layering. Here the stem or branch is again nicked or otherwise has its interior flesh exposed, but instead of being buried in the soil at this point, the wound is covered with a ball of moist sphagnum moss, tightly tied into place. This in turn is covered with a piece of plastic sheeting, again tied in place to keep in the moisture. New roots will grow into the moss and the stem can be cut away from the parent plant below these. It is helpful to sprinkle a little hormone rooting powder over the wound before covering it with the sphagnum moss, for this hastens the root production.

## BUDDING

This is a somewhat more difficult process but one easy enough to carry out after some practice, and one which is widely used commercially for the propagation of fruit trees. Strongly growing plants are produced more quickly by this technique than by most others. It has as its principle the implantation of a bud from the wanted tree on to a suitable rootstock. It is normally carried out in midsummer, but when the weather is moist and showery rather than hot and dry. A fat and healthy bud from the current year's growth of the wanted tree is carefully removed with a sharp knife by cutting out a slim slice of the wood about 5 cm (2 in) long, the bud being in the centre. On the stock plant make a T-shaped cut into the bark, sufficiently deep to allow the skin to be pulled gently back so that the bud can be inserted and the skin folded back again over the 'shield' but leaving the bud projecting. The bud should be carefully tied into position with raffia or tape so that it

adheres strongly to the stock plant and does not dry out. It will be evident by the end of winter whether the budding has been successful; if it has, the whole of the plant used should be cut away from about 2–3 cm (1 in) above the bud.

## GRAFTING

More fruit trees are produced by grafting than by any other method, which rightly suggests that it is a sure and time-saving technique. However, it is also a technique which demands skill and experience together with considerable manual dexterity. There are many types of graft – approach, bark, bottle, bridge, cleft, inarch, inlay, kerf, peg, rind, saddle, side, strap, stub and veneer – each with a special purpose. It seems to us that so much time and space would be expended on explaining the principles and techniques of grafting that it might be wiser to emphasise the problems, and suggest that interested readers determined to try raising fruit trees themselves by this means should consult a more specialist book, or better still go to a fruit expert and get from him the detailed tuition that is really required.

# PRUNING

The main purposes of pruning fruit trees and bushes are:

1. To cut away dead, dying, diseased and damaged branches and stop one branch rubbing against another.

2. To form the tree or bush into the required shape to suit the convenience of the gardener and the site of the tree.

3. To open up the tree to light and air and so assist in the fight against pests and diseases.

4 To control the quantity of the crop so as to obtain large, well-shaped, healthy fruits as a regular yearly crop.

It is important to note that all prunings should be burned to make sure that any pests and diseases they may be carrying are destroyed.

An unpruned tree is sometimes apt to produce fruit heavily, but this fruit will be uneven in size and shape because the branches on which it grows will have too much work to do to be able to give the necessary foods to each and every one of the fruits. And because the tree as a whole will be overworked, it will not be able to produce the buds which should give next year's flowers and then fruit. So in the next year a shortage of fruit on the tree will mean that it has strength enough to produce many fruiting buds, which will lead to a heavy crop, to be followed by a light crop, and so on. There are just a few kinds of trees that have a tendency to biennial bearing, but correct pruning often adjusts this. Details are given in the individual sections which follow these pages.

Styles of pruning differ somewhat according to the age and type of tree. This will be obvious when it is understood that in the pruning of a young and newly planted tree, much of the effort will go into the creation of the required shape. Once the tree is growing happily in this shape, this particular type of pruning can be modified so that it aims not to force the tree into a certain habit of growth, but to maintain this. Usually when one buys a tree from a reputable source it will already be trained and all the gardener has to do is encourage it to continue to grow in the same pattern. In the sections which follow, where guidance is necessary this has been given. One should perhaps point out that as a rule nurserymen will give instructions on what course to follow. Many show diagrams for pruning in their catalogues. Also, by making a few enquiries locally it is possible to find an expert who will give advice should some problem arise.

Those who are looking for interesting gardening might find pruning an absorbing subject, especially when it comes to training, say, an apple tree into a goblet shape or a diamond. Most gardeners might be content to have a fan-trained tree, designed to grow flat against a wall or fence. This means that branches will grow out from the main trunk only at the sides, parallel with the wall, and those buds that point in towards the wall and out, away from it, should be rubbed out. Most fan-trained trees and the other styles mentioned below can be bought ready-shaped.

Similar to a fan-trained tree is one with the side branches trained horizontally instead of outwards in the shape of a fan. Espaliers fit into this pattern. A tree of this shape is of particular value because it can be trained to grow along a mere post and wire fence instead of having to have a wall. The main difference between this and a fan is that the side branches must be induced to grow so that they are convenient to the wire, where they are tied in. This is only a matter of choosing shoots at the required heights and rubbing out the others.

A cordon consists of a single stem, usually grown against a post and wire fence and at an angle of about 45 degrees. For appearance and for convenience it is worth tying a bamboo cane to the stretched wires in the position where the cordon is to grow and to tie in the cordon to this as it lengthens. This will keep it straight.

Once the shape of the tree has been formed and the time has come to begin a cropping programme, the pruning is a less formal matter and consists of cutting out any weak, diseased, crossing or broken branches and seeing that there is space between the others. As time goes on some branches are bound to bend and may get too close to others, in which case some of these may have to be cut back or removed. Generally it is now a question of watching the trees or bushes and cutting back wherever necessary. Learn to differentiate between fruit buds, which are fat and significant, and growth buds, which are slimmer and less noticeable. Different varieties of fruit have different growth habits and the different shapes into which the trees have been pruned will also need different methods of handling. Bushes and standards need the least attention, and the more formal shapes of fans, espaliers and cordons demand more detailed work on them.

Occasionally it is desired to bring back an old and overgrown tree into cultivation. It has probably produced too many fruiting spurs and too little new growth. Some of these spurs can be removed completely and the others cut back to leave just two or three fruit buds. Perhaps most good will come from cutting back a number of the main branches quite severely so as to induce the production of new wood.

Finally, for those without talent or experience, remember that a tree left unpruned is likely to be more productive than one badly or incorrectly pruned.

# THINNING

If a fruit tree, bush or vine sets too much fruit there are several things that can happen. The fruits themselves may be small and with poor colour and flavour, simply because the plant cannot cope with all the work involved in feeding each and every one of the fruits. The development of the fruit buds for next year's crop may suffer. The sheer weight of the fruit can sometimes break branches.

So it is helpful in some seasons, though not necessarily all, to thin the crop out when it becomes apparent that it is going to be heavy. In certain cases, such as with grapes, it is usually advisable to thin out the bunches where they are grown for dessert purposes, although if they are grown for wine this will not be so important. The thinning can be carried out by hand, by using a special pair of scissors for grapes, or by chemical means – by the spraying of certain fruit trees or bushes with Carbaryl or some similar product which will result in the dropping or withering of a proportion of the young fruits.

With many fruits there is a natural thinning process that takes place in early summer, known in Britain for example as the June drop. Where the crop is of average dimensions it might be sufficient to rely on this natural thinning process, and many fruit growers like to wait until this has taken place before deciding themselves whether to resort to a further artificial thinning programme.

Much will depend on the type of fruit you wish to obtain as well as the quantity. Experiments have shown that with apples, and probably most other fruits, thinning about four weeks after blossom resulted in about 40 per cent more large and well-formed apples, whereas waiting until after the June drop and then thinning (some twelve weeks after full blossom) there was only a 25 per cent increase. It is difficult to lay down rules about the thinning of fruits because they differ in their reaction according to variety, and according to climate and soil, but the following information merely suggests what might be helpful towards the production of better fruits.

With apples it is possible to use a system whereby the fruits are thinned until there remains only one apple to every twenty leaves. The laborious counting process is soon overcome by an ability to judge at a glance the approximate number of leaves on a branch, but another and perhaps easier method is to reduce the number of fruits to allow 10–15 cm (4–6 in) between apples of dessert kinds and 15–25 cm (6–10 in) between the larger cooking apples. This really seems the more sensible process.

Pears require rather less thinning than apples as a general rule, and it is usually sufficient merely to allow one fruit per spur. If you wish to have some really superlative fruits, space the pears about 13 cm (5 in) apart, or give them roughly 30 cm square (1 square ft) of space each.

With peaches and nectarines it is better to take the process slowly and carry it out in two or more stages: thinning first before the stones have formed, while the fruits are still only about hazelnut size, and waiting until the stones have formed to reduce the crop once more so that there is about 15–25 cm (6–10 in) between the fruits when the operation has been completed. When peaches are grown on walls, first remove all fruits which are growing towards the wall and then gradually reduce the total number growing until there is a space of about 30 cm square (1 square ft) allowed to each fruit.

Plums, too, should be thinned in two stages – before stoning and after, at first allowing about 2–3 cm (1 in) between fruits and then about 7–8 cm (3 in).

# WORLD CLIMATE CHART

W eather differs in various parts of the world not only according to distance from the Equator or height above sea level, but according to ocean currents and prevailing winds. Minor but still significant differences in weather patterns can be caused on a local scale by such physical features as rivers, forests, hills and valleys.

It is impossible to be specific about the weather in any particular place, because in spite of the regularity of the seasons freak variations occur all over the world. One can, however, generalise on weather types and these have been divided into four patterns or zones for the purpose of this book. The weather chart given here does not claim or even pretend to be precisely accurate; rather it is an indication of what weather may be expected very roughly in the areas mentioned.

The division made here of world weather is based on the conditions required for the growing of fruit. If a certain fruit cannot be grown in the weather zone in which you live, it may be possible to give some protection in winter or to grow the fruit under cover and in warmth. It will be found that in the following pages suggestions to this end are normally provided.

1. *Mild moist winters, warm dry summers*
Mediterranean coastline, California, Chile, south-west South Africa, northern New Zealand.

2. *Winters cool, summers warm to hot, rain throughout the year or more in winter*
Great Britain, western France, Belgium, Holland, south-east and west-coastal Canada, southern Chile, northern Japan, Kamchatka USSR, Victoria (Australia), Tasmania, southern New Zealand.

3. *Cold winters, hot summers, rain or snow throughout the year according to season*
Denmark, Sweden, Germany, Poland, Czechoslovakia, Romania, Bulgaria, Ukraine, Yugoslavia, Austria, eastern France, New York, Pennsylvania, Ohio, Virginia, North Carolina, Tennessee, Kentucky, Arkansas, Missouri, Indiana.

4. *Winters warm and wet, summers hot and wet*
South Carolina, Georgia, Florida, Alabama, Mississippi, Louisiana, Brazil, south-east South Africa, eastern China, southern Japan, eastern Australia.

# PREPARATION AND SOIL TYPES

**M**ost types of fruit will grow in most types of soil. A deep, well-drained, medium loam may be the ideal, but so long as the type of soil is recognised and any possible faults or deficiencies corrected, the extremes of sandy soils and heavy clays can be made to grow good fruit. The sandy soils found so frequently in tropical regions are hungry and thirsty as rain rushes through them quickly, taking with it the essential plant foods in the soil. Clay soils generally found in more temperate regions are heavy and impermeable, wet and sticky in winter, baked hard in summer. Both sandy and clay soils can be improved in texture and hence performance if they are treated with quantities of bulky humus-making materials such as farmyard manure, straw, peat, grass mowings or home-made compost.

Humus in the soil can be regarded as its power element, encouraging bacterial activity to break down plant foods and natural elements into a liquid solution which can be easily assimilated by the plant roots.

The majority of fruits are comparatively shallow-rooting. This being so, deep cultivation of the soil before planting is unnecessary unless to improve drainage, and perhaps in certain circumstances even harmful if it discourages or reduces the worm population.

Weeds are best discouraged by constant heavy mulches, which at the same time increase the fertility and improve the texture of the soil and encourage the advent of worms, which in their turn help drain soil and carry fertilisers down to the roots.

## MULCHING

Perhaps the best material for these mulches is well-rotted farmyard manure which contains a high proportion of straw. When dug into the soil in quantity before planting, good manure can safely allow the reduction by a half of the normal application of straight fertilisers. Never use farm-yard manure fresh, for the ammonia it contains can damage plant roots. Stack it, if possible under cover of some kind, for several months until it has lost its original heat and smell and has become brown, crumbly and friable. Spread this material as a mulch up to 15 cm (6 in) deep around the base of the fruit tree or bush, not close enough to touch the trunk or stems, but reaching out to cover the soil surface under which the roots lie.

## COMPOST

Farmyard manure is not always available to urban gardeners, but a constant supply of home-made compost is always possible. You can make compost merely by throwing on to a heap any soft vegetable refuse you have available, such as potato peelings and the outer leaves of cabbage or lettuce, and general garden debris, such as grass mowings and leaf sweepings. But by using slightly more scientific methods it is possible both to make a superior product and greater quantities more quickly. Compost is produced by the vegetable matter rotting down and this can only happen if both air and moisture are available to get the necessary bacterial activity going.

Make your compost heap of a convenient size, perhaps 1 m (3 ft) square. It can be free-standing, but is better with walls made of stakes, slatted timber, wire netting or whatever comes easily to hand and will both contain the vegetable material and allow air and moisture through to it. On the base or floor of the heap place first a layer of woody branches or some similar material that will keep the main bulk off the ground and allow air in at the base. On top of this throw your vegetable refuse. If you use grass mowings, apply them only in very thin layers, for otherwise they can make a dense mat which will not easily rot down. After some 15–20 cm (6–8 in) of material have been added, sprinkle the surface with a proprietary activator or accelerator to hasten decay and if necessary water this in well before capping this layer with just 2 cm (1 in) or so of garden soil. Then repeat the process, making layer after layer until the top is reached.

In warm climates or summer months when there is plenty of moisture, the vegetable matter will rot down into good, rich compost, black and friable, in a matter of a month or two, but in winter and less favourable districts it may take up to six months or so.

It is probable that the outer surfaces of the heap will not rot down so quickly because they cannot generate the required heat, and that only in the interior of the heap will you find the rich, crumbly compost that is so useful. Scoop out this interior and use the exterior walls to start a new heap. Ideally two heaps should be kept going simultaneously, the first a few weeks ahead of the second, so that as one is consumed the other will be building up ready for use.

Compost made by this method is rich and useful as a soil conditioner and fertiliser in the garden, but it tends to be slightly acid. Where the garden soil itself is naturally acid, it would be well to sprinkle a light dressing of lime at intervals throughout the heap so that the finished compost will be more or less neutral and will not add to any existing problem of an acid soil.

## ACID AND ALKALINE SOILS

Degrees of acidity and alkalinity in the soil can be ascertained by using a small and inexpensive soil test kit; they are measured in a scale known as the pH, with neutral as 7.0. Acid soils have a pH of less than this figure, as far as about 4.5, and alkaline soils have a pH of more than 7.0, up to about 8.5. In general terms the best soil for fruit growing is either neutral, with a pH of 7.0, or very slightly acid, with a pH of about 6.5. Very acid soils can be treated with lime to make them less acid and very alkaline soils can be treated with a chelated iron product generally known as sequestrene. The last, however, is expensive, relatively inefficient for this purpose and suitable for application only on individual plants rather than for the general treatment of an entire area. Continuous cultivation and the regular application of compost and peat will help bring down the pH of alkaline soils and make them more suitable for growing fruit and other crops.

Acid soils are frequently deficient in potash and this can be supplied easily enough where bonfires are lit or where wood is a major source of domestic fuel. Collect the ash as soon as it cools, otherwise it tends to lose its special qualities into the soil where it has been placed or where the bonfire has been.

## FERTILISERS

Plant foods themselves are basically chemicals, mainly nitrogen, phosphorus and potash, but with significant amounts of other elements such as iron, calcium and sulphur and lesser quantities – trace elements – of boron, magnesium, iron, zinc, copper, molybdenum and manganese. Fertilisers usually come ready mixed under a proprietary name in cans, packs or bottles. They are usually known as 'balanced', which does not necessarily mean that the pack contains equal quantities of nitrogen, phosphorus and potash. It is possible to buy high nitrogen balanced fertilisers as well as packs high in the other elements. Where it is necessary or preferred to apply pure chemical fertilisers rather than use the slightly more expensive proprietary mixtures, nitrogen is the most important, for it encourages the lush growth of soft leaves and increases yields of fruit and seeds. It is available in several different forms, probably the most useful being as nitrochalk, a mixture of ammonium nitrate and chalk. It is granular in texture and easy to use at the normally recommended rate of about 15 g per square m ($\frac{1}{2}$ oz per square yd) during spring and summer.

Nitrate of soda is not quite so high in nitrogen, but is very quick-acting, so that the effect of a dressing can sometimes be seen in a matter of days. It should be used in spring and summer at about the same recommended rate to wake up and give a jolt to fruits which have been slow to recover from the winter. It should be used sparingly, never more frequently than once a month, because it can harm the soil structure.

Sulphate of ammonia, another high nitrogen fertiliser, has some interesting reactions according to climate. The best way to apply it is dissolved in water at a rate of 1 teaspoon in 4.5 litres (1 gallon). The ammonia tends to be absorbed by and held by the soil and released only very slowly when temperatures are low, yet much more quickly during warmer days or in higher temperatures. All fruit crops other than strawberries benefit from a dressing of sulphate of ammonia in spring.

The highest rate of nitrogen is available from a product known as urea-form, a long-acting combination of urea and formaldehyde which can be applied to the soil at a rate of 25–55 g per square m (1–2 oz per square yd) and will release its nitrogen for several months, indicating that a single application each year is all that is necessary.

Although nitrogen is the most important chemical factor in all plant growth, it will be found throughout this book that it should not be over-applied so far as fruit is concerned, simply because it tends to encourage the growth of foliage at the expense of fruit. For this reason it is suggested that unless the gardener has reason to believe that his trees are nitrogen-deficient, or unless watering must be carried out to such an extent that it must inevitably be leached from the soil, nitrogen should be applied only at the beginning of the growing season.

# PHOSPHATES
# AND POTASH

A quick-acting supplier of phosphates is super-phosphate of lime, which nevertheless supplies no lime. It is generally used on seed beds or before planting at a rate of about 25–55 g per square m (1–2 oz per square yd) to induce early root formation and to speed up the formation of fruits. Sulphate of potash is probably the best supplier of potash, particularly for soft fruits. Apply at any time of the year at about 15–30 g per square m ($\frac{1}{2}$–1 oz per square yd). Potassium nitrate is another artificial compound, used mainly as a liquid feed at a rate of about 1 teaspoon to 5 litres (1 gallon) of water. It can be used fairly regularly during the growing season.

Potassium is concerned with the manufacture of starches and sugars and so is particularly important for the successful growing of fruits. It improves colour and flavour, benefits the formation and ripening of flowers and increases resistance to pests and diseases. Light soils, peaty and chalky soils, are frequently deficient in potash.

All the fertilisers mentioned so far have been basically single-element fertilisers, releasing specific foods to the plants. Usually, particularly with the growing of fruits, a compound fertiliser will be more useful, providing a more all-round benefit. A good double-acting artificial fertiliser that supplies both nitrogen and potash is potash nitrate, quick-acting and particularly useful in early spring, where the application of nitrogen alone might result in too much soft and leafy growth. It

can be applied as a powder at 25–50 g per square m (1–2 oz per square yd), or 1 teaspoon can be mixed with 5 litres (1 gallon) of water. It can be used two or three times during the growing season.

In addition to pure chemical fertilisers, or in place of them, it is possible to use certain organic compounds, usually of animal origin. We know about farmyard manure, for example, which is both a fertiliser and a soil conditioner. There are also several other forms of animal manure, such as cow manure, chicken droppings and the like, always useful and frequently best mixed with peat or some similar substance.

Organics also provide some of the most useful compound fertilisers, most of them basically similar in their origin and in their use. Boneflour and bonemeal are more or less identical formulations except that the first is more finely ground and hence quicker-acting. Both provide calcium phosphate and a lesser quantity of nitrogen, a compound of particular value to the fruit grower as it promotes good strong root growth. It is most usefully applied in autumn and winter at a rate of about 100 g per square m (4 oz per square yd). Similar, but perhaps with a slightly higher nitrogen content, is meat and bonemeal, a good general fertiliser. Bonemeal can carry anthrax and salmonella, so always wear gloves when handling it, try not to breathe in any of the dust and buy only steamed or sterilised supplies.

Most fertilisers, particularly the artificials or inorganics, have a tendency to absorb moisture from the air, and any stored supply will soon become either a soggy mass or, on drying out again, a solid brick. For this reason they should either be bought only in small quantities which can be used up quickly, or they should be removed from their bags or boxes and repacked in airtight containers, preferably plastic rather than metal because the metal itself will tend to rust and disintegrate.

# FERTILISER DEFICIENCY
# SYMPTOMS

It is impossible to lay down rigid rules about either the types or the quantities of fertilisers required for different fruits, for this will depend largely on soil and climate. It is possible, however, to look carefully at most types of fruit during the summer months and note symptoms that can suggest certain deficiencies. If foliage is small, pale or even yellowish, and the fruits are small, tough and brightly coloured, suspect nitrogen deficiency. Lack of potash may be the cause if the foliage is small and brittle, possibly with brown edges, and if the fruits never seem to mature but remain small and dull. Purple shades in the foliage appear when there is a lack of phosphates in the soil. This is not generally a common occurrence and it is worth checking (a soil analysis will show) to make sure that the shortage is not one of

magnesium. If the latter is the case the purple colour will give way to brown in the centre as well as the margins of leaves and the young shoots will be few, thin and weak. Bright yellow leaves where they should be green is an indication of iron shortage, to be seen in alkaline soils. Fruits will be few and small.

When any of these signals are received, prepare to apply a dose of the necessary restorative at once, but do not apply this at an abnormal rate. In most cases the symptoms will disappear in a matter of days and a significant improvement will be seen very quickly.

# PLANTING AND HARVESTING

Discuss your requirements with your supplier well in advance so that there is plenty of time for you to prepare the site for your fruit tree and for the nurserymen to select and pack your order. If the tree or bush is container-grown it can be planted at any time of the year, merely taken from its container and planted with roots undisturbed, otherwise it will be delivered in winter when the plant is more or less dormant. In this case it should be planted as early as is convenient and when the soil is in good condition, neither too wet nor frosted.

## PLANTING

Dig the planting hole in advance. It should be large enough to take the spread roots of the tree with a little room to spare and about 30 cm (12 in) deep. Dig out this hole completely, loosen the soil at the base and spread here a shallow layer of rotted farmyard manure, compost or peat. Fork this in well and mix it with the soil at the base so that the roots of the young tree do not come into direct contact with it. Lift the soil at the base to form a slight mound and base the roots of the young tree on this. Examine these roots first and prune away any that are split, torn or damaged. Then take out the tree again and insert a stake, where necessary, into the hole, ramming it in securely so that it is vertical and reaches a height just under the main spread of the branches.

Now place the tree in position again and begin filling in the soil to cover the roots. The soil should be that which you have excavated, mixed with a little peat and a handful of bonemeal or some similar slow-acting fertiliser. Scatter this in carefully making sure that all the roots are well covered and that there are no air pockets. Shake the young tree from time to time to settle the soil around the roots. When the roots have been completely covered, press down the soil securely with the foot to firm it over the roots and then fill in the hole, making sure at the end that the soil level, easily determined by the mark on the stem, is exactly the same as it had been at the nursery. Fix the tree to the stake securely, preferably using a special tree tie. Water thoroughly. In dry areas, tropical or sub-tropical regions, make a shallow saucer of the soil around the base of the plant so that when watering, or in case of valuable rain, the moisture will be concentrated where it will do most good.

If there is any danger of attack by rabbits, squirrels, hares, deer, sheep or any other animal, protect the tree with a special collar at its base or with a surround of wire netting firmly fixed into the ground.

This is really the critical period for the young tree. Examine it daily if possible and make quite sure that it is never dry at the roots for the first six months. Make sure also that the tie is secure and that the tree is not rocking in the wind and so tearing its young root hairs. In temperate regions it will make only little growth for the first year or two, spending its energies on sending out new roots, and it is only after this period that you will be able to see evidence of strong new growth. In warmer countries, however, growth can be spectacular almost from the beginning, necessitating even closer after-planting care.

## FRUIT UNDER GLASS

It is perfectly possible to grow several types of fruit with the protection of a cold or heated greenhouse, conservatory, or in some cases even a sunny sun lounge or garden room or porch. However, this is not always a profitable or a practical venture, mainly because of the space required and often also because the fruit plant's needs are different from those of the other tenants. Most often, for instance, an amateur's greenhouse is used mainly for tomatoes, plants whose requirements are unlikely to coincide with most fruit trees. In such cases the fruits should either be those which can be taken out during the summer when the house can be turned over to tomatoes, or they should be chosen from the small fruits which can be grown in pots, such as strawberries, which will occupy bench space for only three or four months of the year, or something like Cape gooseberry or pineapple, with needs much the same as those of the tomato.

The fruits most suited to greenhouse growing, traditionally in the northern countries, are peaches, nectarines, apricots, figs and grapes. To these are added passion fruits, citrus and the occasional tropical fruit by those who have the means and the interest to cultivate them. Although usually selected varieties are chosen for greenhouse culture, most of those in the first section can be grown perfectly well outdoors in most climates so long as they receive some protection when temperatures are low. Often cloches can be used in winter, late autumn and early spring.

Because of the space problem it is normal practice for a grape vine to be grown in the soil outside the greenhouse while the main stem is led into the house through an aperture in the wall and trained close to the glass once inside and long enough. The dappled shade cast by the vine, though too dense for many plants, still allows the gardener to grow a pleasant range of pot plants on the ground or on benches below. Rhubarb can be forced in the dark in every kind of greenhouse.

Peaches and those other kinds are usually grown fan-shaped, pruned so that their branches lie flat against the wall to which they are trained so as to make the maximum use of the wall space available. This presupposes a lean-to greenhouse, built against the wall of the house or perhaps against one side of a walled-in garden. Special peach houses used to be constructed on a large scale in the great private gardens of the past. One gardener we once knew was told by Milady that she would like the whitewashed walls of the peach house coloured sky blue, so that the pink blossom would be more attractively contrasted. Not such good light intensity, perhaps, but it conjures up a pleasant scene.

The advantage of growing fruit under glass is mainly one of obtaining it earlier than it would be available outdoors. There are instances where it might be the only way in which one could grow and ripen certain fruits; persimmons in cold countries come to mind. Whether this advantage outweighs the problems involved is up to the individual gardener. The fruits mentioned can be grown in pots and stood outdoors during the warm weather. This applies to most of the tree fruits, and in fact is one of the best ways to grow citrus, but as a general rule most are grown in soil and must be regarded as permanent residents.

Another advantage is that in some environments a greenhouse can be used simply to create a garden in an area where many factors create an uncongenial atmosphere, such as a small back

yard, a balcony or even a roof in a cold city. Heat and light can then be controlled, moisture provided at the right time, protection given against sparrows and pigeons, all these factors contributing to the creation of a little oasis. In such a spot quite an interesting collection could be made which almost certainly would be impossible out of doors.

A cold greenhouse may be quite suitable for peaches, figs and grapes under certain circumstances, for the heat absorbed during the day will keep the atmosphere warm during the night, and in any case the protection given by the walls and roof will also help to keep the fruits safe from frost. But where frosts can penetrate the house at times when the plants are particularly vulnerable, while in blossom for example, or even in fruit in some cases, it is wise to have available some means of heating the structure and so providing the necessary protection. Heating can also help to hasten fruit production, which is after all the main purpose of growing the fruits in the first place. It should be realised, however, that where it will cost a certain sum to maintain interior heat just above freezing point, say 2–3°C (35°F), each rise of about 3°C (5°F) will cost as much again. In other words, high temperatures mean high costs, and there comes a time when each individual piece of fruit might become so expensive that it really is not worth while growing it.

Because of the high cost of heating it is sometimes advisable to divide a greenhouse into two sections by means of a partition of plastic sheeting or something similar, so that instead of heating the whole house for the sake of just a few plants, it it possible to heat only a single section, which will significantly reduce the cost. Where high temperatures may be necessary to germinate seeds or to root cuttings, a small propagating case can be run at comparatively high temperature at nothing like the cost involved in heating an entire house.

If fruit is to be grown in the soil of a greenhouse this must be specially prepared beforehand. It is no use merely digging a hole in the greenhouse soil and planting a peach or fig, much as one might in the open soil. Instead, a special bed should be made. These fruits will require considerable quantities of water and yet they also demand highly efficient drainage. The drainage must be specially provided, and the best way way to do this involves the removal of about 1 m (3 ft) of soil and the installation of field drains at this depth, or the provision of 30 cm (12 in) or so of rubble 60 cm (2 ft) under the surface. Sometimes a firm and solid base to the bed must be constructed, as is the case with figs.

When the soil is replaced after the drainage has been installed, resist the temptation to provide an enriched mixture, for the combination of rich soil and a protected environment will mean that the fruit tree will take in too much nitrogen and put on excessive soft and leafy growth at the expense of flowers and fruit. Plant in the normal way while the tree is dormant and tie in the shoots so that they develop in the manner required. Treatment is generally similar to that necessary with a tree grown outdoors, except that all watering must be carried out artificially and that there will be fewer opportunities for pollination of the flowers by the normal visitation of insects.

So to start the trees into growth it is generally necessary to flood the soil thoroughly in about midwinter, and thereafter to water as regularly as appears necessary. When growth begins and the buds start to swell it will also be necessary to spray the tree with tepid water once or twice a day until the flowers are open, leaving off at this time to encourage natural pollination. Spraying will help to discourage pest attack as well as providing the necessary humidity.

The house ventilators will generally need to be kept closed on most days during winter, but can gradually be opened as the weather turns warmer, so long as one is always alert to the danger of possible night frosts. The aim should be in general terms to begin growth in a temperature only just above freezing, say 4°C (40°F), and allow this to rise to no more than about 10°C (50°F) in the first month and about 15°C (59°F) in the second. By this time the outside temperature will be rising, and when it begins to exceed about 15°C it will be necessary to begin opening ventilators and damping down the interior of the house, perhaps even to provide some shading in certain climates. When the flowers open it will be advisable to pollinate them artificially. Do this at about midday, using the proverbial rabbit's tail if you have one, or a soft camel hair brush, or even a piece of cotton wool. After you have been over the blossoms in this manner, syringe or spray the trees to bring additional benefit.

As the young fruits form and begin to swell they should be thinned to get a good crop of large and healthy fruits. Stop your spraying programme as the fruits begin to ripen, but as soon as the full crop has been gathered begin again and allow as much ventilation as possible so that the wood can ripen thoroughly. Continue to water the border and to ventilate freely until about midwinter when the trees can be urged into new growth again. Some plants need a chilling period during dormancy.

It is unnecessary and wasteful to feed young trees in their first year or two, but after they have begun to provide good crops of fruit it will be helpful to apply artificial fertilisers at the recommended rate and to provide a good mulch in the early spring, using farmyard manure or homemade compost.

# FRUIT IN CONTAINERS

Many fruits can be grown quite successfully in containers, either completely in the open on a patio or terrace, or transferred to a cold greenhouse in harsh weather. These fruits include apples and pears, cherries, peaches, persimmons, plums, figs and in certain climates citrus and other warm weather fruits, as well as Cape gooseberries, strawberries, pineapples and passion fruits. Those suitable for pot or container cultivation are described in their relevant sections.

A specialist fruit grower should be consulted for young plants, because as a rule these will be better grafted on to dwarfing or some other special stock for obvious reasons. Sometimes nurserymen sell plants already potted. One cannot expect large crops of large fruits, but with reasonable care it should be possible to obtain worthwhile quantities of average sized fruits.

In addition to using specially grown trees, some attention should be paid to soil and to the container, as well as a feeding programme for all times of the year. Because the tree will normally be in the container for a minimum of a year and a maximum of perhaps two or three, the roots will spread and absorb all the goodness from the soil. It should therefore be comparatively rich, yet open in texture and well drained although capable of retaining moisture. This indicates a rich, fibrous loam as the base, with the addition of some peat and perhaps some well-rotted farmyard manure or compost. The container can be a pot, tub, trough or what you will, although it should not normally be less than about 25 cm (10 in) in diameter and about the same depth. The lower 5–8 cm (2–3 in) should be filled with drainage material and the container must, of course, have adequate drainage holes. It is helpful to cover this drainage layer with a thin layer of upside-down turf, or failing this with a piece of hessian or other material, merely to prevent the soil falling down into the drainage layer and clogging it.

Make sure that the plant roots will fit the container and if one or two are too large trim these back neatly. Make a miniature mound of soil on which you can sit the roots and then add the soil gently, firming it as you go so that no air pockets can exist. There need be only 5 cm (2 in) or so of soil above the upper roots, so try to leave a little space at the top of the tub so that there will be no trouble with watering.

If you are going to leave your trees in the open permanently, treat them much as you would trees growing in the soil, with the exception that they should never be allowed to dry out. If they are to go into a cool greenhouse, move them in about midwinter. Apply no heat. Ventilate freely during the day but close down the house early enough in the day for the warmth to be retained for the night drop in temperature.

At the very beginning of spring start spraying and ensure good pollination by carrying out the process by hand. Thin the crop by hand also, for you cannot rely on the wind to do this for you when the plants are indoors. Ideally the trees should be repotted each winter, but unless cropping has been heavier than is good for the plants it will be found that every two years, perhaps even three, will be sufficient. Carefully scrape away a little of the soil at the top of the container and then remove the tree and gently pick away any soil around the roots. Prune the longest roots by up to a half of their length and then repot, preferably in the same container, only using a larger one if this appears genuinely necessary.

# HARVESTING AND STORING

Where fruits can be used unripe in some way or another, it is sometimes wise to begin picking them as soon as they reach a useful size, largely to aid the tree, especially when there is a heavy crop. This is a helpful and convenient way of thinning the fruit. Those which are left on the tree will grow all the better.

Even if you do not pick some of the immature fruits, it is as well to bear in mind that it is unlikely that all the fruits on one tree will reach full development at the same time. Often those on the outside of a tree will ripen before those which are back further in the shade. As one would expect, this is much more marked when the plant is a family tree on which several varieties are grafted. By picking on a number of occasions instead of taking all in one go, you hedge your bets, for you will inevitably select at least one occasion when the fruit is in a perfect state for harvesting. One other point to note is that often fruit on trees which are cropping only lightly will mature before those on a heavily laden tree.

Fruits vary in the way they ripen, and in the speed at which they reach maturity. Any special characteristics in this line have been noted in the respective sections.

It is not really possible to say just when one fruit or another will be ready for harvesting. There are a few pointers to maturity and the grower will find that as he comes to know his plants so he will more readily note any changes which take place in them. This is certainly the case when the plant is in fruit. Usually the base or ground colour of a fruit changes in hue, often quite slowly and unnoticeably at first, and then, suddenly at times, one is aware that the tree or bush has a different appearance. Fruits which one saw or noticed only at close quarters suddenly shine out or are in some other way more conspicuous.

The best test is to taste. Taste a William pear, for instance, and you cannot possibly be mistaken. The fully developed fruit has lost its dry, flavourless hardness or woodiness and will have become succulent with juice. You should also at this time be able to detect the characteristic flavour and sweetness. The pips may be beginning to darken, although this is not always a firm guide because these can change colour early in a dry season. If you look up into a tree or bush so that you can see the fruit against the light, you will see a deeper colour, almost a glow through the fruit when it is ripe. This is especially the case with apricots and some other stone fruits. Many fruits have a more noticeable aroma as they ripen.

Fruits should be gathered when they are dry. Never store wet fruits. On the other hand, do not allow fruit to stand in the hot sun. They should go as cool as possible into a cool place as soon as possible.

Fruits should be handled carefully and never dropped down from a height into a box or basket. Bruising will mark them and spoil them, and damaged fruit rot quicker than those which have been handled with care. Before you use ladders or steps to reach fruit on a tree, pick all the mature fruit within arm's reach. You will find that as the lowest branches are relieved of their fruit they will lift into or out of reach. When many fruits are ripe they generally part readily from their branches. There is often a little 'hinge' in the fruit stalk on which light pressure can be exerted and which will part to allow the fruit to come away easily. Do not hold fruit like peaches and apricots with the fingers, but rather in the palm of the hand. Pull it outwards and give it a slight twist.

Where one is to store fruit depends, of course, on how much fruit there may be, what kind it is and what space one has. If the fruit is one with a short season and it is likely to have its surplus quickly frozen or bottled, then any excess of easily handled crop can generally be stored in some cool, dry place or, if the bulk is small, in a refrigerator. For longer-keeping fruits such as apples and some pears, the store should be dark, although if it is well windowed the fruits can be covered with sheets of paper. The storage place should also be cool, only just above freezing, 2–4°C (35–40°F), for apples and a little higher for pears. A cool upper room or an attic will often suit the latter in temperate regions, so long as it is possible to get to them for the frequent inspection that they require. The store for apples should be slightly moist, which rules out most homes, but if a shed has a stone or earth floor this can be damped down occasionally. Unfortunately a small garage is not always a good place, because of the fumes from petrol and the internal combustion engine which apples are likely to absorb.

It is possible to buy fruit storage cabinets, but a series of shelves can also be fitted into a small floor space. Deep vegetable trays of the type in which lettuces are packed will also serve, anything with a firm base and sufficient head room to allow air to pass over the fruit and which can safely be stacked without damage to fruit above or below.

It is worth while wrapping stored fruits separately, for this keeps them freer from rot and disease. One can buy special fruit wraps, but any clean paper, even newspaper, will do.

# BOTTLING AND PRESERVING

It must be evident to anyone who turns these pages that we share an enthusiasm for the plants, flowers and fruits of the earth. Certainly one of our greatest pleasures when we travel to a new country is to seek out in the local shops, gardens and orchards fruits we may not find so readily, or at the same time of year, at home. For us fruit, more than any other food, defines the character of an area and tells us at a glance, as it were, a great deal about the local way of life.

We have only to talk or think of tasting one particular fruit when we remember others. Talk of the breakfasts at the roadside when we drove through France and ate freshly baked French bread and enthused over the refreshing great peaches is sure to prompt memories of other visits and other places and other feasts: the luscious, magenta-centred white figs of Tuscania, north of Rome; the lozenge-like jujubes in Montelimar; the sugar-sweet oranges we picked from the trees in Perth in Australia; the honey-flavoured Lady's Fingers bananas in Nambour in Queensland; the cantaloupes in the US; the alpine strawberries in Bruges; the quinces in Davos; the mangoes we ate for breakfast on Christmas Day in Sydney.

None of these are just foods. They are for us the fabric of memory, of delight, of romance. Half of our delight was in the places and the people, for some of the foods are a commonplace in markets all over the world. If they are unobtainable fresh, they are to hand canned. So if the ingredients are readily available, all we need are instructions on how to handle them.

But this is not so much a cook book as a book of inspiration. There is not so much of the 'how to' and more of the 'can you?' In other words, it is an attempt to indicate the road rather than arrive at the destination. We have enjoyed discovering, experimenting, tasting, and our hope is that we can pass to readers some of the pleasures and excitements we have experienced.

*NOTE:* Where both metric and imperial measurements are given for ingredients in the recipes, it is important to use only one system consistently, otherwise the proportions will be incorrect.

## CANDYING, CRYSTALLISING AND GLAZING FRUIT

Throughout these pages we have indicated what fruits can be candied, and we have also given some specific recipes for making sweetmeats from and for candying a few kinds of fruit. These recipes, generally speaking, are simple to follow and do not entail a great expenditure of time. In this they differ from the elaborate and time-consuming process needed for candying fruits in a way which most closely resembles the commercial method. This process is described below. The one thing to commend it is that while it is protracted, it is in no way arduous, and the results are well worth while. Most readers will wish to know how to preserve fresh fruits this way, but we should point out that some bottled or canned fruits can be used, notably pineapples, peaches, apricots and firm plums. Their treatment differs a little in that it is not quite so protracted. It is explained later.

**Candying fresh fruit** Once the fruit has been candied it can then be given a crystallised or a glazed finish. Artificial colouring is often added, especially to green plums or gages, small whole pears and cherries, but this is a matter of personal preference. Very many fruits can be candied although, as one would expect, some are better than others. While strawberries are candied, other berries such as raspberries are not, because they are of a different structure. Although texture is important, flavour is more so. This is the main reason why those fruits which have a pronounced or distinctive flavour are best for this purpose. Fruits should be processed in their own kinds (they can be mixed later if wished), and syrup prepared for one kind of fruit should not be used for another. While all the fruits should be ripe, they should not be so ripe that they are excessively soft, or they will not keep their shape. If the fruit is such that it does not have to be peeled, stoned or halved, it needs to be punctured so that the syrup can be properly absorbed by the flesh. Pricking the fruit all over with a silver fork is the recommended method. It is most satisfactory to candy fruit in small batches, a few kilograms rather than many.

The fruit should first be cooked until it is just

tender. This ensures a quick and even penetration of sugar, and this in turn keeps the fruit a good colour. To do this, put the fruit in a pan and cover it with boiling water and then simmer it gently. Take care not to overcook it. Often 3–5 minutes is long enough, but much depends upon the nature of the fruit. Those fruits with thick skins, apricots for instance and some small whole pears, may take much longer. When it is ready, drain the fruit and put it in a bowl.

Make a syrup using the water in which the fruit was boiled. For every 2 cups of fruit use either $\frac{3}{4}$ cup of sugar, or – and this is said to be preferable – $\frac{1}{4}$ cup of sugar and $\frac{1}{2}$ cup of glucose or dextrose, and 1 cup of water in which the fruit was cooked. Boil these together and pour the syrup on the fruit. The fruit should be covered, and where this is not the case, more syrup should be prepared. If necessary cover the fruit with a plate to make sure it stays under the syrup. Allow the fruit to steep in this syrup for twenty-four hours. If artificial colouring is to be used, it should be added at this point.

For the next stage, drain the fruit and put the syrup in a pan; as the fruit has weakened the sugar proportion, add $\frac{1}{4}$ cup of sugar for each 2 cups of fruit being candied. Bring this to boiling point. Pour it on the fruit again and allow it to steep for another twenty-four hours.

This process should be repeated for another five days, i.e. until $1\frac{1}{2}$ cups of sugar in all have been added to the original syrup. On the eighth day, dissolve $\frac{1}{3}$ cup of sugar in the syrup and this time add the fruit and boil all together for 3–4 minutes. Boiling should make the fruit plump. Return all to the bowl and allow the fruit to steep for forty-eight hours. This brings us to the tenth day. The process followed on the eighth day should be repeated, except that this time the fruit and syrup should be simmered until the syrup is thick. It should have the consistency of honey when it cools. Test a little as when making jam. Leave the fruit in the syrup for a further 3–4 days.

Drain the fruit, lay it on a sieve placed over a dish to catch the syrup and let it dry in a cool oven, about 50°C (120°F), or in some other warm place such as an airing cupboard or in the sun, protecting against flies. Turn the fruit from time to time so that all the surfaces are exposed to the drying air. The fruit is dry when it can be easily handled.

**Candying bottled or canned fruit** Drain the syrup from the fruit and place the latter in a bowl. Using the syrup and adding water if necessary to make up to 1 cup, add 1 cup of sugar or, again preferably, $\frac{1}{2}$ cup of sugar and $\frac{1}{2}$ cup of glucose or dextrose. Make sure that the sugar is dissolved. Bring the syrup to the boil and pour it on the fruit. Let the fruit steep for twenty-four hours. Follow the directions given for fresh fruit, steeping the fruit for five days in all. This is less time than taken for fresh fruit, but we have to bear in mind that this processed fruit has already been cooked in sugar. Then follow the eighth- and tenth-day patterns given for fresh fruit.

Some bottling and canning syrups vary, so if the end syrup seems too thin it may be necessary to add another $\frac{1}{3}$ cup of sugar and to repeat the pattern of the tenth day.

**Candied citrus peels** We give a recipe for candying peel with sugar and honey in the section on grapefruit and it is one which we can thoroughly recommend for any pithy-skinned citrus. However, in our opinion the result is best eaten as a sweetmeat. Where peel is required for cakes and other similar purposes, the following recipe may be more suitable. Incidentally, peels saved from squeezed fruits are quite capable of being used this way.

Quarter the peels. Weigh them and reserve a $\frac{1}{4}$ cup of sugar to each $\frac{1}{2}$ cup of peel. First make sure that the peel is well washed. Cover it with water and bring it to the boil. Drain, pour the water away. Repeat. Begin again with fresh water and simmer gently for 1–2 hours until the peel is tender. If it is not tender before it is candied it will become tough.

Add the sugar to the water and peel, stir well until it is dissolved and bring it back to the boil. Take it from the heat and let it cool uncovered. Reboil it the next day and let it simmer very slowly for 10 minutes. Set it aside once more. On the third day allow it to simmer slowly until the peel has taken in almost all the syrup and is of a changed texture and appearance. Drain and dry.

The remaining syrup can be treated in several ways. It can be divided among the quartered peels and poured into their 'cups' where it will harden. This should be done before they are dried. It can be added to fruit salads. It is particularly good in a dried fruit salad. It can be used as a base for creme caramels with a citrus flavour. It can be stored in the refrigerator and used for glazed ham.

Syrups left after candying other kinds of fruits can be used in most of these ways. They can also be given a little butter and made into toffee or toffee apples.

**Crystallising fruit** The simplest way to do this is with a dusting of sugar crystals. Cover a sheet of greaseproof paper with granulated sugar. Treat one piece of fruit at a time. Have a pan of water boiling slowly and quickly dip each piece of fruit into it. Drain off excess water by leaving the fruit on a piece of kitchen paper while one or more pieces are being dipped and drained. Before it is dry roll it in the sugar.

**Glazing fruit** Make a syrup of 2 cups of sugar dissolved in a $\frac{1}{2}$ cup of water brought to the boil. Pour a little of this syrup into a basin and cover the remainder with a lid or a damp cloth. Dip the fruit into boiling water in the manner described above. Using a skewer or a fork, dip each piece of fruit into the glaze and place it on a sieve to drain. After a while the glaze will become cloudy and when this happens replace it with fresh syrup. Dry the fruit as described above.

**Packing and storing** Pack the fruits in layers between waxed paper in cardboard or wooden boxes lined with waxed paper. Alternatively, the fruits can be packed in jars, but neither jars nor boxes should be completely airtight.

If you are not ready to dry the fruits they can be left in the syrup for at least three weeks so long as they are stored in a cool, clean place.

# FREEZING

**Dry, unsweetened pack** Not everyone likes, nor should eat, sweetened fruit, and fortunately many fruits, especially the berries, can be open-frozen and then simply packed into polythene bags or rigid containers in suitable quantities without sugars, syrups or other sweeteners. This entails the very rapid chilling ('flash freezing') of the fruit and will mean adjusting the freezer

controls in advance so that the fruit can be put into a temperature of about $-28°C$ ($-18°F$). Clean the fruit and spread it out well spaced in a single layer on baking sheets or trays. Cover with baking foil. Leave these sheets in the freezer until the fruit is hard frozen, then remove and pack in plastic bags or boxes. This way the fruits remain as individuals instead of becoming massed together in one lump. It is much more like fresh fruit when it is thawed.

Only fruit which does not discolour should be treated this way. Halves and sections of some fruits can be open-frozen.

Freezing results in a slight pectin loss in most fruits, so if it is to be used for jam or some other preserve, allow 10 per cent more fruit than called for in the recipe.

**Sugar pack** Soft fruits, juicy fruits and some larger sliced fruits are conveniently packed in sugar. However, there are certain disadvantages, one being that fruit which is already sweetened is not always suitable for a certain dish, or perhaps for someone's taste. Another is that fruits sweetened and frozen often lose their firm shape and become mushy.

Allow 2 cups of sugar to every 6 cups of fruit. Sugar and fruit can be mixed together, but this sometimes damages soft fruit. In this case they can be packed in layers, with sugar making the final layer.

**Syrup pack** It is not necessary to cook fruit to pack it in syrup for freezing. This is a good method for fruit which does not have much natural juice. Use white sugar and water in the following concentrations:
light (30%) syrup: 1 cup of sugar and 2 cups of water
medium (40%) syrup: 1$\frac{1}{2}$ cups of sugar and 2 cups of water
heavy (50%) syrup: 2 cups of sugar and 2 cups of water
Dissolve the sugar in the water, bring it to the boil and cool it before use.

We should point out to those who like to use brown sugar or honey that the former will affect the colour of the fruit and the latter will affect its flavour.

Use rigid containers for the fruit and cover with

the syrup, leaving a little headspace to allow for expansion. If you care to fill this headspace with crumpled greaseproof paper or special freezer paper, this will prevent the fruit rising above the level of the syrup and becoming discoloured as it sometimes does.

**Discoloration of fruit** Although the colour of most fruits remains good, some fruit becomes discoloured during freezing, in particular apples, bananas and peaches. Sometimes stone fruits become discoloured while they are being peeled and prepared, because their flesh is exposed to the air. To prevent this, lemon juice or ascorbic acid powder can be added to the syrup or to the sugar. It can also be added to the water in which the fruit is kept until it is ready. Usually a pinch of the powder or a teaspoon of lemon juice is sufficient.

**Freezing fruit purée** Purée is so concentrated that it occupies little space in the freezer compared with whole fruits. Furthermore, it can be frozen in convenient quantities, just right for whatever use you have for it.

Some fruits may need to be softened by cooking for a while in very little water – apples, currants and plums for instance – but most can be sieved or blended while they are fresh and ripe.

In these days of electric blenders it is often a matter of two or three minutes to make a purée, and almost every kind of fruit can be prepared this way. A short preliminary spin in the blender will help break down some fruits, blackberries for instance, so that they take less time to push through a sieve to remove the seeds.

**Thawing frozen fruit** Frozen fruit is best thawed slowly while covered. Do not wait until it is completely thawed and at room temperature if it is to be served like fresh fruit, raspberries for instance. Instead, eat it while it is still slightly chilled and still firm. It is better thawed in a refrigerator than in a warm room. Allow about six hours for 2 cups of fruit to thaw this way. Purée does not take so long – about four hours for 2 cups. If a compote is to be made, prepare the syrup and put the frozen fruit into this while it is hot. Poach the fruit very slowly and carefully and it will not break.

**Freezing fruit juices** Pour the juice – of orange, lemon, or any other – into ice trays. When set, transfer to a plastic bag. The cubes remain separated and one may be extracted and used as required.

# FRUIT BOTTLING

Bottling is a means of preserving fruits by sterilisation. Yeast cells and fungus spores present on fruits have to be destroyed to prevent the fruit fermenting or going mouldy. Also the enzymes present in fruits which may cause them to rot have to be destroyed. Bottling involves packing the fruit economically into containers and then processing them in various ways.

Generally speaking there are two types of vacuum jars or bottles in use. One type is closed by a clip and the other by a screw band. Both are obtainable in various sizes. They can be bought with a specially designed vessel in which they can be boiled, complete with thermometer and directions for use. It is also possible to buy tops which can be fitted to certain jam jars. Fruit can be preserved in plain water or in syrup. Usually fruit stored in syrup keeps a better colour and has a better flavour. Fruit bottled in syrup often rises in the jar, but this is no detriment unless you wish to enter a competition.

The average strength for a syrup is 1 cup of sugar to 2 cups of water, which works out to about $\frac{1}{2}$ cup to 2 cups of bottled fruit.

Sometimes cool syrup is poured on the fruit, sometimes hot, sometimes boiling, according to the method used.

The manufacturers of a bottling kit usually provide or offer a helpful book. On the other hand, although the correct kit is helpful it is certainly not essential. For years we bottled fruit by using a large saucepan, sometimes a small galvanised iron bath. A false bottom was made of folded newspapers to keep the jars from making direct contact with the heat. The cold water was poured in up to the shoulders of the jars and brought slowly to the boil. The water was held at simmering heat until we gauged that the fruit was cooked, usually by the fact that it had risen a little. The jars were then taken out and the tops screwed on tightly, or the snap closures put into place.

Our other method was to use the oven, heated at 120°C (250°F, gas mark ½). The prepared fruit was put into the jars with their tops but not their rubber rings, screw tops or clips. The jars were close but not touching each other or the sides of the oven and they rested on thick mats of cardboard. When the fruit was ready it was removed, one jar at a time, topped with water or syrup and closed properly. If the fruit had shrunk a lot, we tipped one jar into another and then topped it up.

There are actually several methods in use, and the reader must follow his inclinations or employ what apparatus is available to him, but in all there are just a few points which should always be followed. It is essential that the bottles should be clean. Sterilise after use and store, closed, in a clean place. Always examine rubber rings for flaws, have them soaking in warm water while awaiting use, then dip them in boiling water before applying. Do not screw the tops tightly before putting bottles in a bath, only lightly. Screw them tightly immediately the jars are taken out. It is unwise to store the bottles with their bands screwed tightly or their clips left on. Not only are these often difficult to remove later, but they sometimes go rusty. So test the jars to make sure that they are correctly sealed by lifting them by their covers. Then remove the screw bands, smear them lightly with a little olive oil and replace lightly. If clips are used, remove these, smear them with oil and store them in a dry place.

## PRESERVING FRUIT WITH CHEMICALS AND SYRUPS

Some fruits, particularly plums and most stone fruits, can be simply preserved by adding sulphur dioxide to them. This is obtainable as a powder and in some countries in the form of tablets, known as Campden tablets. Fruit so treated can be stored for a fairly long period, but before it can be served or used, it must be thoroughly boiled to remove the preservative. Apples can be treated this way, but there are many fruits to which sulphur dioxide should not be added, notably sweet cherries and pears. Salicylic acid and some other chemical preservatives are sometimes used in some countries, but these are not permitted as preservatives in most western countries because it is considered that if they are taken in considerable quantity they can be injurious to health.

**Fruit syrups** These are made from strained fruit juice and sugar, which means that they are clear. Fruit squashes have some of the fruit tissue visible in the liquid. These are both good ways of preserving fruits and they provide a ready means of making wholesome and delicious drinks. Use 1 part of syrup to 5 parts of water, soda water or milk. When milk is used, stir in the syrup slowly, otherwise you may find that the milk tends to curdle.

Syrups can also be used to make table jellies, creams and other desserts. For iced lollies mix syrup and water in equal parts.

The following method for the preparation of a syrup is a simple one for home use. The fruit should be fresh, fully ripe and clean. Only tough-skinned fruits need water added, 1 cup to each 2 cups of fruit. Firm soft fruit such as blackberries, boysenberries and the like need about 1 cup of water to about 12 cups of fruit. Extract the juice without overcooking it, which spoils the colour and reduces the flavour. If this is not done electrically, one of the best ways is to crush the fruit slightly and put it in a covered dish in a moderate to slow oven for about 1 hour. Alternatively, put the fruit in a basin, crush it with a spoon and then place it over a vessel of water and heat this until the juice begins to flow. In both cases crush the fruit with a wooden spoon a second time. Drain it through a jelly bag. Instead of wasting it, the remaining pulp can sometimes be boiled and used for a fruit butter or cheese. Measure the juice and add 1½ cups of sugar to every 2 cups. Stir the juice without heating until the sugar is dissolved. Strain it once more, then pour it into bottles (those with screw caps are best). The syrup should come up to within 2.5 cm (1 in) of the screw on the covers. These bottle tops should have been kept under boiling water for 15 minutes before use. Process the bottles in a deep pan with a false bottom, standing them upright with the water up to the level of the stoppers. Place folded newspapers between them to keep them from touching each other or the sides of the pan. Slowly raise the temperature to about 80°C

Fruit, an indispensable ingredient
for any cook. *(M. Withers)*

Bottled, dried or fresh, it is
possible to have most fruit
at any time of the year.

(175°F) and maintain this for 30 minutes, or maintain it at simmering point, 90°C (190°F), for 20 minutes. Remove the bottles one by one and tighten their screw caps.

It is possible to use corks as stoppers, but these have to be wired or tied down with stout string, otherwise they will be blown out while the juice is being processed. After the bottles are taken out and have cooled, they should be turned upside down and their corks dipped into paraffin wax to make a completely airtight seal.

When the bottles have been opened for use, keep the syrup refrigerated.

Do not use metal basins or other vessels for the fruit juice.

**Using sugar substitutes** Besides preserving the fruit, sugar (i.e. white sugar) helps to keep its natural flavour and its colour. It is possible to use other sweetening agents, but one should realise that these will have an effect on the taste and the appearance of the fruit. This is often not so important if the fruits to be preserved have a strong flavour. For instance, blackcurrants, gooseberries, plums and rhubarb can be bottled in a syrup made from honey or from golden syrup to the proportions 1 cup to 2 cups of water. Dissolve either of these in the water and bring it to the boil. Skim or strain if necessary.

The same strength may be used for glucose or corn syrup mixtures. These add sweetening but do not affect the flavour of the fruit in any way.

# FRUIT CANNING

Where large quantities of fruit are to be preserved the use of a canning machine may be justified, but one should realise that a considerable initial outlay may be involved. Furthermore, one should bear in mind that for efficient canning there should be plenty of clean, cold water available to cool the cans, as well as a suitable source of heat for boiling the water to sterilise them.

There are several types of domestic canning machine on the market, just as there are several types of mechanism for fastening the lids on to cans.

# DRYING FRUIT

It is important that the fruit should be both fresh and fully ripe, so that it will dry quickly, be a good colour and have full flavour. Unripe fruits are not suitable for drying.

Those who live in climates where the sun shines hot and the air is dry can dry their fruits in the sun and open air. Where this is not possible, a moderately warm oven, not more than 60°C (140°F), can be used. A cooling oven, i.e. one in which a meal has been cooked, can be used, but in this case the process will, of course, take longer. A continuous process should take about six hours. The alternative should not extend over more than three days. Fruit can also be dried above a stove or heater, but then one must guard against dust without at the same time impeding the movement of drying air around the fruit.

Usually fruit is laid on trays, easily made from laths and washed cheesecloth or muslin. Wire trays or sieves should have cheesecloth or muslin laid on them, otherwise the fruit is apt to become impressed with the wire pattern. Fruit like apples can be cut into rings and threaded on sticks like kebabs and laid across the trays from side to side of the oven. To prevent fruit – apples and pears in particular – from discoloration, first soak them in salt water, $\frac{1}{4}$ cup of salt to 16 cups ($5\frac{1}{8}$ pts) of water, for a few minutes. Pat them dry with kitchen paper or a cloth.

When dry, apples feel like chamois leather and are springy; pears are juiceless. Plums, prunes and similar fruits should be capable of being squeezed without the skin breaking or the juice flowing. Bananas are very dark and shrivelled.

Chemical preservatives can be used. Apricots, peaches and nectarines can be treated this way if one feels that the other methods are not ideal, but sometimes the fruit discolours. The washed fruits should be halved, then dipped in a solution made up of 32 cups ($9\frac{1}{16}$ pts) water, $\frac{3}{4}$ cup of sodium or potassium metabisulphite, $K_2S_2O_2$, sometimes known as Campden tablets, and 6 cups of sugar. Well submerge the fruit, weighing it down to keep it under the liquid. Let it soak for twelve hours. Then rinse it with plenty of fresh water and place it on trays, the cut side uppermost, and dry in the sun. Fruit can be partially sun- and oven-dried.

All dried fruit should be stored in tightly closed containers in a cool and shady place.

When dried fruit is to be cooked, allow at least forty-eight hours for soaking in plenty of water. Keep them in this water and bring them slowly to the boil. Simmer gently until they are plump and then add the sugar. Sugar added too early will prevent them from becoming as plump, tender and juicy as they might.

# BASIC RECIPES

This chapter outlines the basic recipes for making sweet, savoury and sippable use of fruits in season.

## JAMS, PRESERVES, CONSERVES, ETC

Jams are made by cooking fruit with sugar until it 'jells' or becomes of a firm and jelly-like consistency. Fruit can be left whole, cut into portions or crushed, but it is not expected that the original shape of the fruit will be retained. Jams can be made of one, two or more fruits combined. Juicy fruits need no added water, but fruits which are not very juicy are usually given some water to soften them. This is gradually lost as the jam boils. Usually $1\frac{1}{2}$ to 2 cups of sugar is added to every 2 cups of fruit.

For the sake of convenience we often use the word 'jam' as an omnibus term to cover the following mixtures also.

**Preserves** Preserves differ from jams in that whole small fruits or portions of fruit are cooked in a syrup until this becomes clear and translucent. The fruit is not mashed but is kept clear and identifiable. Only one kind of fruit is used.

**Conserves** Conserves contain a mixture of whole fruits or sections of fruits, usually two or three kinds, often with the addition of nuts or the fruit stone kernels if stone fruits are used.

**Marmalade** Marmalades are generally taken to mean a jam that is made from a citrus fruit, or from some other fruit with citrus added in sufficient quantity to influence the flavour. The citrus peel is an important part of marmalade. This can be cut very finely – 'shredded' – or it can be thick and chunky, according to taste. As a rule the finest peel is used in a clear, jelly-like marmalade. A thick peel takes a long time to soften and cook, which is why more water is specified in recipes for marmalades than for jams. In citrus fruits the pectin, or jelling substance, is present in the pips and the pith (the white inner skin). This is why all the fruit is used in marmalades. As a rule pith and pips are cooked separately, or tied in muslin and cooked with the prepared peel and flesh.

**Jellies** Jellies are made from the strained juices of a fruit or a combination of fruits after these have been boiled in water or cooked in some other way in order to extract as much juice as possible. Sometimes the fruit pulp is boiled a second time for this purpose. Jelly should not be stirred once it has boiled. It should be clear when set and it should be of a firm, stiff texture and not runny. The juice should be measured after the initial cooking and then have sugar added in equal bulk.

In order for it to set properly, jam – or rather the fruit from which it is made – should contain sufficient pectin, a gum-like substance. It is a good plan to keep a store of pectin stock, i.e. acid fruit juice made from redcurrants or similar fruit. This is made by straining the juice and putting it into hot preserving jars, then sterilising them by bottling in the usual way (see p. 27) for 5 minutes, or the juice can be frozen. Commercial pectins can be bought and full directions for their use will be found on the packet. Not all fruits contain the same amount of pectin, and some, like strawberries, are deficient. Slightly underripe fruit usually contains more pectin than ripe or overripe. Pectin combines with the acid in the fruit and later with the sugar. Fruits light in acids, such as strawberries, pears and sweet cherries, can have acid added to them in the form of lemon juice, $\frac{1}{2}$ cup to every 8 cups of fruit.

Pectin is simmered out of the fruit in the early stages of cooking. This is why sugar is usually added after the fruit has been simmered long enough for the excess water to be driven off. If the pectin is boiled for a long time with the sugar it becomes changed into a non-setting pectose, so it is important to cook fruit slowly before adding the sugar and then rapidly for a short time.

Less scum is formed on jams if lump or preserving sugars are used, but granulated sugar is quite suitable. Sugar has a hardening effect on fruits, which is why some fruits, blackcurrants for instance, have to be really soft before the sugar is added. On the other hand, some fruits are kept with sugar overnight before cooking so that they will remain firm. Strawberries and diced fruits such as pears are examples. It helps to warm the sugar in an oven before it is added to the fruit.

To see if the jam is near setting point, spoon out a small amount, wait a minute and then pour it back, taking note of its texture. While it runs back smoothly it is not ready and once it drops in globules it is almost there. Drop more on a cold plate, wait a while and see if it sets.

Always use clean, sterilised, hot jars. Keep them in an oven or warmer until you are ready for them. Stand the jars on a board or on several thicknesses of paper and ladle the jam in. Fill the jars to the top. Preserves, conserves and marmalades should be allowed to cool slightly before being sealed, otherwise the fruit will rise to the top, but others should be covered while hot. Some people use melted paraffin wax to seal the jars to keep out moulds. Others use waxed paper cut into circles which fit exactly on the surface of the hot jam. Some people close the jars with a cardboard-lined screw top, others use parchment or a transparent cellulose paper to close the jars, which generally keeps the jams in better condition.

One last word. Jams made in brass or copper preserving pans have been found to contain less vitamin C than those made in aluminium or stainless steel pans. Enamelled pans can be used, but if these are chipped the jam may burn. Never leave fruit or jams in metal pans for long. When prepared fruits have to be left overnight before cooking, keep them in an earthenware or plastic bowl.

**Butters and Cheeses** These are midway between jellies and jams. They consist of a sweetened purée of fruit. They are not clear like jellies, but opaque like jams. Butters can be used as low-sugar jams. They can be served with bread or scones, but they are also very useful as pie fillings or for spreading in layer cakes.

The sieved pulp should be weighed and 1 to $1\frac{1}{2}$ cups of sugar added to every 2 cups of fruit. Fruit butters are often spiced. Powdered spices can darken the butter – this can be avoided by tying the whole spices in muslin. The pulp should be heated and simmered until it is thick. The sugar and spices should then be added, stirring continuously, until no liquid is seen at the edges of the pulp and the mixture is thick and creamy. Pot the butter like jam.

Cheeses are frequently served at the end of a meal in place of cheese and/or eaten as a dessert or as a sweetmeat. Traditionally, the best fruits for cheeses are blackcurrants, damsons, medlars and quinces. When it is made, the cheese is poured into small jars or moulds from which it can be turned out onto a plate. Some people use small moulds to make individual cheeses. The mould should first be smeared with a little glycerine so that the cheese can be turned out easily and undamaged.

More sugar is used in a cheese: 2 cups to 2 cups of purée. Less can be used, but this entails cooking the cheese for a longer period. The purée should first be boiled and if it seems very liquid it should be considerably reduced. Stir it while the sugar dissolves, then simmer it for $\frac{3}{4}$–1 hour, stirring very frequently to prevent it burning. Test by drawing a spoon across the bottom of the pan. If the cheese is stiff enough, a clean line will be drawn. When cooking this there may well be some spitting and spluttering, so it is prudent to use a deep pan.

## CHUTNEYS AND SAUCES

The more dried fruits, crystallised fruits, golden syrup, honey or treacle used in a recipe, the less sugar will be required. Glucose or corn syrup may be substituted for sugar, but neither of these two will contribute to the flavour. Brown sugars are usually included in dark chutneys.

## SWEETMEATS

Throughout this book from time to time recipes are given for different sweetmeats. Readers who care to experiment may like to know that uncomplicated sweetmeats can be made simply by spreading sweetened fruit pulp, which has been seeded, skinned, sieved and cooked, on to greased trays and then drying it at a low temperature in an oven heated to no higher than about 50°C (120°F).

Fruits which are ripe and very sweet, such as pears and peaches, may need no sugar, or at least very little. Test by tasting. The flavour of the pulp can be changed by the addition of spices and other flavourings, and the texture by adding nuts. Many variations can be played on one theme, perhaps an advisable move when there is a quantity of one kind of fruit to be used.

Instead of pouring the pulp directly on to the greased tray, the tray can be lined with muslin and the pulp spread on this. It will then be easy to turn out, the muslin being pulled off from the under-side. When it is firm enough to handle, test by taking a corner and lifting or pulling it up. Tip the sweetmeat out on to a sugared paper, cut it into shapes and roll it in caster sugar.

These pieces can be chocolate-coated by dipping them into melted chocolate and then leaving them to dry on waxed paper. To store, pack the sweetmeats between waxed paper in non-airtight containers.

# BASIC RECIPES

**Basic Table Jelly** Almost any kind of fruit can be used to make a table jelly, instead of resorting to the familiar packet of synthetic flavoured gelatine. The following jelly is made with lemon juice, but can be adapted for any fruit juice. Less fully flavoured fruits are often improved if some lemon juice is mixed with them. Less water and a greater proportion of fruit juice can be used – it is really a matter of testing by taste.

## Basic table jelly

1½ tabsp gelatine powder mixed with 4 tabsp
    cold water until soft
2 cups boiling water
¾ cup sugar
pinch salt
1 teasp finely chopped or grated lemon rind
¼ cup lemon juice

Mix the moistened gelatine into the hot water until it is completely dissolved. Add the sugar and salt and stir these also until they are dissolved. Add the lemon rind and juice. Pour the liquid into a wet mould or a serving dish. Chill until it is firm. Turn it out on to a dish or serve it in its mould. This jelly can also be poured into individual dishes and used as a basis of a more elaborate sweet, in which case only half the quantity might be needed.

Whole fruits, raw or cooked, can be introduced into a jelly. Arrange the fruit in the mould or dish and pour the jelly on it after it has cooled a little. If the fruit is to be shown in layers, pour in a little jelly at a time to cover the fruit. As one layer sets, make the next layer of fruit, cover this with jelly, and so on.

## Basic fruit sherbet

2 teasp powdered gelatine moistened in 4 tabsp
    cold water
¾ cup sugar
2 cups water less the 4 tabsp used for gelatine
1 cup fruit juice
2 egg whites
pinch salt

Boil the sugar and water together for 10 minutes. Add to it the moistened gelatine and when this has been completely dissolved let the liquid cool. Mix in the fruit juice. Pour all into a suitable vessel (we use a plastic drum with a cover so that only one utensil is required) and put it in a freezer or freezing compartment until it begins to solidify. At this point the sherbet should be well whisked until it is fluffy. This can be done electrically. Take a wooden spoon or spatula and scrape around the edge of the bottom of the bowl, drum or whatever is used, to make sure that no portion remains unwhisked. Whip the egg whites until they are stiff and quickly fold them into the mixture with the salt. Return it to the freezer until it has again become half solid. Bring it back and whisk again, this time making sure that it becomes very light and fluffy and that its bulk increases considerably.

From this point the sherbet can be returned to the freezer and used shortly. Alternatively, a cover can be put on the container and it can be kept for several weeks. The easiest way to serve it is to shave off layers with a large spoon and to heap these frozen curls in individual dishes. If oven-proof dishes are used, these can be prepared a few hours in advance of a meal and placed on folded newspaper in the freezer until you are ready to serve.

**Basic fruit ice-cream** Obviously there are a great number of recipes for ice-creams, many much richer and more elaborate than the one given below. However, we publish it because it is such a simple recipe and because it has always been immensely enjoyed by our guests and our family. We have used a great many different fruits to make it and it is hard to say which is the favourite, but alpine strawberries, blackberries, mulberries and raspberries get high marks. (We also use it to make a cassata by filling a Victoria sponge, cutting it into layers and spreading each layer with a little of the fruit's jam.) If you are short of purée, it is possible to use a fruit jelly, or sometimes even a jam, in which case no extra sugar will be required. Hard-skinned jams such as gooseberry and plum are not good unless they are sieved.

### Basic fruit ice-cream

1 cup fruit purée
½ cup icing sugar
1 teasp lemon juice
½ cup double or heavy cream
½ cup single or light cream
1 egg white, whipped

Add the lemon juice and the sugar to the purée and stir or blend until all are well mixed. Combine the two creams, whisk them until they are thick but not stiff. Blend these with the sweetened purée. Fold in the stiffly whisked egg white. Put into an electric ice-cream maker or pour into a plastic canister. It is not quite so light if it is not stirred while it is freezing, so remove the mixture in a plastic canister a little while before you wish to serve it and let it soften a little in the refrigerator before scooping or spooning it out into individual dishes. If possible decorate it with its own fruits.

## BASIC WINE MAKING

The making of fruit wines can be as simple or as complicated as you wish and there is no doubt that by taking advantage of special ingredients such as purpose-made wine yeasts, a better wine will be produced. But with very basic equipment and very simple recipes it is possible to make drinkable wines from almost all fruits.

Essential equipment begins with a large saucepan or some similar vessel capable of holding at least 4.5 litres (1 gallon), which should be aluminium or unchipped enamel. Wine in the process of preparation should never be allowed to come into contact with any metal, other perhaps than stainless steel. A glass fermenting jar and an efficient airlock, a supply of muslin for straining off the liquid, a length of rubber or plastic tubing

for racking or siphoning it off from one vessel to another, and a supply of bottles and corks are the remaining items of equipment necessary.

Cleanliness is essential and the easiest way of ensuring this is to make use of a simply obtained chemical steriliser known as potassium (or sodium) metabisulphite ($K_2S_2O_2$) which can be bought in crystal form from most chemists or obtained ready made in the shape of Campden tablets. Use two Campden tablets to 500 ml (1 pt) of water to make a stock solution, or crush 150 g (5 oz) of the crystals in warm water and dilute to make 4.5 litres (1 gallon). This solution is for cleaning all the vessels you use, being poured from one to the other, and retained for further use on another occasion. Bottle, cork tightly and label.

The yeast used in wine making can come in several forms, as baker's yeast used in bread-making, as prepared, dried and packeted yeast and in the form of tablets or powder in specialised wine-making forms such as 'port' yeast, 'burgundy' yeast or 'sauterne' yeast, depending on the type of wine one wishes to produce. Obviously one would use a specialised yeast of this type only with a compatible fruit. These special yeasts must sometimes be started into life up to two days before they are actually used, so allowance must be made for this pre-preparation time.

Yeasts need both sugar and acid to work satisfactorily, and as a rule both must be added, although certain specialised yeasts sometimes do away with the need for the latter. The acid, if required, is usually in the form of lemon or orange juice, but can be citric or tartaric acid.

A basic recipe of a simple type, using ingredients obtainable almost anywhere in the world, is for Pear Wine.

### Pear wine

16 cups chopped pears
16 cups water
1 cup raisins
6 cups sugar to each 16 cups juice
1 cup lemon juice
wine yeast

Chop cleaned pears into chunks, including skins and cores. Place with chopped raisins in boiling water and simmer for 5–10 minutes. Remove from heat and cover carefully with at least two layers of muslin, and allow to stand for three days, stirring twice a day. Then strain through muslin on to the sugar, add the lemon juice and the yeast. Pour into the fermentation jar, fit the airlock and leave in a warm, dark place until all fermentation has ceased. Then rack or siphon off into clean bottles and cork tightly.

# FRUIT FOR THE HOME AND GARDEN

## AKEBIA
*Akebia* species

### Origin

The Japanese name of the plant is *akebi*. It is a small genus in the family Lardizabalaceae. The species are *A. lobata*, syn. *A. trifoliata*; *A. quinata* and *A. x pentaphylla*, a cross between *A. quinata* and *A. lobata*. The specific names of these are allusions to the 3- and 5-part leaves which differentiate the species. They are natives of China, Korea and Japan, not well known outside their native countries. *A. x pentaphylla* was raised in 1932 in Japan and America.

### The fruit

Botanically a fleshy follicle, the fruits of *A. lobata* are long, sausage-shaped and a grey-purple, almost like a pale aubergine, and 8–13 cm (3–5 in) long. As the fruit ripens it splits, revealing shining black seeds in white, pulpy flesh. Those of *A. quinata* are similar in colour, shorter – 6–9 cm (2½–3½ in) long – and a little broader.

When grown in Europe, to most people the flavour of the fruit is not remarkable (although it can be enhanced by using a little lemon juice) and this is probably due to the fact that in a cold climate the flavour is not pronounced. In its home countries it is said to be much enjoyed.

### The plant

Akebia is a hardy, vigorous, twining shrub, evergreen in warm localities, deciduous in others. The fragrant flowers are unisexual although they grow together. *A. lobata* has 3 apple-green leaflets which are broadly ovate, with lobed or wavy margins, each some 4–10 cm (1½–4 in) long. The flowers are borne in drooping racemes each about 8 cm (3 in) long, in the axils of the leaves. The numerous male flowers are pale purple and only about 4–5 mm (⅛ in) wide, while the females, usually only 2 at the base of the raceme, are a dark, even lurid purple, and about 2 cm (¾ in) wide. The leaflets of *A. quinata* are attractively spaced on a long, slender, common stalk; there are usually 5 to a stalk, 4–8 cm (1½–3 in) long and oblong or ovate in shape. The flowers grow in a dainty manner on slender pendant racemes, the chocolate-purple females 3–4 cm (1–1¼ in) wide, conspicuous against the tassel-like pale purple male flowers which are only 5 mm (¼ in) wide.

*A. pentaphylla* is a very similar to *A. quinata* in growth and has flowers resembling those of *A. lobata*.

Since the plant is twining and self-supporting, the akebia can be used to cover any erection such as a pergola or to grace the branches of some small tree – an old apple tree, for example. It can be used to make a very light and attractive canopy over a patio. Alternatively, given a trellis or wires against a fence, it can be used as a softening and – in its season – interesting screen. Flower arrangers will find flowering shoots, fruits and even twining stems of great value, especially for those ensembles which call for deep tones and flowing or pendant lines, such as pedestal and wall decorations.

### Cultivation

In spite of its hardiness, this plant does best, and certainly flowers more freely and safely, if it is given the protection of a warm wall. In northern countries it flowers in late spring, a time when the flowers can still be frosted. However, it will grow well in a border in a cold greenhouse. Here it is more likely to flower and fruit well if it is given both warmth and humidity. It should be hand-pollinated. Soil mixture should be equal parts of loam, peat and sand.

Akebia is best planted in autumn. It needs little pruning – simply cut away straggly growths or shoots after the plant has flowered. Propagation is by seed taken from the ripe fruit, but in many regions germination by seed appears to be unsatisfactory, in which case the plant can be increased from cuttings of half-ripened wood inserted in sandy soil in autumn and kept in gentle heat until they root, when they can be potted and later planted. Akebia can also be propagated by layering in early spring (see *Propagation* pp. 9–11).

### Culinary uses

When the fruits are ripe, they burst and they are then ready to eat. This is not the most fully flavoured fruit, and it cannot be used for many purposes. It is good eaten raw. The flavour is improved if a little lemon juice or a liqueur such as kirsch is sprinkled over the fruit. Seeds removed, the flesh can be puréed and made into a cream or a drink.

# AKEE
*Blighia sapidia*

## Origin

This is named after none other than the famous William Bligh, of the *Bounty,* who had much more to do with the transference of food plants from one part of the globe to another than most people realise. This is a genus of one single species of tree, native to Guinea but established and much appreciated in the West Indies. It is very common in Jamaica and is grown in some gardens in Florida.

## The fruit

It is not the fruit that is edible but the fleshy, white arils it contains. The fruit is 3-angled and splits or pops open when mature to reveal the shining black seeds, which are poisonous. It is important that the fruit is allowed to open naturally, for the unripe arils are highly indigestible.

## The plant

Akee makes a striking specimen tree, growing eventually to a height of about 9 m (30 ft), with handsome oblong-ovate evergreen leaves growing in three or four pairs. The upright racemes of hairy white flowers are showy. The pendant fruits, which have been described as being like Christmas tree ornaments, are bright red.

## Cultivation

The akee needs tropical or sub-tropical conditions (climate no. 4 on the world chart, p. 14) to grow well. It can be propagated by seed and by cuttings. The tree usually bears two crops a year.

## Culinary uses

The akee is an important part of the Jamaican diet. It can be eaten raw; if to be cooked, then it is simmered in salted water for 15–20 minutes or until it is tender and evenly coloured a bright yellow. In the West Indies akee is traditionally (though not necessarily) cooked with salt fish of some kind, preferably cod. One method is to soak the fish overnight, then to drain it and wash it well in cold water, or to cover it with water, bring it to the boil and flake it. Bacon rashers are fried in a pan and onions and then tomatoes or peppers fried in the bacon fat. The fish is added to these. The separately cooked akee is then added to the dish, each 'peg' kept whole, and all is mixed together, well seasoned with black pepper. It is served with island vegetables such as sweet potato and green bananas. Sliced raw avocadoes are sometimes used for garnish.

Cooked akee can be mixed with the fish after it has been fried in oil with a little onion and plenty of seasoning. The contents of the pan are then pounded to make a paste. This is used to fill pieces of shortcrust pastry, usually circles which are folded over the filling to make half circles, a little like the pasta ravioli. These little akee pies can be served as hors d'oeuvres. Akee can also be curried and served with rice.

In many ways, in both appearance and texture, the arils of the akee resemble scrambled eggs and do in fact go well with egg. Individual pegs can be dipped in beaten egg, or in well-garlicked batter, and deep fried. Akee can be used in a soufflé.

Cold cooked akee can be served in a vinaigrette sauce. It can also be incorporated in a salad, and goes well with avocado, some people saying that there is a similarity in the tastes.

# APPLE

*Malus* species

## Origin

A member of the rose family and of the genus *Malus*. Any fruit of a tree of this genus, of which there are some 25 species and many varieties, is an apple. Apples are known to have been gathered, eaten fresh, dried and stored – and so perhaps specially cultivated also – as far back as the Stone Age. Today there are thousands of known varieties. Their direct history is not always easy to trace. *Malus pumila,* the common form of the wild crab apple, is to be found growing over a wide area of Europe, western Asia and the Himalayas. Its progeny is very variable although its own fruits are unremarkable and an undistinguished yellow-green. It is therefore surprising to learn, for instance, that it is responsible for some of the decorative, ornamental and very beautiful crabs, such as John Downie, which are grown more for the beauty of their spring blossom and the vivid colours of the masses of small fruits they produce, than for any utilitarian purpose. On the other hand, this species is also the parent of the many important varieties grown for food and drink.

*Malus sylvesteris,* said to be a variety of *M. pumila,* and often found growing wild in northern Europe, is believed to be the parent which passed on its natural acidity to varieties later cultivated. This is an important legacy, since apples were at one time grown in some countries solely for cider-making. Then, no special attention was paid to what varieties were used: all were acid and were mixed as they came to hand. Later, as with wine-making and growing grapes, gradually more attention came to be paid to the selection of those varieties most suitable for the preparation of this apple drink. Propagation was originally by sowing seed, the apple pips. Batches of seedlings would be raised, allowed to fruit and then selected according to their yield and performance.

Of course, from a batch of mixed seedlings – and apple pips cannot be relied upon to grow into trees true to their parents – there would be some which when tasted proved to be sweet and delectable and obviously were worth growing for this reason alone. To prevent waste it would be found that some varieties unsuitable for cider need not be rejected but could be cooked, or even dried and then cooked much later. Others would store well after harvesting and so provide a good fresh food in the long, cold winter months. For a very long time the apple was the only fresh fruit available in winter in northern climates. From these simple beginnings evolved the several groups into which apples now can be classified.

This process has taken centuries. As various peoples moved about Europe and down to the Mediterranean and beyond, it appears that they took the apple with them, all the while improving its quality in some way or another. Apples were cultivated by the ancient Egyptians along the Nile valley in the twelfth century BC. We know that they were also cultivated by the ancient Greeks and Romans. From the fact that a writer in the fourth century AD was able to refer to 37 varieties indicates that they had already been subjected to many centuries of cultivation.

Nearer our own time, at the beginning of the seventeenth century, many varieties of apple from England and France were imported into North America. One writer claims that planting apples was among the first tasks the early settlers carried out. As one would expect, a little later more apples were taken to South Africa and to Australia. From these countries the cultivation of the apple spread even further afield as more areas were occupied. Bismark, a bright crimson cooking apple, was first sent to England from Tasmania in 1895.

Many seedlings raised in these new areas were so good that they were sent back 'home' (one assumes as trees or grafts) but few of them did so well away from their place of birth. Apples are themselves selective about the area in which they choose to grow. Often a favourite in one country fails to thrive in another. Some varieties will do well in one district or area of a country, perhaps in the north but not in the south, and it is for this reason that you will find the same variety recurring time and time again in orchards and garden in one area. This is also the reason why each country tends to rely on seedlings it has grown and tested rather than on imported stocks.

## The fruit

Botanically a pome, the apple matures from summer to late winter. The ripe fruit has a distinctive aroma and exudes ethylene gas. Fruits vary in size according to species and variety. In shape they may be round or globular, flat or oblate, oblong or conical. The 'eye', the term given to the remains of the calyx and stamens of the blossom, is situated in a basin, which may be deep or differently coloured according to the variety. The stalk is in a cavity, and again this may be deep or shallow according to variety.

Apples are divided into two main groups: those which can be eaten fresh (dessert apples) and cooking varieties. These groups tend to overlap in some cases and many dessert apples are delicious when cooked. Apart from these two important sections there are also apples which are most suitable for cider-making and for drying.

Although it surely must be safe to say that anyone can recognise an apple, once familiar with the fruit, it is not always easy to give a particular fruit its varietal name or origin. Varieties differ considerably from each other, in size, flavour, aroma, colour, keeping qualities and uses. Furthermore, the fruits of different varieties mature at different seasons, in summer (earlier and earlier as research and breeding is carried out), autumn and winter. Some mature on the tree. Some do not mature until harvested and stored. Some of these will keep fresh until blossom time comes round again. Some late cooking apples, after being stored all winter, can be eaten raw.

Colours vary from greyish-brown, bright apple green, through golden yellows to orange red and vivid crimson. Many apples are flushed or coloured on one side only. Some have dull skins, some shiny and some oily or greasy, while others are rough and russetted.

In the wild state apples ripen in late autumn and it is obviously to man's advantage to extend the season for as long as possible. In choosing varieties one has to consider that in northern countries where summers are short, only those apples which ripen within ten weeks of flowering will do. Elsewhere, in Mediterranean and other warmer countries, a much longer ripening process can be allowed.

Generally speaking, the earlier an apple matures the softer its flesh and the less likely it is to last long and keep its flavour. Apples produced later in the year are harder and many of these need a long ripening. This can be easily carried out by the amateur, but as one might expect, it is done on a much greater and more scientific scale commercially. Where these long-keeping apples are grown in cold countries they may lack flavour even after reaching maturity, yet in a warm climate under good cultivation, the same variety of apple often becomes delicious. A familiar example is Sturmer Pippin, which many people in Britain know only as an Australian import although it will grow and crop well in warmer areas of Britain.

Some varieties of apple seem to be known universally. One calls to mind Delicious, Jonathan, Granny Smith, Cox's Orange and so on, and there are many, many more in cultivation. One finds that not only each country but often each district has its favourite also. For this reason we think that it would not be helpful to give a list of varieties, especially as names differ sometimes in different countries. Instead we recommend that interested gardeners should seek advice from a specialist nurseryman or supplier, from his local Department of Agriculture, Horticultural Education Officer or even a knowledgeable friend.

## The plant

The apple is a spreading, round-headed, deciduous, branching tree. When allowed to grow naturally it will reach some 6–12 m (20–40 ft) according to its type, its rootstock and its environment. Fortunately, smaller dwarfer and more compact forms can be produced by various methods. The pretty, rose and white flowers are in umbels, appearing with the leaves from mostly downy buds, but here again there may be differences according to varieties. Apples are a good example of our contention that fruit growing can be all things to all men. It can be as casual as one wishes, provided that a great and fine harvest is not expected; or cultivation can be broken down to fit into any daily, weekly or monthly routine; or it can be a full-time occupation particularly suitable and rewarding for those who need a hobby. Pruning alone can be all-absorbing, for apart from anything else there is so much to learn about the various methods. Once learned, these methods can be applied in a manner which adds decoration to any garden, great or small. For instance, an apple pergola can cover a garden path or walk, or a half pergola can cover the path alongside the house with the trees finishing at the house wall. Simple arches, more complex bowers, rooms, mazes, sun traps, all can be constructed from well-trained and pruned trees. Low hedges or edgings to run alongside paths and to mark borders can be made of cordons laid and trained low. An apple tree can be trained into a goblet shape, a diamond, even a great globe. When the trees are bare these living sculptures will remain attractive. They are, of course, a delight when they are in blossom, and careful and proper pruning can ensure that there is always plenty of blossom. All will yield a surprisingly good crop of fruit.

Like many other fruits, apples may also be grown in containers.

Meanwhile, for those who are content simply to allow the trees to grow naturally, blossom can help in flower arrangements for the home. Branches can be gathered as soon as the flower buds show colour. Gathering them gives the gardener a splendid and leisurely opportunity to remove branches which hang too low, which cross, or which seem mishapen or spindly. Such branches often look most attractive in arrangements.

## Cultivation

Generally speaking, apples will flourish in the open or in sheltered gardens, but there are certain points to be confirmed before planting. As with so many plants, vegetables as well as fruits, people get to know a few varieties well by name and will continue to ask for these only, when in fact often another lesser-known variety might suit their garden or their needs better. Obviously some well-known varieties have deserved their high reputation, an example being the English Cox's Orange Pippin, which when grown on the right soils is unsurpassable, yet too often fails to give of its best in private gardens because it is a difficult apple to manage and choosy with its soil. This, like so many fruits, was a chance seedling as was the Australian Granny Smith, which originated as a seedling at Eastwood, NSW, in about 1868. Like the Cox, this variety is excellent for both culinary purposes and dessert. The gardener is advised first to ascertain what varieties are known to flourish locally and from this list to select those which appeal to him.

Sheltered gardens in towns are sometimes heavily shaded at some point or another. Apples will not grow well in the shade cast by a tall building or some densely foliaged neighbouring

tree. Cold and strong prevailing winds also have a detrimental effect and can kill or damage blossom as well as cause fruit to fall. Apples should not be grown in a known frost pocket. Strong winds are not often a great problem in towns, but they could be in certain areas. As a rule apples do not grow well near the sea, where they can be affected by gales and spume. High rainfall, warm winters, acid or clay soils and high altitudes are disliked by most apples.

If you wish to make your garden as ornamental as possible a single tree can be grown, which in blossom time is as pretty as any other. This could be either a cooking variety or a dessert. Where the tree has space to spread itself and where shade would be welcome, a full standard can be grown, with a bare stem or trunk some 2 m (6 ft) high. For those who do not want a full-sized tree there are also half standards with 1½ m (4–5 ft) stems and so-called bushes, trees with a short trunk of only about 50 cm (1½ ft).

However, before planting a single tree, check what other apple trees, if any, grow nearby. Some apples are self-fertile, but even these crop better if their pollen can be crossed with that of another variety. You could do yourself and your neighbours a good turn by checking with them to discover what variety of apple they grow. Some get on better together than others, just like many other marriages. Alternatively, a 'family tree' can be grown, bearing three different but compatible varieties on a single trunk.

Apples are not raised from seed unless a raiser is seeking a new variety. Instead, buds or shoots are taken from the variety the grower wishes to increase and are budded or grafted on to a root-stock (see *Propagation,* pp. 9-11). Modern root-stocks produce neat, compact trees which usually begin cropping from their second season after planting.

Nurserymen also train apple trees into many different forms. The value here lies in the fact that because they have been specially trained and because their growth has to be controlled, they can be planted quite close together.

Pyramid trees, which differ from bushes by the retention of the main stem up through the tree, can be planted quite closely to each other, about 1.5 m (5 ft) apart. These are good plants to use as a screen, across the end of the garden for example.

Espalier-trained trees, with a stout central stem and 'ladders' of four or five branches on each side, parallel and about 30 cm (1 ft) apart, all on one plane, can be grown against a wall or fence or can be supported by wires. They look well this way flanking a garden path. Incidentally, it is not really a good idea to use espaliers as a screen for a vegetable patch, simply because the spreading, searching apple roots thus have access to too much nitrogen, placed there to feed the vegetables. The side stems can be allowed to grow as long as they will, and if you wish to plant more than one, the trees should be about 4–5 m (12–15 ft) apart.

Cordons, which may consist of one or a pair of stems, can be planted where space is at a premium. These can be grown on a slant, supported by a strong cane, or vertically. They can be as close to each other as 60 cm (2 ft). They must be kept well pruned so that fruiting spurs can be produced all along the single stem. It is surprising what heavy crops these compact, controlled trees will bear when they are correctly managed.

Apples can also be fan-trained, in which case they are treated in much the same way as espaliers.

Incidentally, the famous Granny Smith does not respond well to training and there may well be others equally temperamental, so check with your nurseryman when ordering.

A deep, loamy soil is the ideal for apples, but this is not universally available, and one variety or another can be grown on most kinds of soil. It is most important that the soil should not be or become deficient in potash. Watch for symptoms which indicate that there is a deficiency (see *Fertiliser deficiency symptoms*, p. 17) and take measures immediately to supply this essential plant food. Try to carry out simple soil tests at regular intervals. An important factor in good cultivation is that drainage should be adequate, yet one should ensure that in providing this the soil should not be left to dry out seriously in hot summers. In preparing the soil, drainage to a depth of at least 1 m (3 ft) is required.

In spite of the foregoing, it should be stressed that crops can successfully be produced on shallow soils provided you are prepared to go to a little trouble. Fortunately, if the right procedures are followed, soil depths generally improve rather than deteriorate. On shallow soils, ensure that the trees are given all the moisture they require. There are suitable rootstocks for shallow soil cultivation, so select these when necessary.

It is interesting to note that very rich soils, and certainly those which are highly nitrogenous, do not produce good dessert varieties, yet this does not seem to apply in such a definite way to cooking varieties. Dessert apples grow best where the rainfall is about 65 cm (25 in) annually. They do not all grow well where it is heavier than this. Cooking varieties and cider apples grow best in wetter areas.

If the plants are to be lifted from the open ground they should be planted during their dormant season. However, if they are canister-grown they can be planted whenever they are available, although it is prudent even then to buy them in bud rather than in fruit.

If the small tree, however trained, is to bear a good crop of fruit, then it has to be controlled by proper pruning, carried out to encourage the branches to produce fruiting spurs (see *Pruning*, pp. 12-13). Any large tree, left to grow naturally and unpruned, will, if it is pollinated properly, bear fruit. But espaliers, fan-shaped and cordons have to be rigorously and skilfully pruned, with understanding, if they are to be kept compact and fruitful. The larger standard, half standard and bush trees do not need summer pruning, which is really no more than shortening side shoots (easily seen and identified on the trained trees) to 10–15 cm (4–6 in) during late summer. The leader, the main stem at the tip, is left unpruned. When winter comes, these same summer-pruned shoots are cut back to within a few centimetres of their base. This encourages the development of spurs or fruit buds. These are always formed on older branches and at the base of the shoots of the previous year's growth.

So far as the other trees are concerned, they need only be kept tidy and under control. Crossing branches should be cut away flush with a main stem and any dead wood should be removed.

Although one may feel really exalted to see a tree well laden with fruit, it may not be prudent to allow it to remain so. First though, be prepared for the tree to adjust its own matters. Almost inevitably many fruits which seem well set are shed. In Britain apple trees are naturally pruned by what is known as the 'June drop'

Once this is passed it is wise to go over the trees examining the clusters of fruits. First pick off any damaged or misshapen fruits. Interestingly, the fruit which develops from the central flower of a cluster of blossom, known as the 'king' fruit, is usually abnormal, and if you want a crop of good, sound, uniform fruits, you would be advised to take this one off the tree together with any others that do not measure up to your standards.

Ideally, leave one fruit to a cluster with fruits about 15 cm (6 in) apart, if you can bear it. Dessert apples known to grow very large under perfect conditions may suit your purpose better if they remain smaller, in which case leave them unthinned and merely pick off any which seem imperfect.

Thinning can be staggered. If you have an early maturing cooking variety, begin picking the largest fruits as soon as they are a useful size. So far as those cooking varieties which mature late are concerned, thin out by picking the smallest fruits first. Windfalls should be gathered up and not left to lie on the ground in case they harbour pests and spread disease.

As apples approach maturity, their rate of ripening is slower than that of many other fruits, which means that they may seem large and they may even seem coloured (some varieties colour well long before they are mature) but they will not be ripe. Although a great deal depends upon variety, season, locality and climate, generally speaking apples are ripe when their green coloration begins to turn yellow. Then you can tell when a fruit is ready to pick by holding it in the palm of your hand and gently lifting it sideways against the 'hinge' you can detect at the end of the stem; if the apple is ready to be harvested, the stalk will come away clean, easily and unbroken. If the fruit has to be tugged off, it is not ready. (Only pick apples before they are completely ripe if they are to be stored – otherwise leave them to ripen naturally.)

Always pick the fruit on a dry day. Let late apples remain on the tree for as long as possible, but harvest them before the frosts begin. Some of the early maturing varieties quickly fall to the ground when ripe. Straw laid fairly deeply under the tree helps prevent bruising. These early ripening apples should be quickly eaten or processed as they have a tendency to deteriorate rapidly. Late ripening apples can be stored in single layers in boxes, trays or shelves, which can be placed one above the other. Some people wrap each fruit in special fruit papers. Do not lay apples on hay or they may become hay-flavoured. Store only perfect apples untouched by pests or disease.

## Culinary uses

Where there are apples there are the means to prepare an important part of a meal, for apples are a good food fruit, containing carbohydrates and vitamins as well as various minerals. Vitamin C is present in quite large amounts, usually located in the skin or immediately beneath it – one reason why we like to keep the skin on when we bake or purée apples, or slice or grate them for salads. Apples also contain a lot of water, which is why the fruit is so refreshing when eaten raw. This is also why little, if any, water is required when the fruit is cooked. Incidentally some people, especially young children, find apple juice easier to assimilate than orange juice. Apple juice is easily made, and so is apple wine.

Apples can be used for sweet or savoury dishes, for they share a happy adaptability with the tomato. Indeed, one can often use the recipe originally devised for one for the other. Sometimes, but not always, depending on whether the dish is to be a sweet or a savoury, one must substitute salt for sugar and vice versa, although not, of course, in the same quantities. Half a grilled or fried apple is as good with a grill as a half tomato, and often better for one's digestion. Grilled or fried apples and apple sauce can stand in for vegetables. Apples make good jams and they can often be blended with other fruits in this way. Jellies can be plain apple or herb flavoured, using mint, sage, or rosemary to serve with meat. Apples with lemon make delicious marmalade. They can be used in chutneys and pickles. There are also many apple cakes and desserts and puddings, including boiled and baked dumplings, fritters, batters and breads. Apples and rice go well together.

The dividing line between eating and cooking apples is not always sharply defined. Tart, sharp or sour apples are usually best cooked, although sometimes a tart apple will give a certain piquancy to a raw salad. Some tart apples, Bramley's Seedling for example, become sweeter as they age in store. Cooking apples which have a high acid content are usually those which become fluffy or frothy when cooked. Not all dessert apples will cook – some will not soften and seem even to lose their flavour. On the other hand, there are those which are just as delicious when cooked as they are raw. Try using a Cox's Orange Pippin, or some other popular dessert apple such as Delicious, Jonathan, Gravenstein or Baldwin in place of a peach in an Apple Melba recipe. First poach the peeled and cored apple in a vanilla syrup. If you want to ring the changes even more, and with equal success, use a little bramble jelly instead of the raspberry purée.

The choice of apple to use for cooking depends very much on what dish you are making. Apple slices in an open flan, for instance, need to cook to a firmer texture than those in a turnover.

For apple sauce, if you wish to retain the peel, simply wash and quarter the apples, discard the tough cores, put the fruit into a saucepan with only enough water to cover the bottom of the pan to prevent burning, and simmer slowly until the fruit is tender. Then put it in the blender. Alternatively, if you wish to discard the peel, rub the apples through a sieve. At this stage the purée can be either bottled or frozen. To convert into sauce to serve with poultry or meat, add a little sugar, say a teaspoon to 1 cup of the purée, a 5 cm (2 in) strip of lemon or orange peel and a knob of butter. Heat all of these except the butter together, stirring well until the sauce is thick and well flavoured. Add the butter and stir again. Serve hot.

There are many variations on this basic theme, according to the dish with which the apple sauce is to be served. We might add some freshly gathered herb, chervil, chives, mint or dill and sometimes grated horse radish. (Apple and mint are delicious together; try apple, mint and a little sugar in a salad.) One small quince added to 1 cup of chopped apples makes a delicious sauce. Cook the quince first with a tablespoon of sugar and very little water until it is tender.

There are times when spices can enliven the sauce. We like to add a clove or sometimes a little cinnamon, but a word of warning here. Although apples are among the few fruits to which it is customary to add spices, it is important that they be used with discretion, for apples have a tendency to take on other flavours.

Apple sauce is also known as apple marmelade (not marmalade), but this is a more refined version, being made with peeled and cored apples in a little water with a little sugar.

Once you have the sauce you can use it in many ways other than as an accompaniment to a main dish. Try using it as a filling for a small squash which has been halved and the seeds scooped out. Bake all together. Apple sauce can be poured into a flan case, covered with a lattice of pastry and baked. Alternatively, it can be thickened with egg yolk, the white whipped with $\frac{1}{2}$ cup of sugar to top it and put into a pie shell to be baked much as a lemon meringue or a chiffon pie. Make your own adaptations. You can use it plain or mixed with some other food – raisins and almonds for instance – as a pancake filler.

A quick and delicious dish is Apple Mousse à la Chantilly. Flavour the apple sauce with vanilla, preferably by immersing a vanilla pod in it for an hour or two. Cool the apple sauce in the refrigerator before preparing the dish. To every 2 cups of sauce, use $\frac{1}{2}$ cup of thick cream and blend these two together. Pour into individual glasses or one large dish. Top with vanilla-flavoured whipped cream.

Use the sauce for a sweet omelette, first heating it gently in a little butter, or mixing in a little thick cream. Sprinkle icing sugar over the top of the omelette before serving.

Russian Apple Soufflé is simply made. You need ⅔ apple sauce, ⅓ egg white – say 2 egg whites to 1 cup of thick purée. Beat the egg whites until they are very stiff. Add ¼ cup of sugar to each white and mix this in. Fold in the apple sauce and pour into a greased soufflé dish. Bake at 180°C (350°F, gasmark 4), for about 35 minutes.

A variation on this is a cold dish, for which you need:

### Cold Russian apple soufflé

2 cups thick apple purée, sweetened
juice of 1 lemon
1 level tabsp powdered gelatine
2 egg whites, stiffly beaten
1 level tabsp vanilla flavoured caster sugar
½ cup cream, whipped

Begin by dissolving the gelatine in the lemon juice: put the two in a basin over a pan of hot water and stir them. When the gelatine is soft and well mixed, stir in the apple purée. Make sure all is well mixed. Remove from the heat and cool. Fold in the egg whites. Moisten a mould and pour in the mixture. Refrigerate for 2 hours. To serve, turn out the mould on to a dish, surround with sugared whipped cream and decorate as you wish.

You can use apple sauce to stuff peeled and cored apples which have been poached in a vanilla syrup. First sweeten the sauce and flavour it with kummel. Chill well before serving. If you wish, each apple can be stood on a macaroon. As an alternative to the liqueur, flavour the purée with orange juice and add some finely chopped orange peel or chopped candied citrus peel. With the latter the dish is superb.

If you are a raw food enthusiast, apple sauce is quite good raw. Dice or grate some tasty apples, having cored but not peeled them. Add a little lemon juice to keep them a good colour, say a teaspoon to 4 apples. Add a tablespoon of honey or sugar to taste (brown sugar has fine flavour but will darken the sauce). Add a tablespoon of apple juice for each apple and blend all together.

We know that apples go well with meat, so try

Apple Stuffing for pork, poultry and, especially, for duck and goose.

### Apple stuffing

2 good dessert apples, peeled, cored and diced
½ cup stoned prunes, chopped but not soaked
½ cup sliced celery
1 teasp sugar
1 tabsp chopped fresh parsley
1 teasp chopped fresh tarragon or rosemary
½ cup fat, where possible use the fat from the
    meat, make up weight with butter
1 crushed garlic clove or 1 teasp finely chopped
    shallot
½ cup apple juice
⅓ cup breadcrumbs, or alternatively the same
    weight of not quite cooked rice

Melt fat but do not brown. Add apples, prunes, celery and sugar. Simmer until well blended. Add breadcrumbs or rice, herbs and garlic or shallot. Add juice. Remove from heat and allow to cool before use.

### Apple pastilles

10 cooking apples
5 cups sugar
¼ cup ground almonds
1 tabsp rosewater (or other flavouring)
3 egg whites

Peel and core the apples and put them whole into a saucepan. Cover with boiling water and simmer until very soft. Drain thoroughly. Rub through a sieve or blend in an electric mixer. Mix in the sugar, egg whites, rosewater and almonds. Beat well until the mixture is very stiff and thick. Have ready buttered sweet paper cases on baking sheets. Spoon the mixture into the cases. Bake in a cool oven for several hours until the pastilles are set hard and firm.

FREEZING   Apples are easily frozen, for cooking only of course. They can go in prepared but unsweetened if you are to use them fairly soon after freezing. Remember though that once out of the freezer they will discolour unless they are cooked quickly. Otherwise, mix them with sugar – 1 cup to each 8 apples. Peel, core, and then to keep them a good colour drop slices or quarters

Top: Dried fruit *(N. Collins)*
Bottom: Marmalade makings *(M. Withers)*

Top: Granny Smith Apples *(M. Withers)*
Bottom: Avocado *(L. Johns)*

into water containing a little salt or some lemon juice. Alternatively, blanch slices in boiling water until they are just pliable. Drain well, then pack into bags or plastic containers. Apple purée can be frozen unsweetened. Whole apples can be gently poached for a minute or two in a thin syrup and then frozen whole.

BOTTLING   Prepare as above. Pack into jars as rings or slices or purée and follow any of the methods given in the sections on *Bottling* and *Canning* (pp. 27-29.)

DRYING   Apples dry well, but you have to decide whether it is worth while for you, and certainly it will not be if you have plenty in store. On the other hand, windfalls can be dried. Make sure that all the blemishes have been removed. Peel and core the apples and cut them into rings about 6 mm (¼ in) thick. Place the slices immediately in salt water, ¼ cup to 16 cups (5 1/8 pts) of water, to prevent discoloration, for a few minutes only. Drain, and arrange the rings in single layers on trays. Alternatively, thread them on sticks which can either be laid from one side to the other in an oven, or on the trays. Dry in an oven or near a fire or stove. The temperature should be 60°C (140°F). If the process is not interrupted, the apples should be dry in 4–6 hours, otherwise put them into a cooling oven at intervals for 2 or 3 days; it is not wise to stretch the time further than this. Fruit dry enough should resemble chamois leather. After taking the rings from the oven, leave them in the dry air of a room for some 12 hours, then pack and store in a dry place.

DRINKS   Cider is *the* apple drink. It is made from the pure juice which, like that of pears, will with the action of yeast ferment to produce alcohol in roughly 24 hours after it has been expressed from the fruit. Those apples with a high tannin content make the best cider. Usually two or more varieties are blended together to provide bitterness, acidity or sharpness, and sweetness. Fermented apple juice is known as 'hard cider' in America, while 'soft cider' is the name for the unfermented or non-alcoholic juice. Cider is distilled to make apple brandy, the Normandy *calvados* – applejack in America.

For apple juice, wash and roughly chop the apples. To each 2 cups add 2 cups of water. Boil,

cover and simmer until the apples are tender or pulped. Strain through a jelly bag or a lined sieve.

### Apple lemonade cordial

*2 cups apple juice*
*2 cups sugar*
*3 lemons*

Stir juice and sugar over heat until all the sugar is dissolved. Allow to cool. Squeeze all but a half of one lemon and add the juice to the liquid. Peel the half lemon finely and add this to the liquid. Serve on ice and dilute to taste.

Apple wine is a fresh and delightful wine to serve slightly chilled with a meal. There is no need to use your best apples; use any that have been marked or bruised. Save skin and cores from pies and stewed apples; these will keep some days in refrigerator or freezer. Mix as many kinds as you can, including crab apples from the flowering crabs if you have them. A few added quince give a delicious flavour and aroma.

### Apple wine

*20 chopped apples*
*rind and juice of 1 lemon*
*6 cups white sugar*
*yeast*
*1 cup seedless raisins, minced or chopped, add later*

Boil apples and lemon rind in 16 cups (5 1/8 pts) of water until soft, about 15 minutes. Strain into a bucket over the sugar. When lukewarm add the lemon juice and the prepared yeast. Cover well and leave to ferment for 24 hours.

Pour all into a fermenting jar, leave for four weeks and then rack off into a clean jar. Add the raisins. Insert an airlock and leave until you are certain that fermentation has ceased. Cork and leave for six months, then rack into bottles.

# APPLEBERRY
*Billardiera longiflora*

## Origin

A Tasmanian species of an Australian genus of 8 known species of temperate evergreen climbers belonging to the pittosporum family and named in honour of the eighteenth-century French botanist and explorer, Jacques Julien Houton de la Billardière. First introduced into Europe in the early nineteenth century, it was known originally as *B. ovalis*. There is also a white-fruited form, *B. l. fructo alba*.

### The fruit

Botanically, a berry, violet blue when ripe in autumn, about 2.5 cm (1 in) long.

### The plant

An evergreen climber of a twining habit, it grows to about 1.5 m (5 ft) in height. Leaves are lanceolate and bright green. The flowers, borne on solitary stems not in clusters, rounded and somewhat bell-shaped, are extremely graceful. The flowers of *B. longiflora* are yellow-green, usually becoming purple. They bloom in late summer, the fruits following. This is a neat and pretty plant to cover a wall in a small enclosed garden. Apart from the beauty and novelty of its flowers and fruits (especially if you grow the two colours side by side), it provides a leafy decoration throughout the year.

Indoors, so long as it can be given a quarter turn each day so that the light falls on all parts of the plant evenly, the appleberry can be trained into attractive shapes – pillar, pyramid or globe. Alternatively, because of its low height for a climber, it can be used to cover an entire wall at one end of a well-lit conservatory.

### Cultivation

The most favourable climate for this climber is no. 2 on the world chart (p. 14). The plant is described as half-hardy for Britain, although it will grow outdoors in sheltered gardens in mild winter areas. In such gardens it is best grown against a south or south-west facing wall. In any but frost-free zones, it is most prudent to grow the plant under glass in a greenhouse, conservatory or well-lit sunroom. Outdoors it can be planted in open soil. Indoors it can be planted into a greenhouse border where this exists, or it can be container-grown.

Well-drained soil is essential. The plant will grow in ordinary soil but appears to favour a slight acidity. Plants can be raised from seeds saved from the berries and sown in a temperature of about 13°C (55°F). Alternatively it can be propagated by cuttings of half-ripened wood in spring or autumn. These root best in sandy soil in an enclosed environment.

Seedlings or plants should be planted in spring. Support the plants early on with trellis or some similar structure so that the shoots can climb as soon as they appear. Guide shoots to follow any lines you wish. Prune each spring simply by removing all dead shoots or weak and spindly ones.

### Culinary uses

The fruits are ready to gather when they are really shining. Eat raw, as a purée, or add them to a fruit salad.

# APRICOT
*Prunus armeniaca*, syn. *Armeniaca vulgaris*

### Origin

From its native China where it had been known for at least four thousand years, the plant was introduced throughout the Far East and then by the Arabs throughout the Mediterranean. It is still intensively cultivated there as well as in countries in north Africa and south to Rhodesia, as well as in India and Turkey. The Romans brought the fruit into Europe and it later appeared in monastic gardens, the only 'nurseries' or orchards of that time. However, as it was discovered that it could be grown in the open in such northern climates as that of Britain, its popularity increased. In the 1570s it was a common addition to British noblemen's gardens.

Inevitably, as peoples emigrated from Europe the plant was taken to other regions where the climate often proved more conducive to cultivation. In the eighteenth century it had become a cultivated garden plant in the USA and South Africa, whence it found its way to New Zealand and Australia. In some of these regions, far from its original home, the apricot has flourished to the extent that it is commercially produced for export, fresh, canned, dried and preserved in many ways.

The number of cultivars is great. In one publication alone we counted seventy-four. However, to quote the Commonwealth Agricultural Bureau, 'many cultivars are adapted to areas with warm winters, provided other conditions are favourable, but in general it seems that apricot varieties have only a limited adaptability to climates other than those of their origin, and many introductions – successful in their native country – fail in their new sites. In general, the apricot needs a period of chilling during the tree's dormancy which is equal to or greater than that of the peach. Strange as it may seem to those who believe that the apricot will grow only in warm countries, lack of chilling results in blossom bud drop and subsequent poor yields.'

## The fruit

Botanically a drupe, maturing from mid to late summer. It is fragrant and sweet with a high vitamin A content. Fruits vary in size, roughly 4–8 cm (1½–3 in) long, as they do in shape and colour according to variety. Some are rounded with flat ends, some have flattened sides and pointed or even nipple ends. Some are deeply sutured so that the two halves of the fruit are well defined, while others may be sutured only near the stalk. Colour of the skin varies from a yellow-ish green to a brownish orange and is always more deeply coloured on the sunny side, where there might simply be a brownish red flush or mottling of some kind, or a purplish spotting. The flesh is of a different colour from the skin, being almost white, yellow or a deeper, brighter orange. Some varieties have a more juicy flesh than others. The fruits are generally divided into two sections or classifications: those with free stones and those with clinging stones which are most difficult to part from the flesh. It appears that those with clinging stones and pale flesh are less sweet than the others.

The stones also vary in size, character and texture. In some varieties the kernel is sweet, in others bitter. They are sometimes used in cooking. Bitter kernels contain amygdalin and should not be eaten in quantity.

As with most cultivated fruits there are cultivars or varieties with distinctive characteristics. For instance Blenheim, sometimes called Shipley's Blenheim, especially good for preserving and largely used for canning in California, was raised by a Miss Shipley at Blenheim, England, before 1830. Large Early, a late flowering variety introduced from Germany, is especially suitable for small gardens and walls in northern districts. Kaisha, introduced from Aleppo, has an almost transparent flesh, a free stone and a very sweet kernel. There are many more, including the delicious Musk apricot. The so-called Black apricot is a distinct species, *Prunus dasycarpa*.

## The plant

A deciduous tree 4–7 m (12–24 ft) tall, it is sometimes gnarled and twisted, with a dark bark. Flowers appear before the leaves, pale pink becoming white, fragrant. Leaves are leathery, glistening, dark green.

A fan-trained tree attractively clothes the wall of a house: the period of bloom is short, but blossoms are delicately beautiful and fragrant, and the leaves cover the wall all summer. Generally, though, the apricot must be considered more utilitarian than decorative in the garden.

## Cultivation

The fact that the apricot's scented blossoms appear earlier than those of most other fruit trees, after the almond but before the peach in most regions, has considerable bearing on its method of cultivation. Indeed, it also explains its scarcity in some areas. Its frail white or pale pink blossoms are easily damaged in inclement weather and in those places subjected to spring frosts or strong winds at that season, protection in some form has to be provided.

The most favourable climate is no. 1 on the world chart (p. 14). Where the weather is substantially cooler, the critical time is from the moment the buds open until the tiny fruits are set. Where severe and long-lasting frosts are not to be expected, trees can be protected by growing them against a warm, sunny wall. In very cold climates the plants are best grown under glass in specially constructed buildings, and here more time and more gardening skill is required to produce a good crop of fruit. Under glass, planted in soil borders, apricots may be trained against walls, trellis, or allowed to grow as tall or dwarf trees or bushes. They can also be grown as bushes in pots, and in this case they can spend some time outdoors during summer.

Outdoors, where there is space and the conditions are suitable, trees can be allowed to grow naturally, usually as standards. When the plant is grown against a wall it must be trained to grow in such a way that its branches lie close to the warm surface, well back from wind. For this reason apricots are often fan-trained. One can train a young tree or buy it ready shaped.

Trees so trained release space in the greenhouse or on the garden wall for other cultivated plants, for they can be grown attached to horizontally strained wires across the garden and occupying no more space than a fence. For this reason apricots are ideal plants for the small town garden, even backyard or patio.

It is possible to get a crop from a single tree since apricots are self-fertile, but it is usually prudent, especially in northern gardens, to hand-pollinate the blossom. In warmer climates, because of the richness of the nectar, bees seek it eagerly and carry out this necessary task.

Dryness of soil has an influence on abundance of fruit. Where trees are trained against house walls their roots may be protected from rain by the overhanging eaves, and if this is the case immature fruits will drop freely. So, while the soil must be well drained, roots must never be allowed to become too dry. Water well in times of drought, especially during the growing season. Almost any type of well-drained soil is suitable for apricots. They are a good crop for stony soils, as long as their requirements are met. However, the soil should ideally be almost neutral, with a pH of 6.5.

Planting is best done in autumn or winter, according to location. If canister-grown plants are bought at other times they should receive close attention for the first week or two to ensure that their roots are moist at all times.

Apricots differ in their manner of bearing fruit from peaches and nectarines, although their requirements are much the same. Apricots bear fruit on the previous year's growth, but they also bear fruit on spurs, mainly formed artificially by the manner in which the growth is pruned. As with all stone fruits in cooler climates, the woody growth of the apricot should be cut as little as possible. Instead, the little side growths or laterals should be pruned when they are about 8 cm (3 in) long in late spring or early summer, by simply pinching out the leafy tips. This means that the shoot will sprout again from the axils of the leaves which remain. These shoots are also pinched back when they are large enough, to retain just one leaf. This little cluster forms the artificial spur.

Laterals needed to fill in spaces inside the trained fan shape can be left to grow to the required length. These should be tied into position while they are still supple, or they may snap as they are bent at any acute angle that may be necessary. It is wise to thin out fruit in the early stages when they are about 1 cm ($\frac{1}{2}$ in) long.

In poor soils the tree may need feeding, but it is unwise to encourage lush or vigorous growth as this would be at the expense of the fruit crop.

Once the fruits are swelling well, and especially in cool climates, it is prudent to remove any leaves and young branches which may shade or overhang the fruits, so that these can receive the full benefit of light and sun. They will then ripen and colour well. Fruits which are gathered when fully ripe have a far superior flavour to those which are collected unripe and allowed to develop afterwards. A ripe fruit parts readily from the spur and does not tear. It is wise to examine the tree daily and to remove those fruits which are ready rather than allow them to fall naturally or become attacked by birds.

## Culinary uses

Delicious when eaten raw, or as an ingredient in a fruit salad, the apricot, though sweet to the palate (and some varieties are much sweeter raw than others) contains only a very small percentage of usable sugars. It is asserted that the fruit contains 100 times more vitamin A than the average amount found in other fruits.

Many regions of the world lay claim to special varieties of apricot, or have their own special ways of preserving, cooking or treating them. The south of France, Spain and Algeria have the succulent Musk apricot. In the Auvergne region of France a fine jam, sought by gourmets the world over, is made from the apricot which grows there. The varieties most favoured for commercial drying come from north Africa, California, other parts of the Pacific coast and certain areas of Australia. Syria exports a special canvas-wrapped apricot paste in long strips made of sun-dried fruit. Dried apricots have a higher protein and vitamin A content than the fresh.

As with most stone fruits, cooking apricots with added sugar draws out the flavour and emphasises the special blend of sweet and sour which is the characteristic of these kinds. To the imaginative cook this quality opens the way to many unusual yet delicious dishes.

Traditionally this is the fruit most prized and most used by the confectioner and pastrycook. Its name has been used by chefs to coin the verb *abricoter*, anglicised 'to apricot'. One feels that it should be 'to apricoat', since it refers to using a thin glaze made by boiling jam to thicken it, straining it and flavouring it with a liqueur, to cover a cake or some other sweet or dessert. The traditional Christmas cake, where one brushes the surface with apricot jam before adding the marzipan or almond paste is a familiar example.

The fruit can be preserved in many ways: bottled in syrup or brandy, canned or tinned, dried, as jam, conserves, pickles and sweetmeats. It can be made into wines and liqueurs. Perhaps most important of all, it can be dried and so made available the year through. Dried fruits can be reconstituted so well that they can then be used for jams and for many other recipes normally requiring fresh fruits. Tinned fruits also can often be used in the place of fresh.

Apricots need not be limited to sweet dishes. The sweet-sour combination of apricots cooked or prepared with little, if any, sugar, makes them perfect accompaniments to certain meats and savoury salads, such as ham, lamb and duck.

The green fruits can be used in compotes, which means that windfalls or thinnings need not be wasted. They can also be bottled in syrup and brandy, in which case they should first be peeled, since the immature skins are tough.

The sweet kernels are sometimes included in jams, conserves and certain sweet dishes. They may also be added to salads. Where the apricots to be used have bitter kernels, almonds can be substituted. It is not necessary to peel ripe fruits. To fully ripen slightly immature fruits, they are best kept in a dark place or in a brown paper bag out of the sun but at room temperature.

### Fresh apricot purée

*2 cups fully ripe apricots*
*1 teasp lemon juice*
*4 tabsp sugar*
*pinch salt*

Blend so that the purée is smooth and all fruit thoroughly liquified. To keep, place in a covered jar or canister and store in the refrigerator where it will keep for weeks. It can also be deep frozen. Serve with ice-cream, meringues, etc. To make ice-cream, see the basic recipe (p. 33) and add 2 tablespoons of icing sugar instead of 3.

Green apricots make a tasty dish suitable for fruit thinnings once they have reached a good size, or for unripe fruits. Surprisingly perhaps, the flavour is very good.

### Green apricots

*7 apricots*
*1 cup syrup*

Bring the syrup to the boil and add the washed fruit. Allow it to simmer very gently until the fruits are tender but unbroken. Lift them out carefully and arrange them in a shallow dish. When the syrup has cooled a little, pour it over the apricots. Serve cold – delicious with macaroons. These green apricots may also be used to fill a flan, in which case the syrup should be thickened.

To make Crystallised Apricot Fritters, halve as many fresh fruits as you think you will need, put them in a dish and dust them with sugar. Tinned or syrup-stewed dried fruits need not be dusted. Sprinkle with brandy or some other liqueur, allowing sufficient to steep them, turning occasionally for 30 minutes. Drain each fruit carefully until it is dry. Dip into fritter batter and deep fry. Drain on kitchen paper and then arrange on a warmed, ovenproof dish. Sprinkle with caster sugar and glaze, either in a hot oven or under a grill. Serve immediately. Save steeping liqueur for another dish.

An Apricot Salad is a delicious salad to serve with baked or boiled ham or bacon, hot or cold, or with duck or pheasant.

Use ripe peeled apricots according to quantity, or gently poached fruits or tinned, in which case substitute blanched almonds for the kernels. Flavour with tarragon alone or mixed with lemon balm or melissa. Use a cream or yoghurt salad dressing made from tarragon-flavoured vinegar; alternatively bruise a sprig of the tarragon and let this steep in the dressing for an hour or so before preparing the dish. Arrange the fruit in a bowl and pour the dressing over it. Chop the herb or herbs together with the kernels, not too finely, and sprinkle the surface with them.

PRESERVING Apricot jam, made with fresh apricots is the base for the delectable glaze, and it is obviously important to have a small stock in hand at all times. Almonds can be added if the jam is to be served at table rather than used as a base for the glaze.

### Apricot jam, with fresh apricots

40 apricots
3 cups water
12 cups sugar
juice of 2 lemons

Wash, drain and quarter fruit, and remove stones. Crack 25 stones, blanch and split the kernels in half. In the preserving pan place fruit, lemon juice and water. Bring slowly to the boil, then simmer gently until a pulp is formed. Add the warmed sugar. Bring to the boil. Add the kernels. Continue to boil the mixture fast until it sets on testing.

### Apricot jam, with dried fruits

2 cups dried apricots
5 cups water
6 cups sugar
1 tabsp almonds or apricot kernels

Have the water warm but not hot and cover the fruit, leaving it soaking for 48 hours. Warm the sugar in a dish in the oven and put this with the soaked fruit and the water in a preserving pan. Stir well and bring the mixture slowly to the boil. When all the sugar is dissolved, simmer the mixture for 1–1½ hours, until it has set. Blanch the almonds and split lengthwise. Add them to the mixture a few minutes before the jam is ready to pour into hot jars.

A delicious 'cheese' sweetmeat can be made from fresh or dried apricots. These fruits also can be candied.

FREEZING Blanch first by plunging the fruits into boiling water for no more than 30 seconds, then peel them. If you are freezing a quantity, this is best done a few fruits at a time. Halve and remove stones. Pack into rigid containers with the cut sides downwards, leaving headroom. Cover with a syrup made from 2 cups sugar to 4 cups water, with a ¼ teaspoon of ascorbic acid added to every 2 cups of syrup.

BOTTLING To prepare fruit, leave whole or halve and stone. The latter method enables you to pack more fruit into a jar. Follow bottling hints in the main section on p. 27.

DRINKS Apricot Liqueur is a delicious drink for special occasions, to sip occasionally or to pour in small quantities over an apricot mousse or ice-cream.

### Apricot liqueur

15 ripe apricots
4 cups white wine
2 cups white sugar
2 cups proof spirit, Polish white spirit, vodka or brandy
½ tabsp cinnamon

Put the apricots and wine in an enamel saucepan

and bring to the boil. Add the sugar, spirit and cinnamon. Remove the pan from the heat and pour all into a warmed basin. Cover well and let all infuse for four days. Strain into a jug first, then filter and finally bottle and cork tightly.

### Apricot wine, with dried fruits

4 cups dried apricots
2 cups wheat
6 cups sugar
juice of 2 lemons
1 teasp grape tannin
16 cups water
yeast nutrient
pectic enzyme

Chop apricots, put into water, bring to the boil, simmer for 30 minutes and strain well, pressing out all the liquid. Add all the other ingredients when the liquid has cooled. Ferment for 3 weeks in a closely covered china or plastic bowl, stirring daily. Strain into a fermenting vessel, and top up with cold water. Fit an airlock and allow the liquid to complete fermentation.

# ATEMOYA

*Annona cherimolia* and *A. squamosa*

## Origin

This is a new plant, relatively speaking. The atemoya is a hybrid between the cherimoya (q.v.) and the sugar apple (q.v.). It is now grown in America, Israel, Australia and South Africa. Commercially it is known as a custard apple. Its horticultural importance is that the plant will produce fruit in areas where the cherimoya fails to do so.

## The fruit

The atemoya much resembles the cherimoya. This hybrid has already produced many cultivars and so, obviously, is bound to become very important. Among these cultivars are African Pride, which is considered to be the best Florida variety although the fruit tends to split; the Australian Pinks Mammoth, a heavy cropper with large fruit and few seeds; and the Israeli Kaller, which crops twice a year and bears very large, good quality fruits containing few seeds.

## The plant

A low-growing, heavily branched tree, it is very productive, and much resembles its parents.

## Cultivation

As for cherimoya except that it is a little more tolerant about climatic conditions.

## Culinary uses

This fruit is usually consumed raw as a dessert fruit, but it can be preserved and processed. See the section on cherimoya for further details.

# AVOCADO

*Persea gratissima,* syn. *P. americana*

## Origin

A member of the bay tree family, Lauraceae, the genus *Persea* consists of about 50 species of shrubs and trees, mostly natives of Central and South America. One, *P. indica,* is from the Canary Islands and the Azores only. A few are indigenous to south-east Asia. The word *persea* is an old Greek name used by the classical philosopher and botanist Theophrastus for an Egyptian tree, one supposes of this genus. Well-known related species are camphor, sassafras and cinnamon. Although the genus is quite large, the avocado seems to be the only one of any real importance in cultivation for its fruit, although several of the other species are grown for their timber. *P. gratissima* is a native of tropical America. Due to its increased popularity since the days when it first became commercially produced and exported as an unusual and wholesome food, the avocado has become an important crop in many countries throughout the world. Production continues to increase. It is cultivated in Florida, California, Queensland and other regions of Australia, in Israel where the environment has proved conducive to intensive cultivation, and in South Africa, to mention only the most important areas. It grows in gardens in most tropical countries and on islands such as the Bahamas. It is also cultivated in the south of France and in Spain, both in gardens and on commercial holdings, and we can expect to see it spread to other suitable Mediterranean regions where it is already grown as an occasional garden plant. It seems that the cultivars at present grown about the world can be classified into three groups, Guatemalan, West Indian and Mexican in origin. There is a diversity in the times of maturity, some ripening during winter and spring, others in summer and autumn. The Guatemalan fruits have thick, woody skins. Those of the West Indies have a thinner but more leathery skin. Those of Mexican origin are comparatively small fruits with thin, membranous skins. Their leaves when crushed have a distinct anise odour. Fuerte, one of the chief commercial varieties, is thought to be a hybrid of Mexican and Guatemalan parents.

A Mexican variety believed by some to be a distinct species is *P. drymifolia.* This is the hardiest of the avocadoes and has smaller fruits than the type. They have a fine flavour.

## The fruit

Botanically it is known as a large, fleshy berry. The fruit of the species is pear-shaped, about 10 cm (4 in) in length, yellow and brown, often tinged with dull purple. Varieties and hybrids differ in size and shape, some being more rounded, some longer. Some when ripe remain green, others assume yellow or crimson hues. The flesh which surrounds the large, inedible stone varies in colour from a creamy white to a yellow-green, the hue of the green deepening as it is closer to the skin. When ripe the skin is easily peeled off. It is possible to cut around the fruit lengthwise, thus dividing it in half, and the stone can easily be removed. When the fruit is ripe the texture of its flesh softens. If held gently in the hand it yields to the touch as though the skin contains butter. The fruit should never be pressed, for when it is bruised – and it bruises easily – the flesh becomes marked, turns black and is unattractive in appearance, although the dark patches are not, in fact, inedible. The fruit does not ripen until it is harvested, which means that the crop may be left on the tree for some time after reaching maturity. For this reason perhaps, some people find it difficult to gauge when the fruit is mature. This advice was given us by a Queensland grower.

Study the 'knuckle' on the long stalk known as the 'nail'. As the fruit matures this area appears to become dry, and may even change colour. At the same time the glossy appearance of the fruit dulls.

## The plant

The avocado can make an upright or a round-headed tree, not too spreading, generally described as a 'small to medium sized' tree, reaching some 8–10 m (25–30 ft) in time. The tree is an evergreen, although heavy leaf fall does sometimes occur, especially after heavy blossom has been produced. The leaves are usually elliptical and long, sometimes 15–18 cm (6–7 in). They are glabrous, dark green on the upper side and glaucous underneath. *P. drymifolia,* which bears thin-skinned small fruit also has smaller but aromatic leaves.

The flowers, just over 1 cm ($\frac{1}{2}$in) across and green, are borne in small terminal clusters or sprays and are extremely plentiful. Usually a tree blooms outdoors from seed in its fifth or sixth year, but the flowers do not fully develop. As a rule fruits begin to form or set when the tree is seven years old.

In suitable enviroments an avocado fruits heavily, although quite often it produces heavy crops in alternate years. Where the tree becomes damaged – usually because the growing point is destroyed – and it becomes 'stag-headed' instead of growing into a good shape, the crop suffers accordingly.

Avocado stones are often used to produce house plants. These can be satisfactory, even handsome, or they can be straggly and greedy of space. So much depends on how they have been treated in their early stages of growth.

Fortunately it is a simple matter to germinate the seeds, either in the manner described earlier or simply by standing the stone in the mouth of a water-filled jar, rather as one might grow a hyacinth. Once the root and shoot are growing well the young plant can be potted carefully into any good potting compost. Usually the novice gardener is pleased and excited when the shoot grows tall and quickly. However, if this is left it will develop into a lanky, lopsided plant. The normal practice is to nip out the central shoot after three of four leaves have formed. From their axils more shoots will be produced and some (or perhaps all of these) will from time to time also require stopping so as to induce a neat, evenly shaped, round-headed plant. It is important also to give the plant a quarter turn each day so that all sides are exposed to daylight. This helps to promote even growth.

## Cultivation

Generally speaking the cultivation of avocado is the same as for citrus (see Orange). The garden should be frost-free and sheltered from strong winds. Climatic conditions affect fruit setting and tree growth and they also affect flowering times. It is possible for the temperature to be too hot for successful cultivation, so it is important to take advice before planting. Climate no. 4 on the world chart (p. 14) is the most favourable.

Avocadoes planted in poorly drained soil are liable to suffer from a root rot fungus (Phytophthera cinnamomi) and for this reason both surface soil and subsoil should be well prepared. Plants enjoy an acid soil rich in humus and require a lot of water.

Probably the most important point to bear in mind is that avocado trees require careful planting and aftercare. Their roots are extremely sensitive to the drying air and so these must not be exposed any longer than is absolutely necessary. For this reason it is best to plant trees which are pot- or canister-grown, making certain that these are not pot-bound. One must avoid damaging the small, fibrous roots, for any root damage impairs the tree's ability to absorb moisture from the soil. It is important that the plant should not wilt after going in the soil and for this reason some growers reduce the number of leaves on a plant to lessen transpiration.

When a grafted plant is put into the planting hole, the union should be kept above ground level, and as far as possible one should so arrange the plant that the graft side is the one away from the sun. It is the practice of some commercial nurseries to protect the trunk from sunburn with brown paper or some other wrap or cover.

Although the planting holes should be made large and deep enough to take the plant's roots comfortably, there is no advantage in making it larger than required. What is more important is that after planting the soil should be shaped around the tree so that a little basin is formed. This should be filled with water, and regular

supplies should be given until it is obvious that the plant has become established.

The area around the base of the plant should be kept clear of weeds. If a tool is used for weeding, this should be used only on the soil surface and not pushed deeply into the soil where it might harm the roots. From early days one should aim to grow a tree which is symmetrical, with well-shaped branches. These should be strong, because they will have to support heavy crops of fruit. It is the custom at planting to 'head' (i.e. cut) the young plant back just above the strongest of the dormant buds near the growing point. These buds can be expected to make upright growth. When the side branches have been formed, subsequent pruning consists of pinching out the terminal buds to encourage the growth of strong laterals. As the plant grows, all crossed, straggly and unwanted branches or stems should be cut away.

It is not possible to give hard and fast rules on pruning because the amount required or desirable differs according to the variety. For instance, Fuerte has a straggling and spreading habit and so is pruned in such a way as to encourage, even force, growth upwards. Tall-growing varieties such as Hass and Ansheim should be cut to outward growing buds in order to reduce the height of the tree. As the trees grow older, shorten the lower limbs and finally remove them close and neatly to the trunk. This way room is made for the upper branches, which inevitably bear downwards. Some growers trim the skirt of the tree to about 60 cm (2 ft) above the ground each year and mulch heavily to compensate for the loss of shade branches. One can expect a good crop by the sixth year.

Once the transplanted avocado or a seedling plant is growing well, it should be encouraged by watering when the season is dry, by mulching and by feeding.

When avocadoes are grown in cooler countries or under glass, the numbers of fruit which set each year are, as a rule, very few. There is also a tendency for some varieties, including Fuerte, to crop biennially. The reason for this is not fully understood, but it seems likely that it is due to some pollinating defect. Like so many other fruits, seedling avocado trees do not produce fruit which is true to type. Seedlings will vary in habit of growth as well as in the time taken to reach maturity. On the other hand, it has been known for seedlings to grow into good trees. Known varieties are grafted onto seedling rootstocks by the nurseryman. Seed should be taken only from sound, properly ripened fruit. It is not wise to take seeds from fruit which has fallen and decayed. Large seeds generally produce the best plants, possibly because they carry a larger food store in their cotyledons. The seeds do not remain viable for long and they should be sown as soon as possible after they have been taken from the fruit. Seed may be sown at any time of the year; however, that which is sown in autumn or winter may prove slow in germinating. Seedlings of those seeds planted in spring and summer, which usually give the best results, may have to be shaded. Seeds may be sown in the open soil, in which case they should be placed just under the surface with the pointed end uppermost. It does not matter if this protrudes a little above the surface and some growers even think this desirable, especially during winter months. Alternatively, the seeds can be sown in pots or other containers some 30 cm (12 in) deep, in a very open and well-drained compost. If they are to be grafted this should be done when the seedlings are from 30–45 cm (12–18 in) high. Grafting can be carried out at all times of the year. Whip and tongue and cleft grafts are used.

For greenhouse and other non-tropical garden work, seed is best sown individually in pots, with one-third of the stone, the broadest part, in the compost and the pointed end projecting from the compost. The higher the temperature, up to about 30°C (85°F), the better will the seeds germinate. They are best sown as soon as they are taken from the fruit. They germinate quicker if the tunic, or outer coat of the seed, is removed. The compost in which they are sown should be kept moist at all times. Once the root grows, the seed splits in two and the shoot appears.

When the roots fill the pot the plant should be potted on to one size larger. This is best done in spring, when growth begins to be more active.

If the plant is to remain growing in a container, this process should be continued annually until the plant is in its final pot. It needs watering freely in summer and little in winter. Humidity is important. The foliage should be kept syringed daily in all but cool and cloudy weather. Under glass, temperatures should be 25°–30°C (75°–85°F) in summer and about 13°–18°C (55°–65°F) in winter. This means that in good summers plants can be stood outside.

When plants are stood outdoors, see that the area around the containers is constantly damped down and that the foliage is syringed with water from time to time, so that a humid micro-climate is generated.

Some avocado trees will produce literally thousands of flowers yet set only a few fruits. This is because of pollination problems, particularly difficult with the avocado because in the hermaphrodite flowers the male and female organs open at differing times. It is therefore advised that pollinators should be provided; advice about this should be sought from the supplier of your trees.

## Culinary uses

The avocado contains less water than most fruits, but makes up for this in its other ingredients. There is as much as 30 per cent of the fruit's weight in oil. The many vitamins, 14 in all, include A, $B_1$, $B_2$ and C. There are 11 minerals, there is 2.1 per cent protein and a low sugar content. It is estimated that an avocado will provide 250 calories for every 100 g of flesh, roughly 132 for each average sized half. If you are worried about cholesterol, use freshly mashed avocado sprinkled with a little lemon juice instead of butter on your bread. Lemon juice keeps the flesh from becoming discoloured after it is cut.

This fruit can be nature's gift to the busy hostess. Apart from the fact that a simple avocado vinaigrette, in which the fruits are halved, the stone removed and the hollow filled with the sauce, is almost always enjoyed, there are so many variations which can be played on this theme. Lemon in the vinaigrette is better than vinegar for a start, for this improves the flavour instead of dominating it as some vinegars do. Finely chopped shallot, alone or mixed with roughly chopped walnuts, will provide a little contrasting texture and a complementary flavour. A little cream cheese, green with an abundance of very finely chopped fresh herbs, again with a little lemon juice to soften it and make the mixture a little more creamy, combined with the avocado creates a fine bouquet of flavours.

Diners out will be only too familiar with the

ubiquitous prawn or shrimp filling for avocado, yet other seafoods are as good and not quite so hackneyed – crab for instance is delicious. So too is lump fish, the mock caviar. Make an hors d'oeuvre on individual plates with slices of peeled avocado, a little cream cheese and a small heap of the lump fish. The colours contrast in a most appetising manner. Avocado looks and tastes good with black olives.

Smoked fish also can be used as a filling. This includes both the raw and the cooked kinds, such as salmon, mackerel, kipper and haddock.

Often a little avocado can be made to go a long way. For a party snack, for instance, or to serve as a starter away from the table with drinks, little tart cases, pre-cooked, or some plain crackers, can be filled or covered with an avocado and fish, ham, salami, bacon, nutmeat or what you will mixture or spread.

Chilled avocado soup is deliciously creamy. Simply blend together 2 cups of chicken stock with an avocado, adding a little chopped shallot or onion, lemon juice, salt and pepper. Taste and adjust seasoning. Add freshly chopped chives, tarragon and parsley. Chill for at least an hour and serve.

For 'the best baked potato ever', just before you take the potatoes from the oven, mash a ripe avocado with $\frac{1}{2}$ cup of cream cheese and season. Open the potatoes and slash the centre to release the steam and divide the mixture between them. Serve immediately.

Avocado slices rolled up inside thin ham has been a ploy we have fallen back upon when a lunch has suddenly had to be prepared for a guest during a busy time. Tinned ham, shop sliced ham – anything will do, for the avocado gives it just the right touch. With ham the merest hint of aromatic mustard can go into the sauce.

For many years we lived in the centre of the fruit market area of what was then London's Covent Garden and there were occasions at weekends when we would be offered very ripe fruit very cheaply, including avocadoes. Often the flesh was discoloured. We experimented with cooking them and one day found that we had stumbled on a good dish. The flesh becomes a good colour after cooking. Cut the fruit in half and remove the stone. Salt the cut surface. Into each central hollow put a walnut sized piece of butter and a good teaspoon of spicy tomato

sauce. Place the avocadoes under the grill. Serve when the sauce and butter have made the top surface a bubbly brown crisp layer. Alternate this by laying streaky bacon on the avocado and grilling until the bacon is crisp. Or try a kipper filler.

Leaving savouries aside, avocado can be used in many desserts, which is just as well, since so far the best way known of freezing the fruits is in sugar. The slices are good in crêpes or pancakes, and sugar, honey or sweet liqueurs suit them.

One of the quickest sweets to prepare is Avocado with Kirsch. Allow a half avocado per person. Peel and dice it and divide into individual glasses. Sprinkle very lightly with vanilla sugar. Pour on each portion a teaspoon or more of kirsch at the table.

Another way is to blend the avocadoes or mash them finely with 2 tablespoons of lemon juice and 3–5 tablespoons of icing sugar, a matter of taste. Heap the cream into individual glasses and top with nuts, raw or prepared in any way you like. Or use crushed macaroons. Chill slightly before serving.

Avocado Ice-Cream is both delicious and easy to make.

### Avocado ice-cream

2 avocados
2 egg whites
$\frac{1}{4}$ lemon
$\frac{1}{4}$ cup sugar
2–3 tabsp single cream

Put the egg whites in a bowl over a pan of hot water or in a double boiler and beat until fluffy. Add the sugar and beat again until the mixture is lukewarm and the texture of lightly whipped cream. Allow to cool. Take the skin and stone from the avocadoes and mash the flesh until it is quite smooth. Add the lemon juice and mix this in well. Add the cream and again mix well. Fold in the meringue mixture. Pour into an ice-cream maker or into an ice-cream tray. If the latter is used, beat the mixture when it is half set to make sure that it is freezing evenly.

FREEZING To freeze avocadoes, use only flesh which is bright green, free from all blemishes, and just soft-ripe, not mushy. Halve, peel and slice. As the slices are cut put them into a solution of $\frac{3}{4}$ teaspoon ascorbic acid to 4 cups of water. Rinse well before packing in a light syrup with ascorbic acid in it.

# AZAROLE
*Crataegus azarolus*

## Origin

A member of the rose family and closely related to the hawthorn. The Orient is rather vaguely indicated as the place of origin of this plant, but usually one finds that southern Europe is claimed as its home. Certainly it is widespread in the Mediterranean region, where it can be found growing wild in hedges, woods, or sometimes solitary in fields or on their verges. It has been known and grown in English gardens since the seventeenth century, where one would say it has been valued as an ornamental tree rather than for its fruit. However, these may have been used much more plentifully at one time than they are now. The fruits are highly valued in parts of Algeria, France, Italy and Spain, where they are used for various culinary purposes. It appears that the largest fruits grow in Italy, which suggests that there might be a distinct Italian variety. Another variety which has smaller fruits than the species is *sinaica,* from Palestine. None of this family originates from south of the equator and very few come from Japan, China or western North America.

## The fruit

Botanically a pome, the fruit is very similar to those of other hawthorns. The fruits, known as haws, may be yellow or orange-yellow, a darker red like the common hawthorn, or white, according to variety. The globular haws, like the flowers, which are white and fragrant, are produced in little clusters, each fruit being 1–1.5 cm ($\frac{1}{2}$–$\frac{3}{4}$ in) in diameter and consisting of a group of nut-like carpels surrounded by a mealy, fragrant, sugary yet acid flesh, often described as 'apple-like'. This, with the skin, is the edible portion.

## The plant

A deciduous shrub or small tree reaching 4–7 m (12–20 ft), sometimes spiny. It is remarkable for its young, downy shoots and stalks, which give a pleasant, silvery aspect to the plant. The leaves are deeply divided. It blossoms in late spring or early summer.

Azarole is delightful for flower arrangements, whether in the blossom or fruiting stage. For the first, cut the branches while the blossom is in bud, just before it is ready to open. Split the stem ends and stand these in 5 cm (2 in) or so of boiling water. Let them remain until the water cools, by which time the foliage and flowers should be turgid. Before conditioning the stems this way it is always prudent to remove some foliage to prevent later wilting. The best way is to nip off leaf clusters which have no blossom within them. Arrange the stems after stripping the portion which will go under the warm water. Try not to move the arrangement once assembled, for movement causes the blossom to drop. Fruiting branches need conditioning in the same way, but these do not suffer when the arrangement is moved.

## Cultivation

Although the species is quite hardy, it grows best in climate no. 1 on the world chart (p. 18), in almost any type of soil. It likes a sunny position.

Plants can be propagated by grafting on to common hawthorn stock, *C. monogyna,* but such ones are not as long-lived as those raised from seed. Since the species produce abundant seed, this is really the best and easiest way to produce more plants. Be prepared, however, for very slow germination, for sometimes hawthorn seed will lie dormant for four years. The simplest method, where only few plants are required, is to vernalise them by placing a few seeds, washed from their surrounding flesh, half way down in a flower pot or seed pan of sand. Plunge this in the soil outdoors. Let it remain until the second spring. It can then be moved to some warmer place, a frame for instance, where the seeds can be removed and sown in soil where they should then germinate.

No pruning is necessary, but if you wish to keep a plant within certain limitations, the branches can be trimmed in late summer.

## Culinary uses

This fruit has a flavour of apples. It can be eaten fresh; where the season is not always long enough for it to mature fully, then like medlars it can be stored until ready for consumption. It is best used, however, for compotes, jam, butter and in any recipe as given for medlar. It is said to be used in a greatly prized liqueur, but we can find no information about this.

# BANANA
*Musa cavendishii*, syn. *M. chinensis*

## Origin
The family Musaceae, members of which are grown variously for their fruits, plant fibres such as Manila hemp, medicine, dye, alcohol or simply as highly ornamental garden plants, contains about 40 species, natives of tropical regions throughout the world. Intense cultivation has resulted in a great number of varieties and cultivars.

*M. cavendishii* is said to have been brought from China in 1829, but the genus itself is thought to have originated in the region stretching from New Guinea to India. Now it is to be found in all tropical regions. It was most likely introduced into Africa by the Arabs and later by the Spanish and Portuguese to America and to the other tropical regions colonised by them.

Now a food crop of primary importance in most parts of the world between the latitudes of 29°N and 29°S, the banana is thought to be one of the first fruits gathered and cultivated by man, even though the fruits then must have been tasteless and filled with bitter black seeds. When Joseph Banks, who accompanied Captain Cook on his early voyages, described the native banana of what is now north Queensland, he declared that it was 'a kind of Wild Plantain whose fruit was so full of stones that it was scarcely eatable'. Today's fruits, rich in food value, are the results of much selection stretching back down the centuries, and later of hybridisation. They differ immeasurably from the coarse wild product. Many of the modern fruiting varieties are sterile forms and cannot be reproduced from seed. Those grown from seed, some of which are offered by seedsmen, are almost certain to be as inedible as were the first fruits.

Naturally, only those varieties which crop heavily and which travel well when marketed are grown commercially and for export. Many of these are enormous plants, up to 6 m (20 ft) or maybe more, with leaves 2.5 m (8 ft) long. They bear heavy crops of fruit in proportion. These are mostly derived from *M. paradisiaca*, also known as Adam's Apple. There was a legend that this was the forbidden fruit and that the large banana leaves were the first garments of the first man and his mate Eve. Certainly they are large enough to make adequate wrap-around skirts!

This species is extremely variable. The main varieties are divided into groups which include edible dessert and cooking varieties as well as the inedible. They are further variable, some being sweeter, some more fragrant, some apple-shaped, some finger-length and some fruiting much earlier than others.

There are other bananas, not so easily identified, which produce smaller fruits often much sweeter, more fragrant and differently coloured from those which are generally marketed. Some appear to be quite local and are never seen outside an area or district. Perhaps they may be compared to local wines which never find their way to foreign cellars because they are said not to travel well. One wonders sometimes whether it might not be that they are recognised locally as being too good to lose. Fortunately, such plants propagate easily so that those who wish to do so can easily grow their own if they can beg a sucker from an owner.

One type of banana which is well known in many parts of the world is the Cavendish, which grows about 2.5 m (8 ft) high, bearing leaves 1.5 m (4 ft) long by 30 cm (1 ft) wide and which has a medium to large bunch of fruit with 8–12 hands. Its popularity might have something to do with the fact that it is resistant to Panama disease. This banana was once grown exclusively in the Canary Islands and was exported to Europe where for a long time the bananas were known as Canaries (not for their colour as some children believed). There are now several varieties, some with names such as Lady's Fingers, Red Fig and Silk Fig. The plants which produce these fruits, beside being comparatively small, will also tolerate sub-tropical conditions, an important point.

A favourite commercial variety is Mons Mari or William's Hybrid, a tall mutant of Cavendish, with longer leaves and a longer fruit bunch. A variety suitable for the small patio garden is Dwarf Cavendish, sometimes called the Chinese banana.

One of the sweetest of the commercially grown varieties is Lady's Fingers, a tall variety, but with the asset that it is tolerant of cool weather. It also needs no propping, but is, alas, susceptible to disease. Sugar is a banana with a small bunch, 5–6 hands, and short, thin-skinned fruit with a delicious flavour.

## The fruit

Botanically, a banana is an angled berry. The fruit of *M. cavendishii* is 6-sided and seedless, some 10–15 cm (4–6 in) long, although the fruits of some of its varieties may be as short as 8 cm (3 in). The bananas have a delicious fragrance and an excellent flavour.

The fruits are produced in bunches from the female inflorescence and are grouped together in 8–12 layers or hands consisting of some 12–16 fingers. These are really half spirals which grow around the thick stem. These numbers may vary slightly according to variety. The skin of the fruit is green at first, changing colour as it ripens. Although well matured fruit has the finest flavour and fragrance, the bunches should not be left on the plants until the fruit begins to colour, as sometimes the fingers become so full that they tend to split. A bunch is ready to gather when its fruits are evenly rounded and the prominent ribs no longer noticeable. Where a bunch does not ripen uniformly, hands can be cut as they become ready. The remains of the flowers break off readily from the tips of the fruits when these are rubbed. The bunch takes about four months to mature from the first unsheathing of the bell. The flesh is creamy white and, when fully mature, soft to the palate.

## The plant

Although usually called a tree, the banana is really an outsize, broad-leaved, herbaceous perennial plant. The part of the tree that is usually called the trunk is botanically the pseudostem. The true stem is a rhizome which is condensed into a thick, starchy, massive underground structure. Commercial growers confusingly called this structure a corm, a stool or a mat. This rhizome bears rudimentary or scale leaves which contain buds in their axils. From these, suckers or off-shoots are produced. The long, fleshy, cord-like roots, which though tough are easily damaged,

grow mainly from the sides of the rhizome with just a few coming from the base. The pseudostem consists of the expanded leaf bases. These support the crown of the plant, which might be a couple of metres above the ground. The deep green leaves are enormous and extremely handsome, but their texture is so soft that they become tattered and torn when subjected to strong winds and storms, especially hail storms. These leaves emerge in succession, each one beautifully rolled, the light green blade wrapped round and round the sturdy midrib. These leaves are plentiful, the plant producing from 35 to 40 before it fruits. The last leaves to be produced are shorter than the rest, the final very short one usually hanging protectively over the flower bud. The 'leaves' on the flower stalk itself are actually bracts.

Since it is the true main stem, the rhizome produces the flower buds from its growing point and from this area the inflorescence is carried up right through the pseudostem to the very top of the plant. From here, as the flower stem continues to develop, it grows vertically at first and then changes course and hangs below the leaves, with the male flowers or the 'bell' at the very end. The cultivated banana is parthenocarpic, which means that there is no pollination. Thus the fruit is usually seedless. The female flowers, which are situated in double row spirals at the base of the bunch, produce the fruit. These are followed by both hermaphrodite and male flowers. Sometimes the former make a cluster of short fruits immediately below the last true hand, but these are of no value and fall. The inflorescence is strangely beautiful, with the bell in reds and purples.

After fruiting, the stem dies, and meanwhile, as the plant matures, many suckers are produced around it. These too produce fruit and in their turn die. Thus the plant continues to fruit indefinitely, producing a whole crop of stems from one rhizome. It is known that such plants can live as long as 60 years. In commerce 20 years is most likely to be the limit before the plant is replaced or the plantation replanted.

No bowl of fruit for table decoration looks complete without a small hand of bananas, but these can also form a very attractive component in flower arrangement or some plant still-life. Use fruits which are not quite ripe, so that once the arrangement has passed its best they are ready for eating. After all, their thick and attractive skins keep them quite sterile.

## Cultivation outdoors

Gardeners who wonder whether a banana might take up too much space in their plots are reminded that if they follow the commercial grower's practice and allow only one sucker to remain, the plant will be kept well under control. It is also likely to be more productive.

When deciding whether or not to grow bananas, certain climatic conditions have to be taken into consideration. Obviously, freedom from frost is essential, but bear in mind that tall varieties are more tolerant of cold conditions than the dwarf. This is said to be due mainly to their rapid growth during the first year after planting (a banana leaf-sheath grows at 1.1 mm a minute, says Anthony Huxley). This means that the crown is well above the ground, at which level cold air tends to collect during the winter months.

Another essential is adequate moisture and water. Bananas grow best where there is a rainfall of 1.2–2.5 m (4–8 ft) a year. This being so, the most favourable climate for banana production is no. 4 on the world chart (p. 14). The soil must be water-retentive, although it must not on any account become waterlogged. One way to ensure sufficient moisture at the roots of the growing plant is by mulching. Mulches can be as deep as 30 cm (12 in) but should not be close to the main stem. There is no reason why spent banana leaves from healthy plants should not be used for mulching.

Commercial growers usually plant stem cuttings, great hunks of the massive rhizome, sections of which are cut so that each portion has an eye or scale bud. Amateurs are more likely to be able to buy plants in pots. Once the plant has become established it will begin to produce its own suckers, or followers. It is usual to select only one of these so that the fruit on the parent plant will be of good size and quality. First-year bunches are usually small, so sometimes in early years and on soils which are known to be fertile, a plant is allowed to retain two or even three suckers, but after this first spurt only one sucker should be allowed in after years. The best suckers to take are those which produce a bare shoot,

sometimes called a 'sword sucker', rather than one which produces leaves early on. As a rule suckers appear and can be selected before the parent plant fruits. From this point, no other suckers should be allowed to develop until the follower has taken over. Once the parent stem has fruited and the ripe fruit has been harvested, it should be cut down. It is important to remove the surplus suckers in such a way that they do not grow again. This means that the growing point must be destroyed. The best way for the amateur to do this is probably to cut off the sucker just above ground level with a sharp knife. One recommendation is then to gouge out a small portion in the centre and pour a little (about half a teaspoon) of paraffin or kerosene into this cavity, more if the sucker is large and old. Small suckers or 'peepers' can simply be gouged out.

A visitor to some banana plantations in winter and sometimes spring, depending upon the weather, will immediately become aware of the strange sight of hundreds of large, open-ended plastic bags, usually blue but sometimes silvered, covering each great banana bunch as it grows. Fruit so protected becomes less blemished, develops and matures more evenly and gains weight. In town gardens this practice also protects the fruit from damage by birds. The silvered bags are so treated to deflect the sun's rays and so prevent sunburn. It is said that a wide-mesh hessian bag answers the same purpose and that, except for the fact that it is not rainproof, a brown paper bag would also suffice. The bags are placed over the bunch at a time when it can be seen that the fruit is swelling. If the bunches are covered too soon, the bracts between the layers of fruit tend to become mouldy. Often garden banana plants look very untidy because of the number of dead leaves which surround the plant like a mantle. Actually these old leaves keep the pseudostem cool, but at the same time they slow down the rate at which the plant grows. In commerce, the removal of these old leaves is known as 'trashing'. Commercial growers usually trash at the same time as they remove the suckers. It is important not to tear off the leaves because this opens the leaf bases and this could damage and weaken the pseudostem. The leaves are best cut with a sharp knife at the point where they bend over and hang down from the main 'trunk'.

While some varieties of bananas, such as

Lady's Fingers, are strong and sturdy, others need propping against strong winds and heavy rain. The props, usually two pieces of timber crossed at about 30 cm (1 ft) from the end, are placed against the tree to form a V in which the stalk of the bunch is securely held.

Although the male portion of the inflorescence, the bell, is so strikingly beautiful, some growers believe that it is best cut off when the bunch has about half matured. This is done to lessen the weight of the stem and to relieve the plant of some stress. It is also believed that this process causes the fruit bunch to become heavier and can benefit by as much as a kilogramme. The first fruits should be ready to cut from a new plant in some 9–12 months.

## Cultivation indoors

The Cavendish banana can be grown in conservatories and greenhouses where the minimum temperature in winter can be maintained at about 18°C (65°F). If there is a sunroom, large, high and frequently occupied, the temperature here should be ideal so long as there is sufficient space and a relatively high humidity can be provided. The plant may be grown in a greenhouse border where the soil is deep or in a large container, minimum size about 1 m (3 ft) deep and wide. Obviously the larger the container the better.

It is also important that the plant receives maximum sunlight as well as warmth. A little supplementary artificial lighting should be beneficial. Plants grown under these conditions cannot be expected to fruit as rapidly as those grown out of doors, but one should expect fruit after about 18 months from planting.

Watering can be critical. A great deal of transpiration takes place from the enormous leaf surfaces and so the roots must be constantly supplied so that they can maintain the flow. While it is growing well, and as long as temperatures are high, the plant should be watered copiously, and since water leaches out plant foods, it should also be fed once a week with a good liquid manure. In very hot weather it can be given ventilation, but not so much that the temperature falls significantly. As we have explained elsewhere, growing some fruit under glass can be a tricky operation. So far as bananas are concerned temperatures can be critical, especially should there be considerable

fluctuations. Once the fruit is well grown and appears to be ready to ripen, the temperature should not be allowed to fall or the fruit will lose its flavour and fragrance.

If you are growing the plant for pleasure as well as for its fruit, you will no doubt wish to retain the unusual and fascinating male inflorescence. On the other hand, if you feel that it is consuming plant food and moisture unnecessarily, this part can be severed from the whole flowering stem at about 25 cm (10 in) below the upper female flowering portion.

Bananas can be gathered green and allowed to ripen in a warm room, but those gathered freshly ripe will taste best. After the fruit has been harvested, cut down the fruiting stem.

## Culinary uses

As the banana ripens on the tree its flesh becomes sweeter and more aromatic. Be sure to use fully ripe bananas if they are to be eaten raw – the flesh of an unripe fruit is almost tasteless besides being indigestible. (However, cooking renders it palatable and brings out the flavour.) Bananas are not considered as exclusively a dessert – in many parts of the world they are used as vegetables or as items in main courses.

The one great advantage of bananas is that they are all ready, for they need not be cooked for all purposes. Being such a good food they can form the basis of a dish, such as with cottage or cream or other cheeses in salads, with rice and curries where they complement the spicy, hot flavours, on a platter with a mixture of banana duos and trios such as long slices rolled inside very thin ham or a salty salami or very thin gouda cheese. Children enjoy them spread on crackers with peanut butter or a sharp but sweet jam or jelly. They make good sandwiches, especially with wholemeal bread and dates. They go well with all dried fruits.

For a sweet, bananas with brown sugar or honey and cream are about as delicious as anything you can get, but you can take them from this point in a dozen directions and apply them to almost any dish you can think of. They can be used to fill flans, or as layers in cakes; they can embellish ice-creams, enrich meringues, decorate custards, be captured in jellies ... and all uncooked. But that is only one side of the picture. There are banana breads, cakes, pies, fritters, griddle cakes, ice-creams, soufflés, sponges, waffles. One could say, you name it, you can cook it.

Bananas are said to be as rich as tomatoes and oranges in vitamins B and C, and richer in minerals than any other fruit except strawberries. But they are high in calories, a warning for the overweight. Their calorific content is said to be twice that of meat. Undoubtedly it is a good food fruit. It is among the first solid foods to be fed to infants. Because it contains vitamin A it is an aid to digestion. In some countries bananas are dried and made into flour which is said to be more digestible than cereal flours. The characteristic scent is retained in bananas dried in an oven.

Confusingly, cooking bananas are sometimes called plantains, which are really just one type of banana. Green bananas are cooked as vegetables in some countries. They are baked whole in their skins, or in halves and simply forked out when eaten. Some people french-fry them in strips or in round slices.

Those who have barbecues will know also how simple it is to bake a banana in its skin and how delicious it tastes when cooked this way. One of the simplest and most delicious dishes is to bake bananas in the oven while the main dish is cooking. Serve them in their skins so that they can be peeled by the diner, who can then add his own flavourings or condiments, such as melted butter, sugar, honey and nuts, lemon juice or a sharp fruit jelly. For a party, gently poach peeled bananas in a vanilla-flavoured syrup until tender. Lift out and lower the fruits carefully into an oven-proof dish. Sprinkle with any liqueur and flambé when serving.

Alternatively, gently fry the bananas in foaming butter instead of poaching them. Another version of this, without the admittedly wasteful flambé, is to fry the bananas in butter, place in the dish, then add a little brown sugar to the butter and let it caramelise, pour in a little sherry, add a little cream, pour over the bananas and serve.

Bananas can also be grilled and used as a sweet. Coat them first with melted butter. Place them in a single layer on a dish, sprinkle with sugar – brown looks and tastes good – flambé if you wish, and serve with cream or ice cream.

PRESERVING   A useful dish to keep in the larder

is Banana Chutney, using the following.

### Banana chutney

*12 large bananas*
*2 cups dates*
*3 unpeeled green apples*
*4 cups sliced onions*
*½ cup crystallised or green ginger*
*2 teasp curry powder*
*2 teasp salt*
*2 cups vinegar*
*1 cup water*

Chop the bananas, dates, ginger and apples. Slice the onions finely. Place all ingredients in a baking dish in a medium oven, 180°C (350°F, gasmark 4) uncovered for about 2 hours, stirring from time to time until thick and the liquid is absorbed. Pour into hot, sterilised jars and seal immediately.

### Banana and apple jam

*6–8 bananas, mashed*
*2 cups diced or sliced apples, peeled and cored*
*2 lemons, juice and finely chopped rind*
*6 cups sugar*
*4 tabsp water*
*¼ cup blanched almonds*

Mix the lemon juice with the bananas. Put apples, lemon rind and water in a pan and bring slowly to the boil and simmer until the apples are soft. Add the lemon juice and banana. Stir well. Cook for 5 minutes, add sugar and stir until it is dissolved. Bring to the boil and simmer briskly until it sets. Just before the end add the almonds. Pour into hot jars.

FREEZING   To freeze bananas use only mature and unblemished fruits. Peel, slice and mash them or blend. To every 2 cups of purée add 4 tablespoons lemon juice and 2 tablespoons sugar.

DRINKS   Bananas are too mealy, not sufficiently juicy, to be of any great value as the base for a drink. But their flavour is used in the liqueur Creme de Banane and there is said to be a Central African banana wine. Bananas are sometimes used in the making of certain country wines, in particular home-made sherries. We understand that there are some beers made from bananas, but we have not ourselves encountered these.

# BARBADOS CHERRY
*Malpighia glabra*

## Origin

The family Malpighiaceae contains some 25 species consisting of small trees and shrubs, most of which are grown for their ornamental value rather than for their fruits. The genus is named in honour of Marcello Malpighi, and Italian naturalist and professor at Bologna, site of the famous and historic physic gardens, who died in the late seventeenth century. *M. glabra* was introduced into Europe much later, in 1757, from Brazil. It can withstand cool conditions but does best in semi-tropical conditions (climate no. 4 on the world chart, p. 14). In temperate regions it can be grown only in a heated greenhouse. There are several varieties, some of which are grown commercially in the West Indies, and there is some production in New South Wales and Queensland. There are other species with fruit both edible and pleasant to the taste.

## The fruit

The fruit is obviously cherry-like, red to crimson and almost black when ripe, with a thin skin. The pulpy flesh is the same colour, soft, juicy and sweet when well grown, otherwise tending to be somewhat resinous and unpleasant, although high in vitamin C. It has 8 ribs and is about 5 cm (2 in) in diameter.

## The plant

The Barbados cherry is a slow grower which will reach about 3 m (10 ft) in a favourable climate but only about 2 m (6 ft) when grown in a pot in the greenhouse. It has a shrubby habit of growth, densely foliaged, the leaves being a wine colour when young, turning a deep and glossy dark green. The tree is so attractive that it is grown as much for ornamental purposes as for its fruit. The flowers, which bloom over several months, are rose or a bright rosy-purple, growing in little umbels from the axils of the leaves. The tree begins to bear in its third or fourth year. Fruit is borne on the previous year's growth and ripens a few weeks after flowering.

## Cultivation

The Barbados cherry is a tough and versatile plant which will grow in any soil and under most conditions, except that when these are cooler than it enjoys it will fail to fruit.

Plants can be potted or grown in a border of well-drained soil in a greenhouse or warm conservatory. The temperature range required is from 13°C (55°F) in winter to about 24°C (75°F) in summer. In pots the compost should consist of equal parts of sandy loam and fibrous peat, or a good, well-balanced proprietary potting compost can be used. Pots should be watered heavily during spring and summer and lightly in winter. Plants can be cultivated in summer from cuttings of almost ripe shoots inserted in a sandy soil, preferably in a greenhouse propagating case. Grafting is also used, but it is said that as most plantings come true from seed, this is the cheapest and most effective means of propagation.

The fruit should be harvested as soon as it is ripe, and with great care.

## Culinary uses

As well as being high in vitamin C, the fruit contains calcium and iron among its minerals. It can be used in jams, jellies and preserves and in drinks.

# BARBERRY
*Berberis* species

## Origin

'Berberys' is the Arabic name of the fruit, and some say that there is a connection with North African Berbers and the Barbary Coast, yet *B. vulgaris* is a European wild plant. It could be the Crusaders brought back recipes for using the fruit and focused attention on a native plant, for it was once widely cultivated or allowed to grow wild. *B. vulgaris* is just one of a very large family of shrubs which range from 2.5 to 3 m (8 to 10 ft) in height, some of them among the most handsome garden plants. Those which are deciduous change to beautiful foliage colours in autumn, when their fruits add to the blaze of colour. Others are evergreen. All seem to be highly floriferous and fruitful.

### The plant

This is a spiny shrub up to 3 m (10 ft) tall, with long racemes of yellow flowers not pleasantly scented, sharply toothed green leaves, but often coloured differently in its varieties.

### Cultivation

Barberry will grow in any well-prepared soil and under almost any conditions except in sour, waterlogged soil. Pruning consists only of cutting old stems, identified by darker coloured wood, right back to ground level. The plants also sometimes produce suckers at some distance from the main stem. These should be removed, otherwise a thicket is produced. The suckers can be taken with some root adhering if you wish to increase the plant. Shoots can be layered in the spring. Seeds can be sown outdoors in sheltered places.

### Culinary uses

Some barberries are too acid to eat raw, but even so, a few of the ripest can be included in a fruit salad, especially if this includes some insipid fruits. Being acid, they make a refreshing drink. The juice can be used in much the same way as lemon.

PRESERVING They make an excellent jelly, good to eat with meat, especially venison. Use 12 cups of berries, cover with water, cook, and strain to produce 5 cups of liquid. Reboil the berries and strain a second time if necessary to make up the required amount of liquid. Boil this with 6 cups of sugar.

An unusual preserve is made by cooking whole bunches of berries in a thick syrup and allowing this to simmer until the fruit is clear, possibly for 1 hour. Drain and pack into jars. Pour the hot syrup over the fruit.

The green berries can be pickled and eaten as capers.

In many countries or regions the common berberis has been eradicated for agricultural reasons and its cultivation is forbidden. The plant acts as an intermediate host for black rust, a fungus which attacks wheat. Other species of berberis, interestingly, are not attacked by this fungus.

There are several attractive named varieties of *B. vulgaris*. *B. v. macrocarpa* has larger fruits. *B. v. asperma* has seedless fruits and is now a rarity but worth searching for. In Nepal the berries of *B. aristata* are dried and used as raisins. *Berberis angulosa, asiatica, buxifolia, darwinii, haematocarpa* also produce edible fruits.

### The fruit

Botanically, a berry, usually red, ellipsoid, 6 mm ($\frac{1}{4}$ in) or so in length, borne in long, pendant clusters, sometimes with a little blue bloom on the skin, pleasantly acid, containing 2 or 3 small seeds except in *B. v. asperma* described above. Other species and varieties, too numerous to mention here, differ in shape, size and colour, some being blue or black.

# BEARBERRY
*Arctostaphylos uva-ursi*, **syn.** *A. officinalis, Uva-Ursi uva-ursi, U. procumbens*

### Origin

A member of the heather family, Ericaceae, the

plant is to be found growing in the cool or cold regions of the northern hemisphere, but the 'arcto' part of the generic name does not refer to the Arctic. Instead it comes from 'arktos' a bear, while the 'staphyle' part means grape. Bears are said to feed on the plant. It is to be found growing in the north of England and Scotland as well as Canada and elsewhere. It has been cultivated for centuries, not only for its fruit, but more importantly for its leaves, which contain tannin. From them also arbutin, a drug used in the treatment of kidney and digestive disorders, is produced. Actually the plant has many local names. Where it grows on the Burren in Ireland it is known as Burren Myrtle, and elsewhere in that country it is confusingly called Cranberry. The plant grows in little colonies on heaths and moorlands. It is often to be found in gardens, where it is included in heather gardens, on rock gardens or as a ground cover.

Bearberry is included here mainly as reassurance. The fruits, perfectly safe, are sweetly insipid, but are used to make puddings, conserves and liqueurs.

### The fruit

Botanically a drupe, consisting of 4–10 separate or coalesced nutlets, the fruit is a brilliant red

with a smooth, shining skin, about 1 cm (½ in) in diameter.

### The plant

A prostrate, evergreen shrub which spreads rapidly, rooting at the nodes, from which point also arise downy or hairy shoots, some 15 cm (6 in) long, later themselves to become prostrate. The alternate leaves are usually shining and leathery in texture, some 1–2.5 cm (½–1 in) long and oval or rounded. The flowers are only about 6 mm (¼ in) long, pink, urn-shaped and growing in small, pendant racemes at the tips of the shoots in spring. Bleached, dried branches of bearberry are know as Manzanita wood and are highly regarded by some flower arrangers, who buy them ready prepared from florist sundriesmen.

### Cultivation

In the garden the plant grows best in a moist position and in partial shade. The most suitable soil consists of a mixture of peat, leafmould and loam.

### Culinary uses

Use like cranberry (q.v.).

# BENGAL QUINCE
*Aegle marmelos,* syn. *Crataeva marmelos*

### Origin

Aegle is the name of one of the Hesperides, so perhaps the yellow fruit reminded someone of the golden apples of legend. The plant is closely related to the citrus and is of the same family. The fruit is widely cultivated in India and is to be found also in almost every temple garden. The trees are dedicated to Siva and the leaves are used in religious ceremonies. It was introduced into Europe from India in 1759.

### The fruit

Botanically a berry, with up to 15 cells, almost globular, green-yellow when ripe, with a very hard skin which is about 3 mm (⅛ in) thick.

# BLACKBERRY
*Rubus* species

## Origin

A member of the rose family. *Rubus* is an ancient Latin name, probably first given to the red-fruited raspberry, which is also a rubus. *Rubus fructicosus* was the general name given by Linnaeus to all blackberries or brambles.

As this plant has always grown, and still does grow, so prolifically in the wild, it is natural to assume that it must once have formed an important part of man's diet at certain seasons of the year. This assumption has been borne out by scientific discoveries. *Rubus* is an extremely large and widespread genus, not all of whose members are grown for their fruits. Many are highly ornamental garden plants valued for other virtues. However, blackberry species are common in many regions of the northern hemisphere. Specialists have named more than a hundred British brambles alone. The plant is also to be found wild in Australia and South Africa, where, one imagines, it was taken by some means or another by early settlers.

Obviously a fruit's flavour is of great importance. The flavour of some wild species is superior to that of the cultivars. There is no reason why, if a wild plant is found with superior fruits, it should not be cultivated in the garden in most countries. The blackberry has been declared a noxious weed in parts of Australia because it can be so invasive there. One wild species, the cut-leaved or parsley-leaved blackberry, *R. laciniatus,* which has become naturalised in North America, has a fine flavour and beautiful decorative fruits. It has been cultivated in gardens for a long time and is one of the best of all blackberries. It is a smaller plant than some others and has also a neat variety, Norwood, and a sport, Oregon, which is also known as the Thornless blackberry. Both of these are ideal for the small garden.

*R. schlechtendahlii,* another British-European species, also has a fine flavour. American cultivars appear to have been raised from *R. alleghaniensis* and other species. Most cultivars have much larger fruits than the species. Blackberries are cultivated in some regions of the United States, particularly along the Pacific coast. Varieties include

## The plant

This is a small, deciduous, spiny tree which grows to about 3 m (10 ft). The foliage is trifoliate, very narrow, slightly scalloped at the edges and with pellucid or transparent dots. The very fragrant flowers bloom in the spring.

## Cultivation

Outdoors, Bengal quince can be grown as for any other citrus, but indoors in northern countries the plant needs heat and should be grown as a stove tree. Propagation is from seed.

## Culinary uses

The pulp of the fruit is edible and used in drinks. It is known to be an aperient. The dried, unripe fruit is astringent. Bengal quince is used in some form in the treatment of dysentery.

Darrow, which ripens early, Hendrick, Bailey and Lowden. All are spiny.

*R. ulmifolius,* the Evergreen Thornless blackberry, with its variety *inermis,* was produced in California, but is not generally considered to be a fine fruiting kind. The so-called Himalayan blackberry does not in fact appear to have originated in this mountainous region. It is more likely to be of American or European origin and was introduced from Germany in 1899. It is sometimes known as *R. procerus.* A fairly new variety, Nestberry, is a neat, compact plant and very prolific. Scoresberry is much like a loganberry in appearance.

## The fruit

In spite of its name the blackberry is not a true berry, but a collection of drupelets on a cone-shaped receptacle to which they adhere, unlike the raspberry which comes away from its 'hull'. The fruits are borne in long sprays consisting of small clusters on short individual stems, following the style and shape of the racemes of the flowers. Fruits are 1–2 cm ($\frac{1}{2}$–1 in) in length and often conical in shape. They are green at first, becoming redder as they swell, finally maturing to a luscious black. Many rubus grown for ornamental purposes produce fruits of different colours, some edible but not remarkable, some pleasant but insipid, some bitter but not poisonous.

## The plant

The blackberry is a climber, usually making its way upwards by means of its thorns. The stems are known as canes. Most canes fruit in their second year, but *R. laciniatus* often fruits well on first-year canes. Canes radiate from one point and grow erect at first. Where a plant grows away from a support, the canes arch downwards until the tip touches the ground. At this point it takes root and in a very short time forms a new plant. In the wild large thickets of brambles are thus produced. Obviously, tip-rooting is something which should be severely discouraged in a small garden, although it is an easy method of propagating a plant. Once it has rooted, simply sever the new plant from its parent and transplant in autumn.

Species and varieties vary in appearance, some-

times very slightly. The difference may be in the size and colour of the flowers, some being white, some rosy and slightly downy. These are borne on long racemes. There are differences also in the size, texture, hue and form of the leaves, some being in 3 and some in 5 parts. Some plants are deciduous, some turn beautiful colours in autumn before they fall, some are evergreen and some only partly so. Darwin suggested that we were probably witnessing a process in the evolution of the plant in this respect.

Some plants are very prickly, some have few spines or prickles, being more bristly than prickly, and some are thornless. Species and varieties differ also in the size of their fruit and in the size and number of drupelets to each fruit. The largest fruits are not necessarily those with the finest flavour. Modern varieties give high yields. The season of ripening varies, so that there are fruits to be had in late summer right through to autumn, according to species or variety. Blackberries flower late, which means that so long as the plant itself is sufficiently hardy it can be grown in areas which are subject to late frosts. In the garden, with a little imagination the blackberry can be put to fine ornamental use, although one must always have regard for the thorns. For instance, a pillar clothed with canes carefully spaced so that they surround it can look very attractive indeed as soon as the leaves begin to grow. One or two on pergola supports or patio sections will remain handsome for months. To ease work later, have a double set of supporting wires parallel to each other going up the posts or pillars, one for the fruiting canes and one for the new shoots, and tie them in separately. When the old ones are cut down to the ground, the new ones will already be on their way.

The sprays of fruits are delightful in autumn flower arrangements, where they blend happily with the blooms of the other fruits and foliage in season. Try them also as an addition to a bowl of fruits set on the table for dessert. Keep some of their leaves on the stems. Condition them first and arrange the sprays in foamed plastic, which can also be employed to raise and support other fruits in the ensemble.

## Cultivation

Generally speaking, trailing berries grow best in

areas which are not subjected to great extremes of heat or cold. They should not be planted where they may be exposed to hot, dry winds, because these can cause damage to the ripening fruits.

Blackberries like soil which is rich and moist, a condition easy enough to obtain and maintain if, each winter, the soil above the roots of the plants is top-dressed with well-decayed animal manure or home-made compost. Failing either of these, mix a good general fertiliser with peat. Naturally, poor soil should be well prepared and enriched before planting.

The canes are best planted in autumn. It appears that they need the winter months to settle in properly, and certainly later planted canes do not seem to do as well. After planting, cut back the canes to within 30 cm (1 ft) of the soil surface if this has not already been done by the nurserymen or suppliers. As they grow, retain 8–10 canes and cut away the remainder. Keep the largest because these produce the best crop. Canes which grow too long for convenience can be topped in early spring. Take off as much as 1 m (3 ft) if necessary. Strong growing laterals can also be cut back fairly close to the main stem should these prove a nuisance.

The plant requires little room, but it must have ample space to extend its stems. There are several ways of supporting the canes. They can be trained up a strong post or pillar, in which case it may be best to retain just 6 canes rather than 8 or 10. The most usual method is to tie the canes to wire supports, first fanning out the shoots as they grow from the base so that they do not cross each other, and then training them along the wires horizontally. More than one can be tied to one wire. They can also be trained to spread out, fan-wise. Wires for supporting the canes should be fixed firmly to strong posts and they should lie at 4 or 5 convenient levels parallel to the ground. A useful method is to use the lowest wire exclusively for the new canes which appear above the ground while the older ones are fruiting. If these are tied, and taken as they grow further and further along the lower wire, their tips are less likely to be damaged while the fruit is being picked. Later, when the fruiting canes are spent and cut to ground level, the young canes can be untied and spread and trained as required.

Space can be saved or even gained by training blackberries this way along wires which mark boundaries of garden plots. They can also be used to cover sunny walls and fences, but in this case keep them tied to the wires and not to the fence itself. They can also be used to cover a steep bank, but bear in mind that in this case they may be difficult to pick.

Growth is often surprisingly lush, one good reason why those with small gardens should select neat, compact varieties. Plants should not be established so near to a path that shoots are easily brushed as one walks along it.

Modern hybrids give high yields and usually one plant provides sufficient fruit for an average small family. It is possible, where the space is available, to plant sufficient varieties to produce fruit throughout four months, since some varieties crop much earlier than others.

Owners of small gardens would be advised to avoid really vigorous varieties, and nursery catalogues usually give details in this respect. The Evergreen Thornless, for instance, grows very lush and does not really give good enough berries to warrant the space it occupies. Himalayan Giant makes canes some 6 m (20 ft) long.

Blackberries in America are not so hardy as some of their near relatives, such as red raspberries, and they can be grown only in mild districts in the north and in Canada unless their canes can be protected in some manner. In such areas the soil should be very well drained. Heavy clay soils are not suitable. Sterility is a problem with such blackberries and the gardener is advised to buy his plants from a reputable source or to propagate only from those fruits which are known to be productive. Unfortunately, in cultivation many stocks have become weakened by virus infection, another good reason for selecting a strong wild strain if you can find one.

## Culinary uses

The blackberry is a nourishing fruit, containing carbohydrates and a high proportion of vitamin $B_1$. Calcium is present in a higher proportion than with most other fruits and there are also other minerals.

There are few fruits as delicious as really ripe and freshly gathered blackberries. Try them for breakfast with a cereal. Instead of sugared berries for dessert, pour a little thin honey on them. A few blackberries cast on the surface of a fruit salad accentuate the lusciousness of the other fruits. It is worth freezing some berries in small containers for this purpose. An unusual and delicious autumn salad can be made of sliced apples and pears coloured with blackberries and alpine strawberries.

Blackberries are often cooked with apples, but quince and pears will suit them too. Some people find the cooked fruits too pippy, and so it is customary to extract the juice from the berries and to use this to flavour pies or tarts. All kinds of puddings and desserts can be made from blackberries. Try the purée as ice-cream, following the basic recipe given on p. 33.

A short cut we often take is simply to beat blackberry jelly into whipped cream and chill. A simple, easily digested sweet is Blackberry Snow.

## Blackberry snow

2 cups blackberry juice
2 tabsp thin honey
1 tabsp icing sugar
1 tabsp gelatine powder, with 1 tabsp water to mix
2 egg whites

Heat the juice, honey and sugar together. In a large basin mix gelatine and water until the former is soft. Pour the hot liquid over it and stir until all is dissolved. Cool. Put in refrigerator or freezer until the mixture is partially set. Beat up the egg whites until stiff, fold in, put into serving dish and chill. Serve with cream.

Blackberries can be used in the same way as almost any other berries in steamed and baked puddings, charlottes and cobblers. Besides the fruits, the shoots of this plant are edible. They can be used to make bramble wine and they can be cooked and eaten in the same way as asparagus.

PRESERVING When picking blackberries for jelly, take some of the deep red and not quite ripe berries as well, the riper the mass, the more red to use. These contain more pectin and help make the jelly set quickly. There are many recipes for Blackberry or Bramble Jelly, and this one we know to be good.

## Blackberry jelly

8 cups berries
4 medium sized cooking apples, chopped but not peeled or cored
1 cup water
sugar to be measured

The best way to extract the juice is to put the fruit and water in a covered pan in a slow oven. Alternatively, simmer on a stove. Strain through a jelly bag. Add 2 cups of sugar to every 2 cups of juice. Bring to the boil, stirring meanwhile. Once the sugar has dissolved, boil rapidly until the liquid jells. Pour into hot jars, cover when cool.

If you want a spiced jelly, add 1 teaspoon mixed spice with 2 cups of juice and 2 cups of sugar.

Rather less commonplace and equally pleasant is Blackberry and Apple Butter.

## Blackberry and apple butter

8 cups blackberries
6 cooking apples, roughly chopped

Begin with the blackberries, warming and crushing them over heat in a preserving pan until their juice runs. Add apples and simmer both together until all are soft. Sieve, measure and cook until thick.

FREEZING To freeze the berries first grade them, selecting those that are plump and fully ripe. Wash in ice water and drain well. Open freeze and pack into bags or containers with or without sugar. Syrup is not necessary. Purée can be frozen unsweetened or with the addition of ½ cup of sugar to every 2 cups of purée.

BOTTLING The berries can be bottled whole in syrup or without, or as a purée.

DRINKS Blackberry wine can be made in exactly the same way as other fruit or country wines (see the basic recipe on p. 34) and if you have sufficient plants it is even possible to make a bramble tip wine from your prunings.

Less obvious, and a cheering remedy for sore throats and colds, is Blackberry Cordial.

### Blackberry cordial

*2 cups white wine vinegar*
*4 cups ripe blackberries*
*2 cups loaf sugar*
*1¼ cups honey*

Put the blackberries into an earthenware jar. Pour the vinegar on them and allow to stand for a week. Stir occasionally to bruise the fruits and get the juices flowing. When very liquid, strain and pour the solution into an enamel saucepan with the sugar and honey and bring to the boil. Take it from the heat and allow to cool. Bottle, cork and keep in a dark place. Use 1 tablespoon to a mug or glass of hot water.

# BLACKCURRANT
*Ribes nigrum*

## Origin

A member of the world-wide Saxifrage family, this particular genus grows wild in the northern hemisphere, across the whole of Europe to northern Asia as far as the Himalayas. Although it is found wild in Britain, it is believed to have become naturalised after having originally escaped from gardens. Intensive research has taken place during this century in order to improve the strain. The plant is widely grown commercially in many parts of the world and is particularly popular in north European lands. There are many fine varieties on the market.

## The fruit

Botanically a berry, juicy, many-seeded. The berries are round, with the remains of the flower well defined as the 'tops', usually removed when one tops and tails the fruits in preparation for cooking. The skin varies in toughness in different varieties. The juice is generally acid, although some varieties such as Boskoop Giant are fairly sweet. The berries are borne in long sprays and carry from 5 to 10 fruits according to variety. These are not always uniform in the bunch, the largest, possibly because it is the first to be formed, being at the base of the spray. The fruits are valued for their vitamin content, among the highest of all fruits. Like the whole plant, they have a distinctive scent. These are not the fruits which are dried to make currants for confectionary – grapes are used for that purpose.

## The plant

A shrub or bush, sometimes grown on a short stem but usually with many stems rising from ground level, it grows to about 2 m (6 ft) but is often shorter. It is a useful plant for a small garden because it has to be pruned well and so can be kept compact and under control. The palmate leaves have a strong odour, the unmistakable blackcurrant scent, given off by the yellow glands on the leaf undersides. The small racemes of green-white flowers are borne from the leaf clusters.

Modern varieties and cultivars vary in many districts, some flowering and fruiting earlier than others so they are classified as early, mid-season and late, usually arriving over three months or so from mid-summer to early autumn.

Some do better on dry soils than others – Cotswold Cross is an example. Some have erect stems, or more erect stems than others, and some sprawl. Some have few, but large berries to the bunch and some berries are short, some long. Blackcurrants, unlike the red and white, are not trained in any way.

## Cultivation

Blackcurrants do not like hot climates, particularly where these are dry. The most favourable climates are 2 and 3 on the world chart (p. 14). No soil can be too rich for the plants. so it should not only be well dug and prepared with generous portions of manure, but it should be kept mulched so that it is constantly recharged with essential humus. Lawn mowings, home-made composts or well-decayed animal manures can be used for this purpose. Bear in mind that while these deep mulches help feed the plants, they also keep the roots comfortably moist and discourage weed growth.

It is helpful to use artificial fertilisers to maintain the richness of the soil, especially if you garden on naturally poor soils. Feed it in spring with 50 g (2 oz) of sulphate of ammonia per square m (square yd) and in autumn with 25 g (1 oz) of sulphate of potash. Plant in winter while the soil is frost-free. Plant young bushes, 1–2 years old, and plant them so that their roots have roughly 5 cm (2 in) of soil above them when they are finally established. A simple modern method of planting is merely to insert 3 cuttings of the same variety 10 cm (4 in) deep at the point where you wish to have a blackcurrant bush. If you would like several, insert the groups 2 m (6 ft) apart in rows 1 m (3 ft) apart. Cuttings of about 30 cm (12 in) are taken in autumn of well-ripened shoots of the current season's growth. Insert one-third of their length in the soil. No other preparation is necessary.

Blackcurrants produce their fruit on new growth, that is, on shoots made the previous season. They are most easily pruned as soon as the fruit is gathered – or at the same time. Simply cut off the branches just below the lowest bunch of currants. Should there be any shoots that failed to fruit, shorten them. The easiest way to gather the fruit, if you have only a few bushes, is simply to cut the fruiting stems and carry them to a bench or table where you – and others – can sit in comparative comfort and pick off the bunches.

## Culinary uses

Blackcurrants do not always form a neat bunch; quite often there is a large, solitary fruit or two at the top of the cluster which has to be picked separately. There is no need to remove the fruit from the little stalks if the currants are to be cooked and then strained for juice.

The blackcurrant plant, leaves and fruit contain tonic, cordial and blood purifying properties, according to many authorities. They are also said to contain active ingredients therapeutic in the treatment of arthritis, gout and rheumatism among many other complaints. The juice or syrup is often given to young children because it is rich in vitamins, especially vitamin C.

The fruit, fresh, bottled or frozen, can be used in a variety of desserts. It makes good puddings, either with suet or batter crusts, usually the former, used both to line a basin and to top the raw fruit which is set inside mixed with sugar. The pudding is then boiled or steamed.

This is not such a versatile fruit as some, indeed it is often grown simply to make syrup and jams or jellies. Yet it makes good sorbets and ices, and the stewed fruit or purée makes a good accompaniment to rice or any other milk pudding. It is a good plan to grade the fruit, setting aside the largest, plumpest currants to freeze separately in small quantities to add to fruit salads. Once these are stewed, their juice runs and this stains the other fruits. Raw or frozen fruits are not so likely to do this.

Delicious pies can be made by adding a heaped dessertspoon of chopped fresh mint to 2 cups of currants, with sugar to taste of course.

Blackcurrant Brulée offers an unusual sweet.

### Blackcurrant brulée

1 cup prepared blackcurrants
4 tabsp water
$\frac{1}{2}$ cup brown sugar
1$\frac{1}{2}$ level teasp arrowroot or cornflour
$\frac{1}{2}$ cup soured cream

Simmer the blackcurrants in the water until tender, then add the warmed sugar. Bring to the boil and simmer slowly for 5 minutes. Blend the arrowroot or cornflour with another tablespoon of water. Stir this into the currants and let the mixture continue to simmer as it thickens, then allow it to cool. Divide it between four flame- or oven-proof dishes. Top the fruit in each with a layer of soured cream. Cover this with a thin layer of soft brown sugar and cinnamon mixture. Place on a baking sheet and slide under a grill. Let the sugar bubble and become caramelised. Serve cold.

**PRESERVING** It will be seen in the following recipe for Blackcurrant Jam that the proportion of water to fruit is greater than for most other fruits. This is because blackcurrant jam made with insufficient water will contain tough and hard fruits instead of soft and succulent ones more suitable for a jam.

### Blackcurrant jam

*8 cups blackcurrants*
*12 cups sugar*
*6 cups water*

Prepare the fruit and put into a preserving pan with the water. Bring to the boil and simmer very gently until the currants are quite tender, by which time the level should have dropped. Stir from time to time as the fruit thickens. Add the sugar and stir well until this is dissolved. Bring the fruit to boiling point and then boil quickly until setting point is reached.

**FREEZING** To freeze blackcurrants, wash and dry them and strip them from their stems. They may be packed dry and unsweetened in bags, in a syrup or as a purée in rigid containers. The frozen fruits can be used in jams and other preserves. Sweetened blackcurrant purée makes a delicious sauce for meringues and ice-cream. It can also be used to make ice-cream, sherbets and mousse, or diluted and served as a hot or a cold drink.

**BOTTLING** Blackcurrants may also be bottled in the usual way in syrup or as juice or a purée.

**DRINKS** Blackcurrant liqueur, or cassis, the famous and traditional ingredient in the French aperitif, *vin blanc cassis,* is very simple to make, although the mixture needs daily attention for about two weeks. It is not to be confused with the non-alcoholic blackcurrant syrup which is milder, cheaper and less interesting.

Blackcurrant wine is made in the same way as almost all other country wines. To every 6 cups of currants use about the same quantity of sugar and 16 cups (5 1/8 pts) of water. Crush the currants in a large earthenware jar or plastic bucket. Boil up the sugar in the water and pour it still boiling onto the currants. When it has cooled to about blood heat add the wine yeast tablet or your normal yeast type plus any nutrient solution if you use this. Allow to ferment fiercely for about five days, keeping the bucket or crock covered and stirring each day. Then pour into a fermenting jar and fit an air lock, leaving it to stand until fermentation ceases in about three months. Finally siphon off carefully into clean bottles.

### Blackcurrant liqueur

*4 cups cleaned and prepared currants*
*1 teasp each cinnamon and ground cloves*
*11 cups spirit or brandy*
*3 cups sugar*

Mix well all the ingredients but the sugar with a wooden spoon in a large jar. Stand the jar, covered, in the sun and stir every day. At the end of two weeks strain through a jelly bag or muslin and then filter. Add the sugar. Make sure that all of this is well dissolved before bottling the liquor. Usually no more than about a tablespoon of this liquor is added to a glass of chilled, dry white wine.

# BLUEBERRY
**Vaccinium species**

## Origin

A member of the heather family, Ericaceae, the genus contains more than 130 species of deciduous and evergreen shrubs, sometimes but very rarely small trees, inhabiting the northern hemisphere and mainly in North America and east Asia. The name is an old Latin one used by Virgil and Pliny, but there is some doubt that they were really referring to the blueberry or whether they had some other plant in mind, which is more likely in view of the geographical distribution.

The native British plant, *V. myrtillus*, has a great number of local names, three of which are mentioned above; a variety, *V. leucocarpum*, with white fruits, is a low shrub, some 60 cm (2 ft) high, which grows plentifully on moorlands. Its fruits are small and the species is not suitable for garden cultivation. However, British gardeners can now buy American blueberries. Botanically the situation is somewhat complicated and its unravelling does not really have a place in a book of this nature, except to observe that the true blueberries are from a sub-genus in which the species have become so hybridised that botanists have found it almost impossible to classify them.

Although some of these are believed to be of hybrid origin, they have been given specific nomenclature, although they are also known by their trivial or popular names. These include such important species as *V. angustifolium,* syn. *V. pensylvaticum angustifolium,* the Low-bush blueberry, native to the eastern United States; *V. ashei,* a Rabbit-eye blueberry from the south-eastern United States; *V. atrococcum,* the Downy Swamp or Black huckleberry, which grows in eastern North America from Canada to Alabama; *V. australe,* the South Eastern High-bush blueberry, which species, according to the RHS *Dictionary of Gardening,* has 'contributed to the excellent qualities of the modern High-bush commercial blueberries; in fact, until recently, the better varieties were mostly selections of *V. australe,* taken from the wild' – plant history repeating itself in our own time! There are also the important *V. corymbosum,* the Swamp, High-bush or Tall blueberry from the eastern United States, a most variable species, most likely to be a natural hybrid and with its own varieties, *albiflorum* and *glabrum,* sometimes called the North High-bush blueberry; *V. myrtilloides,* once known as *V. canadense,* and more popularly as Canadian blueberry, Sourtop and Velvet-leaf blueberry, growing in Labrador and Manitoba down to Virginia and Illinois; and *V. hirsutum,* the Hairy huckleberry from the south-eastern United States, one of the Dryland blueberries.

The important factor about the commercial production of blueberries is that they have made it possible for thousands of acres of what would otherwise be barren land to be made productive and profitable. In northern regions only the very hardy Low-bush varieties are grown, while elsewhere High-bush varieties, mainly derived from *V. ashei, V. australe* and *V. corymbosum,* are cultivated on land where the water table is about 20 cm (8 in) below the surface, because these plants cannot withstand drought. We have seen them growing in Australia in slightly raised peat beds which are well irrigated. The Low-bush blueberry, hardier than the High-bush, which has been grown commercially in the USA since 1850, is now grown on a large scale in the north-

eastern states and in Canada. Fields of this type of blueberry are often burned over every third year to stimulate rejuvenation and to destroy weeds and pests.

## The fruit

Botanically, a berry crowned by persistent calyx lobes. The fruits of *V. angustifolium,* the Low-bush blueberry, are blue-black, sweet, rounded and some 4–6 mm ($\frac{1}{4}$ in) across, with an attractive, grape-like bloom on the skins. *V. ashei* fruits are very variable and unless one grows a selected form with a good flavour they may even be insipid. The fruits are black or very dull blue, about 6–12 mm ($\frac{1}{4}$–$\frac{1}{2}$ in).

*V. atrococcum,* syn. *V. corymbosum atrococcum,* has large blue fruits according to the variety, rounded, sweet and black. *V. australe,* from eastern North America, has large blue fruits. *V. corymbosum* has blue-black, bloomy fruits. *V. myrtilloides,* the Velvet-leaf blueberry, has sweet, globose, blue-black fruit with an attractive bloom, and *V. hirsutum,* one of the Dryland blueberries, known also as the Hairy huckleberry, has round, purple-black, slightly hairy fruit.

## The plant

*V. angustifolium,* the Low-bush blueberry, is a twiggy, deciduous shrub some 7.5–20 cm (3–8 in) high, with glabrous or slightly downy young shoots. The narrow, lanceolate leaves are small, 1–4 cm ($\frac{1}{2}$–$1\frac{1}{2}$ in) long, and like all blueberries these change attractively in colour in autumn. The flowers are white streaked with red and are the typical bell-shape of this genus, small, about 4 mm ($\frac{1}{5}$ in) long, and are borne in profusion.

The Rabbit-eye blueberry, *V. ashei,* grows much taller, from 1.3–6 m (4–18 ft). The leaves are variable, not only in texture and hue of green, but also because they are sometimes deciduous and sometimes evergreen. The pretty little flowers are white, pale pink, bright pink and sometimes red and sometimes grow as long as 1 cm ($\frac{1}{2}$ in). The Downy Swamp or Black huckleberry, *V. atrococcum,* is a deciduous, branching shrub some 2–3 m (6–10 ft) high. The leaves, 2.5–8 cm (1–3 in) long, are oval or oblong, pointed and smooth above but densely pubescent beneath, which gives the plant its downy appearance. The flowers grow in both the axils of the leaves and at the tips of the shoots in short but crowded racemes, each little bloom about 6 mm (¼ in) long and pink or green flushed with red. A variety, *V. a. leucoccum*, has attractive translucent green or yellow-white flowers.

*V. australe*, the South Eastern High-bush blueberry, grows from 2–4 m (6–12 ft). Its leaves are larger than the others described, some 5–8 cm (2–3 in) in length and 2.5–4 cm (1–1½ in) wide. They are both glaucous and glabrous. The flowers are more cylindrical than bell-shaped or campanulate and are about 8 mm (⅔ in) long, white and sometimes tinged with pink.

The Swamp, High-bush or Tall blueberry, the delicious *V. corymbosum*, grows from 1.3–4 m (4–12 ft) and is distinguishable by its young wood, which is warty and often also pubescent or nearly glabrous. The leaves also are sparsely downy on the undersides and are sometimes ciliate. They are 2.5–7.5 cm (1–3 in) long and roughly half as wide. These become particularly beautifully coloured in autumn.

*V. myrtilloides*, the Canadian blueberry, grows only 45 cm (18 in) high, and as its name suggests, has soft, velvety, hairy young shoots. The leaves also are pubescent, particularly on the undersides. They are small, 2.5–4 cm (1–1½ in) long and half as wide. The flowers, which grow in racemes in their axils, are white tinged with green and sometimes with red, growing in long, cylindrical bells less than 6 mm (¼ in) long.

Blueberries are long-lived. Plants should remain productive for 20 years or more if they are well cared for.

## Cultivation

Blueberry growing presents a challenge because the plants require acid, well-drained soils. They grow best in soils with a pH of 4.0 to 5.5. The soil water level should be at least 30 cm (1 ft) below the soil surface or the roots will suffocate.

Most soils can be made suitable, with special preparation. Sandy and sandy loam soils can be made suitable by mixing acid peat into them and testing the mixture until the correct pH is obtained. This entails mixing roughy 10–15 cm (4–6 in) of peat into the top 15–20 cm (6–8 in) of soil. In some circumstances sawdust can be used instead of peat, and while this does not lower the pH very much, it does provide a suitable medium

for root growth.

On clay soils which are badly drained it is best to make raised beds, using peat blocks, logs, stones, bricks, concrete blocks or even wire mesh to contain the rooting medium. First remove some of the existing soil, say 7.5 cm (3 in), and replace this with drainage material such as gravel, crushed stone or brick or washed clinker. On to this place 20–30 cm (8–12 in) of a soil mixture containing plenty of peat, such as equal portions of acid peat and sandy loam, or soil and sawdust if the soil naturally tends a little towards acidity.

Although blueberries will tolerate a little shade, deep shade inhibits flowering. They do best in a sunny site. It is advisable also to keep them out of frost pockets. Although High-bush blueberries are hardier than peaches, they are likely to be severely damaged or even killed if temperatures drop as low as −29°C (−20°F). Low-bush blueberries are hardier.

Blueberries can be planted 1.2 m (4 ft) apart, and if there is to be more than one row there should be 1.5–1.8 m (5–6 ft) between the rows. Look for the soil mark on the stem and plant them just a little deeper, no more than 2.5–5 cm (1–2 in). Make sure that the roots are well firmed and water them in well without leaving the soil waterlogged. Cut back the branches to 7.5 cm

(3 in). If you can bear to do so, it is best to remove the blossoms which are produced in the first year after planting so that other growth will be stimulated.

Keep the soil over the roots as undisturbed as possible because the plants are very shallow rooting. Mulching is highly beneficial. Use peat, sawdust, chopped bracken, hay or straw to a depth of 7.5–15 cm (3–6 in). Any good complete fertiliser can be used as growth starts in the spring and this can be applied generously, 55 g (2 oz) per plant in the second year after planting and 25 g (1 oz) each following year until the plants have received a total of 150–200 g (6–8 oz).

Check the pH of the soil each year. If it is too high, i.e. above 5.5, apply ground sulphur at a rate of 25 g (1 oz) per plant, either raked or watered in.

Keep watch on the colour of the foliage, for this will give an indication of the health of the plants and the state of the soil. Young leaves are usually a lighter green than the older ones and when the shoots are young these are usually tinged with an attractive red. If the young leaves are yellow and appear stunted, with growth generally poor, this is an indication that they are not getting sufficient iron, a common fault when the pH is, or becomes, too high. Iron deficiency can be avoided and cured if iron chelate is applied to the soil around the plants each spring. Follow directions on the packet.

It is important to provide an adequate and uniform supply of water to the plants from the time they flower until the fruit is harvested. Fortunately, blueberries respond to the trickle or drip method of irrigation, which means that labour and trouble in this task can be cut to a minimum, so long as the necessary expense can be met.

Little pruning is required in the first 2–3 years. Simply remove any dead or diseased wood. After the third year prune annually in spring. As fruit is produced on one-year wood, cut carefully, making sure that plenty of young wood remains on the plant. Watch and cut away old wood which seems not to be making its share of new wood. Cut this close to ground level. Keep weak, sparsely flowering branches cut out, one of the best ways of thinning the fruit. Tips of too vigorous branches can be cut out. Experts vary about pollination advice, some saying that it is unnecessary, others insisting on it. On the principle that most fruits benefit by cross-pollination, we advocate it.

The berries grow in clusters of 5–10 and they ripen during a period of 3–5 weeks. It is not wise to pick them the moment they turn blue, because they will develop a better flavour if left a little longer, say another 3 or 4 days, during which time you may be well advised to protect the fruit from the birds. Berries left too long tend to shrivel or split, so one needs to keep an eye on them. After a time the eye becomes practised in spotting the really ripe fruits, for there are always subtle changes in the appearance.

To pick the berries use the thumb and forefinger and roll the berry off the cluster and into the hand without squeezing it, and thence into the container, which it is helpful to have tied around the waist, thus leaving both hands free.

Once picked, and especially if you wish to gather a good quantity, the ripe berries can be kept in a covered container in the refrigerator for a week or more.

## Culinary uses

There are probably as many recipes for blueberries as there are for strawberries and raspberries. Generally speaking, you can use these in any way that you might use blackcurrants or cranberries. They are more delicious raw than are blackcurrants and are particularly good served with sour cream and brown sugar. They lend themselves to use with spices – cinnamon, coriander, cardamon, nutmeg and ginger. They combine well with apples, pears and quince.

They can be stewed in very little water, sugar and a pinch of salt being added when they are almost tender. Cooked or bottled they can be introduced into many puddings, including fritters, American muffins and shortcakes and pancakes. They go well with cottage cheese and sour cream. Try them in the brulée recipe given for blackcurrants on p. 70. They are good baked, with a crispy or crumble topping.

PRESERVING The following blueberry recipes can also be used for wild huckleberries and wineberries.

To make Spiced Blueberries to serve with cold meats:

## Spiced blueberries

*8 cups stemmed, washed and drained blueberries*
*1 cup red wine*
*1 saltspoon powdered cinnamon*
*5 cloves*
*2 cups sugar*

Mix well in a heavy lined saucepan, bring to the boil and cook for about 30 minutes, skimming when necessary. Lift out the berries with a perforated spoon and allow the juice to continue to simmer until it becomes a thick syrup. Return the berries to the syrup and stir them in well. Allow to cool and put into jars. Cover well. Keep cool.

FREEZING   Simply place the fruit in suitable containers and put in the freezer.

BOTTLING   Follow the procedure described for blackberries (see p. 68).

DRINKS   Blueberry wine can be made in much the same way as other country wines, except that a supplementary nutrient for the yeast should be added to extend the fermentation period and make a better wine.
   An alcoholic dish rather than drink is Brandied Blueberries, requiring:

## Brandied blueberries

*6 cups blueberries*
*1½ cups sugar*
*¼ teasp ground ginger*
*brandy*

Use a glass or earthenware jar with a lid. First mash the berries thoroughly. You can use the blender, but it is best not to make a fine purée. Mix with sugar and ginger and top up with brandy. Keep covered and in the dark for two months, stirring the mixture each week. Then let it rest without stirring for another month. Strain and filter into a bottle.
   There is no need to waste the brandy-soaked fruit. Serve it as a brandied blueberry sauce with ice-cream or bake it as a mince pie. The purée can be saved and frozen if wished.

# BOYSENBERRY
*Rubus* species

## Origin

No one seems to be quite sure how the boysenberry came to be. It is generally assumed that it has mixed blackberry, loganberry and raspberry blood. It was raised in California in the 1930s by Rudolph Boysen. Americans consider it to be their best trailing berry and it is grown more in the USA than anywhere else, although there is a useful production in New Zealand and in some regions of Australia. It has become a significant fruit in the canning industry.

## The fruit

Botanically, an aggregate of drupes. The fruit is large, juicy, first red and becoming dark red and aromatic when ripe, which is in late summer. The fruits are about 2.5–5 cm (1–2 in) in length. There are fewer seeds than in most hybrid berries and the receptacle on which the drupes are grouped is small. The flavour is sweet acid.

## The plant

The boysenberry is a vigorous shrub with thin, biennial canes often 3 m (10 ft) in length. The leaves are dark green and the flowers are produced from joints of the main, one-year-old canes, from which they reach out conveniently. The central part of the cane is the most productive.
   This is one of the fruits that can be used as a piece of garden decoration. It can be trained up pillars or over a pergola, or arch above a path.

## Cultivation

Like the blackberry to which it is closely related, the boysenberry is not a plant to grow in gardens which are exposed to extremes of heat and cold, nor where the prevailing winds are hot and dry. On the other hand, the plant will thrive on a wide range of soils, preferably rich. These must be well drained and deep. It is a plant which is extremely drought-resistant (though like other soft fruits it needs water when the berries are developing) and for this reason can be grown on light soils which dry out quickly and easily.

In areas where the winter is severe, it is possible to protect the canes. Lay them on the ground, cover them with soil and then cover this with straw or litter of some kind. This protective cover should be removed in the spring and the canes then tied to their supports. Although eventually the plant should be allowed to carry several canes, some growers think it is wise in the first season to allow only one strong shoot to develop. At the end of the season this is cut back to just above ground level. This practice is said to encourage more canes to form in the next season. It also encourages the plant to develop a good root system. Two or three of the strongest of the canes are kept. Each year onwards the number of canes can be increased until the plant is carrying as many as 20 if this is convenient.

Other growers allow the plant to make what canes it will and then let them trail on the ground for their first year, allowing them to stretch, but keeping them close to the crown of the plant. Canes can be trained to wires the same way as blackberries. Usually the plant is divided so that some canes go to the left and the rest to the right,

several canes tied parallel to the same wire. An attractive and space-saving method is to train them spread out into a high fan, tipping the canes when they reach the required height. Some growers claim that shortening the cane this way increases berry size.

A support is easily made by using posts and two wires. The top wire should be from 1.3–1.6 m (4–5 ft) from the ground and the lower one 60–75 cm (2–2½ ft). Fan or otherwise spread out the canes in such a way that full advantage is taken of the space provided. Crowded canes are difficult to pick. Cut the canes down to ground level after they have fruited.

Plants do not come true to seed. The best method of propagation is by tip layering, though suckers can also be used.

## Culinary uses

This fruit can be treated in the same way as blackberry and loganberry.

Boysenberry Summer Pudding is a great favourite with many people. It is a good basic

Top: Blackberries *(L. Johns)*
Bottom: Barbados Cherry *(G. R. Roberts)*

Left:  Blackcurrants *(G. R. Roberts)*
Right:  Redcurrants *(G. R. Roberts)*

recipe which can be adapted for most other berries such as blackberries, loganberries and blueberries, as well as the currants, damsons, plums and rhubarb.

### Boysenberry summer pudding

*2 cooking apples, medium size*
*3 cups boysenberries*
*1 cup water*
*¼ cup sugar*
*stale white bread*
*arrowroot or cornflour to be measured*

Wash and drain the berries, peel, core and thinly slice the apples. Put the sugar in the water in a saucepan and boil rapidly for about 5 minutes. Add the fruit, cover and allow to simmer until pulpy (10–15 minutes). Strain. Set the juice aside and press the fruit through a sieve so that the seeds are separated. Add half the juice to this seedless pulp and taste, adding more sugar if necessary. Cover the bottom of a soufflé dish with thin slices of bread and cover them with the purée. Make sure the bread is well soaked. Make another layer of bread, cover with purée and continue this way until the dish is full and all the bread well soaked. This is important, for it should not look like a bread pudding. Cover the filling with a small plate so that it is pressed down when a weight is put in it. Leave this overnight. Measure the remaining juice and add 1 heaped teaspoon of arrowroot or cornflour to each 1 cup. Blend and boil, stirring meanwhile. Let this cool also. Turn out the pudding. Pour some of the sauce over it and keep the rest to serve with the pudding. You can also serve cream or ice-cream.

FREEZING AND BOTTLING   Treat as blackberry and loganberry.

# BREADFRUIT
*Artocarpus incisus*

## Origin

The breadfruit is in the same genus as the jackfruit and native of an area from Sri Lanka to China and Malaya, but cultivated in other tropical regions. (Sir Joseph Banks suggested that Captain Bligh should be sent to Tahiti in the *Bounty* to collect breadfruit seedlings and take them to the West Indies, where, it was hoped, they would provide a staple diet for the Negro slaves.)

## The fruit

Botanically, a multiple fruit with fleshy receptacles which contain a large quantity of starch. The fruits are large, 10–15 cm (4–6 in) in diameter, sometimes weighing 1.8 kg (4 lb), with a rough green skin, becoming tinged with yellow when ripe. In both shape and size the fruit is not unlike a large melon. When fully ripe, the yellow flesh is sweet.

## The plant

It grows to a large tree some 15 m (50 ft) tall, with deeply lobed, 3–9 partite leaves, sometimes cut only in the upper leaf portion, measuring 30–90 cm (2–3 ft) long, deep green on the upper surface and a lighter green on the underside. The flowers, which are monoecious, grow catkin-like.

## Cultivation

The breadfruit must have tropical conditions and has failed to grow and fruit satisfactorily even in the mildest areas of California and Florida. The climate must be warm yet humid, the soil must be rich and constantly moist yet well drained. The large trees prefer to stand in the open away from the shade of other trees and they grow only in lowland areas, disappearing in any country higher than about 600 m (2,000 ft).

Propagation is normally by means of suckers from the roots, which are shallow and wide-spread. A quicker method is to insert root cuttings in a prepared bed during the rainy season.

## Culinary uses

When breadfruit is cooked its taste resembles that of freshly baked bread. It is used a great deal in much the same way as potatoes, i.e. mashed with milk and salt, parboiled and fried until golden, boiled in salt water and combined with bacon and other meats, cooked and diced and made into a salad with dressing.

It can also be used in sweet dishes, mashed with milk and sugar and served with butter or a sweet sauce.

Where seeds do occur in the fruits they can be cooked and eaten like chestnuts.

# BUFFALO BERRY
*Shepherdia argentea*

## Origin

From North America, one of a genus of only three shrubs belonging to the Elaeagnaceae family and so alike in appearance that *S. argentea* is sometimes confused with *Elaeagnus argentea,* a quite different plant which also has edible fruits, but which are silvery, dry and mealy.

The plant grows wild in the central United States. The popular name is said to have been given because the early settlers discovered that the berries made an excellent jelly which could enliven the monotony of a buffalo meat diet, and, so it seems, that of rabbit also.

*S. argentea* was introduced into British gardens at the beginning of the nineteenth century, the other species earlier.

## The fruit

Botanically, an ovoid and drupe-like berry, similar in appearance to redcurrant, growing in clusters among the leaves. There are no cultivars as yet, but one feels that there is room for selection, since the fruits seem to vary from plant to plant, some being red, others orange-red and some being larger than others. The yellow fruits of *S. canadensis* and its variety, *S. c. xanthocarp,* are edible but insipid. As with some grapes, it is said that the berries are all the sweeter for a touch of frost. Occasionally, where there are numerous spines on the bush, the fruit is difficult to gather and it is advisable to wear gloves, but this is not always the case.

## The plant

This makes a tall shrub, growing to some 6 m (20 ft), with silvery, prickly branches and small, whitish leaves. It produces dense clusters of small, yellowish flowers in spring. Male and female plants, one to five or six, are necessary for fertilisation.

Most silvery-leaved plants are ornamental in themselves, but this is a particularly good plant with which to make an unusual and attractive yet fruitful circular or semi-circular windbreak or sun trap.

## Cultivation

This plant will grow in any ordinary soil. Plant during autumn or winter when the ground is in good condition. Once it is established it dislikes being moved. Little pruning is necessary; simply cut away inconvenient growth if you wish to keep the plant within certain confines. Plants can be raised from seed sown outdoors in winter and by layering shoots in autumn.

Like many other silver-leaved plants, this is a good tenant for a seaside garden, an agreeable and adaptable quality it shares with buckthorn to which it is closely related.

## Culinary uses

The fruit is best used to make jellies.

# CALAMONDIN ORANGE
*Citrus mitis*

## Origin

The calamondin is believed to have come from the Philippines and is considered to be a hybrid of lime crossed with kumquat. On the American continent it is grown as a garden tree, but it is most familiar to people in Europe as a house plant. It is also often used as a rootstock for other citrus because of its resistance to disease.

## The fruit

It is small, 4 cm (1½ in) or less in diameter, round, flattened at the poles, with a golden, glossy, loose and edible peel and a strongly acid, lime-like and pleasant juice.

## The plant

A small tree, spineless, with upright and slender branches. The leathery leaves, each on a narrowly winged petiole, are broadly oval. The flowers, small, white and fragrant, are borne singly at the tips of the branches. The tree bears abundantly.

## Cultivation

As for other citrus (see Orange). The plant grows well in the home given a little extra humidity.

## Culinary uses

This can be used in the same way as limes and kumquats, since the sweet, tender peel makes it ideal for pickling or for preserving whole in syrup. It makes excellent marmalade. Calamondin and papaw marmalade is very popular in Hawaii.

# CANISTEL
*Lucuma* species

## Origin

The name is Peruvian, one which is given in that country to just one of the species and has been adopted by botanists for the generic term. This is a genus of about 60 species of trees and shrubs with milky juice belonging to the family Sapotaceae. The plants are indigenous to South America in regions from Chile to Peru, to Mexico and the West Indies, with only a few species in Australia and New Caledonia. The trees are often large. Only a few species appear to be cultivated for their fruits so far, mainly in the warmer parts of America and tropical islands. These are often seen in gardens. The common names often cause confusion. For instance the Canistel, *Lucuma nervosa*, and *L. mammosa*, the Marmalade fruit, are often called the Mammee sapota, a name which really belongs to the true sapote of a completely different genus. We have tried to clarify the situation: see Sapodilla. Lesser cultivated species are *L. cainito*, with translucent flesh; *L. nitida*, yellow flesh; *L. salicifolia*, yellow-orange flesh; and *L. viridis* with red-brown flesh.

## The fruit

Botanically, a berry, usually somewhat egg-shaped. *L. mammosa*, the Marmalade fruit, is globose or elliptical, some 7.5–18 cm (3–7 in) long, with a rusty-brown skin and orange-red flesh, usually one-seeded. The South American *L. nervosa*, the egg fruit or canistel, is more widely grown. There seem to be no distinct cultivars. There is a great variation in the size and shape of fruits from different trees because these are all raised from seed. In Florida and the Bahamas the more nearly round fruits are often called Ti-es.

The longer fruits often have only one seed and it is these in particular that are confusingly known as Mammee sapota. The fruits are orange-yellow, globose to egg-shaped, 5–10 cm (2–4 in) long, with flesh a similar colour to the skin. This is very sweet and mealy, with a slight musky aroma. Harvesting before it is completely ripe tends to reduce the dryness of the flesh. Otherwise there are usually 2–3 seeds, dark brown and shining, in each fruit. *L. obovata,* the Lucuma or Lucmo, from northern Chile and northern Peru, has ovate or globose fruits about 7.5 cm (3 in) long, with a bright, dark green skin and mealy, yellow flesh, with round, large, flattened seeds, usually in pairs.

## The plant

*L. mammosa* grows to a large tree 15–30 m (50–100 ft) tall. *L. nervosa* is smaller, 3–7.5 m (10–25 ft) tall. The long leaves, 10–20 cm (4–8 in), are glabrous and bright green. The small flowers, growing in clusters of 2–5, are produced on the young wood.

## Cultivation

As for *Chrysophyllum* species (see Star apple p. 238).

## Culinary uses

The fruits of these trees are usually eaten out of hand. In Peru they are stored in straw or chaff until they are ready for eating. Canistel is said to be improved by a touch of butter or lime juice to soften the pulp. The sliced fruit can be served with sugar and cream or mayonnaise. The mashed flesh is used in pies, puddings, pancakes and layer cakes and is added to ice-cream. It can be used to make jam.

# CAPE GOOSEBERRY
*Physalis* species

## Origin

Members of the tomato family, Solanaceae, mainly native to Mexico, South America and the southern states of the USA, although the vivid *P. alkekengi,* grown in many flower gardens and known as Chinese Lanterns or Winter Cherry, comes from a region stretching from the Caucasus to China, and although it is grown chiefly for winter flower decoration, its fruits are edible though not remarkable. However, the tough outer husk or lantern, which looks wholesome, should not be eaten. All the physalis are identified by this swollen calyx which surrounds the fruit inside and the number of the popular names suggests that the unusual character of the plant has caught the public imagination.

The best-known species seems to be *P. peruviana,* syn. *P. edulis,* which raises two important questions. In the first place *edulis* seems to be a variety rather than a synonym (see below) and secondly, it seems curious to us that a plant with the specific name *peruviana* should be known mainly as Cape gooseberry, although the latter point appears to be covered by the fact that although it is from South America it was brought in and once extensively cultivated around the Cape of Good Hope. The plant has been in cultivation for some two centuries – time, one would have imagined, for a decision to be made on whether to call it a gooseberry or a cherry! However, the plant has since become naturalised in the Cape as it has in some other warm regions of the world. There are varieties, *P. p. edulis* (see above) which has yellow fruits, and *P. p. violacea,* which has larger, darker purple fruits.

The Mexican Ground cherry, Tomatillo or Jamberberry, is *Physalis ixocarpa,* said by some to have sticky, purple-red fruits and by others golden yellow, large and almost filling the attractive brown-yellow, purple-veined husk. We should perhaps point out here that there are many other so-called ground cherries which grow wild in the southern states of the USA and in South America. Although they share the common name of ground cherry, they also have more localised titles such as Clammy ground cherry, Virginia ground cherry, Prairie ground cherry and so on. The most familiar species in cultivation, known popularly again simply as Ground cherry, is *P. pruinosa,* and this particular one is to be found in parts of eastern and central North America. It is sometimes called the Strawberry or Husk tomato, and sometimes Dwarf Cape gooseberry. In general, like all popular names, these three can be confusing, because they are also given to many other native ground cherries which grow in other regions of the American continent. It should not be considered the only cultivated ground cherry, because the Low Hairy Ground cherry, *P. pubescens,* for example, which is a noxious weed in the southern states, is cultivated in the north. This species has a yellow berry. Of recent years there has been some hybridisation and selection carried out and cultivars of physalis are now appearing in seedsmen's lists under such names as Jamberry, New Sugar Giant, Golden Berry and Sugar Berry. These all have golden fruits. There are likely to be more.

## The fruit

Botanically a globose berry, many-seeded, enclosed in an inflated calyx, the 'bladder' or 'lantern', which is so characteristic of the plant. The fruits can be said to resemble a cherry slightly, hence the name. The berries vary in size according to species, being usually about 3 cm (1 in) in diameter. However, some of the new types are larger, particularly when well cultivated.

As with most fruits, inside the surrounding calyx the berries begin green, changing slowly to their mature colour. As a rule the skin of a ripe berry looks shinier and tighter than one which is not quite so mature, in the same way as a tomato. There is considerable difference in flavour between an almost and a fully ripe physalis fruit, which may account for the reason why some people find them distasteful.

It is quite usual for the filled husk to drop from the plant before the berry is ripe, and while it lies on the ground the berry will continue to ripen. It is wise therefore to search the ground and the surface of the pots in which plants might be grown each day once you find the husks are starting to drop.

The husks, which begin as small sepals around the petals, vary slightly in size, shape and general colour according to the species or variety as they mature. They begin green and change slowly, some being straw coloured, some brownish-grey, some slightly tinged with purple. Some are more pointed than others.

Berries should be left in their husks until required. They can be stored this way and will remain sweet and sound for many weeks. In hot climates they should be refrigerated. The husk can easily be split into 'petals' and these can then be folded back in order to eat the fruit or to remove it. However, fruits vary, especially now that new cultivars are being introduced, and where the husks are obviously packed, or where the fruit actually bursts through or is sticky, it is advisable to soak the whole structure in water for a few moments. They then separate easily.

## The plant

Cape gooseberry, *P. peruviana,* still often listed by seedsmen as *P. edulis,* is a perennial often treated as a half hardy annual, depending on the region in which it is grown. It is an erect plant roughly 1 m (3 ft) tall and as wide and bushy. It is quite hairy in appearance, with attractive heart-shaped leaves having slightly waved and slightly toothed margins. The small flowers are white with violet anthers and slightly spotted petals.

Tomatillo, *P. ixocarpa,* is again a perennial usually grown as an annual. It grows to 1 m (3 ft) or sometimes more, is glabrous, branched and somewhat untidy in appearance unless kept under control. The attractive but small flowers, some

2 cm (¾ in) in diameter, are yellow with five dark purple-brown markings at the throat. The husk is straw yellow, purple-veined.

Ground cherry, *P. pruinosa*, is an annual with spreading branches, heart-shaped slightly toothed leaves, greyish-green and slightly hairy when young. It differs from the other physalis in that the leaves are unequal at the base, so that one side of a leaf is slightly larger than the other, like begonia leaves. The flowers, like those of *P. ixocarpa*, are prettily marked with brown centres. The fruit is yellow, sweet and slightly acid, enclosed in a grey-brown calyx.

When these plants are grown outdoors in pots they need a sunny place, so something can be made of the way they are placed. The cultivars will grow quite tall when grown well, some 1.5–2 m (4–6 ft), with plenty of growth on them, and for this reason they can be used to make a pleasant summer screen.

The plants need to be staked and one of the best ways of ensuring that they do not get blown over by the wind is to tie each supporting cane to a wire or pole stretched along the length of the area where they are to stand, for instance at the side of a path or on the boundary of a patio. In our garden Golden Berry plants were grown along the outside of a large fruit cage. It was a simple matter to tie the supporting cane to the netting. The attractive foliage of the physalis also helped to soften the harsh outlines of this essential but unlovely structure.

Although the husks of the kinds grown mainly for their fruits are nothing like as vivid in colour as the Chinese Lantern, they have their decorative uses all the same. Those husks which are opened up carefully to make 'petals' can resemble dried flowers. They can form part of some composite flower made from other dried materials, for instance a tiny contrasting cone or some button-like flower can be fixed to make a centre in place of the fruit which was removed and consumed. Several can be fixed together to make 'double' flowers. They can also be sprayed lightly with clear varnish and lightly glittered or coloured as you will. This way they can be used in many ways for Christmas or party decorations, in swags, Byzantine cones, garlands, in a hundred decorative designs in fact, depending on the ingenuity and industry of the florist.

## Cultivation

One can take the formula for physalis cultivation generally speaking to be the same as that for the tomato, which means that in regions where summer comes late and autumn early some time under glass, perhaps even the entire season, is necessary. Often in these areas, as for example our own garden in southern England, plants of cultivar Golden Berry were still producing mature and immature fruits and flowers in late September and would be spoiled unless protected. In such cases, if one wishes to crop all the fruits possible, such plants should be brought into a greenhouse or some similar warmed structure where there is good light. For this reason plants are best pot grown.

*Physalis ixocarpa*, *P. peruviana* (often listed as *edulis*) and its cultivars should be treated this way, or they can, like many tomatoes in the northern hemisphere, be grown entirely in a cold greenhouse in pots or by the ring culture method. In sheltered gardens plants can be grown against a sunny wall in a warm border. When physalis is grown this way the plants have to be securely staked, because growth is both plentiful and somewhat lush. If plants are sprayed with clean water during the day, this will encourage fertilisation by increasing the humidity.

Where plants can easily be grown outdoors, it is often best to treat perennials such as the Cape gooseberry as annuals, although this will not apply where night temperatures drop considerably.

## Culinary uses

This fruit is rich in vitamins and although not as versatile as some, there are many pleasant ways in which it can be served, whether raw or cooked. The flavour is distinctive and more pronounced in some species and varieties than in others; it can effectively be brought out if served in a compote as follows. Simmer the fruit slowly in syrup for 5 minutes. Drain it and put it into a bowl with a strip of lemon peel. (Do not cook the peel with it.) Reduce the syrup, pour it on the fruit and peel. Allow to cool.

A purée of the fruits can be used in ways suggested for other fruits. The berries make good jam.

To make glacé fruits in fondant icing, the fondant is flavoured with a liqueur, usually kirsch, or raspberry or pineapple essence, and is left white or coloured pink, yellow or pale orange. Prepare the fruits by opening the calyx. This has then to be folded right back so that it acts as a stalk as one holds it to dip the fruit into the hot fondant icing. Drain and place each fruit on a tray which has been well sprinkled with icing sugar.

Glazed Cape gooseberries are a little more tricky. In this case the fruits are taken out of their husks and each one is rolled in gum arabic. Cook sugar to a degree of crack, 160°C (325°F). Lower in the fruits. Drain with a perforated spoon and place on a lightly buttered tin or marble slab to cool.

# CARAMBOLA
*Averrhoa carambola*

## Origin
Possibly from Indonesia, although not all authorities are agreed on this. However, the plant is widely grown and cultivated and the fruit consumed in the warmer regions of China, India and south-east Asia. It is also grown in South America and in parts of Australia.

Carambola appears to have been introduced into Europe towards the end of the eighteenth century, no doubt as a novelty for the ostentatious stove houses then becoming fashionable among the rich. However, there is no evidence that we can find of the fruit ever becoming popular as a dessert. The genus, which contains only two species, the second being the Blimbing or Cucumber tree, *A. bilimbi,* was named in honour of an Arabian physician named Averrhoes, the Latinised version of 'Ibn Rushd, who lived in Cordova in Spain during the mid twelfth century and who translated Aristotle into Arabic.

## The fruit
The fruits are about 8–13 cm (3–5 in) long, oval or elliptic, with attractive yellow or yellow-brown waxy rind and yellow flesh. They are ribbed in such a way as to make 3, 4 or more usually 5 sharp corners. Cut across, the outline and general shape of the section much resemble a star,

hence one popular name, Star Fruit. The fruits have a clear, watery juice, sweet or pleasantly acid. The flavour appears to vary somewhat from plant to plant and some work is now being carried out to select particularly good fruit trees and propagate from them by layering. Work being carried out in Australia suggests that 3 crops a year can be obtained, producing up to 100 kg (220 lb) of fruit. As these fruits mature and ripen, some turn yellow while others remain green, although there is some slight colour change. They also take on a waxy appearance.

## The plant
This is a small evergreen tree, graceful and well proportioned. The pinnate leaves are compound, the ovate, slender, pointed leaflets being in 4 or 5 pairs and of a pleasant light green colour. The small purple flowers which grow in short racemes at intervals are usually produced from the smaller branches, although they sometimes appear on the larger limbs and even on the trunk. The fruits are produced in profusion and in clusters. Under natural conditions both flowers and fruits are produced continuously, reaching their peaks as conditions suit them.

## Cultivation

Carambola begins to fruit in about 5 years from seed from which it can easily be propagated though with variable results. Much earlier fruit can be obtained and sweeter fruits guaranteed by propagating by layering or grafting. The plant grows well on both light and heavy soils along tropical coasts. It is rather delicate when young, which means that even in the tropics one should ensure that the environment is suitable and has sufficient rainfall and humidity to maintain steady growth, or that it is possible to provide the plant with sufficient moisture. Seedlings and young plants generally can be damaged by cold.

Obviously, when trees are grown under glass it is essential to maintain a high temperature throughout the year, with matching humidity.

## Culinary uses

The fruit is said to be high in vitamin A and C; it can be eaten as a fresh fruit, or made into drinks, jams and preserves.

It is also cooked, pickled, used for chutney and preserved in sugar as a sweetmeat.

# CAROB
*Ceratonia siliqua*

## Origin

A member of the pea family, the plant originates from the eastern Mediterranean, where it grows wild and is indeed a characteristic plant of most dry regions; it is highly valued and appreciated for its kindly shade as well as its sweet fruits, leathery though they may be when dried.

Apart from growing wild, in many warm regions the carob is often cultivated. In fact it seems most probable that there may be areas where the introduced cultivars have taken over from the wild forms. Progeny of these have escaped and have become established, so that in some areas the 'indigenous' plants may be different from the wild species growing elsewhere. Some carobs, those grown in Sicily for instance, have fleshier pods than others. These are thought to have been imported and cultivated by the Arabs originally.

The generic name of the plant comes from 'keration', a horn or pod. This name ties up with an interesting point about the plant. It is of social significance apart from its food value, since it is believed that in time past the carob seeds, which are strictly uniform, were used as units of weight for gold, and that the term 'carat' is derived from the name of the plant.

The name 'St John's Bread' refers to the belief that these were the locusts on which John the Baptist fed when he was in the desert. The pods can be eaten fresh, but are more often used, and are perhaps more useful, when dried. The mature pods are brown, thick, slightly tough and leathery, and in spite of their unattractive appearance, very palatable to those with a sweet tooth. At one time locust beans could be bought in sweet shops in Europe and North America at certain times of the year, and eaten in much the same way as manufactured sweets. They are still enjoyed in this way in many Mediterranean countries. Recently they have been experiencing a new popularity among the foods stocked by health stores. Locust beans are often used as a chocolate substitute. The plant was introduced into southern Europe in 1570 and for centuries it was most highly valued as an animal food and still is as such in some districts, where at the same time it serves as a food for those who tend the animals.

Carob pods are also used in the preparation of a cough linctus by pharmacists. It can also be used in the production of alcohol because of the high sugar content of the pods.

## The fruit

Botanically, a pod, 13–30 cm (5–12 in) in length and about 2.5 cm (1 in) wide, flattened, containing several obovate seeds. The pulp is sweet, with a sugar content as high as 50 per cent.

## The plant

The carob makes a large, spreading tree up to 10 m (35 ft) tall when growing in native surroundings, but otherwise is a comparatively small shrub. The compound leaves have rounded, shining, tough, even leathery leaflets which are dark green above, a paler hue on the underside and about 30 cm (12 in) long. The tiny, unisexual flowers are borne on short-stalked cylindrical racemes, grouped among the leaves and even on the trunk, some 15 cm (6 in) long. The male flowers have a red hue, while the hermaphrodites are green.

## Cultivation

The carob enjoys Mediterranean conditions (climate no. 1 on the world chart, p. 14) and is comparatively resistant to drought. Its roots grow deeply but it has no objection to a certain amount of lime in the soil. It can be grown in particularly mild districts of temperate regions, but will benefit from the protection of a sunny wall, and will never really fulfil its capabilities.

The plant can be propagated by the seeds, which should be sown their own depth in pots of sandy soil in a temperature of about 30°C (85°F) in spring. The seedlings should be transplanted outdoors in suitable climates or potted in summer. Alternatively, cuttings of firm shoots about 10 cm (4 in) long can be taken in sandy soil under enclosed situations in late summer or early autumn. No particular pruning is necessary.

## Culinary uses

Before using the pods, remove the hard seeds.

Possibly the most important feature of this fruit is that it can replace chocolate in drinks and dishes for those who are allergic to this food. If the carob is to be used as cocoa and made into a drink, it should be ground very finely, otherwise the drink may taste gritty. Use the coffee grinder. For those with a sweet tooth, sugar or some other sweetener will be necessary. Honey and carob go extremely well together. Carob is good in ice-cream instead of chocolate and it can be combined with ground or thick liquid coffee in a mocha ice-cream. It can be used in almost any way that cocoa is used. In Bermuda the pods are cooked to make a syrup from which a cordial is made.

Cubed Carob is an interesting sweetmeat.

### Cubed carob

*2 cups sugar*
*¾ cup ground carob*
*¼ cup butter*
*generous ½ cup milk*
*pinch salt*
*1 teasp vanilla essence*

Put all ingredients except the vanilla essence into a heavy saucepan and bring to the boil, stirring all the while. Simmer until the liquid reaches the soft ball stage, 110°C (225°F). Remove from the heat and add vanilla. Beat the mixture until it is really thick. Pour it into a buttered tin or dish and allow it to cool. Cut into cubes.

# CASHEW APPLE
*Anacardium occidentale*

## Origin

This is a plant of doubtful origin, but is believed to be native to tropical Africa, one of a large family, the Anarcadiaceae. Most members are indigenous to the tropics, although there are many which belong to the temperate regions. This particular genus, as far as is known, has 6 species of evergreen trees, of which this particular plant is the best known since it is the source of the cashew nut. The wood is also of value; from it is produced a gum used in the manufacture of varnish. It is grown more widely in the Orient, especially India, where it is held in higher esteem than elsewhere. It is grown to a lesser extent in the warmer localities of Europe.

## The fruit

Botanically, the true fruit is a hard, kidney-shaped nut, described as being seated laterally on a fleshy, wide, pear-shaped peduncle. This last is the so-called 'apple'. The cashew nut is found inside the oddly shaped grey-green or brown fruit. The thick shell contains an irritant oil which will blister the skin if it comes into contact with it. For this reason the nuts are roasted before they are opened and their kernels removed. The part in which we are interested looks like a glossy, bright yellow and red fruit, but it is hard to realise that actually it is the swollen stem. The 'apple' is thin-skinned, soft and very juicy and refreshing. The juice is acid and the apple must be quite ripe or it will be too astringent to be palatable.

## The plant

The tree grows to a height of about 5 m (16 ft). Its notched, leathery leaves, 15–20 cm (6–8 in) in length, are veined and oval or obovate-oblong, wedge-shaped at the base. The small, fragrant flowers are yellow, bright red or rose. The tree is very colourful and ornamental when it begins to fruit. The apples open successively, a few at a time, and while there are flowers still in bloom.

## Cultivation

The plant most enjoys a very warm climate and a rich humusy soil, in which it will flourish. This notwithstanding, much of the world's cashew production comes from sandy and sandy loam soils (which of course should be well cultivated).

## Culinary uses

The fruit can be eaten raw. It can also be sliced and stewed, or cooked in pies and flans. In Ven-

ezuela the fruit is made into a soup much like cherry soup. The juice is used to make a wine and in Cuba is distilled into a liqueur. Stuck with cloves and roasted, it can be used to give a special flavour to a punch. The apples make good preserves, jams and jellies.

# CASIMIROA
*Casimiroa edulis*

## Origin

A member of the family Rutaceae, which also contains the citrus, this is a Mexican genus of 4 or 5 species, the best known of which is this casimiroa. It was first introduced into Europe in 1866, but was earlier known to the Spaniards, obviously through their South American connections, and was named in honour of one of their famous botanists, Cardinal Casimiro Gomez de Ortego, who lived in the late eighteenth century. It is rarely grown outside sub-tropical countries, but can be grown in warm areas in temperate regions and has even fruited in the Channel Islands. It is being investigated by fruit scientists in New South Wales as a possible commercial cropper. Commercial plantations already exist in California and Florida.

In spite of its popular name, 'White Sapote', it is not related to the sapotes, although it does bear a superficial resemblance in some features.

## The fruit

This is green to yellow, sometimes even tinged or streaked with orange, around 7–10 cm (3–4 in) in diameter. The skin is tender and the pulp is yellowish, surrounding 2–5 large seeds, sweet in flavour but sometimes with a slight resinous or bitter flavour.

## The plant

The casimiroa will grow to some 10 m (30 ft), an evergreen with downy young shoots. It has palmate leaves in 3 or 5 parts, roughly 5–13 cm (2–5 in) long and 2.5–5 cm (1–2 in) wide, bright green and reminiscent of walnut leaves in appearance. The flowers, small and green-white, grow variously, either in short clusters in the axils of mature leaves or in long, graceful panicles on the ends of leaf shoots which are a year or more old.

## Cultivation

The casimiroa really needs a sub-tropical climate (no. 4 on the world chart, p. 14) to grow at its best, but as it comes from the high country of Mexico it has been tried with surprising success in less promising regions. Its soil must be well drained and it is tolerant of dry conditions.

In temperate regions it must be grown in a heated greenhouse, preferably in pots, in a temperature of about 18°C (65°F). The plant germinates easily from seed and seedlings should be disciplined to make sure that they do not become too lean and straggly. Cut branches back annually to induce the production of laterals.

Fruit produced from the spring flowers should begin to ripen in early autumn. The fruit drops naturally when it is ripe and it is then ready for consumption. As it ripens, a process that may take several days, the skin gradually becomes a lighter green, even yellow, according to the variety. At the same time it softens as it ripens. One way of staggering the crop, which can be considerable, is to gather the fruit when it is well grown but not mature and store it until it softens and comes to its full flavour.

## Culinary uses

Quite the best way to eat the fruit is to scoop out the juicy flesh from the papery skin, remove the seeds and sprinkle with a little sugar. It goes very well with cream.

# CHERIMOYA
*Annona cherimolia*

## Origin

The generic name means 'yearly produce' and one imagines therefore that the plant grows naturally among those kinds of plants which are perpetually fruiting, or which have more than one season in a year. Since this species originates in Peru, this is likely. The popular nomenclature of this and other plants of the same family is somewhat confusing. The popular name of one species in one country is often applied to another species growing in a different area. Sometimes the names change from one locality to another which is only a short distance away. One finds also that all annonaceous fruits tend to be grouped under the omnibus heading of 'custard apples'. The cherimoya is considered to be the best of the several related species, but it fruits only under specific conditions. While other species are likely to thrive best in the tropics, the cherimoya does best in warm districts outside the tropics. For this reason many hybrids have been developed as commercial crops. In this book we have separated them as clearly as we can and others will be found under the headings Atemoya, Ilama, Sour Sop and Sugar Apple.

The genus contains about 60 species, most but not all evergreen, some with fragrant leaves. Several produce delicious edible fruits. The genus is native to tropical America and the Andes in Peru and Ecuador, but as one might expect, the plants are grown in other tropical regions of the world. It seems that they were brought first from Mexico to the West Indies. More recently they have been grown in tropical Asia, Australia and Israel, where they are being hybridised and grown commercially on a fairly large scale. In Britain and some other northern countries the plants have been and still are grown as stove plants.

A. *cherimolia* was originally named *A. tripetala*.

## The fruit

Botanically, an indefinite number of carpels joined into one fleshy, rounded, many-celled, edible fruit, with a surface covered with concave, U-shaped areas, sometimes smooth and sometimes covered with a small wart. The fruit is generally round, but is variable. It can weigh anything from grammes to kilos. To some people the fruit is at first glance reminiscent of a globe artichoke, although the scales are not separate but massed. Its flesh or pulp is white. The flavour, always difficult to describe, is considered to be that of a cross between a pineapple and a strawberry, but once the fruit is tasted its flavour is unmistakable and usually easily recognised. The seeds within the flesh are large and numerous, black and brown. The fruits ripen in autumn and early winter. Left to ripen on the tree they are likely to fall and spoil.

## The plant

A mature tree will reach about 6 m (20 ft) in height, but some plants vary from the neat, erect and bushy to the tall and straggly. In the main this is an attractive plant with its young shoots covered with a dull yellow velvety tomentum. The leaves are also velvety on the undersides, ovate-lanceolate and strongly scented. The little nodding flowers are also scented, with long green-yellow petals bearing a central purple spot at their bases.

Many commercially grown 'custard apples' are semi-deciduous in habit and shed most of their leaves during the winter and early spring months. There are two stages of flowering, the first just after the buds burst in spring, when many if not most of the flowers fail to set fruit. The late flowers produce the main crop.

## Cultivation

Cherimoya grows well in sub-tropical regions including coastal areas where the temperatures are not excessively high. Generally speaking, where bananas grow well, the cherimoya should also thrive. It is important that there should be fairly high humidity during the flowering period, otherwise the fruit will not set. Late frosts can cause problems, especially to young trees, but the older trees which are semi-deciduous seem able to withstand light frosts successfully.

Cultivation is much the same as that followed for citrus (see Orange). Good, deep, fertile soils of a light texture are best, although the plant may be grown on clay loams provided they are well drained. Shallow soils, especially those that are on a heavy or impervious subsoil, are not suitable. The plants should be encouraged to grow well from the beginning, to avoid problems such as crown rot. Feeding is beneficial, but should not be carried out at planting time. Plant in early spring and water carefully as there is some danger in overwatering. The plant is easily propagated from seed, but seedlings are variable and it is wise to buy grafted plants. Some varieties need pollinators. Since there is so much confusion concerning the various annonaceous fruits it is best to consult local experts and to choose accordingly. It is also possible to propagate from cuttings of firm wood, i.e. ripened shoots with the leaves intact, in moist sand in enclosed conditions. Only young trees should be planted out. These are best pruned at planting time to control the whip-like character of the plant, so far as is possible. When the tree is mature, keep cutting back any branches which rest on the ground, at the same time cutting whip-like terminals on the outside of the tree to about a third of their length. Inside branches which appear to be crowding the centre may be cut away. Pruning should not be carried out in winter, only in early spring, when it can be seen that the sap is beginning to rise.

The fruit is carried on both the current year's growth and, to a greater extent, the old wood. This is due to the fact that the late crop of flowers grows on the lower and more protected parts of the tree, which means that not only do they develop quicker in the more humid atmosphere, but also that they are protected from the sun and so do not suffer from sun scorch. There is not always a strictly defined blossom period. If, for instance, for some reason or another only a few fruits are produced at the main blossoming period, a succession of flowers may follow.

When grown indoors the plant should be placed where it receives good light. including some sunlight, yet it should not be subjected to long periods of the glare of the sun through glass. This may mean that shading should be provided during the brightest periods of the day. During the warmest and best-lit months the plant should be syringed daily to provide added humidity, but this also should not be overdone. Indoor temperatures should range between 13–18°C (55–65°F) in winter with benefit from staying longer at the higher figure. In summer the range should be about 22–27°C (70–80°F).

On the tree the fruits mature at different times. Ripe fruits have a noticeable bloom on the skin. At this time also the carpels separate so that you see spaces or interstices between the corrugations on the skin of the fruit gradually widen until the white flesh beneath is visible. It is best to pick the fruits a little before they reach this stage so they can ripen indoors. After they have reached full ripeness they can be refrigerated.

The stalks are recessed. When the fruit is gathered, the stalks should be clipped and not pulled from the tree. Because of the way it grows, the best method is to cut the stalk level with the shoulders of the fruit. Fruits should be handled very gently to avoid bruising.

## Culinary uses

These notes cover all the different kinds of custard apples.

The fruits can be eaten raw, simply halved and spooned out. A delicious, firm, creamy sauce can be made by mixing the flesh with mashed banana and cream. Test for taste. This can be used as a filling for layer cakes, a base for trifles and a basis for other creamy sweets.

The sweet pulp can be used to make an ice-cream, using the same recipe as given for avocado (p. 55). It is also good in a sherbet. A refreshing drink can be made by mixing the flesh with four times its volume of water. Blend, taste and add sugar or honey as required. Chill before serving.

# CHERRY
*Prunus* species

## Origin

The generic name comes from the old Latin name for the plum, to which the cherry is closely related. Both are members of the rose family, Rosaceae. The genus, which contains about 200 species of trees and shrubs, mainly natives of the temperate regions of the northern hemisphere, is divided by botanists into 7 groups or sub-genera, distinguished by certain common factors. In some, the fruit is grooved on one side, in others, including the cherry, the fruits are generally without a groove or suture. This group is Cerasus, and *Prunus cerasus* is a parent of some of the familiar edible cherries. We shall deal later with the species from which commercial cherries have been derived. Other species that have edible fruits and which are more usually planted as ornamental trees are *P. fruticosa*, syn. *Cerasus sylvestris*, known as the European dwarf cherry; *P. pseudocerasus*, the Bastard or Chinese Early cherry; *P. tomentosa* and *P. besseyi*, which fruits well in warm countries.

Cherries have been in cultivation for so many centuries that it is often impossible to trace the lineage of one variety or another. To add to the confusion there are some names, Blackheart for instance, which have often been passed from one variety to another, and even from one locality to another, although it is believed that there are some varieties which have remained unchanged in any way since Roman times.

Since the early nineteenth century and due to many factors, a vast number of varieties and forms have come into cultivation and are now present in their hundreds. This was due to the establishment of great gardens and fine gardeners working for rich employers and because of more intensive commercial production. For example, today in New South Wales alone there are more than 50 varieties of sweet cherries grown. Great strides have been made in America, Australia and Europe, especially in Britain where the famous John Innes Horticultural Institution raised the now universal Merton varieties.

Modern cherries can be divided very roughly into three groups: those with sweet fruits, those with sour (although actually these are acid rather than sour and bitter), and the in-betweens. The sweet section had originally been divided fairly clearly into two types, the Bigarreau, with firm-fleshed fruits, and the Guigne and Heart groups in which the flesh is softer and more tender. However, these divisions are not now as clearly defined as they were, due to more intensive hybridisation, and we find the two main groups often sub-divided according to their shape and the colour of the skin, flesh and juice.

The sweet cherries are believed to have been developed from *Prunus avium,* the Gean or Mazzard, which grows wild in Britain and other regions of Europe, prolifically in some areas, and across to west Asia. These wild plants are a little variable. All produce small fruits, but some are sweet and some bitter. Obviously it has been the trees with the sweet fruits that have been valued, and since ancient times *P. avium* has been selected for development for this reason and later hybridised.

As one would expect, gifts and exchanges of the best or favourite varieties or forms have taken place between peoples of one district or country and another, so that on occasions better forms of indigenous tree would be imported into a locality and grown in orchards or gardens, while the familiar species would be simply regarded as a not very important woodland plant. However, there are regions, Devon in England being reported as one, where a small, black, delicious form of Mazzard is cultivated and has probably been grown for centuries, possibly because it was the only type which succeeded in a particular area or district.

The Romans are thought to have imported and cultivated their own cherries when in occupation of Britain in about AD 100. No doubt this was because they had discovered how well it grew in other colonies, Gaul for instance.

Today, cherries are produced in great quantities in Italian orchards and form an important part of the economy as exports, even though cherries generally are not considered a good transportable fruit. Romania, Germany and the United States also produce large crops. In Australia the Young and Orange districts of NSW produce four-fifths of the cherries grown in that state. The first commercial orchard was planted at Young as late as 1878. However, of all peoples the French appear to value more highly and to use cherries with more flair and resourcefulness than any other group. They produce 100,000 tonnes per year and apparently consume 2.5 kg (5½ lb) per head. It is there and in European countries generally that cherries have been and still are used most widely for culinary purposes. It is mainly the so-called sour cherries that have been most cultivated there (or gathered) and used for desserts, conserves and foods of many kinds including confectionery and drinks. These sour cherries can be divided into two groups according to the colour of their juice. They are the Kentish or Amarelle cherries with colourless juice, with varieties including Montmorency, Meteor and Early Richmond, and the Morello or Griotte cherries with red juice and darker fruits than those in the first group and with varieties including the English Morello and Northstar.

Originating in south-east Europe and western Asia, the sour cherries appear to have been developed from two species, *P. cerasus austera* and *P. c. caprioniana.* Another species, *P. marasca,* a variety of *P. cerasus,* is the source of maraschino liqueur. Incidentally, *P. cerasus* is also the species from which many of the beautiful ornamental flowering cherries have been developed, although few of these produce fruits of any significant value.

The third group is of hybrid origin, crosses between *P. avium* and *P. cerasus,* and the fruits have inherited some qualities of both the sweet and sour groups. These are sometimes known as Royals, more often as Dukes. It is said that there are as many as 100 varieties originating from this hybridisation, but it would not be surprising if there should prove to be considerably more than this number. Like the sour cherries, the Dukes, generally speaking, flower later than the sweet types. These cherries are particularly valued for their hardiness in unfavourable climates.

### The fruit

Botanically a one-seeded-drupe, the fruits vary considerably according to the variety. In shape they vary from round, through ovate to heart-shaped. Oval fruits have shallow stem cavities; heart-shaped fruits have deep stem cavities and prominent 'shoulders'. Size varies according to variety from just over 1 cm to just under 3 cm (½–1 in.) Stem lengths also vary from about 2–7 cm (¾–3 in). The cherry stone may be free or semi-clinging. Experts can identify some varieties by the characteristics of the stone as well as by their appearance. Both skin and flesh colour differ according to variety. It can range from a creamy-yellow through yellow and cerise to so deep a red as to appear almost black.

All cherries of all forms and varieties become mature in a relatively short period. As they approach maturity their weight increase accelerates. During the last 12–14 days it is said that they may increase as much as one-third of their total final weight, conditions being favourable. The harvest is greatly influenced by rainfall or by the amount of water available to the plant. With insufficient, the cherries will begin to dry on the tree after they have ripened. Too much moisture, on the other hand, can result in fruit cracking at about the time of harvesting.

Morello cherries, *Prunus cerasus austera*, are smaller than the sweet cherry and are borne on longer and thinner stems. Although the fruit is often described as black, in fact it varies from dark red to almost black. The flesh is a deep, crimson red, tender, juicy and bittersweet, too acid for most palates when eaten raw, but delicious when cooked or preserved in some way or another. The stones are small in proportion to the size of the fruits.

The Amarelle or Amarella cherries, *P. c. caprioniana*, which are often confused with morellos, are similar in appearance, but they have lighter coloured fruits with less acid, yellow flesh tinged with red such as in Kentish Red or yellow as in Flemish. They have the small stones and slender stems of the morellos. And confusingly they are sometimes called Red Morellos. Varieties of Amarelles, 'Griottiers' as they are known in France, are used in confectionery in many ways and are highly recommended for Cerises à l'eau-de-vie.

### The plant

Cherries are among the most decorative of all fruit trees, but they come in great variety. The species can be clearly described, but cultivars differ greatly. Apart from anything else, differences arise when a tree is grown as a standard or a bush or is fan-trained. *P. avium*, the Gean or Mazzard, is naturally a pyramidal tree which will grow as high as 20 m (75 ft) or more, with a silvery-grey bark that peels horizontally. It has smooth shoots. The leaves are oval to ovate, 8–13 cm (3–5 in) long, slender, pointed, irregularly toothed and on stems some 5 cm (2 in) long. Cherry blossom is beautiful and often a tree appears to be smothered with flowers. Those of this species are white, up to 4 cm (1½ in) in diameter, growing in stalkless umbels each with several flowers. This species is distinguished from *P. cerasus* by the fact that there are no leafy bracts at the bases of the blossom umbels, as well as by its non-acid fruit and the habit of the plant. The leaves and fruit of the sweet cherries are larger than those of the other species.

All sweet cherry varieties are self-sterile.

The morello cherry is a pendulous, vigorous, slightly spreading little tree, often bush-like, reaching some 6–8 m (18–22 ft), with a small trunk and drooping branches. Its red-brown trunk also strips transversely in time. The leaves, smaller than those of the sweet cherry, are also smooth and glossy. The blossom is white. The morello is self-fertile, as are all commercial sour cherries. They will, however, cross-pollinate with any sweet variety which happens to be in blossom at the same time.

The Amarelle is just a little more tree-like than the true morello. It is not quite so vigorous in growth nor does it produce such a full crop. Unlike the morellos, these cherries usually crop best when they are cross-pollinated, although they may be described as self-fertile by the nurserymen. Bees assist pollination of all cherries.

The fact that the Duke and sour cherries can be fan-trained against a wall or some similar vertical surface offers the gardener an opportunity to extend his garden space and to decorate his surroundings at the same time. Furthermore, the fact that sour cherries will tolerate a sunless or almost sunless wall means that it is possible to clothe what is often a problem area both prettily and profitably. Incidentally, one should bear in mind that fan-trained plants are the easiest to net against birds.

We once saw one side of a drive in from front gate to garage made attractive by cherry planting. A wall divided one house from another. The drive, which ran parallel to the wall, was flanked by a narrow border in which the trees had been planted. This was edged with a low growing plant, London Pride (*Saxifraga umbrosa*). When we saw it the wall was white with cherry blossom from the three fan-trained plants which covered it from gateway to garage door. These made a dull entrance attractive and made what is usually a barren area productive. Because the trees were near the house they were under constant observation when the cherries were ripe, for small boys and girls are known to delight in cherries just as much as birds. The area was also easy enough to cover with a net.

Practically all cherries have an attractive copper-brown bark and some have the habit of peeling bark which exposes a fresh, gleaming surface underneath. *Prunus serrula* is probably the best example of this attractively peeling bark.

Cherry branches look delightful in flower arrangements, either in flower or in fruit.

## Cultivation

The cherry can be grown in cooler regions than the plum. It does not like very hot summers and prefers climates in which there are no sudden extreme changes of temperature. In order that the trees should produce well the soil must be right. Cherries prefer a light, deep, well-drained loam, but they will grow on most soils except heavy loams. There are growers who claim that the condition of the soil is more important than its initial fertility, since poor soils can more easily be corrected. Cherries, incidentally, require high nitrogen and plenty of potash if they are to continue to bear well. Everything should be done to ensure that the soil is well drained. The subsoil should be cultivated so that it is friable before planting. It is important also that the site should be protected against frosts or strong winds. Cherries blossom early and the flowers can become damaged by frosts, which can mean the loss of an entire crop. Ripening cherries become bruised and damaged by strong winds and the trees grow lopsided.

Generally speaking, gardeners would do best to grow the sour cherries. Sweet cherry trees can be very large indeed, much too large for a small urban garden. Unfortunately there are as yet no true dwarfing stocks on to which cherries can be grafted. Unfortunately also cherries cannot be cut so severely as some trees when they are grown in certain regions of the world, Britain and North America included. We have seen many 'small' trees well under control in Australia, and indeed on one occasion these were grown as a close screen at the end of an orchard. In this part of New South Wales young trees are headed back after planting and 'topped' for the first few years of growth. One grower we visited whose trees could be harvested without the use of a tall ladder

Carambola *(G. R. Roberts)*

Cape Gooseberries *(G. R. Roberts)*

old us that he gave his trees a 'haircut' each year to restrict their growth. In that same area the official Department of Agriculture advice was that when a cherry tree had been allowed to grow too tall, a practice which 'tends to elevate the bearing area with subsequent loss in much of the lower fruiting wood', the tree should be reduced in height. This done, of course, not only is harvesting easier but general care and spraying also. However, even there local growers were advised to avoid winter pruning because at this time the trees were more susceptible to bacterial canker infection.

In many other countries it is important to appreciate that once the tree is well established and well shaped, the less pruning it receives the better. Excessive cutting of the wood leads to 'gumming' and this in turn lays the plant open to attack of silver-leaf, a fungus disease which is so deadly that in some countries it is a notifiable disease, obligatory to report to the local department or ministry of agriculture.

In all countries, however, summer pruning of young trees helps to shape and develop the trees' framework and also encourages earlier cropping. Any leader that is growing too quickly can be checked at this stage by pinching out the terminal bud. Pinching should be confined to the young and tender tips of the shoots. All cutting of wood should be kept to the absolute minimum. Any branches which look as though they are going to cross or rub against others or crowd the centre of the tree should be removed while they are young. Old wood should be cut out since this is likely to carry or harbour disease. Therefore, before ordering or buying a cherry, the gardener should take advice and make sure that he or she knows what the ultimate height of the tree can be and whether or not it would be a safe practice to prune it hard should this become necessary. It is possible, as with most fruit trees, to buy a bush, half standard or standard, and from some growers it will even be possible to pick up a fan-trained plant, although these too will grow large in time without attention to annual pruning.

We have seen a standard sweet cherry tree in a suburban garden, the remaining member of an orchard which once covered the land on which the houses were built, and although it bore a good crop, it caused considerable difficulties and inconveniences. Apart from the fact that it was virtually impossible to save the fruit from the birds (smaller trees can be netted, even grown in a fruit cage) it occupied a great deal of garden space besides casting a large area of shade under which little else could be grown.

Some sweet cherries can be pot-grown and thus restricted in size, but this is a fairly skilled horticultural operation and we feel that there are better and easier ways of growing this fruit. Some nurserymen sell 3 on 1 and other 'family tree' cherries. These help pollinate each other and are not difficult to grow.

However, in the main it is probably true to say that except in particularly favourable climates sweet cherries are best left to the commercial growers. These fruits are fastidious as to situation, soil and climate. Unfortunately they also suffer from more diseases than most fruit trees, the most virulent of which is bacterial canker in temperate climates. For this reason it is always important to go to a good and reliable source, and also to buy virus-free stocks.

Cherries do not grow well on soil where other cherries have previously grown, neither should they be planted after or too near tomatoes and potatoes or other members of the same family in case of the transference of verticillium wilt fungus.

Consult your nurseryman for suitable varieties for your own district and where necessary spend time in preparing the site. Enrich the soil, remembering that for cherries old leafmould, burnt garden refuse and mortar rubble can safely and advantageously be incorporated into the soil.

Usually trees are sold when they are four years old and it usually takes another two or three years before they are properly established and can carry a good crop.

If the sour cherries are to be grown as bushes in the open soil, or fan-trained in some way, they should be planted some 4 m (12 ft) apart. Since drainage is so important, where the plants are to be trained against a wall it is prudent to bank the soil so that it slopes away from the wall in order to drain it well.

Like the sweet cherries, the Dukes form spurs freely. Sour cherries fruit mainly on wood produced during the previous year. This means that the two need different forms of pruning. For the former, restrict pruning to cutting out dead, dying or unhealthy looking branches and to removing any which cross each other. Do this in spring and early summer.

Dukes trained on walls should have their laterals cut back to about 6 leaves in summer and in autumn these can go back a little further to 3 or 4 buds or leaves to induce the development of spurs. Do not cut back the leaders. If these are too high for your purpose, bend them down, tie them if necessary, and later you can cut them back to a weak lateral growing at a height convenient to you. This side growth will then become stronger and will develop in the direction you require it to grow.

Sour cherries should be pruned in such a way as to encourage the growth of fresh shoots each year, so that these will ripen and produce fruit the following year. The best way to do this is to cut out one or two of the oldest branches to induce the production of, and make way for, new shoots, but take care not to overdo this.

For fan-trained cherries, select the shoots you intend to replace the old at any time during early or late summer as they appear or offer themselves as improvements on the old shoots. Ideally, choose one which arises near the base of a fruiting shoot, and another at its tip. This draws up the sap to the fruit. Pinch out all the other shoots while they are quite small. When the tip at the top, the terminal shoot, is about 8–10 cm (3–4 in) long, pinch out its tip. After the fruit has been picked, cut back the fruiting stems to the shoots which are to take their places. The new ones can then be tied in within the pattern of the fan.

In spite of its apparent vigour, a cherry tree needs feeding in some way or another. Any type of tree can be mulched with well-rotted farmyard manure or home-made garden compost in the spring. This will not only help to feed it, but will keep its roots moist. Supplement this with an application of 50–80 g (2–3 oz) per square m (square yd) of nitrochalk in the spring and in the autumn with 25–55 g (1–2 oz) of sulphate of potash per square m. Plants which are trained against a wall often need a little more attention. It is essential to watch over them so that they do not become very dry at the roots in hot spells, as they tend to do. Be sure to water them from time to time, and give them an occasional feed at this time with a liquid

fertiliser.

When picking cherries it is important for the sake of the fruit and the tree that the stalks are retained on the fruit. The stems should not be roughly pulled off or damage may be caused to the spurs from which they grow. Damage to these affects the following year's crop. Be careful also not to strip the leaves from the tree.

## Culinary uses

Cherries can be used in many ways, not only as a raw dessert. Perhaps one of the nicest ways is to stone them beforehand and serve them with vanilla ice-cream or clotted cream. They can be made into jams, jellies, preserves, conserves, confections, pickles, chutneys, cheeses, cakes, pies and puddings galore. They can be bottled, frozen or dried.

Cherries go well with meats. Those which traditionally have a slightly sweetened fruit served with them – for instance pork with apple sauce, ham with peaches, poultry with cranberry – can be served with cherries. These can be stewed, but in these days of electric blenders a quickly prepared and delicious sauce can be made by blending stoned ripe cherries with a little sugar and a dash of lemon juice. Serve cold with cold meats or heat if preferred.

A cherry stoner is an essential tool if you have lots of cherries. Don't forget to strain the juice from the stones at the end of the operation and add it to whatever jam or dish you are making.

The kernels inside the stones of cherries are used in some recipes. In this case the kernels should be blanched. Pour boiling water on them, leave for a minute or two and then skin.

Turkey with Cherry Sauce makes an unusual dinner party dish.

### Turkey with cherry sauce
*thin slices turkey breast*
*butter*
*wineglass Madeira wine*
*4 cups cherries*
*1 teasp mixed spices*
*2 tabsp sugar*
*1 or 2 tabsp water*

Stone the cherries and put them in a saucepan with the sugar, water and spices. Cook very slowly until they are reduced to a pulp. Sieve or blend. Season the turkey slices and sauté in a little butter and the madeira. Heap the cherry sauce in the centre of a shallow dish and arrange the turkey slices around it.

Cherries are delicious in a savarin, or more modestly in a sponge flan. Stone 4 cups of sour cherries and place them in a dish. Crush 12 of the stones and tie these in a piece of muslin and put in with the cherries. Sprinkle all with sugar. Leave for an hour or so. When the juice begins to flow fairly freely, tip into a heavy pan, cover, and cook the cherries over a low heat. Cool and drain. Pour the juice into the centre of the cake or flan. Pile the cherries in the centre of the savarin or spread them on the flan. Top with whipped or Chantilly cream, flavoured, optionally, with cherry brandy.

In spite of its name, Cherry Soup is served as a dessert.

### Cherry soup

*3 cups dark cherries*
*2.5 cm (1 in) stick cinnamon*
*3 cloves*
*2 cups water*
*¼ cup sugar*
*finely peeled rind 1 lemon*
*pinch salt*
*½ cup claret*
*squeeze of lemon juice*
*2 level tabsp cornflour or arrowroot*
*sour cream to garnish*

Wash and stone the cherries and put them in a saucepan with the cinnamon, cloves, water, sugar, salt and lemon rind. Cover and simmer until the cherries are soft. Remove the cloves, the cinnamon and a few cherries. Put the remainder through a sieve or blender. Return the pulp to the saucepan and add the cornflour or arrowroot blended with the wine. Stir until thick. Add the lemon juice, taste and correct if necessary. Serve in individual bowls topped with a teaspoon of sour cream and the reserved cherries. The Danes say that the best mixture for this dish is really made up of equal quantities of redcurrants, raspberries and cherries.

Many kinds of sweetmeat can be made from cherries. Glacé cherries, used for cherry cake, are also used in Florentines and for decorating all kinds of desserts. To make them, prepare a good heavy syrup of sugar and water. Let it boil and put in the stoned cherries. Simmer until soft. Leave them standing in the syrup for three days. Drain and place them in a bowl. Bring the syrup to the boil again and pour it over the cherries and then leave them for another three days. Drain and dry them on a sieve. Store in greaseproof paper in jars.

White cherries, poached until they are tender, or bottled fruits if you have them to spare, can be made into a sweetmeat to be eaten immediately, although they will keep for a day or two in a refrigerator. Drain them and simply replace their stones with a toasted hazelnut. They should then be rolled in sugar and served with coffee. In place of the hazelnut, a core of marzipan can be used.

Cherries in brandy can also later be dipped in chocolate to make a delicious sweet. Dark cherries are best, firm and perhaps not quite ripe. Shorten the stalk and pack the fruits, stem end upwards, in a glass jar which can be sealed later. Prepare the brandy by dissolving sugar in it, to the proportions 1 cup to 4 cups brandy. Cover the cherries with this. Seal the jar and store in the dark.

PRESERVING Sweet cherries contain little pectin and for this reason sour cherries are usually picked when not quite ripe for jams and other preserves. Redcurrants are also used, both to provide pectin and to add colour. Apple juice and redcurrant juice can be used when cherry jelly is to be made.

The Morello cherries and other sour or acid cherries are really the best for jam, although the variety May Duke is excellent for this purpose. As a rule the black cherries are better for bottling than for jams, mainly because cherries contain little pectin, which means that the jam made from the sweet varieties does not set well, but as we said earlier, you can add redcurrant juice, 2 cups to every 6 cups of stoned fruit.

An easy way to make Morello cherry jam is first to measure the cherries and an equal quantity of sugar. Place the stoned cherries in a dish, sprinkle a little of the sugar over them and heat in a covered dish in a warm oven until the fruit is soft. Heat the sugar in a dish in the oven. Transfer the cherries to a preserving pan, add the sugar and boil together until the jam sets when tested.

### Black cherry conserve

4 cups black cherries, stemmed and stoned
6 tabsp lemon juice
3½ cups sugar
6 cloves
¾ teasp ground cinnamon
2 oranges

Slice the oranges thinly and remove seeds, but do not peel. Put into a pan and barely cover with water. Bring to the boil and cook until the skin is very tender. Add the rest of the ingredients. Stir well, bring to the boil and simmer until the conserve is thick and clear. Pour into hot jars.

### Cherry butter

16 cups black cherries
2 lemons finely chopped, or grated rind and juice
8 cups sugar

Stone the cherries and crack some of the stones to give about a ½ cup of kernels, blanch and skin these. Place the cherries, lemons, kernels and sugar in layers in a bowl, cover and leave overnight. Then bring to the boil and simmer for 15–20 minutes, finally boiling fast until the mixture is very thick. Pour into hot jars. This is very good served with scones and cream, or as a dessert with vanilla ice-cream.

Pickled, or sweet-sour cherries are simply covered with a vinegar, sugar and herb spice solution. De-stalk almost ripe Morello cherries and fill a preserving jar or jars with them. To 4 cups vinegar, use 1⅔ cups light brown sugar, 2.5cm (1in) cinnamon stick, saltspoon grated nutmeg, 3 cloves and thyme, bay and tarragon to taste. Boil these ingredients together, allow to cool, pour over the cherries, cover, and they will be ready to eat in about two weeks. Serve with cold meats.

FREEZING   Cherries are easy to freeze. It is advisable first to soak the fruits in ice-cold water for an hour before freezing, regularly adding more ice as necessary. This firms the fruit well. Dry the cherries, remove the stones because these will flavour the fruit with the kernel flavour, and pack in rigid, but not waxed, containers. Allow 1 cup of sugar to every 4 cups of stoned cherries. White cherries are likely to become discoloured during freezing unless ascorbic acid is added.

DRYING   In these days of easy freezing, one wonders whether it is worth while going to the trouble of drying cherries, but there may be times when the freezer is full and you wish to hold on to all the fruit you can. In hot, sunny climes, cherries will dry on the trees, becoming prune-like. Elsewhere they have to be dried in a cool oven, about 60°C (140°F). Leave the ripe cherries on their stalks. Place them on trays or tie them to sticks. Watch over them to see that they do not change colour.

BOTTLING   When bottling black or white sweet cherries, it is recommended that about ⅛ teasp. citric acid is added to every 16 cups (5⅛ pts) of syrup, roughly ½ teaspoon per 4 cups.

DRINKS   Cherries are widely used in the preparation of drinks, especially liqueurs. Genuine maraschino, kirsch and cherry brandy are made by distilling the juice of fermenting cherries, a process which is neither legal nor practical for most of us and we make do with simpler measures which nevertheless can produce some delicious results.

Ratafia is a fruit liqueur made from almost any kind of fruit. The name is said to have come from the celebratory drink served at the ratification of a treaty (rata fiat). So far as we are aware it is not made commercially today, possibly because it is so simple for the average amateur.

Use black cherries. Remove stalks and stones. Crush half with a fork and pound or blend the remainder. Put all in an earthenware crock and allow to stand for 12–24 hours. Then pour this through a sieve into another jar and measure the volume. For every 4 cups of juice allow 1½ cups of sugar, 4 cups of brandy or vodka and a small stick of cinnamon. Pour into a glass or earthenware jug and allow to stand for ten days or so, then strain and bottle.

Cherry Brandy can be made in much the same manner. Porportions of cherries, spirit and sugar can vary according to taste.

# CHINESE GOOSEBERRY
*Actinidia chinensis*

## Origin

The botanical name comes from 'aktin', a ray, a reference to the way the styles grow in the flowers. The plant is in no way related to the true gooseberry, *Ribès grossularia,* but the fruit of actinidia when sliced does vaguely resemble the flesh of this much smaller fruit and some people see a similarity in the hairy skins. The French, on the other hand, call the plant *souris végétale* and say that the fruits resemble a mouse hanging by its tail.

The Chinese gooseberry is one of a genus of about 40 species of hardy, deciduous, climbing shrubs of the Actinidiaceae family. Only three species produce edible fruits, *A. chinensis, A. arguta* and *A. kolomikta,* the first undoubtedly the best. The species is indigenous to China, where it grows on the margins of forests in the Yangtse valley. It has been cultivated in European gardens since its introduction in 1900, although it is said to have been discovered by the botanist Robert Fortune as far back as 1845. As a commercial fruit the Chinese gooseberry is a comparative new-comer to the world's markets. Cultivation is said to be extensive in the USSR and, one presumes, in China, and more recently in France, Italy, Spain, the United States and Israel, both on a commercial scale and in private gardens. However, nowhere else in the world to this date, it is claimed, has the fruit attained the commercial acceptance that it has done in New Zealand. It was first grown there by Alex Allison, who is believed to have received the seed soon after the turn of the century from a Mr James McGregor, who brought it from China where he had seen plants cultivated. Vines grown from this seed first fruited in 1910. All the New Zealand varieties of this plant are descended from these vines. The potentialities of the fruit as a useful commercial crop were first considered in about 1940 when several small plantings in the Bay of Plenty region came into production. Since then there has been more and more land taken under cultivation. With some initiative and no doubt some personal pride in their achievement, the New Zealanders named the Chinese gooseberry 'Kiwi Fruit', thus laying some kind of national claim to it. Many people today know it by no other name. With its growth as a commercial crop, the plant has received more attention from nurserymen who see it as a decorative and productive climber for the amateur gardener and sales in this area have increased considerably in the past few years.

A cross between *A. chinensis* and *A. arguta,* which has smooth fruits, has been produced in the United States.

## The fruit

Botanically, a juicy berry containing many small seeds. Fruits of modern varieties are much larger than the type, which is some 4 cm (1½ in) long, egg-shaped, with a thin, rough, hairy, russet skin. Fruits vary somewhat according to variety. Some are quite rounded, others flattened in cross section. Some are longer and therefore more cylindrical than others. The flesh is a beautiful bright green, paler in some varieties, sweet and slightly acid. It has an agreeable perfume which seems to be a bouquet of several other fruits – grape, fig and, once again, ripe gooseberry. When sliced, the small seeds make an attractive pattern.

## The plant

This is a vigorous, deciduous climber which will reach 10 m (30 ft) in length, with shoots attractively shaggy with red-brown hairs. The plant climbs by twining round its supports and not by means of tendrils. The leaves are heart-shaped, 13–20 cm (5–8 in) long and almost as wide on non-fruiting shoots, less wide on the others, covered with small, stiff hairs on the upper surface, downy beneath. Male and female flowers are borne on separate plants, so it is essential to grow a compatible pair. Female flowers are easily recognised by the small fruit swelling at the base of the petals.

The flowers are attractive, clustered on short axillary branches 4 cm (1½ in) across, white at first, becoming creamy as they grow older. They are sweetly scented and honey-rich.

While this vine is usually grown on trellises, arches, walls and pergolas, it can also be used very attractively and efficiently to cover a tree stump or an unsightly building. Make sure first that any support is strong, because the sheer weight of a vigorous plant such as this can be quite considerable. Begin by training and securing the leaders in the direction you wish them to travel. After this prune rigorously to keep the plant under control and fruiting well.

Ken Muir, the leading British supplier and expert, says, 'Chinese gooseberries will do exceptionally well grown in large (30 cm (12 in)) containers under glass. A heated greenhouse is not necessary. The flowers will have to be hand-pollinated and the plants liquid-fed at regular intervals during the summer.'

## Cultivation

It is most important to realise that the root system of this plant is both fibrous and shallow. Soil should be well prepared and have plenty of bulky organic matter incorporated, so that it is constantly moist yet well drained. Every care should be taken to ensure that the roots do not dry out in hot, dry periods. Actinidia prefers a mild climate with adequate rainfall, but trickle irrigation has been tried with this crop and found to suit it perfectly. (Incidentally, this is a cue to the many people who live in urban centres, possibly with nothing but a backyard and a few plants growing in pots, who find that because of limited root room these plants dry much too quickly. A trickle irrigation system will answer their problem immediately, and for those who declare with distaste that it is unpleasant to see that quantity of plumbing in the garden, we can only suggest that it is no real problem to remove it and tuck it away on the occasions when visitors are expected.) Mulching is also beneficial, especially as this helps to keep weeds down as well as hold moisture in the soil. A frost-free, sheltered site is also essential. Although commercially grown on pergolas and trellises, fortunately this plant can be used to cover a wall, and where this is facing the right way and so long as it will not become too hot, it can be used profitably and attractively for this purpose. When the plant is to cover an arch, or even a tree stump, ensure that it will not be exposed to strong hot or cold winds, which would break off at their bases the tender young laterals which make such prolific growth in the spring. Proper shelter also avoids wind rub on the berries while they enlarge and mature. Severe rub can cause dark, depressed, unsightly blemishes on the skin of the fruit. The Hayward variety appears to be especially susceptible to skin rub. Although the plant is surprisingly hardy and leafless growth is unlikely to become damaged, the young shoots are very tender. Fruit also can be damaged by autumn or winter frosts.

Being deciduous, a Chinese gooseberry is best planted when dormant. The young vine should be cut back to leave about six buds when it is planted. This encourages the production of good leaders. Plants bought from specialist nurserymen are usually already cut back. If the plants are to be grown on a specially constructed overhead trellis, this should be prepared before planting if possible, certainly not after the first season of growth, or it will become impossible to train the plant as required. A pergola is the best form of support, with the vines planted on two sides and trained on wires overhead. Take care when planting that the vine is not set too deep. Remember that it has a shallow rooting habit.

The plant should be pruned regularly if it is not to become out of control, for it is a very vigorous grower. During the first years the leaders can grow unchecked and they can be trained into the required positions. These will produce laterals or side shoots which should be cut back hard to keep them neat. The crop is produced on the first three or five buds of the current year's growth, so the aim of pruning should be to keep this cropping growth close to the leaders. Laterals which have fruited are pruned to the second bud beyond the previous season's fruit buds, but only when the plant is dormant. Because growth is so vigorous, laterals become overcrowded and these can be cut away entirely. Three-year-old leaders, which bear only at the tips, or have a straggly growth, can also be cut away and new ones tied in place instead.

It takes four or five years for a vine to begin bearing a worthwhile crop, and perhaps seven or eight to come into full production, but plants are long-lived. Because of the vigour of this vine the urban gardener should make certain that he has space enough to accommodate two climbers – remember that pollinators must be provided. For up-to-date information on suitable pollinators consult your local expert or supplier. The actual transference of pollen is carried out mainly by insects and it helps if there is a local beehive or two. Inadequate pollination results in many undersized fruits.

Tomuri, which has a late flowering season, is often used as a pollinator and this variety suits Hayward very well. Hayward is one of the latest of varieties to bloom. It is easily identified by its large, pale green-brown, broadly oval fruit, often slightly flattened on the sides and densely covered with fine silky hairs. This is said to be the best flavoured variety with the best keeping quality.

Matua is another male clone and one which flowers more prolifically than Tomuri and for a longer period. It coincides with the blossom period of most of the named fruiting varieties, but unfortunately the peak of its flowering period is usually past before the flowers of Hayward are ready for pollinating. Incidentally, when the plant has produced a very heavy fruit crop, it may be prudent to thin this out in order to obtain full sized fruits at maturity.

Chinese gooseberries are easily raised from seed, but until they flower it is not possible to distinguish which are the male and which the female. Therefore as a rule seedlings are used as root stocks on to which scions of known varieties or selected plants are budded or grafted.

When the fruits are ready to be harvested they should be firm enough to handle but not hard. The flesh will be juicy and the flavour fully developed. The fruits can be stored well under cool, draught-free conditions for as long as eight weeks, longer under specially controlled refrigeration. However, they should not be stored near other fruits, especially apples, because even small quantities of ethylene gas normally respired by some fruits will hasten their maturity.

## Culinary uses

These fruits are rich in vitamin C; it is said that one fruit provides as much as is to be found in ten lemons. They also contain protein, iron, calcium and phosphorus salts. They make a good light starter to a meal, halved and the flesh spooned out. Their flavour can be enhanced by a little lemon squeezed on the cut surface. On other occasions a dash of liqueur will help.

The firm, rough skin is easily peeled off with a knife. The fruit should be cut into slices, crosswise, for use in most dishes. The bright green flesh and the radial pattern of the seeds in the flesh give the fruit slices a most attractive appearance. The most can be made of this by using them to decorate a fruit salad, a fruit cream, a mousse or a cake, especially if more fruit has been used inside as a filling. The fruits lend themselves particularly well to ice-creams and sorbets, and when these are made from them the appearance of the dish is always improved if some of the fruit slices are displayed. Slices can be used to fill flans and tart cases. They can be glazed with apricot jam, warmed and applied with a pastry brush, and can be used to good effect in an upside-down cake.

Like so many faintly acid fruits, Chinese gooseberries go well with meats, and can actually be used as a meat tenderiser. They can be used in a side salad, and can be served together with all kinds of cheeses. Cream cheeses and yoghurts can be combined with the slices in sweets and salads alike. Use honey to sweeten for a change. Chinese gooseberries can be used for jams and pickles.

### Chinese gooseberry frozen salad

*4 Chinese gooseberries*
*3 tabsp icing sugar*
*¾ cup cream cheese*
*¼ cup glacé cherries, some quartered, some halved*
*¼ cup roughly chopped walnuts*
*¾ cup cream*

Have ready a loaf tin or a similarly sized plastic freezing box lined with kitchen foil. Peel and quarter the Chinese gooseberries lengthwise, remove any core and then cut the quarters crosswise into small pieces. Reserve one of the fruits and slice this crosswise to give you a number of slices to decorate the base of the mould. Use some of the cherries here also if you fancy them. Mix the chopped Chinese gooseberries with the icing sugar in a bowl. Cream the cheese further and to it add the quartered cherries, walnuts, sugar and Chinese gooseberries. Whip the cream until fairly stiff and fold this into the mixture. Pour this over the patterned fruit slices and cherries. Smooth the top with a palette knife. Freeze until it is firm or you are ready to serve. The advantage of making this in a plastic container is that it can be prepared well ahead of time.

# CITRANGE
*Citrus sinensis* x *Poncirus trifoliata*

## Origin
This fruit is the result of a marriage between the sweet orange and the hardy poncirus, which has the popular names of Trifoliate orange or Golden apple. This same hybrid was crossed with a species of *Fortunella*, and this gave us the kumquat (q.v.).

It was first raised by W. T. Swingle in Florida in 1897, and was given its name in 1905. The great thing about it is that the plant is almost hardy and will grow in northern gardens where these are in mild and sheltered districts. There are several varieties, some of which are grown mainly for the beauty and scent of their flowers. Those worth growing for their fruit include Rusk, with red-orange fruits 4–5 cm (1½–2 in) across and Morton, which produces orange-coloured fruit weighing sometimes more than 450 g (1 lb). The Troya citrange is grown for rootstocks.

## The fruit
Botanically, a berry 2½–10 cm (1–4 in) across, almost round, skin lemon-yellow or red-orange, smooth or hairy, often with an abundance of essential oil which is unpleasant to the taste. The flesh is juicy and aromatic, acid or sub-acid.

## The plant
The evergreen shrubs have three foliate leaves, the lateral leaflets of which are much smaller than the terminal one. The fragrant flowers are very large, more than 6 cm (2½ in), which is larger than most orange blossom, although the fruits are smaller. These flowers are white, with long, narrow petals.

## Cultivation
See the section on Orange for cultivation details of all citrus fruits.

## Culinary uses
Citranges can be used in the same way as oranges (q.v.).

# CITRON
*Citrus medica*

## Origin
The name is derived from the Greek *kitron*. The plant is closely related to the orange, lemon, tangerine and all those we know as citrus fruits, members of the family Rutaceae, which includes such differing plants as rue (the Herb of Grace), the scented Australian boronia and skimmia. It is believed to be one of the first of this family of fruits to have been introduced into the Mediterranean from its native Far East, somewhere around 500 BC. It is possible that it was first brought to Israel from Babylonia after the Exile and was thereafter incorporated into the ancient Jewish festival of Sukkot given to celebrate the harvest, especially of fruit.

The Jews popularly identify the citron or Etrog with the forbidden fruit of Eden. They also believed that to dream of it means that one is precious before God and that if a pregnant woman bites an Etrog she will bear a male child.

It was, and perhaps still is, used for perfuming rooms in China and Japan, for the skin of the fruit is fragrant. It is cultivated mainly for the production of candied peel and is grown especially for this purpose in Corsica, Greece and Sicily, but it can be found growing wild along the Mediterranean. It is cultivated in gardens as far west as the French and Italian Rivieras.

There is a variety, *C. m. sarcodactylis,* known as the Fingered citron because of the irregular outgrowths or separate segments which grow on the surface of the fruit.

## The fruit

Botanically, a hesperidium, a special kind of berry in which the peel, easily separated from the fleshy portion of the fruit, is made of two parts, outer and inner portions. It is very large compared with most other citrus fruits, especially the lemon, to which it is very closely related. Green or lemon-yellow in colour, it is vaguely lemon-like in shape, though not in texture. The rind is rough and warty. The fruits grow 15–25 cm (6–10 in) long and 10–15 cm (4–6 in) in diameter. The rind covers a very thick inner white skin or pith, and it is this whole skin and not the pulp that is of culinary value. It is candied and used in confectionery. The quantity of sour pulp is very small compared with the size of the fruit. The skin of the fruit is fragrant when fresh, and when dried, like that of other citrus, can be used in the preparation of pot pourri.

## The plant

A small, evergreen tree some 2–5 m (6–15 ft) tall at the most. The branches bear short, stiff spines. The leaves are large, 10–18 cm (4–7 in) in length, oblong in shape and saw-edged. They differ from the foliage of most other citrus species in that their short leaf stalks are not winged. The flowers are large, the buds tinged with red, and when fully open purple-red outside and white within.

## Cultivation

See the section on Orange.

## Culinary uses

As the outer rind of the citron is so thick, this leaves little room for the flesh. This need not be wasted, of course, but it is the thick rind that is of the greatest use. Commercially it is candied and sold in slices.

PRESERVING  Citron Preserve is a dessert.

### Citron preserve

*3 cups diced citron rind*
*1 lemon, sliced very thinly and seeded*
*4 tabsp lime juice (or lemon juice)*
*1 cup water*
*3 cups sugar*
*½ cup preserved or crystallised ginger*

Pare the outer green skin from the fruit and dice the rind. Put it into a bowl with the other ingredients and allow them all to stand overnight. Put into a preserving pan, bring to the boil stirring meanwhile and then allow to simmer until the citron is clear.

DRINKS  There is said to be a liqueur called cédratine made from citrons in Corsica and citrons can also be used to make Citron Wine.

### Citron wine

10 cups citron pulp
16 cups warm water
½ cup lime juice
1 cup raisins
4 cups sugar
yeast

Pare off the citron rind and slice and mash the fruit pulp. Cover it with the warm water, add the chopped raisins and leave for a week, stirring daily. Strain the liquid into a fermentation jar and add the sugar, previously dissolved into a syrup with some of the mixture. Add the yeast and the lime juice, fix a fermentation trap and leave to work to a finish before bottling.

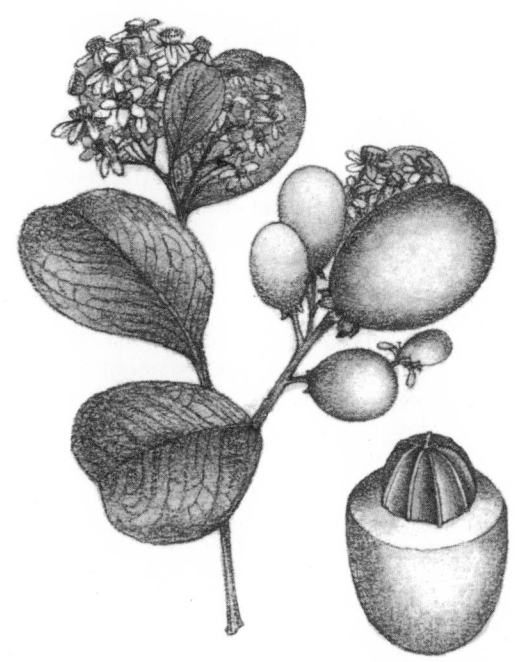

# COCO PLUM
*Chrysobalanus icaco*

### Origin

This genus has probably only three species of West African and Florida trees or shrubs closely related to the prunus and belonging to the rose family. There is a smaller coco plum, *C. icaco pellocarpa,* which grows wild in swampy areas.

### The fruit

*C. icaco* has fruit about the size of a plum, almost egg-shaped, usually purple with a bloom on the skin, but sometimes pale pink, magenta red or black. *C. icaco pellocarpa* has dark purple, oval fruit, 2.5 cm (1 in) or less in length. The sweet, white, cottony-textured flesh has an insipid flavour when raw and clings to the stone.

### The plant

This makes a large shrub or a small tree with leaves about 5 cm (2 in) long, obovate, thick, and a deep glossy green. Flowers are small, white, growing in ancillary racemes.

### Cultivation

The fruits of those plants found growing wild in tropical America and the West Indies have a low market value. Cultivated trees are grown from seed sown in moist, rich ground and transplanted.

Mature trees grow to about 7–9 m (25–30 ft).

Great care should be taken when picking the fruit because the skins are so thin and the pulp so soft that the plums soon become dented and marked. This does not affect their use, only their appearance.

### Culinary uses

The fruits can be eaten fresh, but as they are not very fully flavoured, they are better combined with others in a salad or some other dish.

The most popular way of cooking the plums is to peel them and stew them gently with plenty of sugar. They then become an attractive wine red. A little lemon juice offsets the sweetness. In Cuba, the fruit is made into a sweet preserve and served in restaurants as a *sobremesa* or dessert.

When fruits are used in preserves, the kernel can be used. The custom is to pierce the stone with an ice pick or sail needle so that the syrup can penetrate and flavour the kernel. It appears that the stone is left in the fruit but removed when the preserve is served and the kernel eaten.

The stones can be cracked when raw and the kernels roasted and eaten like nuts.

The plums make good jams and other preserves. They can be dried, and used in the same way as prunes.

# CORNELIAN CHERRY
*Cornus mas*

## Origin

One of a genus of about 40 species distributed throughout the temperate parts of the northern hemisphere, the Cornelian cherry is a native European plant, although it and its varieties are now to be found in gardens in many other parts of the world. Its specific name means 'male' and the plant is sometimes called the male cornel because when grown from seed it begins by producing male flowers only and often takes as long as 15 years to produce both male and female flowers and, therefore, fruit. It has been cultivated for centuries in European gardens, originally for its fruits alone, which were often pickled rather than eaten raw, as still happens today in some parts. Nowadays it is usually planted as a flowering shrub, valued for its winter blossom.

In France, before the introduction and general cultivation of the peach, apricot and other exotic fruits, the Cornelian cherry was to be seen in orchards along with apples and medlars.

There are varieties of the species named for the coloration of their leaves or the size of the plant. Thus we have *aurea, aurea elegantissima, nana, variegata* and *xanthocarpa*, but *C. mas* is still the best for the fruits.

The reader may be reassured to know that among other cornus that are grown as ornamental plants, both *C. kousa*, which has lovely strawberry-like fruits, and *C. officinalis*, which is very similar to *C. mas*, have edible fruits. Those of the first are so beautiful and so strawberry-like that any child is likely to sample them and they will do no harm.

## The fruit

Botanically, a drupe, bright red, oval, 1.5 cm ($\frac{5}{8}$ in) long, with a pleasant, slightly acid flesh, ripening in late summer.

## The plant

*Cornus mas* forms either a deciduous shrub or a small tree and in either case it is a spreading plant. When it forms a tree, the grey-brown trunk is often twisted. In spring (and in Britain this can sometimes be as early as February) each branch becomes smothered with clusters of tiny, tassel-like yellow flowers. These persist for some weeks on the plant unless a particularly frosty spell sets in and lasts for several days.

The flowers are followed by the leaves, which are oval, 4–6 cm ($1\frac{1}{2}$–$2\frac{1}{2}$ in) long. The branches are good-looking, being a lively green tinged with red on the sunny side. These leaves turn colour in the autumn but are more likely to be a dull wine purple than a brilliant red.

This is an attractive plant, which when placed with thought can furnish a garden most attractively. Since it blooms so early, it is among those trees and shrubs which are worth placing within sight of one or other main windows of a house. In our own garden we grow it at the end of a pergola-covered walk where in spring it fills the area at the end with a mass of blossom. In summer it helps create a pleasant vista when the mass of leaves forms a backcloth for a tall stone vase.

Because the plant blooms early it is of great value for the flower arranger. Branches can be picked as soon as the buds are seen to be swelling and the flowers will open slowly indoors. Both the leaves and the branches grow opposite each other, which means that for arrangement branches which seem too stiff need to be pruned a little. For instance, laterals should be removed from one side of the branch and not the other.

## Cultivation

Best grown in a sheltered spot where the soil is moderately moist or the roots are shaded. Either buy mature trees or take cuttings from trees which are known to be fruiting. Cuttings will root if they are taken from firm shoots and placed in sandy soil outdoors in autumn. Plants can also be layered in spring.

No pruning is required except to remove old, untidy and straggly growth, although on the other hand new growth should be encouraged, because this produces the flowers of the following year. Naturally a growing plant is continually making new growth, but if branches are picked to force into flower for indoor decoration, this will encourage the formation of new growth.

## Culinary uses

The fruit contains a useful amount of vitamin C.

A syrup is made from it that looks and tastes exactly like grenadine.

PRESERVING   It is often used to make a good, sharp jelly, with the addition of lemon juice. It can also be preserved in syrups of sugar or honey. At one time it was often preserved in brine in the same way as olives.

# CRANBERRY
*Vaccinium macrocarpum* and species

## Origin

Closely related to the blueberry which belongs to the same genera, the cranberry is a member of the widespread heather family. There is some confusion about the origin of the generic name which was used by both Virgil and Pliny, and it is believed by some to be a corruption of hyacinthus. Others claim that the fruit may have been named after the cow, *vacca* in Latin, and certainly one species, *V. vitis-idaea,* which grows wild in north-west America and in north-east Asia, is known as the Cowberry. There is also some disagreement over the common name 'cranberry', which is an old British name for *V. oxycoccus,* which grows in many regions of the northern part of the northern hemisphere. It was only natural that should have been given by the early settlers in America to the species they found growing there. We have no record of the American Indian name, although we know that the fruit was used and prized by them. One theory is that it is so called because cranes could be seen feeding among the plants. Another is that the name was given because the pink blossom buds resemble cranes' heads.

The early settlers must have been glad to find a familiar fruit, which apart from anything else is an effective preventive of scurvy. The berries can be successfully stored and thus used in winter or on long sea voyages. Certainly they would have been welcome as an easily harvested fresh food. *V. macrocarpum* is the Large or American cranberry, with synonyms *Oxycoccus macrocarpus* and *O. palustris, var. macrocarpus.*

From this have been derived several selected forms now in cultivation. There are other wild cranberries such as the European *V. microcarpum*

and *V. oxycoccus,* both called Small cranberry, the American Southern Mountain cranberry, and those which are known by such names as Foxberry, Partridgeberry and Ligonberry.

One Captain Henry Hall is said to have been responsible for the domestic cultivation of this fruit in the early 1800s in Dennis, Cape Cod. Since then the commercial production has increased a thousandfold. To quote the Royal Horticultural Society's *Dictionary of Gardening,* 'The genus has considerable economic importance in the US and Canada where many thousands of acres of otherwise barren land with acid soil are used for the cultivation of Blueberries and Cranberries . . . Several forms of *V. macrocarpum* have been selected and are cultivated on a large scale in the east USA in cranberry bogs, the water level of which can be artificially controlled so that from December to April the plants are under a foot of water, but are above water level during their season of growth.'

## The fruit

Botanically, a berry crowned by persistent calyx lobes. The scarlet fruit is rounded or sub-ovate. Its size varies from the type to cultivars and may be from 1–2 cm ($\frac{3}{8}$–$\frac{3}{4}$ in) in diameter. Each berry is carried on a slender stalk bringing it well out from the leaves. When quite ripe the fruit will bounce, hence one of its common names. At that stage it will be both acid and astringent on the tongue.

## The plant

A neat, creeping, evergreen shrub with ascending shoots and slender stems. The leaves are small, usually less than 1 cm ($\frac{3}{8}$ in) long and about half as wide. The flowers, which may grow singly or in groups of as many as ten on a single shoot on slender stems arising from the leaf axils, are extremely dainty, white, rose-tinted and just under 1 cm ($\frac{3}{8}$ in) in length. The corolla is divided into four lobes which resemble petals. These roll back as they mature and in doing so expose the eight stamens which give the little flowers such attractive centres and a general appearance of daintiness.

## Cultivation

Since the plant grows wild only in wet, peaty,

very warm and sunny, and in summer and subsequently from time to time as appears necessary, but never in winter. The rooting medium should never be allowed to dry out completely but should always feel moist to the touch. It is insufficient to give small amounts of water.

The plants can be propagated from cuttings 13–25 cm (5–10 in) long. These can be pushed down through the sand into the peat below.

## Culinary uses

Cranberries contain a significant proportion of vitamin C, slightly less of A and traces of others and of mineral salts. People living far away from the frozen north do not generally realise how important a fruit is the little cranberry. Look through any northern cook book and you will find cranberry recipes galore. One Canadian cook suggests ten ways to use cranberries, ten good ways, on which we suggest certain variations. As a cake filling alone or with apple sauce; as an icing, just add to standard butter icing; as an addition to a salad; as a filler for halved fruits such as pears and peaches (there's no reason, we suggest, why these should not be the dried fruits stewed – certainly the cranberries would give them a welcome fresh fruit flavour); an addition to vanilla pudding, sweetened and chopped (and, we could suggest, to all custards, milk puddings and ices); for a mixed pie, half apple and half cranberry (use pears also this way, we suggest); in an upside-down cake instead of tinned pineapple, and use them also in the bottom of a basin for a steamed sponge pudding; as a Cranberry Cobbler instead of the cherries often used (also try a cranberry crumble instead of an apple crumble); for an applesauce cake, use instead at least two-thirds cranberries and apples for the remainder (we suggest doing this for all applesauce recipes, apple soufflé for example); and finally in a meat loaf substituting cranberry sauce for the liquid called for in the recipe (an inspirational touch), or try it in a rough pâté campagne some time.

You can see from this what an adaptable fruit the cranberry is. Apart from the jams, jellies and butters, you can make spiced cranberries, relish, sherbet, ice-cream, cocktail starters and a thousand pies, tarts, puddings and the rest. It seems that given the fruit the remainder is up to you. Certainly the cranberry should not be

bog conditions, it follows that if it is to be cultivated in a garden a similar environment must be created. Although the plants will not give the same return as some other fruits, they do offer the owner of a problem plot an opportunity to make this both profitable and attractive. The plants cover the ground well once they are established. The soil in most gardens, even small ones, often varies considerably from one part to another. Where a moist situation naturally exists, these are plants which could be grown successfully so long as the soil is acid enough.

One of the best methods, and certainly one which is essential where there may be lime in the soil, even if only a trace, is to construct a raised bed using peat bricks and filling this with a mixture of peat and leafmould. Alternatively, on neutral soil a bed can be excavated to a depth of 60 cm (2 ft) and the soil removed to be replaced with a peat and leafmould mixture. The plants should be placed about 60 cm (2 ft) apart. They are best planted in spring or autumn, although canister-grown plants can be put in at any time of the year. The soil surface can then be covered or mulched with sand at a depth of about 5–7 cm (2–3 in). This will prevent the peat from drifting and help to keep the rooting medium evenly moist. Immediately after planting the bed should be flooded, preferably with rainwater. It should then be flooded again in spring if the weather is allowed to play for ever in the single role of an annual sauce for turkey, as it does in some countries.

## Cranberry nut loaf

1/4 cup butter
3/4 cup sugar
1 teasp salt
1 egg
1 teasp bicarbonate of soda
1 teasp baking powder
12 tabsp sour milk
2 cups flour
2 cups chopped cranberries
1/4 cup roughly chopped pecans or walnuts

Cream the butter, sugar and salt together until pale and creamy. Beat in the egg, and add the milk. Sift the flour, soda and baking powder together and fold into the mixture until all is well blended. Fold in the fruit and then the nuts. Have ready a buttered loaf tin. Bake at 180°C (350°F, gasmark 4) for 1 hour. Test by piercing with a skewer – if this comes away clean take out the loaf and let it cool in the tin. After turning it out wrap it in foil and store in an airtight container for a few days to mature. Serve sliced with butter. This loaf freezes well.

One point to remember: do not cook cranberries too long or they become bitter. Stew slowly until the berries pop, about 10 minutes.

In jams and chutneys cranberries can be combined with various fruits and even vegetables. For instance, you can cook the berries with apples, pears and quince, separate or mixed, with lemon or orange, white grapes, carrots and pumpkin. They are good with raisins.

PRESERVING   Unusual, economic and delicious is Cranberry and Carrot Jam, made from equal quantities of each. To every 4 cups of cranberry purée or crushed berries and diced small carrots, use just over 5 cups of granulated sugar. Cook these all in a preserving pan, stirring continuously until the mass is liquid. Allow to simmer, stirring from time to time, for about 20–30 minutes. When the mixture sets, pour into warm, sterilised jars.

Cranberry Delights are a delicious sweetmeat that we can thoroughly recommend.

## Cranberry delights

2 cups cranberries, or the equivalent in purée
4 cups granulated sugar
3 tabsp powdered gelatine
icing sugar for coating
4 tabsp water

Put the berries and water in a saucepan and cook until the pop stage. Add the sugar and cook until the mixture becomes thick, stirring from time to time. Blend or strain. Combine the gelatine with another 4 tablespoons of water, and when it softens (in about 5 minutes) add it to the hot fruit juice. Stir until all the gelatine is well dissolved. Have ready a lightly oiled pan and pour the syrup into this. Cool and then chill. Test for firmness, and when you can handle the delight cut into shapes and roll each in the icing sugar to coat well. Chill again. To store, pack between waxed paper in an airtight container.

FREEZING   Cranberries can be frozen without previous processing.

BOTTLING   They should be bottled like redcurrants (q.v.).

DRINKS   Cranberries are one of several fruits that need the addition of a nutrient to get the yeast working when making wine. Here, rice is suggested as an alternative.

## Cranberry wine

12 cups cranberries
12 cups water
1/4 cup rice
6 cups sugar
yeast

Bring the water to the boil and pour it over the berries. Allow it to cool gradually and when it is just lukewarn add the rice and the yeast. Cover and keep warm for a week, stirring and mashing the berries every day. Strain into a fermentation jar and add the sugar. Leave fermenting until all is finished, then bottle.

# CUSTARD APPLE
*Annona reticulata*

## Origin

See the section on Cherimoya. The custard apple is probably the best known of the nine species in cultivation, although many fruits from this family are known by this popular name. This one is also known as Bullock's heart, because of both shape and colour, although these can be somewhat variable. The first name describes the sweet, custard-like pulp which can simply be spooned out and eaten. It was introduced from tropical America to Europe in 1690, where it must be grown in hothouses.

## The fruit

Botanically, it is formed of many carpels. The fruit varies a little from plant to plant, being heart-shaped, round or asymmetrical. The smooth skin has a netted pattern and is dull yellow, becoming red or brown on the sunny side. The flesh is yellow-white, sometimes tinged with brown, and its texture more solid and granular than that of some of the other annonaceous fruits. It varies in weight from 225 g to 2.25 kg (½–5 lb).

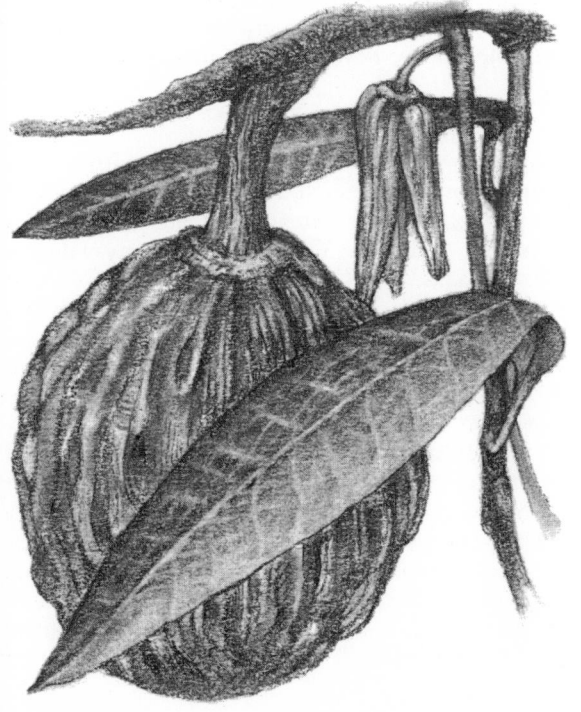

## The plant

One of the deciduous species, a small tree growing to 5–8 m (15–25 ft). The young shoots are covered with a rufus brown, but as they grow the stems and leaves become smooth. The leaves are oblong – lanceolate, acute, smooth or nearly so. Flowers are produced in clusters in the axils of the leaves of the current year's growth, outer petals fleshy, olive or yellow, usually tinged with purple and with a darker purple blotch within.

## Cultivation

As for Cherimoya.

## Culinary uses

See Cherimoya.

# DATE PALM
*Phoenix dactylifera*

## Origin

The name itself is an ancient one, used by Theophrastus in about the second or third century BC. The family Palmaceae includes about ten species, many of which are variable and most grown for their decorative qualities, in homes, gardens and under glass. The common date, *P. dactylifera,* is the only species which produces fruit for food. For this purpose it has, in certain regions, been cultivated since ancient times. There are records going back at least 5,000 years in the Middle East. As one would expect from a plant grown for so long, it has produced varieties of the species. Also as one would expect, such a rich and important food has found its way to other countries and regions from where it was first found growing wild.

It is not a good crop for humid climates, producing poor yields only. Dates are grown generally from Morocco to India, in dry sub-tropical areas, but with the aid of irrigation. The most important Middle East countries producing, using and exporting dates are Iraq, Saudi Arabia, Algeria, Iran and Egypt. They are now also being grown on a somewhat smaller scale in areas of the USA such as Arizona and California, and in Israel, wherever suitable conditions prevail.

Dates can be grouped into three kinds; soft, semi-dry and dry. Countries into which dates are imported seldom see soft, ripe dates, although of late years some supplies have been available in specialist stores. Most of the soft dates are pressed and sold in blocks, it being then impossible to separate one date from another. These dates are very sweet and are often used in confectionery. Semi-dry dates are usually sold ready packed in long boxes. These are usually special varieties such as Deglet Noor or Deglet Ennour, which is said to be the world's most popular date. Israeli dates are usually the luscious Chiyani, which are exported the year round.

Dried dates, which can be stored for a long period, ground into flour or softened by soaking, are used locally by people in Arab countries and are not, so far as we know, exported outside Arab countries, although Israel exports dried Halawi and Chadrawi dates.

## The fruit

Botanically, a drupe with one grooved seed, egg-shaped or cylindrical-elliptical, some 2½–5 cm (1–2 in) long. When ripe the fruits are a dull yellow and the flesh is soft and buttery. When dried, the skins of the fruits darken. The dried fruit remains wholesome for a long period. Fruit is produced on 'strands', each bearing some 25–35 dates. There can be as many as 40 strands in a bunch and several bunches on a tree. A good yield is between 45–70 kg (100–150 lb) of fruit to a tree.

## The plant

Tall, evergreen and unbranched, a date palm will grow higher than 30 m (100 ft) in natural surroundings but usually about 25 m (80 ft) under cultivation. The pinnate grey-green fronds are arching, each leaflet some 20–40 cm (8–16 in) long, irregularly spaced in two rows on each side of the main stem. The trunk, tall and slim, covered with fibres, is surrounded from the ground upwards with the bases of the earlier formed leaves, while the living leaves top the tree in a handsome terminal cluster. Male and female flowers are produced on separate trees in spadices of dull yellow-brown or yellow-white leathery flowers.

Miniature plants of *Phoenix dactylifera* make excellent house plants which will live for many years without outgrowing their place in the home. It is possible to grow one from seed without any special facilities other than the warmth of a radiator and the enclosure of the pot in a sealed polythene bag.

## Cultivation

Palms can begin bearing some 5–6 years after planting, but it may be 15 years before they are capable of full production. As their life is around 80 years, a great deal of fruit can be obtained from a single tree, and even after its fruiting life is over a tree can be tapped to provide a sugary sap which can be reduced by boiling into a syrup or used to make a palm wine or toddy.

Female plants need to be pollinated before they can bear fruit, but a single male will suffice for up to 50 females. The small-scale, backyard date palm owner can ensure pollination of his tree if he can obtain a few clusters of male flowers from a friend or neighbour and hang these in his tree.

One warning, the ends of the leaf fronds are needle sharp! As the foliage is frequently shed, date trees can be dangerous if grown where children play. Dates can be grown from seed, but then the plants are not likely all to be of equal quality. Female plants in particular are liable to be inferior. Suckers taken from plants of proved bearing are the best means of propagation.

## Culinary uses

This is a very nutritious food fruit with a high sugar content, as much as 70 per cent in dry and 60 per cent in soft dates. The fruits also contain vitamins A, $B_1$, $B_2$, C and D and many valuable mineral salts.

Fresh dates can be kept for several days in a refrigerator. Fresh, semi-dried or dried, dates are a versatile fruit as well as a wholesome food. Being sweet to the taste, one might be tempted to use them only in sweet dishes, but they can play an important role in salads. They go very well with cheese, especially cream cheese, with which they can also be stuffed. Use them for topping a cheese cake, too.

The dates are good with savoury fillings, such as chopped cooked bacon mixed with nuts and chutney; cold cooked lamb with finely chopped shallot and mint or mint sauce; apple, mustard

**Chinese Gooseberry** *(G. R. Roberts)*

Top: Cherimoya *(Thompson & Morgan)*
Bottom: Citrange blossom *(L. Johns)*

and finely chopped cooked pork. If you have stuffing left over from a bird, use this to stuff the dates and serve them with the hot or cold meat.

Like most dried fruits, dates combine well with all kinds of nuts, especially almonds. They can be stuffed with peanut butter, when they can be either included in a salad or rolled in sugar and served as a sweetmeat. Dates can be used in the same way as other dried fruits, i.e. in breads, cakes and buns, and in rice dishes and curries.

Make a creme caramel type dish, using dates instead of caramel. Use 1½ cups of milk and 2 eggs. Beat these together. Line the bases of the individual dishes with the finely chopped dates and divide the custard between the 4. Dust with grated nutmeg. Stand the dishes in a baking tin and pour in water round them almost up to their rims, and then bake at 140°C (275°F, gasmark 1) for an hour.

Dates are easily made into sweetmeats, the most usual being stoned dates stuffed with almonds or marzipan. All kinds of fillings can be devised, including crystallised fruits mixed with chopped nuts and fondant. Chopped or minced dates can be mixed with nut meats, rolled into balls and then dusted with icing sugar.

When whole dried dates are to be used for this purpose they can be made more succulent by being steamed for 10 minutes or so, or by being steeped in lemon or orange juice, in wine or in brandy.

### Date and lemon chutney

*3 cups chopped dates*
*2 cups finely chopped onions*
*3 lemons, pith removed, sliced and peeled, finely*
  *chop the peel of 2*
*1 cup sultanas*
*3 cups sugar*
*¾ cup treacle or molasses*
*¼ cup salt*
*5 cups vinegar*
*generous pinch cayenne pepper*

Boil vinegar, sugar, treacle, salt and pepper. Add the fruits, simmer until thick, about ¾ hour.

# DEWBERRY
*Rubus caesius*

## Origin

This is very closely related to the common blackberry and is indigenous to Europe. In the wild it is a small shrub with sparse though luscious fruits which mature before the blackberry. However, cultivars produce much larger fruit, particularly the American varieties which appear to have been derived from crossing many American species with *R. alleghaniensis*.

Notes on the plant, its cultivation and culinary uses are as for Blackberry.

# DURIAN
*Durio zibethinus*

## Origin

A native Malayan tree, now widely cultivated throughout Asia, it is rarely seen outside this area.

## The fruit

Very large, weighing 2.25–4.5 kg (5–10 lb), of which only about a third is edible. The fruit is covered with a thick skin which bears a number of rough spines. When this is removed a cream-coloured flesh is revealed. This fruit is famous (or notorious, whichever way you look at it) for its aroma. This is offensive, particularly when the fruit is overripe, but the flavour of the flesh is in no way spoiled. It is, in fact, not unlike that of strawberries and cream, with a suggestion of almonds.

## The plant

The durian makes a tall tree, 20–40 m (65–130 ft) at maturity, with a straight trunk and many low branches. The flowers are borne on leafless branches on the main trunk and on the limbs. An unusual feature is that the flowers are pollinated while they are in the bud stage. The leaves are oblong, with short petioles, and are covered on their undersides with silvery or coppery scales. The tree fruits twice a year, in June to August and November to February.

## Cultivation

The tree is grown in the tropical lowlands in deep, well-drained soil. It will not tolerate cool conditions.

## Culinary uses

At harvest time, much fruit is eaten casually at the roadside from local stalls. Some of the thrill of eating a durian is probably in opening the fruit. The thick, horny, hard skin has to be slit at segment joints so that the fruit can be pressed open easily. This can only be done with a sharp knife and experience as the thorns are sharp.

Besides being eaten fresh, the fruit is cooked with Indonesian rice and meat dishes. It is also fermented. Cooked with flour and sugar, durian cakes are made in Penang, and it is used to flavour ice-creams as well. Furthermore the durian is claimed to have aphrodisiac properties.

# ELDERBERRY

*Sambucus* species

## Origin

A member of the honeysuckle family, Caprifoliaceae, the genus includes both herbaceous plants and deciduous shrubs and small trees, widely distributed throughout temperate and sub-tropical regions. The name is believed to have come from sambuca, a musical instrument. Elder wood, which is close-grained and polishes well, was once extensively used for making various types of musical instruments, mainly woodwind.

The Romans may have imported the black-fruited elder along with the vine into some of their colonies, including Britain. The plant has for centuries and in many countries been highly regarded for its many uses. Every part of the plant which grows above ground has been and can be used in some way or another. The elder has also been held in awe for its supposed magic powers.

The American elder, *S. canadensis,* demonstrates a change in attitude to many wild berry plants. It was usually to be found growing wild and plentifully on or near roadsides in many places, and from these areas the fruit was picked and used in pies and preserves of many kinds. However, due to the increased use of herbicides to control wayside weeds and shrubs the number of wild plants has greatly declined. But because of continuing demand for the fruit, the plant is now grown commercially in many areas of the United States and in some places in Canada. This being the case one feels that the elder also deserves a place in gardens. We were further encouraged on visiting the Agricultural Research Station at Bathurst, NSW, to find growing there a selection of elderberries, including named varieties Monster and Ratty Red.

Below, some of the names of ornamental elders are listed, but they do not include *S. racemosa,* which bears red fruit and is not as palatable as the black ones. Generally speaking the best fruits are the black. A further point is that those who grow elders often use the flowers to make wine and a sambocage (elder flower fritters). The aroma of the flowers varies from plant to plant and it is prudent to pick only those flowers with a pleasant scent, for it will be found that some are so strongly scented as to be unpleasant to some tastes.

# AMERICAN ELDERBERRY, OR GOLDEN ELDERBERRY

## Botanical name
*Sambucus canadensis,* syn. *S. pubens*

## Origin
Canada, eastern United States.

## The fruit
Botanically a 3–5 seeded berry, a deep purple-black when ripe, similar in appearance to *S. nigra,* but the berries are larger, juicier, better flavoured and more abundantly produced, hanging in heavy clusters.

## The plant
A shrub, growing up to 4 m (12 ft) tall, with smooth young branches. It has the characteristic compound leaves, with leaflets, usually 7, sometimes 5 or even 11, oval, 5–15 cm (2–6 in) in length, tooth-edged, bright green but slightly downy on the underside, with the lowest leaflet often lobed. The small white flowers are in convex umbels some 10–20 cm (4–8 in) across.

There is a handsome variety, *S. c. aurea,* with golden yellow leaves and cherry-red fruits. *S. c. maxima* is a very vigorous variety with compound leaves as long as 45 cm (18 in) and flower umbels the same length. *S. c. xanthocarpa* has golden berries.

# EUROPEAN ELDERBERRY

## Botanical name
*Sambucus nigra*

## Origin
This species is native to temperate Europe and is now to be found widespread and recognised as a wild plant.

## The fruit
Black and shining when ripe, in the same shaped cymes as the flowers, but often drooping with the weight of the berries.

## The plant
This a shrub or tree according to how it is treated. If it is allowed to grow naturally it will form a prettily shaped small tree; some have been known to reach 10 m (30 ft), but this is rare. In bloom it can become smothered with the creamy white cymes of blossom, 13–20 cm (5–8 in) across, which have a delicate muscatel fragrance. Its compound leaves are large, with usually 5, though sometimes 3 or 7 leaflets, individually 4–13 cm (1½–5 in) long, their edges markedly toothed though soft and smooth. In autumn this foliage sometimes becomes beautifully coloured, according to the season, soil and general envi-

*American Elderberry*

*European Elderberry*

*Western Elderberry*

ronment. One great point in its favour as an urban garden plant is that it will thrive in the heavily polluted atmosphere of industrial districts. Like the American elderberry, the common European species has produced many varieties so that the gardener can, if he wishes, introduce variety in foliage and fruit colour, although in our view, for sheer practical use with a good measure of beauty thrown in, you cannot beat the species.

The varieties are so diverse that we suggest it would be wise to see them growing, or on show at a botanic garden or perhaps at a garden centre, in both flowering and fruiting seasons, before making a choice of which to grow. There are a number with creamy-white or yellow markings on the leaves in one pattern or another, for example one with white-bordered foliage, another with cut leaves, with bright golden and with yellow-spotted foliage. There are varieties which weep and those which stand with stems stiffly upright. Some have rose-tinted flowers, some white and greenish fruits.

From the flower arranger's point of view the blossom is elegant and can be used in many different styles of decoration. Like most blossom, elder will take water faster and will last longer in an arrangement if some of the leaves are removed. Fruit clusters are also worth arranging, either green – especially in monochrome ensembles – or when fully ripe to bring a touch of opulence to an arrangement.

# WESTERN ELDERBERRY

*Botanical name*
Sambucus caerulea

*Origin*
Western North America.

*The fruit*
Botanically a 3–5-seeded berry, blue-black and densely covered with a bloom like some grapes

and sloes, larger and juicier than the fruits of *S. nigra,* the common elderberry, about the size of a pea. Produced in late summer through to autumn.

## The plant

This is a shrub or small tree growing up to 3 m (10 ft) or so, but sometimes much larger when found growing wild under ideal conditions. Shoots are smooth, slightly glaucous, leaves compound and quite large, with 5–7 leaflets, the individuals from 6–15 cm (2½–6 in) long. The flower cymes are more yellow than white, 10–15 cm (4–6 in) across and convex. It has a good muscatel scent and flavour.

## Cultivation

The elder is a hardy plant which can be used as a windbreak, perhaps simply to protect one or a group of less vigorous kinds of plant or as a hedge or screen. However, if used for the latter purpose, be prepared for a large area to look very bare in winter.

The plant prefers a nitrogenous, moist soil, one reason why it does so well in wild hedges and copses. In this it will produce lush foliage, thick stems and a heavy crop of fruit. Generally speaking, however, it will grow in almost any kind of soil, and in sun or semi-shade. More specifically, variegated plants prefer moist soil and a sunny position if they are to be well coloured. Should the winter and spring be dry, it is helpful to give the plant at least one good soaking before it breaks bud.

Elders need little attention. If you wish to keep the plant fairly compact, simply cut it back annually in winter. Shoots can be cut to ground level or simply trimmed to a pair of buds. Varieties with ornamental foliage, whose beauty must be taken into account as well as their utility value, are best pruned in late autumn or in early spring before growth begins. This done, the new shoots will be brightly coloured. The elder responds to treatment so quickly that after a year or so even the least skilled gardener will have discovered the best way to handle his plant so as to get the desired result.

Should you take over an old, neglected garden, where a plant has grown out of control, you can

if you wish cut it back severely, even saw it down, and it will soon shoot again.

If you encounter difficulty in obtaining a plant from a nursery or garden centre, you can raise what you want by taking cuttings from wild plants. Find one which looks good to you. There are several methods.
1. Take bare shoots of old wood in autumn, some 25–30 cm (9–12 in) long and root these in sandy loam in the open ground.
2. Take heeled, half-ripe shoots in summer and root these in sandy soil in frames or in pots.
3. Take hardwood cuttings consisting of 3 double buds in early spring. Insert these in the soil so that only the top pair of buds is above the surface. Lift the plants and move them to their permanent sites the following spring.

If you wish to grow your plant as a tree rather than a bushy shrub, select the strongest shoot from a plant and let this grow as high as you want the trunk of the tree to be. The other shoots should be cut away. When the chosen shoot has reached its required height, pinch out the growing tip to induce branching. Remove any other shoots which may appear at ground level.

At harvest time, pick the fruits by the bunch rather than individually as we once found an urban guest doing. Then remove the individual fruits by combing down the bunch with a fork so that they fall into a bowl beneath. Wash the fruits first in their bunches.

## Culinary uses

Praised for centuries by country people as a wine fruit, the elderberry in fact can be cooked in other ways, mainly in the same way as the blackberry. Some people find its flavour too strong and when it is used with apples, pears or quinces, for example, it is better to use half the quantity one would use of the other berry. Of course much depends on personal tastes. As well as the fruit, the buds and flower heads can be used, the one as 'capers' and the others as fritters or as a flavouring in gooseberry and rhubarb dishes to which they bring a muscatel flavour, and for elderflower champagne.

FREEZING It is possible to quick-freeze bunches of elderberries and then to shake them over a container when the berries will fall off.

Pack into bags. Alternatively prepare a syrup as below and pack with this in rigid containers.

BOTTLING   For bottling, pack the fruit into jars and make a syrup of their juice and sugar rather than the usual sugar and water. Pack in small jars to have small quantities available for mixing with other fruit.

DRINKS   The traditional Elderberry Wine of the countryman can be made in a number of ways. The simplest recipe is probably the following.

### Elderberry wine

*16 cups elderberries, stripped from their stalks*
*32 cups water*
*⅓ cup stem ginger*
*24 cups sugar*
*yeast*

Boil all except the yeast together until the berries have lost their juice, then strain and put in a jar or bucket. Leave until lukewarm and then add the yeast. After the first fermentation pour into fermenting jars and leave until all action ceases, then bottle.

There is also an Elderberry Port which we used to make some years ago and of which we have happy memories.

### Elderberry port

*8 cups elderberries, stripped*
*16 cups water*
*1 cup raisins*
*7 cups sugar*

Boil water and elderberries for about 15 minutes, strain and add sugar and raisins, pour into a bowl or bucket and allow to ferment for 2 weeks before straining again into jars with a fermentation lock. Bottle only when all fermentation has stopped. Keep and allow to mature for at least a year.

# FEIJOA
*Feijoa sellowiana*

## Origin

A monotypic genus, which means that this species is the sole representative. A native of Brazil and other areas of South America, it is named in honour of Don da Silva Feijoa, a San Sebastian botanist. Its specific name is in honour of the German explorer Sellow, who discovered the plant in 1819. It was not introduced into Europe until 1890. It was brought back from South America by Edouard André, a famous French horticulturist. He grew it in his Riviera garden. It has become widely established in many sub-tropical gardens, notably in Australia, America and New Zealand. It was introduced into California in 1900. There are some varieties in existence, particularly in the south of France where the plant grows wild, but comparatively little is known about it, which is a pity since it is both useful and productive.

## The fruit

Botanically, an ovoid berry. The fruit, sometimes oblong, sometimes more rounded, is pineapple-scented and more like a passion fruit in appearance than a guava. It is about 5 cm (2 in) long, green when ripe, with a thin, tough, waxy skin and white or yellow-green granular flesh around a jelly-like pulp, in which the seeds are embedded. This has a rich, guava-like flavour with a hint of strawberry and pineapple, hence the common names. The fruit usually falls to the ground before it is ripe. For this reason some gardeners gather them a little early and hold them in store until their full flavour has developed. At this point their aroma will be stronger. In some countries, depending upon the season, fallen fruits tend to ripen very quickly and unless picked up immediately and used they will deteriorate.

## The plant

This is a bushy, attractive evergreen shrub with whippy stems and white felted shoots and glossy green leaves with grey or white felt on the underside, 4–8 cm (1½–3 in) long. Under suitable conditions it will reach tree stature in time. The solitary flowers are beautiful and plentiful, borne in one or two pairs at the base of the current year's shoots. They are 4 cm (1½ in) across and consist of 4 felted sepals, 4 round and concave petals, grey-mauve outside and red within, with erect, crimson stamens and yellow anthers.

## Cultivation

The feijoa will grow in almost any ordinary soil, even tolerating a little chalk. Although it has been known to withstand low temperatures, it really should be grown in a frost-free site. Too cold, it will not bear fruit. Where nights are likely to be cool, the plant is best grown against a warm wall. It can be contained and grown in a greenhouse and brought outside in summer.

It has been found that trees grown alone do not always fruit well, which suggests that cross-fertilisation is advisable where possible.

Feijoa can be raised from seed. Varieties can be propagated by layering or by grafting, using a cold frame in summer.

## Culinary uses

This fruit is rich in vitamin C and has a sugar content of about 6 per cent. The whole of the fruit is edible except for the thin outer skin. It can be eaten raw and is excellent in fruit salads. The feijoa can be used in the same way as a guava.

PRESERVING  It makes good marmalade, jellies and other preserves. The flowers are also edible and can be crystallised or used in salads.

# FIG
*Ficus carica*

## Origin

The fig, a member of the mulberry family, is one of the most ancient plants in civilisation. It is believed that there exist some 700 varieties of the species. The plant is most likely to be a native of western Asia, but because it proved to be such a useful and valuable food, it early became an important part of the staple diet in many countries of the old world. Like the date, its food value improves with drying, and drying means that it can be stored. It grows best in the northern warm temperate and sub-tropical regions, climate 1 on the world chart (p. 14). The Phoenicians probably introduced it into India and China. Wherever the colonising Romans introduced the vine into those countries which lie much further north than its original habitat, they seem also to have planted the fig, in most cases with great success. From a plant so given to producing varieties, it was inevitable that some should be much more hardy than others. Naturally it would be these which would have been selected for other climes.

The fig is now being produced much more widely than ever before, both commercially and in private gardens, and recently it has been planted on a commercial scale in new regions such as Madagascar, South Africa and Australia. It is good to see it well featured in nurserymen's catalogues for amateurs in many countries. Areas producing the greatest quantities of figs commercially are Turkey, Greece, Italy, Algeria, Portugal and California, where Calimyrna (*California* and *Smyrna*) figs are grown among other varieties suitable for fresh dessert and for canning. The famous Smyrna figs are said to have been produced for more than 2,000 years.

The exact lineage of such an ancient plant,

with so many varieties, is extremely difficult to trace. In some countries, such as Britain, it is likely that after the Roman occupation it may have disappeared, later to be reintroduced possibly as different varieties some centuries later, when there was a mainly monastic interest and revival in gardening. Even today there is occasionally some confusion, simply because one variety of fig is given several names which vary from country to country or even from garden to garden.

Anyone greatly interested will find the botanical life of *Ficus carica* makes fascinating reading, but for the urban gardener who simply wishes to grow a fig tree or two, we feel it is not necessary here to go into great detail. The important fact hinges on the way in which some figs are pollinated. At one time it was not possible to have a plant produce fruit without the aid of a tiny fig wasp, which, to put it briefly, wandered in and out, and indeed bred and lived, inside the intricate flowers (which are of three types, male, female and neuter), and by so doing transferred the essential pollen from one to another. Fortunately hybrid figs were bred, which set fruit without the aid of pollination. This is important, because the fig wasp cannot live in all the climates in which figs are now grown.

## The fruit

Botanically, a hollow, globular or pear-shaped fleshy receptacle, having at its tip an orifice closed by small scales. This receptacle, in fact, encloses the many tiny flowers which grow and mature away from daylight, completely enveloped by the fruit.

Figs are produced singly or in pairs in the leaf axils. They are classified by the colour of their skins, and so there are 'white', 'purple', 'black' and 'red' figs, but these are loose descriptions because the appearance of the skin varies considerably from variety to variety. Some are rounded and turbinate, some more egg-shaped or pear-shaped, like the popular Brown Turkey. This variety, incidentally, is one of those which, no doubt due to its great popularity, has many synonyms, including Common Purple, Brown Naples, Blue Burgundy, Lee's Perpetual and others in English alone, for in other countries it has other names. Some of the pear-shaped figs have long necks. Some of the fruits are ribbed. In almost all the

skin is fine and since the fruit is not really ready to eat until the skin begins to split, it can easily be understood that figs generally do not travel well if properly ripened.

However, the skin is really the least important part of the fruit, for it is the flesh that is so delicious. This also varies considerably according to the variety. The hardy, dwarf, prolific, pear-shaped Brown Turkey has a rich, sugary, white or yellow-green flesh tinged with red at the centre. Some figs have a dark red, thick syrupy flesh. Some white figs, such as Col di Signora Bianca, have a thick, yellow-white skin with a syrupy dark red flesh inside. Celeste, grown widely in the south-western fig areas of America, is violet-coloured and like others of this type, and those with violet-black fruits, has a light-coloured flesh, white, light pink, pink-buff or rose-coloured, which is firm, juicy and sweet. White Adriatic is another American variety.

White Marseilles, one of the hardiest of all varieties, has a thin, almost white skin when ripe, with almost transparent flesh which is extremely rich and sweet. This variety is another of those known by other names, among which are Figue Blanche, Ford's Seedling, White Genoa and White Naples. American growers can select Magnolia Fig, one of their hardiest species, which has very large straw-coloured fruits. One of the famous black figs is Black Mission, grown in California.

## The plant

The common fig will grow into a large tree or shrub, as tall as 5–10 m (15–30 ft), although cultivars generally are less vigorous and many of these can be trained against walls. In nature the plant tends to spread out rather than reach up. It is deciduous, with palmate leaves of usually three and sometimes five lobes. They are rough-textured on the upper side and slightly downy on the under side. The plant is a handsome one and is an ornament to the garden regardless of the manner in which it is grown.

Cultivated varieties or hybrids differ from the wild forms and some of these varieties produce no male flowers but female only. This means that their fruits develop parthenogenetically, i.e. without pollination. The young trees, propagated in various ways, quickly bear fruit. The Smyrna and most varieties grown in the Middle East are likely to produce three crops of fruit in the year. In other countries, and under certain conditions, fig trees will produce two kinds of fruit, the first maturing in early summer from tiny fruits or figlets which were produced the previous year and which persist during the winter, and the second crop maturing in the autumn. Usually these two crops vary, the first producing the larger fruits, and the second, though prolific, smaller and less succulent fruits. One must stress, however, that a great deal depends upon the climate as well as the variety grown. More usually only one crop a year is produced when the plant is grown outdoors and this crop can be expected to be prolific in good summers and if the plant has been protected against any possible frost.

In colder climates where the protection of a wall is sought, or where figs are grown under glass, the plants are usually fan-trained and can be bought this way from the nurseryman. Obviously a fan-trained tree is always an ornamental feature on a patio or some place near the house.

## Cultivation

From the urban gardener's point of view the fig is an ideal plant, mainly because if its roots are restricted it will bear a better crop of fruit than if they were allowed to roam. This indicates that it is an excellent container plant. Large pots, at least 25–30 cm (10–12 in) in diameter, as well as tubs and other containers, can be used. How these pots are displayed depends entirely upon the environment and the climate. In some areas it may be possible to have them standing as a patio plant, in others they have to be grown in a greenhouse, where under certain conditions it might be possible, or even convenient, to allow them to stand out of doors for part of the year.

Where there is room for a fig tree outdoors in the open ground, in all but warm climates the plant should be given the warmest, sunniest, most protected spot in the garden, preferably near a wall. Here again one should try to restrict the roots. It may be possible to construct a slightly raised border, following the old gardener's method of making a trough, some 1 m by 2 m and about 1 m deep (3 ft×6 ft×3 ft) with some section of the brick or concrete wall below the surface. Alternatively, the plant can be grown in a narrow border against a suitable wall which flanks the path along a house or some other building. The wall will support the plant and the pathway, if paved in some way, will help to keep the roots confined to one area.

One old and proved method of restricting root run, against outside walls or in greenhouses, was to make a 1 m (3 ft) wide border, remove the soil to a depth of about 75 cm (2½ ft) and then compact the base of this trench with lime rubble or chalk beaten down really hard. The roots were then restricted, although the drainage was not impaired when the trench was refilled with the recommended mixture. It should be possible to follow this process easily enough in other situations, such as on a patio.

Soil for figs should not be rich in nitrogen, so do not grow the plant too near certain vegetables which need to be fed with nitrogen from time to time, and for the best flavour there should be a lime content in the soil.

A good and simple yearly tonic is to every square m (square yd) of border apply 170 g (6 oz) of basic slag, 43 g (1½ oz) of sulphate of potash each autumn. Every other year apply 225 g (8 oz) of ground chalk.

Ideally a potted fig should be repotted every autumn, but should you be growing a plant in a large container this will be found to be a major operation. Instead, carefully scrape away the surface soil until you begin to reach the roots and replace with fresh soil. If you have fed the plant regularly the existing soil should be fairly rich.

Being a deciduous plant, the fig tree has a dormant period while it is leafless. Water it very little at this time. Once you see that it is beginning to come into growth again, begin to water more freely. This applies to all trees, including those in the open ground that may be in dry soil or during a dry season. When standard or half standard trees are grown in the open, the soil should be prepared by deep digging, simply to improve drainage, but take care that it is not too rich, otherwise your plant will be leafy but unproductive.

As you would expect, where soil has to be well drained yet fruits produced from it must be juicy, water should not be spared. During the growing season give plenty of water to root-restricted plants. They can be given a little bone-meal in spring if you fear that too much plant food is being leached out, and plants grown in borders can be mulched to conserve moisture. As many mulches provide nitrogen, avoid using a rich manure or compost, using instead moist peat or some similar less active material. When the fruit is bearing heavily, however, it is helpful to add a little tonic food in the form of some liquid manure.

Little pruning, but a certain amount of pinching out is demanded. Pruning consists only in cutting out dead, deformed or weak branches, and perhaps any that are inconveniently placed. Cut these back to the main trunk to encourage new growth. In midsummer pinch out the tips of vigorous young shoots so that they make plenty of good, strong growth. Remember that figs come to maturity only on new or recently ripened wood. So it should be the gardener's aim to see that this is forthcoming.

In cold climates these precious shoots have to be protected and in areas where winters can be severe it is the custom to protect the branches in various ways. In Switzerland we have seen spruce branches laid over the plant. In other places bracken or heather are used, canvas, rush mats, hurdles and all manner of things according to the climate or the severity of the latest weather forecast. Some gardeners in cold climates remove the branches from their supports in cold weather, bundle them gently together with a straw packing and envelope the whole in a thick coat of straw or matting. When any cover is provided, it must gradually be removed in the spring, a counsel of perfection being to remove the packing during the day and replace it at night until the weather improves. Growing or forcing figs under glass is a somewhat skilled operation, and given the right treatment it is possible to produce two or perhaps even three crops in a year. We suggest that this might be an engaging and rewarding occupation for someone with time and money to spare, the latter being necessary because high temperatures must be maintained during winter.

Propagation is by layering or cuttings. Layers should root in a season. Detach them from the plant when the pot into which they have been led is well filled with roots. For cuttings select short-jointed shoots of the previous year's growth in spring, some 15–25 cm (6–9 in) long, preferably with a heel. Plant these in pots of sandy soil, preferably in a propagating case in a greenhouse, and maintain the young plants in warmth until they are seen to be sturdy and growing well, when they can gradually be introduced to the outside world. If they have been grown well they should fruit while still young.

## Culinary uses

When fresh, figs contain some 80 per cent water and 12 per cent sugars, but when they are dried the sugar rises to 50 per cent. One authority suggests that all recipes for apricots are suitable for figs. When they are to be eaten fresh, figs are usually peeled, but this is a matter of personal taste and is not essential. A ripe fig is a deliciously succulent fruit with its own characteristic flavour. In Italy and in Italian restaurants it is sometimes served on its own as an antipasta, sometimes with thinly sliced prosciutto in the same way as melons. It is good with freshly ground pepper. Another way of serving figs as a first course is to fill them with various mixtures, cream cheese or the more flavoured cheeses such as Stilton and Dolcelatte, creamed by mashing with a fork and with a little wine added. Fennel seeds or fresh chervil add flavour to this and go well with the figs. The ham mentioned above and other kinds of ham and cooked sausage or sausage meats can also be used this way.

An unusual fresh fruit salad can be made from peeled figs, apricots, peaches and plums all cut small and left to marinate in their juices for a few hours before a syrup made from sugar and lemon juice is poured on them. Fresh figs can be sliced and made into a table jelly.

Dried figs are extremely useful. They can be used in many kinds of puddings, breads, cakes, biscuits, and cookies, as well as in desserts, mousses and ice-cream. When they are used as a compote the flavour can be enriched if a little wine, liqueur, lemon peel, redcurrant jelly or some crystallised fruit such as citrus peel or ginger is added. Dried figs can be stuffed with nut meats and citrus peel in the same way as dates. If they are to be cooked they are best if they are first plumped up a little in ways recommended for dates. Try covering them with honey and then baking them in a covered dish until they are tender.

### Stewed figs in honey and wine

*2 cups firm green figs, slightly under-ripe*
*1½ cups dry white wine*
*1 cup honey*

Wash the figs, trim the stems, place in a saucepan and cover with the white wine. Bring slowly to the boil and then stir in the honey. Cover the pan and simmer for about 15 minutes or until the figs are tender. Drain with a perforated spoon and place in a serving bowl. Meanwhile, boil the syrup for about 10 minutes to reduce it and slightly thicken it. Pour it over the fruit. Cool and then refrigerate for at least an hour before serving. Serve with whipped cream or vanilla ice-cream.

PRESERVING  Fresh or dried, figs can be made into jam, marmalade, chutney, pickle and preserves, or they can be spiced.

### Fig jam

*3 cups figs*
*5 apples*
*2 lemons, juice and rind*
*4 cups sugar*

Slice the figs, and peel, core and slice the apples. Put all the fruit in a pan and cook slowly until all are tender, then boil fast for 10 minutes. Add sugar, stir it in well, then boil fast again until the jam sets.

DRYING  Figs can be dried at home if you have a good supply. In some countries this is done quite simply by spreading really ripe fruit out in the sun, turning them frequently so that all surfaces are exposed. Take them in at night. They can also be dried indoors in a hot, dry atmosphere, commercially in special drying rooms. A hot, sunny windowsill can be used. Fruits can be strung and hung in the warm air.

Fig Roll Slices are loved by children – if the adults leave any.

### Fig roll slices

*2 cups chopped, dried figs*
*½ cup blanched almonds, chopped, i.e., roughly halved and quartered*
*1 tabsp icing sugar*

Pound or blend the figs and almonds until they make a rough paste. Pat and fashion this into a long roll. Coat with the icing sugar, using all and adding a little more if the coat seems to need it. Wrap in foil and chill in a refrigerator. To serve, cut into slices. Serve with coffee and liqueurs.

FREEZING  To freeze figs use only sweet, soft, ripe fruits. Wash, remove stems, peel if desired. Crush, slice or use whole. For whole fruits use a syrup pack or an unsweetened pack. Crushed fruits can be given a dry sugar pack. All must have ascorbic acid.

BOTTLING  For bottling, remove the stems and peel if desired. Add ½ teaspoon citric acid to every 2 cups syrup. Pack with an equal weight of syrup.

DRINKS  The Germans have a fig brandy by the name of *Feigenbranntwein* and in Tunisia and certain other North African countries one is sometimes served *boukha*, sometimes called *mahia*, which is a powerful eau-de-vie made from figs, drunk either before a meal as an aperitif or with the coffee as a liqueur.

There is also a Fig Wine made from dried figs which is said to be suitable for drinking soon after it is made. Take 1 kg (2 lb) of dried figs cut into quarters, 10 dried juniper berries and 10 litres (18 pt) of water. Put all into a large bowl, cover and allow to stand for a week. Strain and bottle. Let the liquid settle for 4 or 5 days before using.

# FUCHSIA
*Fuchsia* species and varieties

## Origin

These plants are natives of areas as far apart as central and southern America and New Zealand. The genus of about 100 species of shrubs and trees was named after the botanist Leonard Fuchs (1501–66), who is particularly remembered for a beautifully executed book of woodcuts of plants.

Since its introduction the plant has proved popular with gardeners everywhere and there is now a great range of cultivars derived from the various species, which means that modern varieties inherit the most useful characteristics of their parents, and varieties can be found for almost any situation in most gardens.

The reason for the inclusion of the fuchsia in this book on fruit is largely to reassure readers who may believe that the berries which form on their pot or garden plants could be harmful to those who eat them. There is no cause for alarm. The berries are in fact delicious.

## The fruit

Botanically, a berry with several small seeds as a rule. The size and the shape of berries of cultivars vary considerably and one can give no definite type. Often a gardener is aware of the fruits only when he or she has neglected to deadhead the flowers. In their places are swollen seed boxes, green at first, later red or even as black as a cherry. The richer the colour the better the flavour. Some species have purple fruits. such as *F. corymbiflora* and the tree fuchsia or kotukutuku, and the New Zealand konini, *F. exorticata*, a species, incidentally, which in northern countries is almost hardy.

## The plant

According to the species, fuchsias vary from ground level shrubs to trees some 6 m (20 ft) tall in their native habitat, but cultivars are usually smaller and bushier. Some can be trained to grow tall to use for covering pergolas and archways. They can be grown in containers, as standards, ground covers, for arches and towers, as cascades, as climbers and splendidly in hanging baskets. This is a highly versatile and most attractive fruiting plant.

## Cultivation

The method of cultivation should fit the type of plant. For instance. *F. magellanica* and its varieties, originating from the cold areas of South America, are hardy. These are often used as hedges, and in some countries such as Ireland even appear to be wild. Others, mainly derived from *F. fulgens,* need warm, sunny conditions, and are the types grown in greenhouses or in sunny beds and borders.

As a general rule most fuchsias need or favour either complete or partial shade. White varieties and those with the lightest colours are definitely shade lovers, and if grown indoors under glass must be given shady conditions when the sun is hot and strong.

Those planted outdoors in cold zones usually need a protected or comparatively warm site. They do well at the base of a wall which faces the sun. It is wise in severe winters to protect the bases of the plants with dry bracken litter, dry fallen leaves, peat or even ashes from the bonfire heaped over them. This protective cover should be moved away from the bases when the plants are pruned back hard in early spring. In less cold areas the stems usually just die back a little and in this case one should cut away the old damaged wood until good buds are reached. All well-rooted fuchsias can stand vigorous cutting down to ground level.

Those grown in pots should be planted in spring, although young plants grown from cuttings can be potted as they are ready. From spring to midsummer it may be necessary to keep the containers under glass, according to the climatic conditions under which one gardens. As a guide the temperature should be no less than 4–7°C (40–45°F) during winter and some 13–18°C (55–65°F) afterwards. They can then be moved outside to a sunny place until the cool nights of autumn come round again. The plants should be watered very little during their dormant period, and a little more freely as they begin to make growth and finally very freely when they are in full growth. Once the plants begin to flower give them a regular liquid feed. During the growing period the plants also respond to a daily spray or syringe with plain clean water.

All fuchsias make new growth at the ends of the branches and for this reason one should pinch back young growth so as to make the plant bushy and productive. The pinched out shoots can be rooted if so desired. Fuchsias grow easily from cuttings. The best are taken from new, unflowered shoots some 10–13 cm (4–5 in) long.

## Culinary uses

Eat raw or use for jams and jellies.

# GOOSEBERRY
*Ribes grossularia*

## Origin

A member of the Saxifrage family, this plant is another of the genus to which currants also belong, but it is distinguished from them by its spiny character. The plant grows 'wild' in many parts of Europe, mainly in the north, but it probably originated in the mountainous regions as well as in North Africa. Actually, many of the so-called wild gooseberries growing near communities are most likely to be seedlings or descendants of cultivars.

The plant has been in cultivation in northern countries for centuries. It was enormously popular at one time, but it now seems to be suffering a decline, possibly because its spiny stems make it such an inconvenient fruit to gather. It may also be that it appears to be a host to a fungus that attacks the American white pine, and for this reason imports and cultivation are prohibited in certain areas. It is, however, an extremely useful plant since the berries can be used in their immature stage, early in the summer, as well as when they are fully ripe. Furthermore, as explained later, there are many ways of growing the plants to make picking easier.

The American gooseberries differ from the above. They have mainly been derived from a native species found in eastern North America, *R. cynobasti,* and others. The Worcesterberry is a *Ribes* species and is a small black fruit. The plant is immune to mildew. Unfortunately, the European gooseberries are badly affected by American gooseberry mildew, which appears to be an unfair name when one considers that the American species appears to be immune to it! It is for this reason that most American gardeners and growers use hybrids raised from their native species. However, some European varieties are favoured, such as Clark, with very large red fruits, and Fredonia, also red, but ripening a few days later than the first. An American variety which is also grown in Canada is Captivator, which has small red berries. The gooseberry is hardy enough for most northern gardens.

In cultivation the European gooseberry has produced many varieties – the Royal Horticultural Society has listed more than 400 varietal names. Briefly, one should record that at one time in England there were Gooseberry Clubs in many villages and towns, the members of which dedicated themselves to competition in growing the largest single fruit. Special gooseberry scales were designed and constructed to record infinitesimal differences in weight, and these are now collector's pieces. The history of the clubs makes fascinating reading. In the main, however, the ordinary gardener grew those varieties which were of the greatest culinary value and the same applies today all over the world.

One wonders how the only variety grown commercially in New South Wales came to be named. It is Roaring Lion!

## The fruit

Botanically, a berry. Unlike the currant and the American gooseberry, *R. cynobasti,* var. *inerme,* the fruits of some groups are hairy, and their relative hairiness has a bearing on the way in which the varieties are classified. Other factors involved are the colour of the fruit when ripe, i.e. green, white, yellow or red, as well as the shape, size, flavour (which one would imagine should be the most important) and, lastly, by the habit of the plant or bush.

Generally speaking, the largest fruits are not as well flavoured as the smaller varieties. It is worth recording that a great deal of choice of variety depends upon what use is intended for the fruit.

All varieties can be picked young and cooked, and this is usually a good way of thinning the fruits. The early ripening amber and yellow varieties include those with the finest flavour. These varieties are also, like the green-skinned kind, likely to have thin skins. The latter differ considerably in size according to variety, and some of the smallest have the richest flavour. One of the best-known white varieties is Careless. Red-skinned varieties generally are considered to be more acid than the rest. This class includes some varieties which can be stored for autumn eating, and so for this reason valued. One such is the large-fruited London.

## The plant

Gooseberries vary considerably in their mode of growth and in their general appearance according to their variety, although one might say that any gooseberry bush is unmistakable. Some varieties tend to become very pendulous.

The species is a deciduous, spiny shrub some 1.2 m (4 ft) high. It has a variety, *uva-crispa,* with fruits not hairy or bristly as those of the species are. The plant may grow upright, spreading or pendulous. Fortunately the gardener can control growth to a certain extent by selecting shoots for retention. The young leaves are edible and good in spring salads.

## Cultivation

Almost any garden soil will grow gooseberries, but it should be understood that on heavy soils the plants are much more liable to succumb to disease because they produce soft, coarse growth. For this same reason one should not be over-generous with nitrogenous fertilisers. If the soil is thin and poor it should be well conditioned with plentiful supplies of well-rotted manure, and this can be added to by applying good mulches of organic matter. Gooseberries are particularly susceptible to potash deficiency, and to keep the plants productive it is recommended that ½ cup of sulphate of potash to the square m (square yd) should be applied to the soil in late winter each year. Indications of a potash deficiency are an early leaf fall and the discoloration of the leaf margins, which appear to be dead.

When gooseberries are grown as bushes they are best if they stand on a leg or short trunk: usually 15 cm (6 in) is sufficient. This means that the lowest branches, which tend to droop lower when they are fruit-laden, are clear of the ground. This not only means that the fruits are kept clean, but also that there is sufficient space for the hands to go freely under the plant when the fruit is being picked. Varieties with a pendant habit are best grown as bushes. Select upright shoots while plants are being pruned. Shorten year-old, extra-pendulous shoots by snipping off their bending tips.

The gooseberry fruits on the previous year's growth as well as on short spurs and old wood. Fruiting quality declines as the latter two age. To rejuvenate old bushes shorten laterals to just a few buds.

The urban gardener can grow fruits more easily and save more space by concentrating on trained trees. These can be cordons or fan-trained. The latter can be grown on sunless walls. But for this purpose pruning is slightly different since new shoots are selected and tied in place each year, while cordons are restricted to spur pruning. If a late crop of berries is required the same site can be used for single, double or triple cordons. You can stagger the harvest this way if wished, planting some in sunny positions for early ripening. Cordons should not be grown on a wall or other structure which receives fierce sun all day long. In hot areas the fruit is best grown in bush form since the top branches help shade the fruits below which can become scorched.

It is wise to consult a nurseryman before selecting varieties to grow, because much can depend on district and site. For instance, in cold northern areas those varieties that flower late, when planted in a north border, usually escape injury from late frosts when they are in bloom. It is also important not to plant gooseberries in low-lying land which is apt to become a frost pocket during cold periods.

Bushes tend to grow very dense and need plenty of space. Plant them 1.2 m–2 m (4–6 ft) apart each way. Cordons are spaced as redcurrants, 30 cm (12 in) for singles, 45 cm (18 in) for doubles and 60 cm (2 ft) for triples. The plants are also pruned in much the same way. Traditionally, they are winter pruned. However, if you find that birds peck at the young buds it may be best to delay the pruning until spring. Cut back the main or leading shoots by a third and shorten side shoots to 2–5 cm (1–2 in). Where gardeners want large dessert fruits only, they often cut right back to two buds. Cordons, much simpler to see and handle, are best pruned by cutting all the side shoots to about 2 cm (1 in).

As stated earlier, the fruits can be used when they are immature. One can begin picking them as soon as they are a useful size, bearing in mind that they will need topping and tailing so that they should be large enough to handle conveniently. This is usually in early summer. You can make this a thinning process and take time spacing the fruits so that they can develop without being crowded.

Propagation is very simple, and if you would like to try your hand at training a tree into whatever form, this can be done by first taking cuttings. Choose well-ripened shoots in autumn, some 20–23 cm (8–9 in) in length. Remove the lower buds. Plant 10 cm (4 in) deep in a slit trench with sand at the base for good drainage.

## Culinary uses

In many countries this fruit is used mainly as a dessert, but in France, where it is known as *Groseille à maquereau,* its use is limited almost entirely to a sauce for that fish. Although gooseberries may not be as versatile as some fruits, they can serve as the basis for many more dishes than that of one sauce for mackerel. However, to make the sauce – and it is really good with this rich, oily fish and any other of a similar nature – boil 2 cups of gooseberries in very little water and when the berries are tender, blend and strain them. Put them into a heavy pan and mix with them 3 tablespoons bechamel sauce, ¼ cup butter, seasoning and a little grated nutmeg, adding sugar if you must. We like to add a little fresh fennel.

Gooseberries are good cooked with honey instead of sugar. We like them carefully cooked this way so that they remain whole, in various salads. They go especially well with potato and can take the same kind of dressing. This kind of salad is also good with fresh dill. Try using a few gooseberries with a little cooked rice and freshly chopped chervil to stuff tomatoes. Mix the tomato pulp with the rice. Carefully stir in the gooseberries. Top with cream or cottage cheese and finely chopped chives.

Gooseberries have traditionally been made into purée and used to make Gooseberry Fool, which is no more than equal parts of pulp mixed with milk, or half milk and half cream, and sweetened to taste.

Cooks will find a stock of gooseberry purée quite useful, not only for the two dishes mentioned above, but for many others including Chiffon Pie, small open tarts topped with whipped cream, or sponge puddings, where the mixture can be poured on the purée before baking or steaming, or the gooseberries can be poured over it as a sauce. We find gooseberry ice-cream excellent, refreshing and something a little out of the ordinary. Make it following the basic ice-cream recipe given on page 33. The purée can also be used as the base of a trifle.

The whole gooseberries, topped and tailed, can be used for many dishes also, not only for a com-pote but also in pies, tarts and puddings of many kinds.

One of our favourite ways of serving really ripe gooseberries is to wash the fruits and then squeeze their pips and juice into individual dishes. The fruit is then covered with thin cream and sprinkled with chopped almonds. The dishes are chilled slightly before serving. There is no need to waste the skins. They can be mixed with rhubarb or apple to make a little jam. Even one potful will prevent them being wasted.

Gooseberry and Elderflower Syrup, which tastes so strongly, some say, of muscatel grapes that it is sometimes called muscat syrup, is well worth making, not only for summer drinks, but also to flavour fruit salads and to make sorbets and water ices.

### Gooseberry and elderflower syrup

8 cups gooseberries
6 cups sugar
2 cups water
12 corymbs of elder flowers

Put the sugar and water into a saucepan on slow heat. When the sugar is dissolved add the gooseberries and simmer slowly for 5–10 minutes or until tender. Turn off the heat. Wash the elderflowers and tie in muslin. Throw into the syrup and let them stay in it until it is well flavoured. Drain through a sieve or muslin. Filter or strain again through muslin to clear the syrup. Pour into jars or bottles and sterilise these for 10 minutes. There is no need to waste the pulp. This can be used for Fool or for a gooseberry cheese or butter.

PRESERVING The young berries have the highest pectin content. Use some of these when making gooseberry jam. Alternatively, when the berries are ripe, add redcurrant juice to them, 2 cups to every 8 cups of fruit, for jam or jelly. The ripe fruits are quite suitable for chutneys and for sauces. Gooseberry jam makes an excellent and unusual jam omelette. Make a sweet omelette, stuff it with the jam, sprinkle the top with icing sugar and serve. For a special occasion, while it is still in the pan pour over it 2 tablespoons of kummel and set the liqueur alight.

Gooseberry Chips are a sweetmeat, not a veg-etable. You need a purée made from green and unripe but well-grown berries. To every 2 cups of pulp allow half as much sugar. Heat the purée and stir in the sugar while it is simmering very slowly. When it is quite dissolved, pour the pulp on to a lightly oiled slab or into flat meat dishes to make a sheet only 2–3 mm ($\frac{1}{8}$ in) thick. Set this in the sun to dry. Test, and when it can be handled, cut and/or twist into shapes. To store, pack between waxed paper in a tin or some other airtight container.

FREEZING   To freeze gooseberries first grade the fruit so that you get batches of roughly equal size. Pack unsweetened in bags. Fruit in syrup tends to break, but it can be frozen this way, as can purée.

BOTTLING   Green varieties picked while the fruit is still hard are best for bottling. If they are to be preserved in syrup, their skins should be ruptured in some way or else they shrivel. Either cut a tiny slice from one end of the fruit while it is being topped and tailed, or prick each fruit with a cocktail stick.

DRINKS   For some reason unknown to us, gooseberry wines seem to have a greater tendency than most towards effervescence and they are therefore called gooseberry champagne or sparkling gooseberry wine and bottled with corks wired down or placed in casks with loose bungs. We have had some experience of the dangers of wired down corks and few of us today have a sufficiency of strong, empty champagne bottles, or indeed of casks which one is advised to 'rinse out with brandy'.

Let us merely say that still gooseberry wines can be made in exactly the same way that other country wines are prepared (see basic recipe for guidance, p. 34).

# GOUMI
*Elaeagnus* species

## Origin

*Elaeagnus* is a genus of about 40 species of deciduous and evergreen shrubs and trees, many of which are spiny. Their native homes are widespread and range from China and Japan to North America, western Asia, the eastern Mediterranean and southern Europe and elsewhere. Not all of these plants produce edible fruits. In spite of the name *elaia,* Greek for olive, the plant does not belong to the olive family, though some fruits resemble the olive in size and shape, hence some popular names.

In most gardens, elaeagnus are grown as ornamental plants and any harvest is incidental. Many readers may not even realise that the fruit of some particular species is edible. However, it should be pointed out that this genus does offer a good potential so far as food is concerned. Goumi, *E. multiflora,* syn. *E. edulis,* in the opinion of some growers is well worth greater attention from selectors, hybridisers and fruit specialists generally. Some research into the plant is being carried out in the USA, where it is hoped that new hybrids will eventually be produced, superior to many of the most popular berries, not necessarily of this family, such as redcurrants and cranberries.

## The fruit

Fruits are a dark orange, speckled with small white spots, about 1½–2 cm ($\frac{1}{2}$–$\frac{3}{4}$ in) long, oval, with flat ends. As they mature they soften and sweeten.

## The plant

Elaeagnus do make handsome garden plants. Many have attractive evergreen foliage, sometimes variegated and sometimes silvery. Most have fragrant, fuchsia-like, tiny flowers. Some of the deciduous group are notable for their unusual appearance, like the silvery *E. angustifolia* with its attractive, edible, drupe-like fruits.

## Cultivation

The deciduous species will grow well in any ordinary soil so long as this is a little on the dry side. They are well able to resist drought. They cannot tolerate waterlogged or too moist root conditions. Sandy soils suit them, but if they are grown near the sea, give protection against strong winds blowing inland. Evergreen species appreciate shade or partial shade, most especially when they are growing in warmer climates. These kinds cannot tolerate either too arid or too humid conditions. In northern latitudes, although the plants are described as hardy, it is prudent to

Top left: Fruiting Figs *(L. Johns)*
Top right: Fuchsia flower and berry *(L. Johns)*
Bottom left: Feijoa blossom *(L. Johns)*
Bottom right: Feijoa fruit *(G. R. Roberts)*

Gooseberries *(G. R. Roberts)*

provide some protection for all kinds. The plants thrive best where they are planted in a warm border with other plants rather than in isolation. They should be protected from cold winds and can be grown against a warm or sunny wall.

The deciduous species should be planted in autumn and winter, the evergreens in spring or early autumn.

Propagation is by seeds sown in boxes of light soil in spring in a temperature of 13°C (55°F). Plants can also be layered in spring.

M. Yamaguchi 1979

## Culinary uses

Use as suggested for cranberries (q.v.), in tarts, pies, sauces, jams and jellies.

# GRAPE

*Vitis vinifera*

## Origin

This is one of the oldest plants in cultivation. *Vitis* is the ancient Latin name for the grape vine. It is applied to a genus of some 60–80 deciduous and evergreen shrubs, mainly of a climbing habit, supporting themselves by tendrils.

The plant is closely related to other climbers familiar to gardeners in sub-tropical regions and to those who grow house plants: ampelopsis, cissus, columella, parthenocissus and tetrastigma. At one time botanists included these in the same genus as vitis. They are now classified within their own genera.

The common grape vine, *Vitis vinifera*, which is hardy, is probably a native of Caucasian areas, but it is also found growing wild in western Asia, southern Europe and parts of northern Africa. It has produced certain varieties: *apiifolia*, the Parsley vine with divided and deeply lobed leaves, hence its name; *corinthiaca*, from which are produced the currants baked in cakes and are simply the little black grapes dried; *incana*, the downy Miller grape, sometimes called Dusty Miller; and *purpurea*, or Dyers grape, with leaves which become a deep purple red.

There are other vitis native to America. These include *V. aestivalis*, the Summer grape, the source of important cultivars; *V. labrusca*, the Fox grape, parent of several varieties of vine which produce fruits of a reddish-brown (foxy) or amber colour; *V. rotundifolia*, the Muscadine, with tough skin and a musky flavour; and *V. rupestris*, the Bush grape, a plant which is more a bush than a climber.

As with the rose, no one knows just how long the vine has been cultivated. It seems impossible to study any history of civilised man without finding reference to the vine. Records go back for centuries and as archaeology uncovers yet more evidence of past civilisations, so we learn a little more of the antiquity of the grape vine and the part it has played in civilisation. When wine was first made no one can tell, but there are Egyptian records of its production which date back 6,000 years, yet even though wine was important, the fruit itself was valued as a nutritious and refreshing food, particularly where the climate was hot and dry. The dried fruit – raisins – provided, and still do provide, good wholesome food. These are particularly important because they can be stored and used in winter.

Viticulture, the cultivation of the grape, probably began around the Caspian Sea, and from there, with the movement and the conquest of peoples, it became widely distributed. Roman colonists introduced the plants westwards into France and thence to Britain in about AD 10. Vineyards soon became established and these were maintained for centuries. After the Romans left Britain and gradually withdrew from France, these were maintained by the monasteries, but through the centuries, vineyards declined in number and acreage as the monasteries themselves declined. The fall of the Roman empire had its effect in many countries and on the cultivation and processing of the grape. During the Middle Ages viticulture again became widespread and has continued to grow from that time.

Although it is only of late years that vineyards have become established in Britain once more for the production of wine grapes, grapes under glass as a dessert fruit received a great boost with the introduction of heated glasshouses at the end of the eighteenth century. At one time, in large private gardens, the vinery range and the grape room where fruits were kept were important features. The Royal Horticultural Society *Dictionary of Gardening* describes some famous greenhouse vines such as the Black Hamburgh vine at Valentines, Ilford, Essex, which was planted in 1758 and flourished until well into the twentieth century. This plant was the parent of the famous Hampton Court vine, planted in 1769 and still bearing fruit which is sold to the public each year. Nowadays many a small garden boasts a little greenhouse and a vine, and many amateurs cultivate a 'vineyard'.

### The fruit

Botanically, a pulpy berry containing 2–4 usually pear-shaped seeds. Some cultivars, such as Sultana from Anatolia, are seedless. The size of the fruit and the colour of its skin vary considerably according to both species and variety.

The skin of the fruits is usually divided into 'black' and 'white', but actually skins can be a deep purple, sometimes a red–purple, sometimes blue like a sloe, pale green, apple green and green flushed with a purple tint. Some grapes seem to be smooth and even a little waxy, while others will be pruinose or bloomy, some having a much more distinctive coat of bloom than others so that they appear to be blue. Some grape skins can be very thick and tough, others fine and silky. The flesh is juicy and again varies with species and varieties, sometimes being firm enough to be cut and sometimes so loose as to be almost liquid. Such grapes are often difficult to peel.

The fruit bunches follow the shape of the inflorescence, becoming pyramidal, conical or even cylindrical. Some grapes have tightly packed bunches and others are looser, with the individual grapes on longer stems. Shape also differs, for some grapes are oval or egg-shaped, and some are round. There are a few exceptions. Fruits of *V. vinifera* can be oval or round, black with a blue bloom or amber coloured. *V. aestivalis* fruits are just 1 cm (⅓ in) wide, round, black and with a bloom, borne in elongated bunches. *V. labrusca*, in spite of giving rise to red and amber grapes, itself produces purple-black fruits, 2 cm (⅔ in) wide and with a musky flavour and only a faint bloom. Fruits of *V. rotundifolia* are large, up to 2.5 cm (1 in) in diameter, a dull purple with no bloom, a tough skin and a musky flavour, hence the name Muscadine. Almost round fruit is produced by *V. rupestris,* purple-black, 1.5 cm (½ in) wide and pleasantly flavoured.

### The plant

A vigorous deciduous climber, reaching some 15–25 m (50–80 ft) if allowed, according to species and variety. The plant is, however, amenable to severe pruning. It produces a long, thick, twisted trunk. Vines with trunks more than 60 cm (2 ft) in diameter have been known. Buds producing leaves and shoots are produced along its full length. Its palmate leaves, usually simple, lobed and toothed, grow alternately. The tendrils by which the vine supports itself as it climbs, by coiling them around any nearby support, grow opposite the leaves. The very small flowers, green and sweetly fragrant, grow in panicles or racemes opposite a leaf. Their little green petals are joined at the tips. When these fall they remain unseparated. Most vine leaves turn colour in autumn, some being much more spectacular than others.

### Cultivation outdoors

The grape vine thrives best in warm areas. On the other hand, its roots are hardy enough to withstand quite cold winters so long as the shoots, and consequently the buds, are not too exposed. If they become badly frosted the buds will be killed and the vine will not make new shoots early enough for its fruits to ripen. For this reason, in cold areas plants are sometimes trained against a warm and sunny wall, where if necessary extra protection can be provided, or grown in such a way outdoors that they can be covered with cloches or kept in cold greenhouses.

On the other hand, so many specialised cultivars have now been produced that grapes can be grown without special protection in the most unlikely parts of the world. We have seen many acres of grapes growing in Ontario, Canada, near Niagara-on-the-Lake, and without any special protection while fierce winds covered them with snow in temperatures way below zero. It is little known that Canada has a flourishing wine industry and produces some excellent and interesting wines. We have also stood in a vast vineyard in Griffith, NSW, in a temperature of 40°C (105°F) and eaten grapes from the vine, sun-warm, sweet and refreshing. The range and the quality of Australian wines is today too well known to warrant comment.

Obviously some varieties or species are hardier than others and some of the commercial types are not always available to the amateur grower unless he has special contacts. Modern French early maturing hybrids are proving excellent in many cold districts. It is important for the beginner amateur to consult a commercial grape grower or a reputable specialist nurseryman before selecting a variety for his own garden. Fortunately grape vines are self-fertile.

One other point we think should be stressed is that the proper cultivation of a grape vine is no pastime for the gardener who cannot or is not prepared to spend a considerable part of his time on his plants at certain seasons of the year. Daily attention is vital, for a grape vine makes an astonishing amount of growth each year and shoots must be pruned constantly if the fruits are to develop properly.

Obviously the selection of the correct site is important. This should be sunny. Ordinary soil is quite suitable, but it must be both fertile and well drained. Organic matter such as well-rotted farmyard manure or home-made compost should be dug in before planting to make sure that the soil will both drain well yet hold moisture, and towards the latter end it is also worthwhile to mulch vines heavily after they have been planted. Fertilisers rich in nitrogen should not be used, but doses of potash at intervals on established vines can only do good.

Vines are best planted in winter when they are dormant. After planting, the soil should be well firmed and the vine cut back to about 30 cm (12 in) from the ground. Most vines are sold in pots or canisters. Since their roots can so easily become damaged, it is sound practice to break the pot to extract them rather than risk injuring them.

The greatest factor in the success of viticulture lies in the correct training and pruning of the vine. The methods used will depend on how and where the vine is to be grown. It is possible, for instance, to grow a row of grape vines, just as one would grow a row of any fruit bushes. In this case, rows should run north and south, with 75 cm (2½ ft) between the rows. The plants can be trained as cordons, espaliers, fans and even bushes. Cordons can be as long as you wish, or as long as the vine will extend itself. The single stem which is the cordon is sometimes known as a 'rod'. There are many ways of accommodating a cordon, some of them quite attractive and interesting.

Where the grape vines are to be grown in rows, the pruning method most often recommended is the Guyot system, probably the simplest and most effective. The vine trunk is a short stump. Each year two shoots are grown upwards. In winter one is cut off to just over 1 m (4 ft), bent down and trained horizontally on the wire. The other is cut back to just two buds. This one will provide the new shoots for the following year and is not allowed to bear fruit. The other shoot is encouraged to produce fruit on all the shoots produced from its buds. During the summer these are kept under control and pruned back occasionally to about 15 cm (6 in) above each bunch of fruit. The following winter this fruiting stem, the longer bearer, is cut out at its base. The two new upright shoots are then treated in the same manner as above. There is no question that the best grapes are produced by the amateur who can spend time on his vines. Ideally they should be looked at carefully each day, because new buds are constantly appearing which will result in new shoots unless the buds are brushed off.

Pruning of old wood once growth has begun in the spring can sometimes lead to severe 'bleeding' which can weaken the plant.

Where one would like to grow a vine on a wall and there is little space, the plant can be kept to one main stem or cordon and then zig-zagged up the wall, covering it from one side to the other. The vine should be planted to one side or the other at the foot of the wall. The stem can first be taken along horizontally to the left or the right, then upwards for 30 cm (1 ft) or more and then trained horizontally in the opposite direction but parallel with the lower stem portion. Taken to the end of the wall the process is repeated until sufficient space of the wall has been covered. When the plant is not in leaf wide areas of the wall may appear to be bare, but once the vine shoots the whole surface will be covered. In a similar fashion, a grape vine can be trained to form an oval or a circle on a wall. The centre of the circle can be almost filled in as the shoots grow and are trained, or the outlines of the circle can be kept well defined. Some gardeners take a cordon right along a house wall from one end to the other at a suitable or convenient height, and when it reaches the end, instead of stopping the stem, they take it along another wall. Alternatively, they turn the cordon and take it back parallel with the first but at a higher or lower level.

Shoots grow from this main cordon stem, and these are usually thinned so that they grow singly 30 cm (12 in) or so apart. Each winter the shoots are cut back to one bud only.

The espalier is perhaps the most popular method of growing grape vines, and for this wires are necessary so that the stems can be supported. Usually only two or three tier espaliers are grown. The branches which are allowed to develop from the main stem begin about 30 cm (12 in) apart.

Fan shapes are suitable for training on wire or plastic trellis or on a wall. In this case, five to eight shoots are encouraged to grow from the short main stem in the manner of canes.

A bush vine is the simplest style, but unfortunately the untidiest and the least convenient when it comes to harvesting. This consists simply of cutting back the branches each year to about 2.5 cm (1 in) of the main stem.

Where two or more grapevines are grown together, the distances between them should be approximately 1 m (3 ft) for upright cordons, 1.3 m (4 ft) for horizontals, 2 m (6 ft) for espaliers and 2.6 m (8 ft) for fans.

In some districts of Ontario where the temperature can sometimes fall below −28°C (−20°F),

fan-training is recommended so that the plants can be given some degree of necessary protection. The trunk is kept well below the bottom wire. Each autumn the arms of the vines are unloosened from the wires and bent to the ground. They are then laid flat under the wire and covered with 8–10 cm (3–4 in) of soil. In the spring the vines are uncovered, three to five canes selected from the previous season's growth and tied to the wires. They are then cut so that some three to six buds are left. Every few years, as the arms become thick and difficult to bend safely, renew with a cane selected from or near the head of the trunk, thus establishing new arms from which to select the canes. In cold climates where the gardener hopes to raise dessert grapes from plants grown in the open, it is wise to use cloches. These need to be tall enough to allow some 60 cm (2 ft) of headroom. The vines can be cordons or similarly trained. Cloches are said to advance the ripening of the fruit by as much as 30–40 days in a good year, besides which larger fruits are produced. They need to be capable of being opened, or to have slots at the top so that the actual fruiting shoots can grow in the open while the fruit hanging from them is protected inside the cloches. Good varieties for this purpose to be grown in Europe include Muscat Hamburgh, Golden Chasselas, Chasselas Rose, White Frontignan and Chasselas 1921. The Chasselas grapes are extremely useful because they continue to hang ripe on the vines under the cloches for a long period, in northern climates sometimes extending the season for fresh grapes until Christmas.

In these climes the fruit usually begins to ripen in early autumn in a normal season. If the grapes are to be used for wine, they should be left to become very ripe, even remaining on the vines until well after the first frosts.

## Cultivation indoors

Many types of glassed structures will prove suitable for the cultivation of one or more grapevines. To save space and for cultivation purposes the vines are frequently grown in the open ground just outside the glasshouse and the main stem led through into the house. Some varieties do best in a heated greenhouse, but there are plenty which will grow well in a cold house. A

lean-to garden room, sun porch or similar structure will do so long as the vine is in the sun and so long as the roots can be grown in fertile soil. Vines can be grown in pots, but in this case the main stem or rod should not be allowed to exceed some 1.5 m (4–5 ft).

Time should be spent on preparing the soil which must be well drained as well as fertile. It should be kept in good condition with mulches of good organic matter at regular intervals.

If the vine is growing in a heated house, it is important that the air should not be allowed to become too dry. The atmosphere should be kept moist by spraying both the plants and the soil at least once a day.

Generally speaking, vines start into growth when the early spring temperature is raised to 7°C (45°F), from which time it should rise steadily to about 16°C (60°F) at the end of three weeks. The temperature should be kept down to about 18°C (65°F) on sunny days and at this time the house should always be well ventilated. Less ventilation is given at the end of the growing season, when the fruit has swollen and is ready to ripen. Increased warmth will hasten this process.

## Culinary uses

Wine, of course, must be the major subject for discussion when mentioning grapes, for to be strictly accurate wine can be made from nothing else. But before we reach this major topic, let us have a brief glance at the production of Grape Juice, a non-alcoholic drink much in evidence in some parts of the world but not in others.

It is simple to make. Use black grapes and pick them from their stems and place them in a saucepan, covering with cold water. Boil until they are split and you can see the seeds. Strain once or twice through a jelly bag so that the juice is quite clear. Measure the juice produced and to every 2 cups allow ½ cup of sugar. Boil the juice and sugar together for 20 minutes. Bottle the juice and keep it in a refrigerator. It can also be frozen or sterilised in bottles.

Red wine can be produced only from red or black grapes, whereas white wine can be made from any grapes. Depending on variety and location, it will normally take between 20–30 cups of grapes to make about 16 cups of fermented wine. If the climate is warm and the grapes have an opportunity to ripen well, they will need little if any sugar to ferment to a strength of 10–15 per cent of alcohol by volume, and if your attempt at wine-making is to be a serious one it will be helpful to have a hydrometer with which to measure the specific gravity and so obtain wine of the required strength. But even without it is possible to attain a fairly high alcohol figure by forcing the fermenting juice to produce more with the addition of sugar. Plastic, ceramic and glass vessels are recommended for all phases of winemaking. Enamel or stainless steel are the only metals which will not taint or flavour fermenting liquids.

To make a white wine, pick the grapes from the stems, discarding any that are mouldy, and crush or squeeze the juice from them by hand or by means of a press. If you have a hydrometer take a reading. The specific gravity will probably be between about 1050 and 1100, the lower figures demanding more sugar and the higher less, the quantities varying roughly from about ½ cup per 16 cups of juice to about 2½ cups, to obtain alcohol at about 15 per cent of volume, a reasonable figure to aim at. If you have no hydrometer it is simple enough to guess more or less the quantity of sugar required and to add about 1 cup at this early stage. Even if you are working to hydrometer figures it is wise to add up to a half of the sugar required at this stage and use the balance later.

It is now necessary to make up your mind whether to allow the wild yeasts on the skins of the grapes to carry out the fermentation process for you or whether to introduce additional yeast, perhaps of some specific type such as a chablis (dry) or a sauterne (sweet). It will give you greater control over the end product if you introduce some yeast and perhaps even some yeast nutrient to get it working well. To be on the safe side it is also helpful before the yeast is added to ensure that the must is pure by adding a sodium or potassium metabisulphite tablet, known in some countries as a Campden tablet.

It is probable that the fermentation will quickly be evident and that the activity will last only a day or two in the first place, a sign that more sugar is needed. Add another ½ cup at this stage and where necessary up to two more supplements of the same quantity as the days go by. When all the fermentation has finally ceased you can rack off the wine into clean jars and then finally into sterilised bottles and cork.

To make a red wine follow exactly the same process except that the grape skins are retained in the mash for about ten days to give the necessary colour. It is important that they be submerged in the liquid rather than floating on the top, so some means of holding them down must be devised. The best way is to make a cap or top which will slide up and down in your container without leaving too much at the sides yet being capable of moving easily. If necessary weight this down with some object that will not affect the fermenting juice. At the end of ten days or so remove the skins by straining, making sure that all the juice is extracted. Thereafter follow normal processes, remembering to rack the red wine finally into dark or opaque bottles to prevent it losing colour.

Grapes should always be fully ripe before they are cut. Test by tasting. The interest shown in the crop by birds is a good indication that maturity has been reached. Grapes can be left on the plant in a greenhouse, so long as the atmosphere is cool and dry. A little heat may be necessary sometimes to keep out the damp. Once they are picked it is not easy to keep ripe bunches in good condi-

tion for a long period. Some gardeners cut the bunches from the plant with a little of the main stem retained and keep this portion of the stem in plain water just as one might a flower. Grapes to be dried should be picked when fully ripe and dried in the sun.

All grapes, the dessert varieties or those grown for wine, are good to eat. The late maturing kinds can have very tough skins. These are highly nourishing fruits, fairly rich in vitamins, containing a really good percentage of carbohydrates in the form of glucose and fructose as well as many mineral salts. The white grapes are said to have more vitamin B than red or black. Grapes have both therapeutic and digestive properties, which no doubt is one reason why they are taken to invalids. Before serving, the whole bunch should be washed in cold water and drained. To help oneself, the little sub-bunches should be cut off with scissors rather than torn off, since this is sometimes apt to tear or break some of the berries and disfigure the bunch.

Some of us only meet grapes in a savoury dish when we sample Sole Véronique, yet they can be used to great advantage with certain meats. The white grapes, pipped and skinned, are used for this purpose. One of the easiest and most satisfying ways is to incorporate the grapes in a sauce which has been made by deglazing a pan after roasting or frying the meat. The grapes need not always be cooked, merely heated. Often nuts, usually almonds, are added to the sauce. The great thing about these grapes is that their texture and taste offer such a pleasant contrast to a rich dish. They make a good sauce, just as cherries do, to serve with tongue. They go well with duck, partridge, pheasant, quail and game generally. They are excellent with liver dishes, especially chicken livers. They are good served with rich, cold pâté.

To complete a meal few things are better than cheese with grapes – indeed, with a good loaf these two can make a meal. Grapes go with cheeses of all kinds, and are particularly good in salads with cream cheese. You can quickly make an excellent salad dressing by halving pipped and peeled grapes and stirring them into seasoned yoghurt. Mint goes well with grapes and so does lemon balm. Either or both of these, freshly chopped, suit this type of dressing. It is a theme capable of limitless variations.

Grapes can be used in savoury aspic moulds or salads, often lemon-flavoured, alone or combined with asparagus, celery or segments of really fresh and nutty cauliflower. If you want to make a beautiful aspic salad, spend a little time making a pattern from grapes and slices of Chinese gooseberry. Turn the mould out on a bed of lettuce leaves and use contrasting cream cheese for a little decoration, but don't overdo it.

As one might expect, grapes, or rather their juice, make an excellent dessert table jelly into which one can always incoporate a few of the fruits for interest or decoration.

Grapes can be used as an ornament on many desserts which need not necessarily be made from grape juice or the grapes themselves. They are attractive in fruit salads. The peeled green grapes make an excellent brulée. They look and taste delightful made into flans, large and little tarts and glazed. They can be made into pies. The grape thinnings can be used this way also, but may need a little more sugar.

PRESERVING   Like most other fruits, grapes can be used for jams and jellies. The latter can be herb-flavoured and spiced; use 4 cups of juice to 1 cup of apple juice. Cheeses, preserves, conserves and pickles can also be made. Black grapes are usually best because their skins give such a good colour.

To make Glacé Grapes, have ready small bunches, twos or threes of green grapes each tied to a thread. Make a syrup of:

### Glacé grape syrup

¾ cup golden or corn syrup
1 cup Demerara sugar
¼ cup unsalted butter

Boil until when tested in water the syrup hardens. Take from the heat. While the mixture cools, lower the grapes into the syrup so that they are quite coated. Hang the thread on a string so that the grapes are suspended and allow them to dry. Store between waxed paper in an airtight container in the refrigerator. To serve at the end of a meal, arrange the bunches on grape leaves.

For Frosted Grapes use only thin-skinned kinds. Wash and dry. Dip the grapes into egg white and then dust them thickly with caster sugar, shaking off the surplus.

Lay the grapes to dry on paper dusted with the sugar.

FREEZING   Black and green grapes freeze well, so well in fact that they can be used as fresh grapes once they have thawed. Wash them and drain them so that they are dry and then detach them carefully from their stems. Put into bags or other containers. Grapes can also be peeled and pipped ready for use before they are frozen. They can be frozen in a syrup pack and grape purée can be frozen. When grape juice is frozen, tartrate crystals may form, but these can be removed on thawing by straining the juice.

BOTTLING   Skinned grapes can be bottled in a syrup. Grape juice should be poured into jars and boiled for 10 minutes.

# GRAPEFRUIT
*Citrus paradisi, C. grandis, C. maxima uvacarpa*

## Origin

Confused. Botanists disagree, and what makes the subject even more difficult for the layman is that *Citrus maxima,* with the synonyms *C. decumana* and *C. grandis,* is known both as Pummelo and Shaddock, while *C. paradisi* is known by a similar sounding popular name, Pomelo. Actually there exists very little difference between the two species and we get a clue to one of the causes for the confusion when we read that the Pummelo was taken to the West Indies by a Captain Shaddock.

*C. paradisi* is believed to have originated in East Asia, while *C. grandis* or *C. maxima* is thought to have come from Polynesia. However, *C. paradisi* is believed by some authorities to have appeared in the West Indies as a sport or as a hybrid. It was given species recognition in 1830. Although grown locally in certain countries for years, commercial cultivation of the grapefruit did not begin on a large scale until 1880 and this was in Florida. The story is that the fruit was introduced into Florida by the chief surgeon in Napoleon's army. He was captured at Trafalgar in 1805 and sent as a prisoner to the Bahamas, where the grapefruit and other citrus grew abundantly about him. When he was freed two years later, he journeyed to Charleston, South Carolina, and there he practised medicine, but not apparently without dreaming of the delights of the islands where he had been forced to stay. Some time about 1823 he moved to Florida and established a citrus plantation, propagating seeds he had brought or was sent from the Bahamas.

Some 60 years passed before the fruits began to be grown to any important extent in other regions, Arizona, southern Texas and California. However, by 1895 the grapefruit was considered of sufficient importance to be considered as a commercial crop and came to be cultivated on a grand scale. In 1914 it was introduced into Palestine.

It grows in tropical or sub-tropical regions, wherever there is no fear of frost, which means that altitude must be taken into consideration. Many other countries about the globe now have important grapefruit-producing areas. These include, the West Indies, central America, Brazil, South Africa, Israel, Greece and Spain.

Meanwhile, the fruit is being grown more and more in gardens in suitable climates. Occasionally *C. maxima* can be found growing wild in Mediterranean regions.

## The fruit

Botanically, a globose berry known as a hesperidium. If the prefix 'grape' puzzles you, as well it might, you will be interested to learn that this is a reference to the manner in which the fruits grow naturally on the tree, in great clusters similar in shape to a very large bunch of yellow grapes. It is only fair to say, however, that this explanation appears to astonish every authority or expert to whom we have put it as much as it astonished us when first we heard it. However, no other explanation has been forthcoming.

As one would expect with a fruit so widely cultivated, there are now greater differences between species and varieties. *C. paradisi* has fruits which are almost globose, although sometimes they may be flattened at the top and base. They are thin-skinned, yellow and have very juicy flesh divided like most citrus fruits into segments.

The fruit of *C. maxima* is 10–15 cm (4–6 in) across, somewhat pear-shaped, with a smooth and pale yellow rind which is very thick and covers a firm pulp. Most grapefruit have a very pale yellow flesh, although the thickness of the skin differs from one variety to another. It appears that the name Shaddock was given originally to those fruits produced by *C. maxima,* which have a pinkish flesh, and Pummelo to those which were extra pear-shaped, though not necessarily with pink flesh. Grapefruit grown in Texas is likely to have a pink-tinted flesh. Some varieties of grapefruit are seedless.

## The plant

*C. maxima* grows into a tree of about 5.5 m (18 ft), evergreen, symmetrical, with a rounded head. There are sometimes spines, and when these appear they are flexible, slender and blunt. The large oval leaves, 8–15 cm (3–6 in) long, are glossy green, downy on the underside, with broadly winged stalks. The flowers are white, large 2–4 cm (¾–1½ in) long, fragrant and may be either solitary or clustered in the leaf axils. When young the plant is very sensitive to the cold, but appears to be less so as it matures.

*C. paradisi* is much like *maxima* but it has more slender shoots, which are almost glabrous.

## Cultivation

See the section on Orange.

## Culinary uses

This is a good food fruit, rich in vitamins and mineral salts. The inner skin of the grapefruit is one source of quinine, so no wonder there is sometimes a bitter, though not necessarily unpleasant, taste.

Thin-skinned fruits are usually the best value since they contain more juice than the thick-skinned varities. Even so, this thick skin is well worth candying and the resulting sweetmeat is much better than that made from most other citrus fruits. Russet marks on the skin usually denote extra juiciness and flavour. The pink-fleshed grapefruits have less of the characteristic flavour than the white-fleshed fruits.

Grapefruits, or their juice, are popular breakfast dishes. Sometimes one of these two is served as a first course at lunch or dinner. One friend of ours says that her heart sinks when she goes to a house for a meal and catches a glimpse of the table laid ready with the first course at each place, a halved grapefruit. She claims that this unimaginative approach gives warning of a dull meal to come – and she may be right. Wholesome as the plain fruits and juices are, there can be other ways of serving them and the imaginative cook should be able to invent other dishes to add to these. Some people keep the idea of the grapefruit halved for a first course, but dress up the fruit by sprinkling the cut surface with brown sugar, sometimes also a sprinkling of port, and grilling the fruits until they are glazed. They are then served.

Keep a peeled grapefruit in the refrigerator so that it is always ready to add to a salad. Peeled, the pith and fibres when dry can easily be detached from the segments. Grapefruit is particularly good with shredded cabbage, the juice of the one complementing the nutty texture of the other. Raisins, dates, cream cheeses and yoghurt combine with these two very well.

Grapefruit can be blended with cream cheese or yoghurt to make a refreshing salad cream dressing. Depending on with what type of meat, cheese or fish the salad is to be served, we like to add some fresh chopped herbs – fennel, tarragon or sage, for instance – with fish, poultry or pork, or chives with cheese. Finely chopped celery, walnuts or radish can also be added. For a more piquant dressing, add a little mustard, a shallot finely chopped, a little olive oil or some other oil and a little honey for those with a sweet tooth. Chopped preserved kumquats are delicious with grapefruit.

For a fuller first course than the plain halves, but refreshing all the same, serve Grapefruit Prawns. First halve and take the pulp from the fruit, allowing a half grapefruit per person. For four, finely dice 1–2 apples, 1–2 dill pickles or the equivalent of diced fresh cucumber depending on personal tastes; 1 tablespoon tomato sauce beaten into 2 tablespoons mayonnaise, yoghurt or cream; seasoning and prawns. Reserve a few prawns for a garnish along with a little chopped parsley, chervil or fennel, whichever you like most. Halve or make smaller the segments. Blend the tomato sauce with the mayonnaise or alternatives, add the grapefruit, cucumber and apples. Mix in the prawns, halved or chopped smaller. Divide the mixture among the grapefruit shells. Garnish, chill slightly and serve.

For another starter, try Spinach Florida. You need 4 grapefruit shells, but the flesh from one grapefruit only, ¼ cup butter, 2 cups cooked spinach, well chopped. Melt the butter, stir in the spinach, mix in the grapefruit. Put into the fruit shells placed ready on a baking sheet or dish, top with a very little cream, heat in the oven and serve.

Soufflé made with some grapefruit juice also can be packed in the shells and served straight from the oven.

Apart from using the juice and segments in a fruit salad, for a delicious dessert first skin the grapefruit segments. Float them in a little heavy syrup, garnish with bright pomegranate seeds and serve with vanilla ice-cream.

Grapefruit makes an excellent table jelly into which the fruit segments should be blended. Use 4 tablespoons each of orange and lemon juice and water to 1½ cups grapefruit juice, and sweeten to taste.

PRESERVING Grapefruit can be used alone for marmalade or mixed with oranges and/or lemons in a two- or three-fruit conserve.

Candied Grapefruit Peel, a sweetmeat, may also be coated in chocolate. Use:

### Candied grapefruit peel

*2 grapefruit, peel only*
*1¼ cups sugar*
*¼ cup honey*
*1 cup boiling water*
*water for preliminary boiling*

Wash the grapefruit peel and cut it into narrow strips as uniform as possible. Put into a saucepan and cover with cold water, boil for 10 minutes and then drain. Repeat this operation, this time cooking the peel until it is tender, which may take longer than 10 minutes. Drain. In a heavy saucepan, combine the sugar, honey and boiling water. Stir well, bring to the boil and boil for 1 minute. Add the cooked peel to the syrup, bring to the boil and then simmer very slowly until most of the syrup has been absorbed, which may take an hour. Lift each piece of peel from the syrup with a skewer and lay it on a sieve to drain and dry. Put a large dish under the sieve to catch the drips. These can be scraped off later. The drying process may take 24 hours or longer. When the peel seems dry on the surface it can either be rolled in caster sugar to coat it, or it can be dipped in melted chocolate, in which case it should be placed on waxed paper and allowed to dry again. To store the sweetmeats, pack them between waxed paper and store in a covered container in a refrigerator. Save the remainder of the syrup. It can be used in the base of little oven dishes to make a flavoured creme caramel, or it can be used to glaze a baked ham. It keeps for weeks in a refrigerator.

FREEZING  To freeze grapefruit, peel and divide into segments, removing all pith and as much skin as possible. Use a dry sugar pack or a medium or heavy syrup pack, according to taste and convenience. If the juice alone is to be frozen, take care that as the fruit is squeezed the oil is not pressed out from the peel. It is best to remove this first. Sweeten with 2 tablespoons of sugar to 4 cups of juice. Add a scant $\frac{1}{4}$ teaspoon of ascorbic acid to every 4 cups of juice.

BOTTLING  To bottle, the segments should first be peeled, packed into jars and covered with a syrup, according to taste.

# GUAVA
*Psidium* species

## Origin

Related to the fragrant myrtle and in the same family as the eucalyptus, psidium is a genus of deciduous and evergreen trees and shrubs native to tropical and sub-tropical America. The best known of the fruits is probably *P. guajava,* which grows naturally from the West Indies to Peru. It was brought back to Europe by the conquering Spaniards. It has now become established in most tropical and sub-tropical regions of the world. It has become the raw product of an important fruit juice trade and is used in many forms of preserves. It is grown on a small scale in Florida and California.

This particular species appears to be more variable than the others. It has varieties: *aromaticum, pomiferum* and *pyriferum,* which, incidentally, is known in France as the guava pear and is there highly appreciated and said to be the best of all. There are also many named cultivars such as Patnagola and Parker's White. At the moment there is research being carried out into selected plants in Hawaii, Australia and other countries, where it is hoped to raise the commercial status of the fruit.

The Purple or Strawberry guava, *P. cattleianum,* native to Brazil, has a variety, *P. c. lucidum,* sometimes called the Yellow guava, a popular garden shrub in many regions. A nearly related species, but with leaves which are narrower towards the base, and differently shaped fruit, is *P. littorale. P. friedrichsthalianum,* the Cos or Costa Rica guava, is sometimes called *P. laurifolium.*

## The fruit

Botanically, a berry, which may be white, yellow, green, purple or red according to species and variety. All fruits are highly scented, some very musky and in number overpowering. They may be globose, ovoid or pear-shaped. Some resemble a lemon as they grow, being first green and then becoming yellow. Some are crowned with the remains of the calyx, which gives the fruit a similarity to a pomegranate. The pulpy flesh, which contains many hard, kidney-shaped seeds, varies from white to yellow and from pink to red-purple. The skins may be smooth and waxy or slightly ridged. Most have very thin, even papery skins which are not easily separated from the flesh. The fruit ripens over a long period.

*P. guajava* bears a white or yellow globose fruit which may be 2.5–10 cm (1–4 in) in depth. The fruits have a musky aroma. The outer wall is naturally thick, but some of the newer varieties are thin-walled. The pulpy flesh is sweet-acid. The fruits of the variety *P. g. aromaticum* are the size of a cherry. Those of *P. g. pomiferum* are round and resemble small apples with green skins and a firm, pleasantly acid flesh. These are excellent for conserves. *P. g. pyriferum* is pear-shaped, sulphur yellow with pink flesh and about the size of an egg.

*P. cattleianum,* the Strawberry or Cherry guava, has round fruit 2.5–4 cm (1–1½ in) in diameter, deep wine-red, with a very thin skin. The perfumed flesh under the skin is tinged with the same red-purple, becoming paler until at the entre it is white. The flesh is juicy and has a similar texture and flavour to a strawberry, hence the popular name. Many people believe this to be the finest flavoured guava. The variety *P. c. ucidum* has sulphur-yellow fruits, larger than those of the species, which are highly aromatic.

Fruits of the Costa Rica guava are small and acid but are highly esteemed by those who use them to make jelly and other preserves.

## The plant

*P. guajava* is a small, branching, deciduous tree, which grows 2–5 m (6–15 ft) and has 4-angled branches. Its bark tends to peel in longitudinal strips. The leaves are handsome, oval or oblong, hairy on the underside. The flowers, fragrant, white, numerous and attractively downy, bloom in summer. Varieties differ in small ways.

*P. cattleianum* is a compact, evergreen shrub of some 3–6 m (10–20 ft) in height, with smooth, rounded branches. Its leaves are smooth, glossy, leathery and about 5–8 cm (2–3 in) long. The white flowers, borne close to the stems, bloom in late spring, but sometimes the tree blooms a second time in late autumn.

*P. friedrichsthalianum* grows into a tall tree, in time as high as 8 m (25 ft). Its branches are also 4-angled, the bark dark. The long oval to oblong leaves, 4–8 cm (1½–3 in) long, tapering to prettily pointed tips, are smooth and glossy, deep green on the surface, downy on the underside. The solitary white flowers appear in the axils of the young branches.

The urban gardener will soon appreciate that an evergreen flower- and fruit-bearing plant which will flourish in a container is bound to have some ornamental value, if for no other purpose than that of a patio plant. The guava can also be trained as an espalier, which means that it can be used in various ways. Other means of training can be tried by the enthusiastic and experimental gardener.

## Cultivation

Any kind of soil is suitable so long as it is well drained. The plant fruits best when grown as a bush. Guavas are suitable for screens, when they can be planted 2 m (6 ft) apart.

Perhaps one of the most important reasons for the guava's popularity away from its homelands is its ability to tolerate extremes of climate. Indeed, it is said that where it is subjected to extremes of temperature its fruit is of a finer flavour. However, the plant cannot stand low temperatures for long and is susceptible to frosts. In regions where there is high humidity the fruit is likely to develop an insipid flavour, yet when grown indoors humidity is of some importance. As a guide to climatic requirements, it is interesting to note that *P. cattleianum* thrives out of doors on the Cote d'Azur, where its blooms open in May and its fruits ripen in November.

In cold climates guavas have to be grown indoors. Fortunately, this is a plant that responds to container cultivation, and has been grown this way for many centuries in Europe. Obviously, once contained, plants can be moved outdoors, should this be convenient, when the weather is suitable. Contained plants can also be grown outdoors permanently where the climate allows. On the other hand, it is a neat tree or shrub for the small garden where space can be found in the open ground.

To grow plants indoors really warm conditions are necessary. They can be kept bush-like and trimmed to shape, or the branches can be trained to the walls as peaches are. It is possible to use the wall of a vinery for this purpose. Here they can be grown also in beds as well as in large pots or other types of container. In either case it is important that drainage is perfect. Old potting soil recipes give two parts fibrous sandy loam, and one part of equal proportions of dry cow manure, leafmould and silver sand.

The plants reach the peak growth during summer and rest during the winter. From mid-spring to early autumn, or at any time when it is obvious that growth has begun again, the plants should be watered freely. This applies whether the containers stand outdoors or under glass. After this hold back gradually until the plants are receiving only moderate amounts of water. From spring onwards until the fruit begins to ripen, spray freely. Once the fruit ripens, keep the foliage dry. When the berries form the plants can be fed with weak liquid fertiliser until the fruit ripens.

Repotting is best carried out in early spring. If necessary, and if you wish to keep it in the same size container, the roots can be pruned at this time also. Contained plants can be pruned into shape in early spring or late winter. It is suggested that a pot plant is best pruned into a goblet shape, using three or four good branches and removing the remainder. Suckers which spring up at soil level should be removed.

Propagation can be carried out in various ways. Seed is taken from a ripe fruit. It tends to come true to parent types and will fruit in about three years. It can be sown in a moist compost, and in cold climates kept in a warm place. Once germination takes place water with care. If the guava is to be grown outdoors, plant out the seedlings before rainy seasons, if these can be determined.

Root cuttings, of about 15 cm (6 in) in length, are recommended by one authority. These can be grown in pots and kept contained, or planted outdoors as desired. This method, like cuttings, is advised where you wish to propagate a specific guava. Cuttings taken of shoots which are just becoming firm at the base may be placed in sand and grown under enclosed conditions. Outdoors, plants can be propagated from suckers from good varieties.

## Culinary uses

The guava is reputed to be richer in vitamin C than the orange. The fruit can be eaten raw – just cut it in half and remove the flesh from the skin.

Although sugar is usually added to cooked guava to sweeten the fruit, honey can be used and is very pleasant, one flavour seeming to suit the other very well. To make a compote, halve the fruits, cook them in a little water until they are tender and then sweeten to taste. Simmer a little longer and allow to cool. From this point guava sauce is made by sieving or electrically blending the cooked fruit. This purée can be used for a variety of desserts.

Guavas need not be limited to sweet dishes. Stuffed with cream cheese they are good with a green salad.

PRESERVING  Guava jelly is rightly held in high esteem. It is excellent eaten with any of the blue cheeses, especially Roquefort and Stilton. After making jelly the pulp can be used to make a guava cheese.

### Guava jelly

*6–8 cups whole fruit*
*8 cups sugar*
*juice of 1 lemon*

Peel the guavas and remove the seeds. Cover skins and seeds with water and boil. Cut the remainder of the fruit into small pieces, add a little water and boil until soft. Add the sugar allowing 2 cups of sugar to every 2 cups of fruit. Strain the liquid from the seeds and skins and add to the fruit and sugar, then boil until it jells. Add lemon juice.

BOTTLING  Guavas are best halved and bottled in syrup.

# HOG PLUM
*Spondias* species

## Origin

A small genus of tropical trees, probably not more than twelve, in the family Anacardiaceae, to which the mango also belongs, most of which are indigenous to the West Indies. Their fruits, known generally and, so it seems, collectively as Hog plums, are produced by most of the species and are eaten. Some are said to be superior to others.

The name of the genus is derived from an ancient Greek word for plum, which the fruit much resembles, though not in any way related to the plum or the prunus family. Some of the species are now fairly widely distributed in tropical countries, where they are quite common and are known by local names, making identification difficult. Probably the best known is *Spondias dulcis,* a native of Polynesia, known as the Sweet or Otaheite apple, widely cultivated in the tropical lowlands. It has the synonym *S. cytherea* as well as many common names such as Ambarella, Vi apple and Hog apple, the last in place of Hog plum used for the other species. Perhaps this is because the fruit of this particular species is not plum-like, being fairly large, with a russetty skin. The flesh of the fruit also has an apple-like flavour when fresh.

*Spondias lutea,* sometimes known as *S. mombin,* the Yellow mombin, the Golden apple, the

Jamaica or Hog plum, is a native of tropical America. Another species, *S. pinnata,* the Malayan mombin, is widely cultivated in Indo-Malaysia, and can be seen heaped high on the fruit stalls there. Another, which is much favoured, is Imbu, *S. tuberosa,* which does not appear to be well known outside its own locality although it is listed among those species which might be worth cultivating as a commercial crop in Australia. *S. purpurea,* another American species, sometimes called the Purple, Red or Spanish mombin, does not grow quite as tall as the other species.

## The fruit

The fruits of *S. dulcis* are golden yellow, with a thin russet skin on the sunny side, some 5–8 cm (2–3 in) long. They have a firm, yellow flesh with a flavour much resembling that of a pineapple, surrounding a large seed similar to that of a mango.

*S. lutea* has fruits which vary from yellow to deep red, ovoid, some 5 cm (2 in) long, with a sweet acid taste and an aromatic flavour. The flesh is firm, though not so plentiful as the above, and the fruit is generally considered to be inferior to that of *S. dulcis.*

*S. pinnate* has yellow, ovoid fruits, 4–5 cm (1½–2 in) long, which ripen on the tree after the leaves have fallen. These have an excellent flavour, even though the flesh is thin.

The fruits of *S. purpurea* are strangely shaped when young, following the outline of the knobbly seeds they cover. Later the fruits become rounded but retain an oddly shaped 'lip' which covers the protruding apex of the large seed. The skin is deep red sometimes tinged with purple, firm, glossy and tough. The fruits are some 4 cm (1½ in) long. The flesh is slightly more acid than the others mentioned; it is plum-like, bright yellow and juicy, delicious when cooked.

The fruits of *S. tuberosa* resemble a greengage, but with a thick skin.

## The plant

The Jamaica plum tree, *S. lutea,* grows to a height of 9 m (30 ft) in the open ground under favourable conditions. It has attractive compound leaves. The pale yellow flowers, growing in graceful panicles which are often longer than the leaves, bloom in summer. Thorn-like outgrowths are produced on the bark of the tree.

*S. dulcis* grows even larger, up to 15 m (50 ft), yet this is the species most often grown in greenhouse borders. It also has compound leaves 5.5–13 cm (2–5 in) long, 1.5–5 cm (⅝–2 in) wide, in 4–12 leaflets. These give off a resinous smell when bruised. The flowers, which grow in spreading panicles, are green-yellow. They bloom in early summer.

*S. pinnata* is a much smaller tree, 3–4 m (10–12 ft). As its name suggests, it has attractive pinnate leaves. *S. purpurea* grows to 9 m (30 ft). It also has compound leaves, the leaflets usually toothed and blunt. The flowers are produced in much shorter clusters and in smaller numbers in each raceme, which are much shorter than the leaves. They are yellow, like the fruit sometimes tinged with purple, and they bloom in summer.

## Cultivation

Outdoors, the plants need a well-drained, friable

soil, and where frosts do occur, a sheltered site. A minimum winter temperature of about 13°C (55°F) is required for these plants where it is not possible to grow them out of doors. They do well in conservatories, especially those which are lofty enough to allow the tree to grow to a good size.

The plants can be easily raised from seed. They may also be raised from cuttings, which is most likely to be the only way one can acquire a stock, unless some enterprising nurseryman has set up business in your area. Take half-ripened shoots and root them in enclosed conditions.

### Culinary uses

This is a pleasantly flavoured fruit which can be eaten raw. Try it peeled, halved and marinated for a while in its own juice and brown sugar. Serve with cream and a little rum or liqueur.

It makes good jams and can be pickled.

# ILAMA
*Annona diversifolia*

### Origin

This species resembles the cherimoya (q.v.). It differs in its choice of environment, the cherimoya growing well up to altitudes of 1,800 m (6,000 ft), while this species grows in the lowlands. It is a much favoured plant in central America and Mexico.

### The fruit

Like the cherimoya, it is conical, ovoid or round, with a rough, sculpted surface. Generally it is much larger, sometimes weighing as much as .675 kg (1½ lb). It lives up to its specific name by being diverse in more than foliage and in fruit colour, for it can vary from the soft pale green of the sour sop to a deep magenta pink. Like some of the other species, the surface of the fruits is covered with a heavy white bloom. The flesh varies with fruit variation. In green fruits the flesh is sweet and white, in pink fruits it is more acid and pink. There are as many seeds in the ilama as there are in the cherimoya, but they are larger and easily removed.

### The plant

When grown naturally it follows form and still is diverse, being tall, slender and erect, or bushy and spreading.

### Cultivation

See the section on Cherimoya.

### Culinary uses

Use for desserts of many kinds, for layer cakes and trifles, ice-cream, drinks, jellies and other preserves.

# INDIAN FIG
*Opuntia* and other cactus species

### Origin

We are concerned here mainly with *Opuntia* species, for an entire book would be required to describe the multitude of other cactus species. However, we should point out that the fruits of species and varieties of cacti, both in the wild and when under cultivation, are edible. A few notable kinds are listed under Pitaya (q.v.), including Strawberry pear. Some people claim that they are the most delicious of all fruits.

The cactus family is almost entirely restricted to the Americas, but its members have spread through importation to almost all parts of the world. The so-called Indian fig (American Indian, incidentally), *O. ficus-indica,* comes possibly from tropical South America where it is held in high esteem. It is believed to have been brought back to Europe by Christopher Columbus. It is now so widespread in the Mediterranean and other temperate regions that it is considered a native plant there. It is often used as a dense hedge against wandering animals. It was introduced into California by Franciscan monks and it is now abundant in that region, especially around old missions.

It is likely that it, and other opuntias including *O. vulgaris,* was originally much more widely cultivated for its fruits than it is today, when the interchange of so many kinds of fruits between countries is so great. However, in a number of countries – India, Italy, Malta and Sicily, to name just a few – the plant is cultivated in small-holdings and gardens alike. The fruit is often to be seen on sale in Mediterranean countries and less frequently in large centres in major cities throughout the world.

One unhappy aspect of opuntia cultivation was experienced in Australia, where plants were grown not for their fruits but to farm an insect, to which the plants are host. In the early days of settlement opuntia was introduced in order to nurture the cochineal insect from which was produced the red dye needed for military uniforms. By the 1920s the opuntia, the prickly pear, had become one of Australia's greatest problems and it was finally brought under control only by importing another predator, a moth, which fortunately did not become a problem itself. Some species of opuntia are now banned from Australia. Elsewhere it seems to have been kept under control well enough by climatic and other factors. In some countries at certain times it has been cultivated for food.

## The fruit

Botanically a berry, the fruit differs in size considerably according to species and variety. Some cactus berries are very tiny and are produced in a ring or garland around the top of the plant body, mixed with open flowers and buds. The fruits of the opuntia under discussion, O. ficus-indica, can be very large, about 6–8 cm (2½–3 in) long, and of O. vulgaris, about 4 cm (1½ in). They vary in colour from yellow to orange, from brick red to purple. The pulp or flesh is very sweet. Some flesh is white, some tinged with pink, some yellow, some orange, some red, again according to plant. Usually the flesh encloses seeds, large seeds in the opuntias, but there are fruits, possibly of cultivars which are seedless. The seeds are edible.

## The plant

Indian figs or prickly pears are distinguished by their spiny, leafless pads or flattened joints, oblong, egg-shaped or spoon-shaped. These can be small or very large, as much as 60 cm (2 ft) or more in length. Sometimes the young pads are covered with a fine, white bloom, sometimes with tufts of 'wool' and tufts of yellow bristles or glochids. Great care should be taken when handling the plant without gloves, in case any of these glochids penetrate the skin, for being barbed they are difficult to extract. One method we have found effective is to lay a sticking plaster or piece of transparent tape over the affected spot; when this is peeled off the glochid will usually come away with it.

The flowers of these cacti, as with most others, are most beautiful. Those of O. ficus-indica are yellow and can be 8–10 cm (3–4 in) across. Those of O. vulgaris are golden yellow and smaller.

The flowers and subsequently the fruits are produced on the margins of the joints. The plants grow erect and can be tree-like, sometimes reaching 4 m (12 ft), with thick trunks and heavy branches.

## Cultivation

All cacti have a great tolerance for dry conditions. They will withstand both long periods of drought and high temperatures. Their plant bodies are constructed to act as reservoirs. They must have a well-drained soil and plenty of sunshine. Often they can be grown on stony soil and rocks. They call for little cultivation, but will not tolerate wet, moist or shady situations.

Opuntias grow so well under some conditions that they may need supporting or staking, not always an easy task. Where there are prevailing strong winds, the best thing is to grow the plant in the lee of a wall or fence.

Propagation is simple. Simply break off a mature pad, or a portion of plant. Insert this so that 2 cm (1 in) or so of the base is under the surface of a sandy soil, in a pot or in the open according to climate. If the pad is large, support it by pushing in a cane on each side of it. These opuntias can be grown in a greenhouse, but they can occupy a great deal of space in time. They should be grown in special cactus soil in a large, heavy pot, or in a border. They should not be grown in a greenhouse that must be kept humid for other plants.

## Culinary uses

The best way to prepare this fruit is to wash it, making sure that the spines are removed in the process. A stiff brush will do the trick. Cut a slice from top and base, slit downwards, peel off the skin and slice.

The raw fruit is succulent and with a sweet aroma. One of the best ways to serve it is simply sliced and accompanied with fresh lime or lemon to squeeze on it as one sometimes does with melon. It goes well with cream.

The fruit can be used as a compote, but the disadvantage of this is that the seeds become hard and unpalatable.

Made into a purée and sieved, the fruit can be served with ice-cream or used in various desserts.

PRESERVING  The pulp of the fruit can be made into jam or, with the addition of citrus juice and peel, into marmalade. As a rough guide, use:

### Indian fig marmalade

2 cups fig pulp
½ cup orange juice
1 tabsp lemon juice
1 cup sugar

If the orange peel is used, treat it as julienne first. Alternatively, candied peel is good in this.

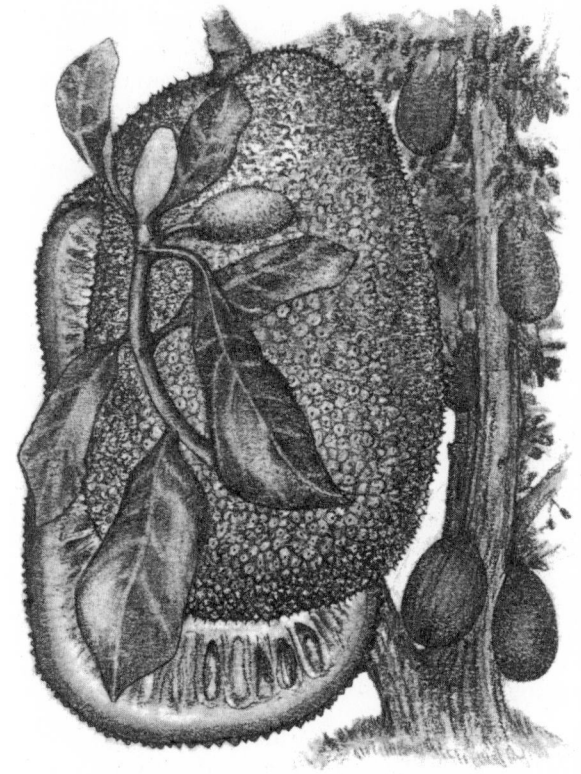

# JACKFRUIT
*Artocarpus integrifolia*

## Origin

A native of the mountainous districts of India and the Malayan archipelago, now widely cultivated throughout the tropical lowlands of the world in Asia, Africa and America. It is being grown experimentally in Australia. In Ceylon a small type known as the African breadfruit is cultivated for its seeds, which are ground into a meal and used in the preparation of various dishes. Several distinct forms are recognised, two especially: a soft-skinned and a firm-fruited kind, the latter most popular in Asiatic countries.

*Artocarpus integer*, the cempedak or champedak, has fruits which resemble Jackfruits, but are smaller and have a stronger odour.

## The fruit

These are very large, barrel-shaped. Some fruits weigh as much as 22–23 kg (50 lb) and are 1 m (3 ft) long. The skin is rough, with hard, pointed studs all over the surface, brown-yellow in col-

our. The flesh is soft and juicy and contains large white seeds. It has a pungent odour. The fruit takes from 6–8 months to ripen. Fruit of the type is oblong to oval, about 45 cm (18 in) long, but the shape and size vary from tree to tree.

## The plant

This makes a large, handsome, striking tree, some 20 m (65 ft) tall at maturity, bearing deep green leathery leaves, often grown for ornamental purposes. The flowers are monoecius and catkin-like.

## Cultivation

The jackfruit will grow in most soil types, but does best where these are deep and well drained. It must have hot and humid conditions the year round. Very little attention is required once the plant becomes established.

## Culinary uses

The fruit may be eaten raw. Simply remove the

Lemon Guava *(Thompson & Morgan)*

Top left: Indian Fig *(L. Johns)*
Top right: Various shaped Limes *(L. Johns)*
Bottom: Ogen and Galia Melons *(L. Johns)*

skin and serve the pulp. The seeds are embedded in the rind. However, not everyone finds the fresh fruit palatable, particularly those who are accustomed to European foods.

The flesh is often cooked in oil and served in or with a curry. It may also be preserved or dried. The seeds can be roasted like chestnuts.

Cempedak or champedak has smaller seeds than the jackfruit. It is often coated with batter and deep fried in oil and sold at banana fritter stalls in street bazaars in Singapore and Penang.

# JAMBOS
*Eugenia* species

## Origin

A member of the fragrant myrtle family, one species, *Eugenia uniflora,* is sometimes called the fruiting myrtle. This genus was named in honour of Prince Eugene of Savoy (1663–1736), who took a keen interest in botany. Perhaps the best-known member of this genus, by its popular name at least, is *E. aromatica,* the pungently scented flower buds of which when dried become cloves.

Eugenia species are to be found growing wild in both tropical and temperate regions. They are most abundant in eastern Asia and South America, less so in Africa and Australia and absent from Europe. They are evergreen trees and shrubs, often attractively coloured when the foliage is young. There are possibly 700 species in all, but less than 30 are in cultivation and not all of these are grown for their fruits. A native plant and a familiar garden tree widely distributed in Australia, the Lillipilli, is *E. smithii.* Athough grown generally for its decorative and adaptive qualities, its fruits are edible, although they are inferior to those of other species. It has been suggested that this species could be hybridised with imported types. One authority suggests that a species of *Eugenia* was possibly the first fruit sampled by Captain Cook's party in Australia. Joseph Banks at Botany Bay recorded that Cook and Solander 'found also several trees of the Jambos kind, much in colour and shape resembling cherries, of these they eat plentifully and brought home also abundance which we eat with much

pleasure tho they had little to recommend them but a light acid'. The acid was no doubt greatly welcome after a monotonous ship's diet, perhaps it was even craved by their bodies as an antidote to scurvy. They may have become familiar with the jambos at home, for it is recorded as having been introduced into Europe from the East Indies in 1696. It was for some time known as *Jambos vulgaris.* Then again they may have found it growing in some other parts they visited on their long journey. *Eugenia jambos,* syn. *Sysygium jambos,* also called Jambul and Rose apple, is now to be found naturalised in many warm countries. Its name Rose apple comes from the fact that the ripe fruits are rose-scented and for this reason are used in confectionery, usually as crystallised fruits. As a dessert fruit it is poor.

The Malay apple, Santo Domingo apricot or Ohia, is *E. malaccensis,* and as its name suggests, the plant is a native of Malaya. It was originally listed as *Jambosa malaccensis.* It was first introduced into Europe in the mid eighteenth century, and has since then, in cold countries, been cultivated as a warm greenhouse plant, being valued as an ornamental plant of distinction.

This particular species represents a dilemma in which the botanical researcher often finds himself. One would expect, for instance, *E. jambolana* to become trivialised into 'jambul' or something like it, rather than the preceding species, but no. It is known sometimes as Java plum, in addition to a number of local names. It has a botanical synonym, *Syzygium cumini.* This is a popular fruiting plant widely grown in tropical countries.

More confusion in nomenclature comes in the wake of *E. uniflora,* syn. *E. michelii,* a native of the South American tropics and known as the Pitanga. Yet there is a species with the specific name of *E. pitanga,* native of Brazil and Argentina. Also confusing is the fact that this fruit is sometimes called Brazilian cherry, a trivial name applied also to *Malpighia glabra,* a completely different fruit. Acquainted with these facts, surely even the layman will agree that one needs the full botanical names to determine just what plant is being discussed.

*E. uniflora,* Pitanga, possibly the most popular species, is grown in many warm countries about the world, sometimes as a garden tree, sometimes cultivated commercially on a small scale. We are told that the scented leaves, odorous when crushed, are sometimes scattered on the floors of Brazilian homes as strewing herbs. It is a popular fruit in India and is also grown in small areas in Florida and California. Recently it has been suggested as a potential horticultural crop for tropical Australia under the popular name Pitanga. It seems most likely that cultivars exist, but no names are published that we can discover, yet while some trees produce fruit of excellent flavour, others have been known with fruit which is resinous and unpleasant.

Since Australians are showing interest in this imported species, one ought to mention that of their native species, *E. coolminiana* is considered to be well worth eating, and *E. luehmannii,* which bears red, pear-shaped fruit abundantly, is so pretty when in young leaf that it is also highly decorative in the garden. *E. moorei* has showy red flowers and large, cream-coloured fruits. No doubt the day will come when we shall see hybrids of these and others. All of the fruiting species are attractive, even ornamental plants.

## The fruit

Botanically a berry or a drupe, according to species. Those of *E. jambos* are somewhat apple-like in appearance, but smaller, usually about 4 cm (1½ in) in diameter. They are pale yellow, often tinged with pink, not unlike an apricot in colouring. The fruit is a berry containing 1–3 seeds. These tend to be polyembrionic. The flesh is roughly the same colour as the skin, firm and juicy. The fruits are rose-perfumed. The skin is waxy and edible.

The fruits of *E. malaccensis* are generally described as being as large as a hen's egg, although the fruits are pear-shaped. They are a lovely pink or rose to dark purple.

*E. jambolana* has oblong to round fruit, a deep purple-black in colour, with a shining skin, 2–4 cm (¾–1½ in) long and one-seeded.

The Pitanga, *E. uniflora,* is a drupe with a large stone. The fruits are very attractive visually. Basically round to egg-shaped and a little turban-like in appearance, 3–4 cm (1–1½ in) wide, they have 8 deep longitudinal grooves dividing the fruit into sections. Each fruit is topped with a persistent calyx. They are light green at first, turning as they mature through reds until they are almost black, like a cherry. The darker the fruit the more pronounced in flavour. The flesh is the same colour as the skin and is soft and juicy with a sub-acid flavour in the best sorts. The flavour of the fruit varies, being resinous and unpleasant in some plants without apparent reason.

## The plant

*E. jambos* is a tall, evergreen tree 6–12 m (20–40 ft) in the wild, smaller in cultivation. It has handsome, dark green and glossy leaves, oval to oblong, 10–20 cm (4–8 in) long and 3–5 cm (1–2 in) wide and pointed. The flowers, green-white or yellow-white, 5–8 cm (2–3 in) across, with attractive, long, numerous stamens, grow in terminal clusters.

*E. malaccensis* is an attractive evergreen shrub or small tree growing to some 1.8–2.5 m (6–8 ft). It has handsome leaves, shining on both surfaces, which are 15–30 cm (6–12 in) long and 6–10 cm (2½–4 in) wide, mainly oblong in shape. This plant is one of the few of the genus which is brilliant in flower. The flowers are lovely, red-purple, set in clusters, each bloom 5 cm (2 in) wide, with rich red stamens and bright yellow anthers forming a cluster nearly 3 cm (1 in) wide. On the tree the flowers appear tassel-like.

*E. jambolana* is a tall glabrous shrub or small tree. It has oval to oblong leaves some 10–15 cm (4–6 in) long and about half as wide. Its flowers are red, small and fragrant. They grow in rounded heads forming collectively pyramidal panicles which grow up to 12–20 cm (5–8 in). Their petals fall away in one piece.

*E. uniflora* is a glabrous, evergreen shrub, sometimes a small tree growing to some 3.6 m (12 ft), though smaller in some arid regions. It is often used as a hedge, when it will still produce fruit. It is a neat and compact plant with ovate leaves 5–6 cm (2–2½ in) long and 3–4 cm (1–1½ in) wide, copper-coloured when young. These shoots have a pleasant pungent scent when bruised. The fragrant, white, 4-petalled flowers about 1 cm (½ in) wide, sometimes bloom twice a year in warm climates, but only once in northern latitudes. The plant is slow growing and will take about 20 years to reach 3 m (10 ft). It begins to bear in its third or fourth year. The fruit ripens a few weeks after flowering.

## Cultivation

The method of cultivation is much the same for

all species. In warm countries where the plant can grow out of doors it is easily cultivated in all kinds of soils. The Pitanga can withstand occasional cool conditions without suffering damage, but fruit production appears to be limited when it is grown in cool regions. However, the plants are not hardy out of doors in gardens in colder countries, and where in these circumstances they are grown in a greenhouse, the temperature should not be allowed to fall below 10°C (50°F).

Propagation from seed usually results in plants coming true to type. The seed should be taken from ripe fruit. Cuttings can be taken of ripe wood in summer. Grafting and budding are also successful. *E. uniflora* will grow from suckers.

*E. jambos* grows well in wet, tropical regions. It prefers deep loam soils, but appears to get along well enough in most types of soil. Generally speaking, pruning should be restricted to keeping the plant within the desired shape.

These plants can be grown in containers in a conservatory or similar structure where the light is of sufficient intensity and where the plant can be sprayed or syringed with clear water daily. If necessary they can be stood outside in summer.

Pitanga and some of the other species are said to make excellent hedges in the tropics. Pitanga trims to shape well, which suggests that it could be used for some forms of topiary. It can be controlled at any height between about 1 m (3 ft) and 3 m (10 ft).

## Culinary uses

It is important that the fruit is really ripe. Under-ripe fruits have too strong a flavour. This decreases to one which is pleasantly aromatic when the fruit is ready for eating. The flesh should then be crisp and enjoyable when eaten out of hand. It is also important that the stones or seeds of the fruits are removed before these are cooked, since they are unpleasantly astringent. It is not necessary to peel the fruits unless the skin is blemished. The seeds and calyx should be removed before the fruits are sliced or halved for use in salads or as a compote.

The finest varieties of jambos are eaten raw. They are also cooked in tarts, pies and puddings. In a delightful book, alas undated, but published one would imagine in the early 1800s, of a selection of Rare and Curious Fruits Indigenous to Ceylon (from drawings made in the island and coloured from nature), the author J. W. Bennet, FLS, tells us that *E. malaccensis,* whose illustration shows a beautiful pear-shaped fruit, soft green streaked with pale magenta, 'forms part of the usual dessert at European tables. It is also stewed and baked after the manner of pears in Europe and occasionally preserved as a sweetmeat. In order to give it a pink or deeper red colour, to resemble baked pears, the native cook employs the petals of the Shoe-flower, *Hibiscus rosa sinensis,* var. Duplex (so called because its bruised petals are occasionally used as a substitute for blacking).'

PRESERVING   Jelly made from the green fruit, usually called pitanga jelly, is thought by some people to rival guava jelly. Syrups made from the juice, as well as wines made from the fruit, are said to have some medicinal value.

In some countries the fruits are preserved and candied.

# JAPANESE QUINCE
*Chaenomeles* species

## Origin

This is a genus of four deciduous shrubs native to northern Asia. The plants are closely allied to the quince with which they were at one time grouped and named, so that the plants are still known by some people as cydonia. There are, nevertheless, botanical differences, the most obvious being that chaenomeles have toothed leaves. There are now many cultivars derived from the species known popularly as ornamental quinces. These also sometimes fruit, quite plentifully in certain seasons, and their fruits are as comestible as those species listed here.

Many people like to call these shrubs 'Japonica,' which is in fact the specific name of one of the species, *C. japonica,* also sometimes called Maule's quince. This plant was first thought to be a pear and was, in fact, first named *Pyrus maulei.* It has two varieties, *alba,* with white flowers, and *alpina,* which is smaller than the type.

Another chaenomeles, possibly the most popular, is known as Japanese quince, just to confuse the issue a little more! This one is the lovely *C.*

*lagenaria*. Numerous varieties have been raised from this type, but many of these have disappeared from nurserymen's lists. If you know of a good plant and would like an example for yourself, it can easily be propagated by layering.

If you are ready to sacrifice a little beauty for utility, the Chinese quince, *C. cathayensis,* which originates from central China, produces fine fruit for jellies. There is a variety, *wilsonii.*

*C. sinensis,* syn. *Cydonia sinensis,* less hardy than the first three, also from China, is another very handsome plant.

## The fruit

Botanically, a pome, with the cells of the fruit many-seeded. *C. japonica* has apple-like fruit about 4 cm (1½ in) in diameter, very short-stalked so that it seems almost sessile on the stalks. The fruits, when ripe, are yellow and fragrant.

Fruits of the Japanese quince, *C. lagenaria,* are green-yellow and speckled. They can be either globose or pear-shaped. They are larger than those of *C. japonica,* some 5–7 cm (2–2½ in) long and broad. They have the characteristic pleasant quince odour, which is often very strong.

The Chinese quince, *C. cathayensis,* bears very large and very heavy fruit, which is a dull green, and to some people nothing like as attractive in appearance as the former. However, the fruits, which are 10–15 cm (4–6 in) long and 6–9 cm (2½–3½ in) wide, make a most excellent jelly.

*C. sinensis* produces egg-shaped fruits 10–15 cm (4–6 in) long, deep yellow in colour.

## The plant

*C. japonica* is a low, spreading shrub with spines, growing to a height of about 1 m (3 ft), but spreading much wider than this. It can become smothered in orange-red flowers, which are produced singly or in small clusters on the previous year's growth, opening as all do, before the leaves. Even in cold climates these will sometimes bloom in early winter. As explained earlier, the variety *alba* has white flowers, and *alpina* has a much dwarfer growth.

The Japanese quince has been one of the most popular of garden shrubs since its introduction, not least because of its propensity for flowering in winter. In the northern hemisphere it is often in bloom by the new year, and will go on blooming, the weather being favourable, into the spring, or, according to how it is grown, even until summer. It is a rounded shrub, widespreading, dense in habit and somewhat spiny. The long ovate or oblong leaves, evenly and sharply toothed, are a dark and glossy green. The scarlet or blood-red flowers, 4–5 cm (1½–2 in) wide, grow in clusters of 2 or 4.

*C. cathayensis* is not as endearing a plant as either of the former. It grows 2.5–3.5 m (8–10 ft) tall and is armed with short, spiny shoots. Its leaves are quite attractive, 8–13 cm (3–5 in) long, very finely toothed, with a pleasant ruddy coloration on the undersides. The white flowers, which bloom later in the spring than those described above, grow in short clusters of 2 or 3 and they are about 4 cm (1½ in) wide.

Probably the most handsome of all is *C. sinensis,* because if it is growing in the right conditions it will grow into a tree of some 6–12 m (20–40 ft). This species, like some prunus, has a peeling bark, which adds to its attraction. The young shoots are hairy, and the long, finely toothed, obovate to oval leaves are downy on the undersides when young. The 3–4 cm (1–1½ in) wide pink flowers are almost sessile on the branches and are solitary, not in clusters as in the other species.

Flowering quince can be used to cover a wall most attractively. Apart from the beauty of the early flowers, the young growth of the foliage is also often interestingly coloured, much depending upon the site and the season, and the leaves persist until late autumn.

First establish a framework of branches, best done by fixing them to a support. Once this is satisfactory, shorten the branches after flowering. In late summer cut back all outward pointing shoots.

Where there is space to spare this plant will make an attractive hedge, and when it is so used its flowering season is much prolonged. Where the climate is mild, or the garden pleasantly sheltered and warm, the plant makes a good solitary specimen as a lawn or patio shrub. It can be trained and disciplined into a neat and rounded shape by discreet pruning.

The blossom is delightful for flower arrangements. It may be cut as soon as the flower buds can be seen and the flowers indoors in their vases will gradually open in the warmth of the house.

Although the fruits are most attractive, and ideal for flower and foliage arrangements in which fruits can be featured, take care that they are not mixed with carnations, and watch for their effect on other blooms. Like apples, they give off an aromatic gas which affects some flowers and causes them to become 'sleepy', even if they are freshly gathered. This also sometimes happens if the fruits are left in a closed room in which there are flowers.

## Cultivation

These ornamental quinces are mainly hardy and easily grown in any garden soil, although they seem to enjoy one in which there is some lime. If the full benefit is to be gained from their early blooming, it follows that they will do best in cold countries if they are given some protection, and for this reason they are usually planted against a wall. A sunny position ensures a good performance. If it is considered necessary to restrict the size of the plant, it should be pruned in early autumn, spur pruning as for apples. Otherwise, remove surplus growth after the plant has flowered. It can be propagated by layering in the autumn or, should you wish to raise new var-

ieties for yourself, by sowing the seed of some cultivar. Cuttings of half-ripened wood can be taken in summer, and plants can also be increased by suckers.

## Culinary uses

Treat as quince (q.v.).

# JUJUBE
*Ziziphus jujuba,* syn. *Z. vulgaris* **and species**

## Origin

Ziziphus is a genus of about 40 species of tropical and temperate evergreen and deciduous trees and shrubs and is a member of the buckthorn family, Rhamnaceae. The actual origin of the jujube is obscure. Its name is derived from the Arabic Zizouf, by which name one species, *Z. lotus,* was known.

Some believe the plant originated in the Mediterranean region, probably in Syria. Certainly it can be found growing wild around this sea. Others believe it came from China and India. It is an important crop in India where it is known by many common names, Ber or Bor being just two of these. It has been cultivated in China for centuries – there are records of it there which date back to the third century BC. So widespread has been its cultivation that by the seventeenth century there were apparently 43 varieties known to gardeners; hundreds of varieties are grown now.

It is believed that the jujube was introduced from China to the Philippines. Whether from China or Syria, it has spread throughout Persia, Arabia and Asia Minor as well as southern Europe and to all warm countries. In Russia it is cultivated in the dry sub-tropical regions and rates as an important crop.

One sees a great difference in the many jujubes on sale in different countries. It is impossible to say how numerous now are the cultivars grown throughout the world – and more still are being produced. Improved varieties are being grown in the USA. Frank N. Mayer, agricultural explorer, was responsible for the introduction of scions of large-fruited jujube varieties into the USA in 1908.

It was introduced into Britain in 1640, where it will grow as a hardy plant only in the mildest areas. Other species of the genus are grown as hothouse plants.

*Z. mauritiana,* a tropical plant of Indian origin, known as the Indian jujube or Chinese apple, has excellent fruits and is highly esteemed in its own country. In some parts of Australia where it was imported, in particular in northern Queensland, it is considered to be a weed. The Jujube lotus, *Z. lotus,* which is both cultivated and found growing wild, to the extent that it is a weed in Algeria, flourishes on a dry, stony terrain in many Mediterranean countries and north Africa, but its fruit is of poor quality being small and dry.

There are many other species, all with edible although not significantly useful fruits. Perhaps one day plantsmen will work on them.

## The fruit

Botanically, an ovoid or oblong fleshy drupe. The common jujube, which can be found growing wild, has egg-shaped fruit 2–5 cm (¾–2 in) long, which is at first shining green, then red, and finally almost black when ripe. Cultivars vary somewhat in the colour of ripe fruit, many becoming dark brown or rust-coloured. Their appearance is that of a fresh date or olive. Each fruit contains a single, hard-shelled stone. The white flesh is mucilaginous and for that reason the fruits are allowed to wither for some time so that the pulp becomes dried out. It is then crisp and sweet.

*Z. mauritiana* has a smaller fruit, which when dried has a date-like flavour.

## The plant

The jujube is a deciduous shrub or small tree, which under suitable conditions will grow to 9 m (30 ft). The branches, zigzag in shape, are armed with spines, which grow in pairs at each node, one short and hooked, the other longer and straight. The spines are a characteristic of this genus. There is a species known as *Z. spina-christi,* which can be seen growing around the old city of Jerusalem, from which some believe the stems were taken to make Christ's crown of thorns. Happily there are spineless cultivars. The leaves are mainly oval, 2.5–6.5 cm (1–2½ in) long, shining and glabrous on the undersides. The

H. Yamaguchi 1979

flowers are insignificant and of a yellow hue, growing in twos and threes in the leaf axils of the current year's young growth. These bloom in summer and the fruit matures in early autumn. The plant should reach its full fruiting capacity in fifteen years from seed, but in about five from a grafted plant.

*Z. mauritiana* is much the same in size. It, though, is evergreen, with the undersides of its leaves very hairy. The plants tend to send up numerous suckers in certain conditions.

## Cultivation

Although the jujube can withstand light and short-lived frosts when it is dormant, it will be killed if frosted when in leaf. It is safest where the temperature does not fall below 10°C (50°F). In cold areas it can be given the protection of a glasshouse, but it is not usually a good container plant. It grows best in dry regions, especially those which have hot, dry summers. Humid conditions tend to encourage disease as well as lessen fruiting capacity.

The type of soil is not important, but where it is good the fruits grow large and lush, as they are said to do in China. A deep, sandy loam is considered to be the best medium. However, the great thing about the plant is that if the climate is right it will grow, even on badly drained and poor soil. Its rooting system is such that it can tolerate both drought and excessive waterlogging, though it does need sun.

Pruning is not essential. Obviously it is profitable to encourage the plant to make plenty of young growth, since the fruits are produced on this. Any pruning is best carried out when the plant is dormant. As time goes on, old and weak branches should be removed and the principle of keeping the centre of the plant from overcrowding followed.

Plants can be raised from seed, but there seedlings take some 15 years to fruit. Superior varieties are grafted on to seedling stock. Seed has to be stratified to soften the hard shell.

## Culinary uses

Most fruits become deep brown when fully ripe, but some varieties can be eaten while still green. Test by tasting. For those which are to turn brown, gather while they are still firm but orange-red, with just a hint of brown in their skins (some say as soon as the first brown spot appears) and allow to finish ripening off the tree, unless they are to be used as a compote. Jujube fruits are rich in vitamin C.

Although they are sweet they need not necessarily be reserved for sweet dishes; in some countries they are used in fish dishes and soups, usually in a dried form. They can be used in puddings, cakes and breads.

PRESERVING   The fresh fruit makes an excellent jelly and cheese. It can be candied as well as dried. First puncture the fruit all over before it is boiled in the syrup. Dried jujubes are used in much the same way as dates.

They are used in pharmacy to sweeten medicines. They are also among the fruits most soothing to the throat and chest. For this reason the juice and decoctions made from it can be given to those with colds and sore throats.

FREEZING   Jujubes can be stored in open containers in a freezer for as long as 45 days, becoming damaged if the containers are closed.

# JUNE BERRY
*Amelanchier* **species**

## Origin

A member of the rose family, and closely related to the apples and pears, the genus takes its botanical name from the French popular name, *amelanchier*, given to *A. ovalis*, *A. vulgaris*. In English, this is the Snowy Mespilus, one of the few species native to central and southern Europe. The majority are natives of North America. One, *A. asiatica*, with fine, blackcurrant-like fruits, is native to China, Korea and Japan.

Most amelanchiers are shrubs and small trees. The shrubs are so neat that in countries like Holland and Germany one sometimes sees them massed in beds in town parks or around municipal buildings.

They are not really important as fruit trees, although the fruits of most species are delicious. Like the unexpected fruit of the fuchsia, they are included in this book to bring them to the attention of beginner gardeners and to reassure those who may worry that the little fruits are poisonous. Those who have the trees already and those who buy the plants for their beauty can make the most of the early maturing fruits, although if you wish to benefit fully from the crop you may have to beat the birds to it.

The fruits appear to have been used whenever available by the early American pioneers, who gave the various species such names as Shad bush, Service berry and Swamp pear.

## The fruit

Botanically, a berry-like pome. *A. alnifolia*, the Western shad bush, has juicy fruit of a similar size to that of the other species, about 1 cm ($\frac{1}{3}$ in), and is black with a purple bloom, as is fruit of *A. florida*, syn. *A. oxyodon*, and it is for this reason perhaps that this species is so often confused with *A. alnifolia*. The fruit of *A. asiatica*, as already described, is black-purple and somewhat like a blackcurrant in appearance. The Shad bush, *A. canadensis*, also known as Service berry, has purple-red fruits and its hybrid, *A. grandiflora*, a cross between this species and *A. laevis*, has sweet purple fruits which are larger than those of the type. *A. laevis* is often confused with *A. canadensis*, but its purple-black fruit is rounded but flat-

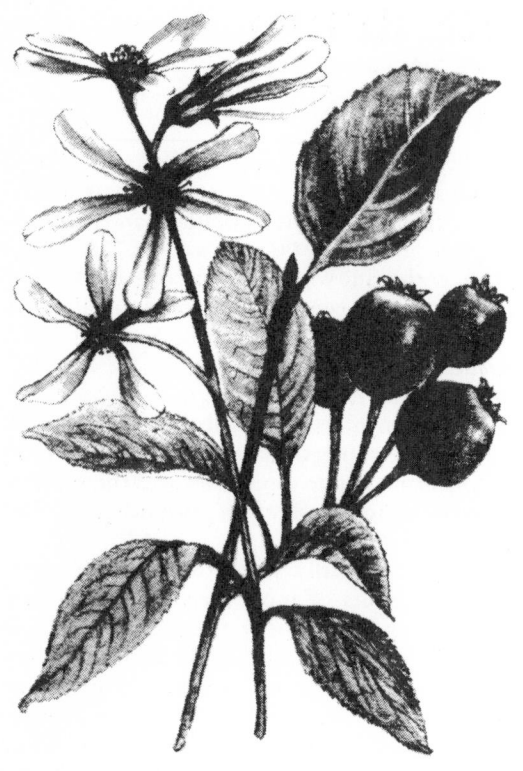

with a fine, loose down, turn brilliant colours in the autumn.

Higher than most, the Shad bush normally reaches some 6–9 m (20–30 ft) but has been known to grow twice as high. Like many of this genus it bears shoots which are woolly when young, in this case on both surfaces. The flowers are carried in drooping racemes of usually 6–9 blooms, each about 2 cm (1 in) wide. In autumn the foliage turns yellow.

*A. grandiflora* produces young downy foliage tinged with purple. In autumn the leaves are beautifully coloured. Its flowers are larger than those of its parents and are also white, although there is a pink form which is known as *rubescens*. *A. laevis* also turns to a vivid, rich red in autumn, by which it differs from *A. canadensis,* with which it is so often confused. Its flower racemes are erect. *A. florida* grows more as a shrub, although it sometimes makes a small tree some 6–9 m (20–30 ft) high, with erect branches and rounded-oval leaves. The flowers also grow in erect racemes.

Make the most of the brief life of the amelanchier blossom and gather branches of newly opened buds for flower arrangement. Take this opportunity to remove from the tree any spindly or crossing growths. These may not look good on the tree, but they will prove both useful and decorative in floral designs.

## Cultivation

These are easy plants to grow, ideal for small gardens. All are hardy. They seem to grow on all kinds of soils, including chalk. Certainly, where apples and pears can be cultivated, so can amelanchier. Even so, the plants will do best on a rich, loamy soil and in a sunny position.

They are easily propagated. One can detach and plant suckers, make layers or sow seed. Bushy shrubs can also be lifted and divided. Take care not to buy plants grafted on to hawthorn or medlar stock, for this, not the amelanchier, may shoot or sucker.

## Culinary uses

Fruits are cooked as though they were little apples, in puddings and pies, and are used in juice form in desserts, including sherberts, jams, jellies and butters or pastes and cheeses.

tened and about the same size as most of the others. The fruit of the Snowy Mespilus also looks like a blackcurrant and is blue-black.

The Swamp sugar pear is *A. oblongifolia,* and has particularly flavoursome fruits which were highly esteemed by pioneer cooks, who made them into fruit puddings which much resembled plum puddings of the old days. Others such as *A. spicata* and *A. stolonifera* have excellent fruit, but because they increase untidily by suckers and eventually make thickets, these are not really suitable for urban gardens.

## The plant

*Amelanchier alnifolia* is a shrub, some 1–2 m (3–6 ft), with downy young shoots. The leaves as they open are densely hairy. The white flowers grow in erect racemes of 6 to 8 blooms.

*A. asiatica* is a delightfully graceful tree, 3–10 m (15–35 ft) tall, with slender branches which in late spring are covered with racemes of loose-petalled fragrant white flowers. The long, oval, slender leaves, which are at first covered

# KUMQUAT
*Fortunella* species

## Origin

The fruit has long been cultivated in China, Japan and Malaya, but is still little known in other countries, although it is often seen in Australia. It was introduced into Europe in 1846 by Robert Fortune, who spent in all 19 years in the Far East, collecting plants for the Royal Horticultural Society. This little genus, containing so far as is known just four species, was named in his honour. It was originally included in Citrus, to which it is closely related. It was introduced to the United States in about 1850, where it slowly became appreciated and is now grown commercially for preserving in California and Florida.

As one would expect, in those countries where the fruit has been cultivated for centuries, there are many local varietal types with their own names. There are also hybrids, not only from crosses within the genus, but with closely related plants such as citrus and poncirus, two other members of the same family, Rutaceae. Thus we have such strange fruits as Citrangequat, a hybrid obtained from crossing the Citrange (which is itself a hybrid from a crossing with a sweet orange and *Poncirus trifoliata*) and a species of *Fortunella;* the Limequat, from a crossing of lime and *Fortunella,* and Lemonquat and Orangequat, the parentage of which should be obvious. These are known as inter-generic hybrids.

## The fruit

Botanically, a berry like the orange, and in appearance kumquats are also much like small oranges. They differ from the true citrus in that their rinds are thin and edible and that the fruits can be divided into only 3–6 sections rather than into the 8–15 of the citrus. The fruits are slow to colour and ripen.

*F. japonica,* the round or Marumi kumquat, still sometimes known as *Citrus japonica,* has round, golden yellow fruits, about 2.5 cm (1 in) in diameter, with a thin, waxy skin. It has an acid-sweet, juicy flesh. *F. margarita* is the oval or Nagami kumquat, about 4 cm (1½ in) long and 2 cm (¾ in) in diameter, more orange-coloured when ripe.

There is also a species known as the Malayan

kumquat, in that country called limau pagar or hedge lime, which is *F. polyandra*. There appears to be some doubt about this species, which may, in fact, be the Limequat, a hybrid with some variety of citrus.

*F. hindsii,* the Hong Kong wild kumquat, has many native names and a variety, Chintou, the Golden bean kumquat. This is believed to be a cultivated variety of a wild species. This has small fruit, about 2 cm (¾ in) in diameter, not quite round, and is a bright or almost scarlet orange.

## The plant

All kumquats are evergreen. *F. japonica* is a small tree or shrub up to about 2 m (6 ft) tall, with spinous branches and glossy, ovate leaves pointed at the tips. All parts of the plant are scented. The flowers are white and firm, usually growing solitary rather than in clusters. It and *F. margarita* are much alike.

The flowers of *F. hindsii* do not open as widely as the others and they are short and broad. This is a spiny shrub or small tree. The oval leaves have winged stems or petioles.

Kumquats make ideal pot plants and can be used not only out of doors as patio plants in those areas where the climate permits, but they can also be grown as greenhouse and house plants generally. As all parts of the plant are sweetly scented, it can easily be appreciated what pleasant tenants they will be for well-lit living-rooms. In the greenhouse one should strive to keep the temperature above 4°C (40°F), and preferably at about 10°C (50°F) during the winter. The usual open potting mixtures will suit these plants.

Where they can be grown outdoors, consider using them in little groups on their own.

## Cultivation

The kumquats in the main are cultivated in exactly the same way as citrus fruits. See the section on Orange. However, they are more resistant to cold than orange trees and can stand cool conditions for some time. However, the disadvantage of growing them cold is that growth slows down when the temperature is lower than about 13°C (55°F).

## Culinary uses

These little fruits can be eaten raw when quite ripe. The skin is edible. Generally regarded as a sweetmeat, they can in fact be used in many savoury dishes. The experimental cook will find them useful in sweet-sour dishes, and they can be used in the same way as preserved stem ginger, in which case they should be sliced and seeded. They can be pickled in vinegar like cucumbers or small melons, using the same recipe. When served as a savoury, they are most often cooked and used to garnish dishes, notably pot-roasted or braised duck and other wildfowl.

Although kumquats can be eaten raw, they are most often cooked in some way and served cold, or recooked in a sauce or sweet. To prepare them for this purpose cover 4 cups of kumquats with water in a saucepan and bring the water to boiling point. Take the pan off the heat and drain the fruit through a colander. Repeat twice – three boilings – except that in the last water the fruits should continue to simmer until they are tender. The classic test is to see if the head of a pin will go through the skin easily. Make a syrup of

2 cups of sugar and a scant 1 cup of water for 5 minutes. Add the kumquats and boil these also for 5 minutes. To store, put them with the syrup and refrigerate. Alternatively, put into jars, adding a little brandy to each jar and topping up with syrup.

From this point they can be served individually with cream or ice-cream. They can be chopped and used in ice-creams (use the syrup as a sauce also), desserts, puddings, cakes, what you will. They can be used in sauces for meat or as a garnish. They can be incorporated into salads. For the latter purpose the fruits can be split, seeded and stuffed with cream cheese and served with a green salad and a vinaigrette dressing.

PRESERVING   A somewhat unusual Kumquat Marmalade can be made like this:

### Kumquat marmalade

*2 cups kumquats*
*1½ cups sugar*
*4 cups water*

Slice the fruit, put it into the water and let it stand all night. The next day boil the fruit until it is tender, pour into a bowl and let it stand all night again. On the third day add the sugar to the fruit and water and boil it until it jells, which is usually after about ¾ hour. Pour into warm jars and seal.

### Preserved kumquats

*4 cups kumquats*
*4 cups water*
*1 cup additional water for later boiling*
*2 cups sugar*
*good pinch cream of tartar*
*granulated sugar for coating*

Prick a hole in the stem ends of the fruits. Put them in a saucepan and add 4 cups of water. Bring this slowly to boiling point. Simmer the fruits until tender, which should take anything up to 15 minutes, but give them longer if necessary. Drain through a colander. Meanwhile, make a syrup from the cup of water and the sugar. Stir this until it is dissolved and add the cream of tartar. Boil until the thread stage is reached. Add the kumquats to the syrup and simmer for 10 minutes. If the syrup does not quite cover them, turn the fruits about in it from time to time. Lift the kumquats from the syrup and drain on a sieve with a platter beneath. When the fruits are cool, roll them in the sugar.

# LEMON
*Citrus limon,* syn. *C. limonium*

## Origin

The country of the lemon's origin is not known for certain. It is most likely to have come from certain regions of east India, Burma and south China. The names Lemon and the French *limon* are thought to have been derived from the Hindu word *lemoen*.

Although Theophrastus, Virgil and Pliny praised the qualities of the lemon in their own time, it appears that this admirable fruit was not cultivated by the Arabs, whose civilisation later dominated the ancient Greek and Roman worlds, until about the fourteenth century. However, it was they who, having at last popularised it in their own lands, finally brought the plant to North Africa. Like so many other fruits and nuts, the lemon was brought even further afield, to Europe, by the returning Crusaders. Just when it came to Britain no one is quite certain but there is a record of it growing there outdoors in summer, indoors in winter, as far back as 1577. From Spain the lemon was carried across the Atlantic by Christopher Columbus in 1493 to Haiti, so it is claimed, but it was not necessarily from this country that it spread to the Americas. There is a story, for example, that the highly praised and widely grown variety Eureka originated from a seed from a fruit from a box of lemons imported from Sicily to Los Angeles in 1858.

Most authorities are agreed that the Mediterranean regions provide the best growing conditions for the lemon, and certainly they are produced commercially in many areas there, in Italy, Sicily, Cyprus, in Israel and North Africa, as well as further afield in Florida, Texas and California. Australia grows lemons commercially and a tree is to be found in many gardens there.

## The fruit

Botanically, an oblate, spherical berry known as a hesperidium. The fruit is oval or oblong, in some varieties rounded, with a spical protruberance, usually 8–13 cm (3–5 in) long, pale yellow, with a definite rind, more or less rough in texture although some varieties are smooth, and dotted with oil glands. The pulp is abundant, fleshy and acid.

The plant has given rise to many varieties and cultivars and the fruit of these can differ considerably. There are also a number of oddities or curiosities such as the Ponderosa, which can weigh as much as 1 kg (2½ lb), but which has little juice and is lacking in the characteristic lemon flavour; this hybrid was raised in the USA where it is known as the American Wonder Lemon – it is a good tub plant. There is also the Turk's Head, which is said to be the size of a man's head, with sweet pulp and juice; and the Monachello, or Little Monk, and the Spadafora.

'Rough' lemon, the original lemon type, has bland tasting fruits, often round, which are sweet when ripe and without the characteristic acid taste. Rough lemon is known as the Mazoe lemon in South Africa and as Jambhiri in India.

## The plant

The lemon makes a small tree, sometimes a spreading bush, a tendency which follows its raising from seed. It grows about 2.5 m (8 ft) to 3.5 m (12 ft) high, according to environment and variety. It has irregular, somewhat pendant branches, much more pendulous than other citrus. These are armed with short, stiff, stout spines. Some varieties have few or no spines, for example Villafranca and Genoa. The leaves are glossy, green and small, some 5–10 cm (2–4 in) in length, oblong-oval, with pointed tips and toothed margins. Their stalks are sometimes narrowly winged. The young shoots are tinged with magenta-red. The small, fragrant flowers, 1–2 cm (¼–¾ in) long, are borne in the leaf axils and are either solitary or in clusters. Their buds and the outer sides of the young petals are tinged with magenta-red. In some areas the plant is in flower and fruit the year round, but in others, such as the Cote d'Azur, the plant flowers in May to produce fruits which are harvested in winter, and flowers again in October for fruit the following year.

As the lemon does not need a great depth of

soil, it follows that it is an ideal subject for container gardening. Even in Italy, where the plant flourishes outdoors, one often sees lemon trees growing in handsome pots and used as decorations in some of the lovely formal gardens in that country. The pots can be plain and simple, in which case the traditional clay pot, 30 cm (12 in) across at the top, will prove suitable.

## Cultivation

Generally as for other citrus (see the section on Orange). Nurserymen sell grafted trees, usually on a rough lemon stock.

The lemon requires less heat than some members of this genus, but on the other hand it does not stand intense cold or sudden icy spells. Young tips may be killed by frost, and the plant will not recover quickly from such attacks. On the other hand the lemon has been known to grow outdoors in mild districts as far north as England, where they can be given some protection, such as a wall. There are lemon trees which have been growing outdoors for years at Dunster Castle in Somerset in the west of England. These are a great attraction to visitors to the castle, since lemons and their blossom on the trees is a novel sight to those used only to hardier fruits such as apples, pears and plums. In cold climates lemons are more often grown with other citrus fruits in an orangery.

When grown in greenhouses in winter, the temperature should not be allowed to fall below 4°C (40°F) at night and should be maintained at least at 7°C (45°F) by day. Spring temperatures are rather critical, because it is important to induce the plant to grow, and the rate of growth slows considerably once the temperature falls below 10°C (50°F), or if it stays at or near this point for any length of time. Ideally, it should keep rising until it is 21°C (70°F) by early summer. If the plants are container-grown, they are best stood outside for the summer, since they need both air and light. The plants should be sprayed daily and watered carefully. The roots must never be allowed to dry out.

If a plant is grown in a greenhouse border, the temperature should not be allowed to rise above 29°C (85°F), so give plenty of ventilation during summer.

## Culinary uses

Lemons are rich in vitamins, especially vitamin C, as well as in mineral salts. They are generally therapeutic. Among its other qualities the peel of a lemon is anti-bacterial, for which reason the lemon is considered a medical plant.

One could write an entire book in praise of the lemon. It is an essential food in our kitchens where it is put to many uses. We value it highly as a meat tenderiser and restorer of quality, espe-

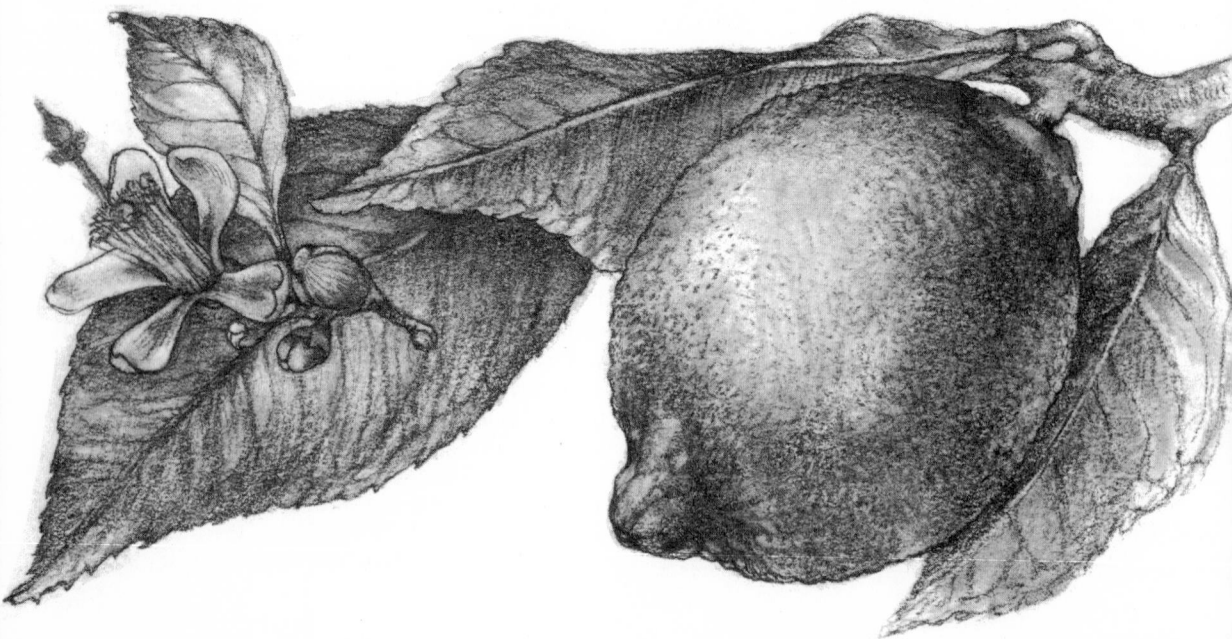

cially when frozen meat is to be cooked. Mix any kind of prepared mustard and lemon juice in equal quantities to coat some meats before baking, for example chicken joints, turkey, pork chops and veal. Lemon brings out the flavour of foods; be liberal with the juice. Hold a lemon under the warm water tap for a few minutes and then roll it in the hands before squeezing it to make the juices run more freely. When only a little lemon juice is required, rather than cut the fruit, pierce it with a fork and squeeze out only as much as you need. The skin will close later.

The juice contains citric acid. It is said that 28 g (1 oz) of juice contains approximately 40 grains of the acid, one reason why lemons are not the best fruits to eat raw like an orange. It is this acid which acts on other fruits and helps them to keep their colour, fruits like apples, bananas, pears and avocado, which become discoloured when exposed to the air after peeling. Lemon juice can be squeezed over them, or they can be soaked for a time in water with added lemon juice. Lemon juice in strawberry jam keeps it a good colour and prevents a greying of the fruit. A slice of lemon or a little juice should be used when boiling sweet potatoes, Jerusalem artichokes, stems of Swiss chard, seakale, or anything you see that becomes discoloured. Lemon juice makes a better vinaigrette and mayonnaise than does vinegar. Whenever possible in uncooked dishes substitute lemon juice for vinegar, for it aids the digestion and is better for one's health. Lemon juice has a good neutralising effect. Serve lemon wedges always with any kind of deep fried food.

Not only the juice but the peel or zest aids many forms of cooking. Save lemon peels after the juice has been squeezed from them and either dry and powder them or chop finely and freeze for future use. (These can also be candied.) The white pith under the skin should be pulled away, because if lemons are cooked with this they may add a bitter touch. Rather than grate the skin, an operation which is wasteful because so much remains stuck to the grater, remove the peel finely by using a potato peeler. Then cut the peel in strips and chop it finely to dry or freeze. If it is to be used julienne, cut it into fine strips, blanch it, drain and dry before freezing or using in the dish. Lemon juices can be added to sauces for fish or meat. It can also be used in Greek lemon soup.

Lemons can be used in a thousand desserts and in a thousand ways from a mere twist of the peel in a baked rice pudding to an elaborate mousse. Lemon makes a good table jelly. Lemon-flavoured puddings, baked or boiled, are excellent.

Lemons can be made into table jellies (see basic table jelly recipe p. 33), blancmange and various creams. If you want a good sweet in a hurry, try making one by whipping cream, adding lemon juice and icing sugar to taste. If there is time, top at the last moment with almonds browned in butter and sprinkled with brown sugar to give them a slight toffee finish. Lemon meringue pie is a classic dish.

Lemon juice makes an excellent sherbet (see the basic recipe on p. 33). This can also be used as a basis for other flavours, for instance with chopped mint, later strained as a mint jelly; with blackcurrant leaves as a blackcurrant ice and with elderflowers as a muscat ice.

### Lemon soufflé

*3 eggs*
*juice of 1 lemon*
*finely chopped rind of ½ lemon*
*½ cup caster sugar*
*1 level teasp powdered gelatine*
*1 tabsp water to dissolve gelatine*

Dissolve the gelatine, making sure that it has been properly softened. Separate the eggs, beat the yolks well, add the lemon juice and rind and sugar. Beat the mixture well. Add the gelatine liquid. Whip the egg whites until they are stiff and fold them into the mixture. Heap this into a serving dish. Chill. Top with whipped cream decorated with lemon slices.

PRESERVING   Lemon juice and peel are used in many jams and jellies in which other fruits take the major role, such as melons, apricots, figs, grapes and pears, as well as on their own in lemon jam, marmalade and a special lemon preserve, Lemon Curd.

### Lemon curd

*2 lemons, squeezed, and the peel finely chopped*
*½ cup butter*
*2 cups sugar*
*3 eggs*

Put the juice, butter, sugar and lemon peel into a basin or jar and stand this in a pan of boiling water. Stir occasionally until the sugar is dissolved. Beat the eggs well. Add these gradually to the mixture and stir continuously until it thickens. Pour into hot jars. Cover lightly and seal when cool.

FREEZING    If you like to serve slices of lemon with drinks, pack them in small quantities, film-wrapped and frozen.

Lemon juice can be frozen. A good method is to use plastic ice trays. When the juice is frozen, release the cubes and pack them into bags.

BOTTLING    Lemons can be bottled in the same way as grapefruit, or they can be bottled as juice. They tend to become thick and cloudy after they have been stored for some time, so although they can still be used in this state it is best to make small quantities that can be used quickly.

DRINKS    Lemons are traditionally the great thirst quenchers and lemon drinks the most refreshing. A slice of lemon in some drinks, gin and tonic for example, brings out the flavour as lemon juice does for food. A twist or zest of peel adds a delicate piquancy to a dry Martini and to many other drinks.

It is possible to make a Lemon Wine in just the same way as other country wines, but as the essential flavour is lost this way, it seems much more sensible to enjoy the real thing and make Lemon Squash.

### Lemon squash

*2 cups lemon juice*
*6 cups sugar*
*3 cups warm water*
*1 teasp citric acid*

Wash the lemons and squeeze them. Finely chop the peel of half of them. Add the peel to the sugar and water. Stir until the sugar is dissolved, warming slightly if necessary. Strain. Add the lemon juice and citric acid and mix well. Bottle and sterilise in the usual manner.

# LIME
*Citrus aurantifolia, C. limetta, Limonia aurantifolia*

### Origin

Uncertain, but it seems most likely that the plant originated in tropical Asia, possibly in the East Indies, although today it is cultivated in the West Indies probably even more extensively than in its homelands. It is also to be found growing wild in those islands. The Arabs are most likely to have begun the distribution of the fruit, introducing it into India and Persia. Its progress then became much the same as that of the lemon, being brought to Europe by the returning Crusaders and also by being taken to the New World, which includes the West Indies, by Christopher Columbus. It is now grown in many tropical countries, where it often replaces the lemon. Mexico and Egypt and Israel produce limes extensively. More are produced in Florida and along the Gulf coast, to be known as Key limes, from a variety first produced in the Florida Keys.

### The fruit

Botanically a globose or oblate-spherical berry known as a hesperidium. Like the lemon, the roughly 5 cm (2 in) fruit has an apical protuberance, and in the lime this is somewhat blunted. The rind is very thin. The pulp is abundant, juicy and green, the famous lime-green. The juice tastes much like that of the lemon, but has an elusive scent, flavour and personality of its own.

### The plant

The lime makes a small tree, 2.5–4.5 m (8–15 ft) tall, and like the lemon has irregular branches, but is a little more bushy and spreading. It has very short, stiff, sharp spines. The leaves are long, 5–8 cm (2–3 in), light green and crenate. The stalks are narrowly winged. The scented flowers are white, in small axillary clusters, growing for most of the year.

### Cultivation

Similar to that of the lemon (see the section on Orange for details). One should bear in mind that this is a tropical plant and is therefore more tender than the lemon.

## Culinary uses

One can almost say that wherever lemons are used – juice, flesh or peel – they can be substituted with limes, and yet there are occasions when the subtle difference matters. The flavour is perhaps a little more pronounced, particularly in the peel.

Like the lemon, the lime is rich in vitamins, especially C. Varieties of limes differ in size and colour. The bright green fruits are usually thin-skinned and heavy. Yellow-skinned limes are not so acid as the green fruits, nor is the lime flavour so pronounced.

Lime juice has a digestive or cooking action on fish and it is used in many tropical recipes for this purpose. In the Bahamas it is used particularly on conch fish. Basically, the flesh of the fish is cut on the bias, that is across the grain, into very thin, uniform slices. The flesh is then mixed with very finely sliced onions and put into a deep dish. Lime juice is then poured over the mixture, which is turned occasionally (never with a *metal* spoon or utensil) so that all the surfaces of the fish come into contact with the juice. A little coconut milk is added. When the fish is considered to have been well turned, fresh tarragon is sprinkled over it. Altogether the dish marinates for 20–60 minutes before it is served.

Like lemons, limes go well with eggs and cream. Lime Cream Cloud is an unusual and excellent cream to serve with sweets, especially with those that often have lemon juice or lime squeezed on them, such as bananas, strawberries and pears. Try it with Chinese gooseberries. It can also be used to top a flan, or to top the pomegranate jellies described on p. 217. Garnish the top with a little star of the bright pomegranate grains.

### Lime cream cloud

*3 tabsp lime juice*
*¼ cup honey*
*2 eggs, well beaten*
*½ cup heavy or whipping cream*

Mix the lime juice and honey until well amalgamated. Stir in the eggs. Put the basin in a pan of boiling water and cook until the mixture becomes transparent, stirring continuously. Allow the mixture to cool. Fold in the cream. Chill.

Limes are particularly refreshing when made into drinks and sorbets or water ices. The flavour can be dominating when the peel is used, so bear in mind that a little will go a long way. When any kind of dried fruits are made into compotes, their own flavour is greatly enhanced if after the fruit is cooked lime juice is added at a rate of the juice of one lime to every 2 cups of fruit uncooked. Where limes are scarce, the juice of half a lemon makes a good substitute.

Limes make good table jellies into which other fruits, particularly bananas and Chinese gooseberries, can go. Slices of the latter arranged in a pattern can give the jelly a most attractive appearance.

PRESERVING    Limes can be made into marmalades, jellies and mixed with other fruits in these preserves and quantities used can be much the same as with lemons, except for the peel, with which one should perhaps be just a little more diffident. Limes can be preserved whole or peeled in syrup and can be pickled for use as an accompaniment for meats.

FREEZING AND BOTTLING    Both for freezing and for bottling, limes can be treated as lemons.

DRINKS    You can make a pleasant and refreshing Lime Julep with:

### Lime julep

*4 sprigs fresh mint*
*8 limes, squeezed*
*sugar to taste*
*½ cup brandy*
*soda water*
*ice*

Bruise the mint in a claret jug and pour in the lime juice, brandy, soda water and several ice cubes. Taste and add just sufficient sugar to take the edge off the acidity of the limes.

# LITCHI

*Litchi chinensis,* syn. *Nephelium litchi, Scytalia chinensis*

## Origin

This is a member of the same family, the Sapindaceae, as the Longan or Lungan, a genus in which only two species are recognised and only one, *L. chinensis,* is grown for its fruit. It is often confused with *Nephelium,* but there are botanical differences. The plant originates from China, where it has been cultivated since ancient times, one writer describing it as being grown in Kwantung along dykes and canals. There is now no known wild form of the species, although as one might expect there are occasional escaped plants to be found.

There are many varieties and cultivars in cultivation, more these days than a few years ago, since the plant is now being grown either commercially or experimentally in Australia, India, Japan, New Zealand, South Africa and certain regions, mainly Florida, in the United States.

## The fruit

Botanically, a cordate berry. When ripe, the skin of the fruit has a pleasing texture, dark, red-brown and rough, even scaly or warty. It is often described as being like a plum in shape. The fruit is 3–4 cm (1–1½ in) long, and grows in bunches, sometimes as many as 20 or so together. Under the shell-like skin, brittle and easily peeled, the translucent flesh is pearly white and jelly-like, though firm. Actually the flesh is botanically the aril of the fruit, covering a hard, shiny brown seed. The flesh is very sweet, with only the faintest taste of acidity.

## The plant

An evergreen tree, slow-growing, often reaching 10–12 m (35–40 ft) under natural conditions, usually with a low, spreading crown, a short trunk and crooked branches. It has attractive, pinnate leaves of a shining leathery texture, the leaflets in 2–4 pairs, tapering to both ends and glaucous and lighter coloured on the underside. When young these are pink, orange or copper tinted.

The small flowers, which may be unisexual or bisexual, green-white or green-yellow, are without petals but with shaggy calyces. They grow in a long, wide panicle of several hundreds, only some actually producing fruit since most of the flowers are male. They bloom in spring and in great profusion. Subjection to a cool period during the winter induces the plant to flower well.

## Cultivation

The litchi needs certain climatic conditions before it will thrive. Distinct seasonal variations are considered necessary for the plant to fruit well. It is considered beneficial and inducive to flowering if the tree is exposed, in dry atmospheres, to brief periods of cold, between 2–4°C (35–40°F). However, young trees cannot stand frosts and are soon killed while older trees are likely to be badly damaged. One authority observes that 'the climatic conditions of its native China are ideal for it: a large part of the year is moderately hot and humid and there is a period in winter which is foggy, continually cool but free from any frost'.

M. Yaimaguchi 1979

Top: Jambos, Lillipilli *(S. Macoboy)*
Bottom: Japanese Quince *(M. Withers)*

Top: Lychees *(G. R. Roberts)*
Bottom: Loquats *(G. R. Roberts)*

The plant will tolerate many kinds of soil, but it does best in those which are both moist and acid. It will thrive in deep, well-drained loams if these are rich in humus. Although it requires an abundance of water, especially when in fruit, and is tolerant of damp, it will not grow in damp, stagnant soils.

Litchis can be raised from seed, which should be sown as soon as it is removed from the surrounding flesh, since it does not remain viable for long. However, such seedlings are not likely to become productive until they are 7–12 years old, and even then are frequently unsatisfactory croppers. For this reason air layering is most often used for propagation.

Litchis have a tendency towards a weak root system when they are young, but if they are planted in well-prepared, deep soil and cared for after planting, never allowed to become dry and want for water, they should grow into vigorous plants.

In some areas, Hawaii for instance, gardeners ring bark or girdle their trees to encourage fruiting. It is advisable to take expert local advice on this matter, since not all varieties are suitable for this operation.

Once they reach maturity and ripen, the fruits quickly change colour, some varieties becoming a rosy red. Apart from testing by taste, the readiness of the fruit can be gauged by the appearance of the skin. The tubercules become flattened and ripe fruits have a smoother appearance than the others.

The fruits should be picked in clusters or bunches. They last longer in store if a little of the main stem and even a few leaves can be taken at the same time. The fruits should not be pulled from their stems. There is a danger also of trying to pick them individually, because the stem may be pulled from the skin, thus rupturing it. This will cause rot to set in. Clip individuals from the bunches, leaving each with a portion of stem.

There is no advantage in picking the fruits before they are ripe, because they will not then mature and the flesh will be flavourless. Once they are ripe they will not keep long under normal conditions. However, they will keep for three months or so in a refrigerator or freezer at a temperature of −1 to 7°C (30–45°F).

## Culinary uses

Litchis can be eaten raw, but these fruits are most often served cold after they have been poached gently in a syrup for a sweet. They blend well in a fruit salad, and are a refreshing complement to cream and ice-cream. Litchis can be used in sweet-and-sour dishes in Chinese cooking.

BOTTLING   They are best bottled in a medium syrup.

DRYING   When dried, the fruits are often called litchi nuts, yet actually they resemble raisins more. They should be removed from their stones before drying. They can be used like raisins.

# LOGANBERRY
*Rubus* species

## Origin

A member of the rose family, the plant is said to have originated in the garden of Judge J. H. Logan, in California in 1881. It was first thought to be the result of a chance cross between the cultivated form of the American blackberry, *Rubus ursinum vitifolius,* and a raspberry, most probably Red Antwerp. Subsequently it was declared by some botanists simply to be a red-fruited variety of the American blackberry. However, recent experiments in breeding have shown that it is probably the true hybrid after all, and one of the first known of the hybrid brambles.

In America it has been named *Rubus x loganobaccus*. The fruit was first exhibited in England by the famous fruit nurserymen, Bunyard's of Maidstone, in 1897. It is now widely grown both in private gardens and on a commercial scale.

In America it is grown on the Pacific coast but not in the east because it is not sufficiently hardy.

## The fruit

Botanically, a berry composed of numerous round, one-seeded drupelets. The dull, wine-red fruit is oblong, often as much as 5 cm (2 in) long and resembles a large raspberry. However, the individual drupes are much larger than those of the raspberry.

can be up to 12. These should be tied to supporting wires stretched above, one at roughly 1 m (3 ft) and the other at 1.5 m (5 ft) above ground level. Growth should not be allowed above the top wire. Fruit is produced on the previous year's canes, so none should be expected in the first year. As soon as the fruit is picked, the old canes which have borne the fruit should be cut down to ground level and the new canes spread out in their place. (See the section on Blackberry for notes on training new canes).

The best means of propagation is by tip-layering.

## Culinary uses

Treat as blackberries or raspberries (q.v.).

# LONGAN
*Euphoria longana,* syn. *Nephelium longana*

## Origin

A native of India, this is now widely cultivated, especially in China and in many tropical and sub-tropical countries. It is related to the litchi and the rambutan and is cultivated in countries where one or other or both of these fruits are popular, usually in areas which are too cool for these fruits.

## The fruit

It is similar to the litchi in appearance, about 2.5 cm (1 in) in diameter, with a light brown outer shell. The flesh, botanically the aril, is white, with a sweet, pleasant flavour.

## The plant

It makes a neat tree some 10–12 m (32–40 ft) tall, with a low trunk and a spreading crown, densely foliated. The flowers grow in upright clusters.

## Cultivation

Longan is a little more adaptable than the litchi since it will grow in poorer soils and will tolerate colder conditions. Indeed, it requires some chilling temperatures before it will crop well. It can withstand several degrees of frost. Although not all the flowers set, it is still advisable to thin the

## The plant

It produces strong, prickly canes which rise up from the base. These carry 3–5-lobed leaves, also prickly. There are thornless varieties freely available which are more pleasant to handle. The blossom, which opens late in the season, is white and is borne in long sprays. The fruit is produced in summer and early autumn.

## Cultivation

This is a good plant for heavy soils rather than light or chalky ones, which tend to induce iron and manganese deficiencies. However, even heavy soils should be well drained, and cannot be too rich; they should be generously manured with liberal amounts of nitrogenous matter. Once established, mulch around the crowns of the plants annually in late autumn. To this can be added a feed of about 55 g (2 oz) of fish manure and 25 g (1 oz) sulphate of potash to each square m (square yd). Ideally the plant or plants should be trained to run north-south and the best site is a sunny, open and sheltered one.

When planted, the canes should be cut back to encourage new growth. Three to six new canes should be produced in the first season. Later there

fruit, otherwise it will be of an uneconomic size. It is wise to water the plant well during the fruiting period.

## Culinary uses

The fruit is delicious fresh and raw, but many believe it to be improved by cooking. It can be canned and bottled in syrup, and also dried. Treat it as you would a litchi. Some people say that preserved longan is superior to preserved litchi.

# LOQUAT

*Eriobotrya japonica*, **syn**. *Photinia japonica*

## Origin

The plant belongs to the Rosaceae, the same family as that of apples and pears, and is one of the very few sub-tropical plants in that group. The botanical name is derived from 'erion', wool, and 'botrys', a cluster, a reference to the slightly downy fruits. The loquat was at first thought to be a mespilus, or medlar.

Like so many plants that originate in China, the loquat is also confusingly named japonica or Japanese. Actually, it is a native of central China, introduced to Japan and widely cultivated and highly esteemed in both countries for centuries. In India, too, the crop is of considerable importance.

It was brought to Europe in 1787, not for its fruit but for the beauty of its foliage. It has become naturalised in many areas and will fruit freely in mild regions, though not frequently in Britain except sometimes after an unusually hot summer.

There are now many fine cultivars. The fruit is widely grown throughout sub-tropical regions. It is cultivated in parts of America (especially California), Australia and southern Europe and is planted widely in Mediterranean countries, where it is often seen as a decorative garden tree.

## The fruit

The loquats, which are borne in loose clusters of ten or so, are ovoid, sometimes slightly pear-shaped, with yellow or yellow-orange, slightly downy skins. In the type they are small, some 4 cm (1½ in) long. The flesh is white to yellow-orange, softly acid, sweetly perfumed. Many cultivars have really strongly scented fruits, but unfortunately many of these have very large pips in proportion to the amount of flesh. However, there are varieties with smaller seeds. There is usually one large seed, sometimes two, in each fruit.

The fruits mature in spring and early summer, a valuable asset since this means that by growing a loquat with other fruits one can extend the season for fresh fruits.

## The plant

A small evergreen tree which can reach 6–9 m (20–30 ft), but is usually much smaller than this, about 3 m (10 ft). The handsome leaves are large, 15–30 cm (6–12 in) long and some 7.5–15 cm (3–6 in) wide. They are firm and strongly ribbed or veined, dark, glossy green above and downy on the underside, with a woolly stem. The flowers are white, faintly tinged with yellow, 5-petalled, about 2 cm ($\frac{3}{4}$ in) wide and closely packed into a stiff terminal panicle 8–15 cm (3–6 in) long. These flower in late autumn and winter. They are so strongly scented that some people find them overpowering. There is also a variegated form.

## Cultivation

Although the plant itself is fairly hardy, it does not fruit well in cold climates. One has to bear in mind that the flowers open at a cold time of year, from autumn to the beginning of winter, and these can be damaged more easily than the tough foliage. For this reason, even in the milder regions of southern England and Ireland, it is given the protection of a south-facing wall, or it is grown inside in a cold or slightly heated greenhouse. The loquat has been known to fruit in London, which like most other cities can often offer a warmer home to some plants than could be found in the open countryside, and this gives one a guide to its capabilities. Obviously, it does better in warmer climates, and although subtropical, it can be grown successfully in the tropics at medium elevations, above some 1,000 m (3,000 ft) or so.

The plant will grow well in a great variety of soils, but does best in one which is light and loamy and deep. This should not hold a great proportion of lime. In cold climates a good place to grow the plant is in the ground against the high wall of a cold or slightly heated greenhouse or conservatory. A vigorous plant known to us and growing near our home flourishes in an open lean-to, but has never fruited. No doubt this is simply because it needs just a little more heat in winter.

Where a plant is grown this way, it should be watered freely from spring to early autumn and after that, more moderately. It should be sprayed with clean water daily in the warmer months and in early spring it is helpful to neaten the plant by clipping away wayward shoots.

Trees are usually grafted or budded, the rootstock often being a quince, which both dwarfs the plant and hastens an early fruiting. Layering can be carried out in spring and cuttings can be taken in summer.

Fruit is sometimes thinned, especially where it is wished to harvest fruit as large as possible. It is also thinned to maintain an even harvest. Like some apples, the loquat has a tendency to produce a large crop one year, become exhausted by this, and then produce a very small one the following year. Some people cut off the flower panicles (save them for flower arrangement), while others thin out the flowers by cutting through the cluster when pruning, or wait and thin out the fruit.

Loquats should be picked when fully ripe, because only then is their sugar content at its greatest. Ripe fruits should be well coloured and have a slight bloom on the skin. Loquats which are allowed to remain too long on the tree are particularly susceptible to fruit fly and so should be gathered when ready. Some regions in Australia have sections under the Plant Diseases Act which give obligatory dates for harvesting, e.g. before 31 October in coastal districts, 15 December inland. For this reason also the loquat is not recommended as a garden tree in some areas.

## Culinary uses

Loquats are refreshing, easily digested fruits, not highly nutritious but with many uses all the same. It can be eaten fresh, as it usually is, but it can also be made into a compote, by pouring syrup over the prepared fruits. These mix with others quite well. An agreeable combination can be arranged by adding to the loquats an equal quantity of mixed fruit, containing for example mango, papaw, pears, apples, oranges, peaches and apricots. The flavour of the fruit can be brought out by adding a little lemon juice. Ginger, preserved or candied, cut into fine slices, and finely cut candied citrus peels suit loquats.

PRESERVING    The fruits can be candied, and in some countries this type of sweetmeat is held in high esteem. Loquat jelly can be boiled down to make a fine-tasting paste.

When confronted with an abundance of loquats, we suggest that it would be worthwhile following some of the recipes usually applied to cherries.

To make a loquat jelly, wash and wipe the fruit, cut it up and cover it with cold water. Boil without stirring for 2 hours. Pour into bowl and allow to stand for 24 hours. Strain and measure the juice. Use equal quantities of sugar, i.e. 2 cups to 2 cups of liquid, with the juice of 1 lemon. Put all into a pan, stir well until the sugar is dissolved and then boil until the liquid jells, which is usually about 1 hour.

FREEZING   To freeze loquats place in a sugar syrup after peeling and removing seeds. Cook until tender, then chill. After chilling the cooked fruit, pack in a freezing container and cover with cold syrup. Seal and freeze.

DRINKS   There appear to be one or two local drinks made from loquats, and in particular a loquat liqueur made in Bermuda, but we have no experience of any of these.

# MABOLO
*Diospyros discolor*

## Origin
It is believed to have originated in the American tropics and it grows generally in the warmer regions of sub-tropical areas.

## The fruit
It is usually round, about 6–8 cm (2½–3¼ in) in diameter, rather similar in appearance to a flat persimmon, except that the skin has a velvety appearance due to the reddish hairs with which it is covered. The flesh is cream-coloured, sweet and of a dry texture. It contains several large seeds. There is a seedless form with a sweeter and moister flesh. The fruit has a strong aroma.

## The plant
Usually, this is grown just as a medium sized ornamental shade tree, for only a few fruits appear on each plant (these, however, often produce throughout the year). The leaves are 10–20 cm (4–8 in) long, have shining upper surfaces, and are pubescent beneath.

## Cultivation
The plant is usually raised from seed, but the seedlings develop slowly and may not be large enough to plant out until they are three years old.

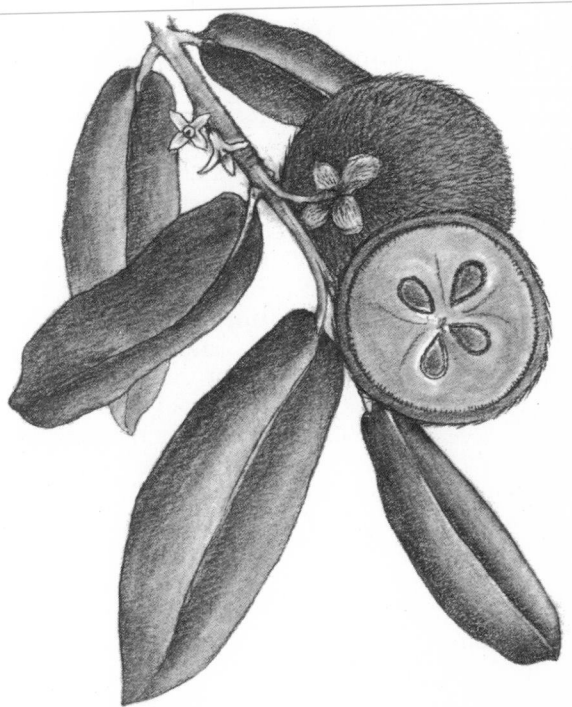

## Culinary uses
The uses of this fruit are fairly limited, a challenge to the imaginative cook. It is at its best served as fresh fruit juice. This can, or course, be used in a fruit salad as well as in sherbets and table jellies.

# MANGO
*Mangifera indica*

## Origin
A member of the same family, Anarcardiaceae, as the Jamaica plum and the cashew nut, the mango is one of a genus of a dozen or so species of evergreen trees believed to be natives of the East Indies and Malaya. However, it has been cultivated so long in India, for more than 4,000 years, that it is often believed to have come from that country, as its specific name suggests. Certainly it is one of the earliest known tropical fruits.

The fruit seems always to have attracted the attention of both travellers and growers. It seems most likely that it was the Portuguese traders who started it on its worldwide travels, taking the fruit with them to Africa and across to South America, where it was probably introduced first into Brazil. During the eighteenth century it came into the West Indies and central America and thence through the tropics and the warmer sub-tropics. Commercial production is carried out today in India, south-east Asia, the East and West Indies, central America, South and central Africa, the Persian Gulf region, Israel, Spain, the Canary Islands, Madeira, tropical Australia, the Philippines, Hawaii, Florida and California – almost everywhere, in fact, that the climate permits. Grown under ideal conditions it is highly productive. The country producing the greatest amount of fruit is India. It is claimed that five million tonnes of mangoes are produced each year there, most of this for home consumption.

The mango appears to be divided into two groups, those originating from India and those from the Philippines and America. Those of the first group are monoembryonic and those of the second, polyembryonic. It is therefore important to select a good variety to grow. Those of the Indian group are considered to yield the finest fruit. Alphonse is in this group, along with Julie, Peters and Mulgoa. Heyden or Haden mangoes, a Bahamian friend tells us, are very large, have firm flesh and are not so stringy as others. They have a good flavour, though not necessarily the best, but they are easier to eat. One should say in passing that it is difficult to eat a mango without getting sticky. Israel produces Haden, Maya, Mabruk and others.

## The fruit

Botanically, a drupe. Mangoes vary considerably in size, shape, colour, flavour and fibre content, usually according to variety but also according to maturity. Some fruits are ovoid and beaked, sometimes grooved from the stem end to a projection on one side known as the 'nak'. Some are kidney-shaped. Often they are large and heavy, weighing 170 g–680 g (6 oz–1½ lb), according to quality and variety. Fruits are a dark green initially. Some become a uniform yellow-green when ripe, some straw-coloured, while others are orange or red. Many combine more than one colour very attractively and are often prettily flushed. Colour differences are not always due to

varietal difference. Environment also affects the intensity of colour within a variety.

The fruit of the common mango is long, yellow-green, thin-skinned and with a very fibrous, but sweet, well-flavoured, light orange flesh. Elongated mangoes are sometimes called banana mangoes, possibly because of their colour as well as their shape. Others are known locally as Peach, Strawberry and Apple mangoes for various reasons. One of the very best varieties is the so-called Apple mango, represented by the mid-season variety Bowen, or Kensington. The fruit weighs just under 450 g (1 lb). It has skin of a finer texture than usual. This is bright orange with a rosy blush at the base and on the side exposed to the sun. This variety is grooved and beaked. The flesh is deep orange and free of fibre.

The flesh of the mango is naturally fibrous, but some modern cultivars have few fibres. The fibre content depends largely upon the structure of the large seed which the flesh surrounds. The varieties just mentioned have small seeds compared to the size of their fruits. However, many people feel that fibre content is less important than taste, and so many of the modern cultivars have been developed mainly for their flavour and are widely cultivated accordingly.

Usually the mango skin is tough and is not eaten. When fully ripe, good varieties are pleasantly aromatic, but inferior fruits are unpleasantly scented, best described as turpentine-like. Such kinds also have a fibrous and unpleasantly acid flesh.

## The plant

A dense, evergreen tree, medium sized or large according to the conditions under which it is grown. It can reach 18–20 m (60–70 ft). The shape of the tree varies. Some mangoes grow upright and tall, some are round- or oval-headed, and some have a broad base and a conical or pyriform top. The leathery, narrow, dark leaves, simple and entire, and often 38 cm (15 in) long but only 5–8 cm (2–3 in) wide, give a tufted appearance to the branches. The small pink flowers, about 6 mm (¼ in) in diameter, grow in terminal panicles which are much branched and surprisingly light and dainty when one considers the size of the fruit ultimately produced. There are always more individual flowers than there are finally fruits in a cluster. Both male and bisexual flowers are produced. Flowers near the apex of the panicle are most likely to set fruits. Blossoming usually takes place in early spring, but in some regions, north Queensland for example, there are two flowering periods. The fruits develop a very long stalk which reaches well down below the leaves in most cases.

The mango, in common with some other members of the same family, possesses a caustic sap. This is released when the fruit is picked, squirting out from the fruit stalk. It can cause irritation to eyes and skin, so gardeners are advised to wear sun glasses and rubber gloves, or to take other precautions.

## Cultivation

This is a tropical tree, so climate is of great importance, although it will grow in sub-tropical regions. It will not thrive in areas where the rainfall is continuous, but likes moderate moisture. It appears to do best in regions where there is a definite dry season, ideally in spring, since rain during the period when the tree is in blossom influences fruit setting and can bring disease. At the other end of the scale, heavy rains when the fruit is ripe cause the mangoes to split.

Although the mango is not frost hardy, and revels in a warm climate, it should be observed that where light ground frosts occasionally occur, a plant will eventually come to tolerate these, so long as it is covered and protected against them while it is small and young. Most kinds of soils will prove suitable, but these should be well cultivated beforehand, so that they are deep and fertile. Good drainage is essential. The mango roots have a tendency to roam in search of water, and for this reason are fairly adaptable. Nevertheless, while the young plant is becoming established it should not be allowed to want for moisture. As one authority says, 'a stable water table is an advantage'.

Mangoes can be produced from seed, but there are some disadvantages. Many good varieties, Bowen (or Kensington) is an example, produce polyembryonic seeds, which means that one seedling develops from the fertilised ovule, while the rest grow from vegetative buds which are present in the ovary. The majority of these seedlings will be similar to those of the parent plant

from which the fruit was gathered and the seed saved. Seeds of the monoembryonic mangoes, however, produce only one plant from a seed, and this seedling is most likely to deviate from type because of cross-pollination. These appear to be mainly the Indian types. For this reason, varieties of this nature are propagated by grafting, budding or some other vegetative method.

If seeds are sown they should be freshly taken from the fruit and not allowed to dry out. The seed should then have the husk removed, otherwise the root may be deformed. One can then see also if the seed is sound, for sometimes it is affected by the mango weevil.

The seedlings should be planted during a wet season as soon as they are large enough to handle, and always only when the plant is resting between spurts of growth and when the terminal shoots are dark green in colour. Great care should be taken not to injure the fibrous roots. Nurserymen grow the seedlings in a frame which has a floor, usually of concrete, so that there is no chance of the taproot growing down into the soil and becoming damaged on transplanting.

One can buy grafted trees. These should come into bearing in about three years after planting. They should also be ready trained. Naturally, the mango begins to branch somewhere about 1.8 m (6 ft) from the ground. Often when a plant is grown from seed it races away to form a long trunk which might be too tall for convenience. For this reason it is best to pinch out the top of the seedling at about 1 m (3 ft). It will then branch at this point, and although the trunk will continue to elongate, it will not be as tall as it would have been unstopped. Fruit-laden branches tend to droop to the ground, so one has to keep this fact in mind also.

Little pruning is necessary unless the tree looks as though it would be improved if some of the weaker shoots in the centre were removed. One Queensland gardener we know who does not want a large mango prunes his tree quite hard and it continues to bear well, but the usual practice is to thin out overcrowded branches and to shorten any limbs which hang too low.

The tree should be kept well fed, particularly in its early years.

## Culinary uses

Mangoes are rich in vitamin A and contain significant quantities of B and C. The fruits have about 10–20 per cent sugar.

Once you have managed to peel and stone it, the mango can be used in many ways. The easiest way to peel the fruit is to cut it lengthways into three slices, around the fruit from top to base on each side of the stone. These portions should be separated and you should then be able to remove the remaining portion from the stone. If you can crack the stone, the seed inside can be dried and eaten. When preparing mangoes for cooking it is wise to hold the fruit over a basin in order not to waste the juice.

A fully ripe mango can be served raw on its own. It is best to leave guests to tackle the fruit their own way. Provide spoons and a small dessert knife and fork. Provide finger bowls also, or a moist towel and an extra napkin.

A mango contributes plenty of fruit juice, and for this reason alone is good to use in fruit salads, but it loses its aroma quickly and should be eaten soon after it is peeled. When used in a salad, cover the dish until you are ready to serve it.

The fruit can be used in jams, cakes, preserves and fruit sauces. Try a purée of mango over meringues or ice-cream. With the purée one can make Mango Fool, which can be used in ice-cream, sherbets and mousse. The fruit can be made into a compote – just pour the syrup on the raw fruit. Almonds added to this provide a contrast in texture.

The vitamin C content is said to be greatest when the fruit is green, which is a pity in some ways. However, green mangoes are the best for chutneys. These are usually served with curries. Mangoes can also be cooked in curries; salted mango is used in fish curries. Here again the green fruits can be used.

A Mango Sauce for barbecued beef is made up from:

### Mango sauce

*2 ripe mangoes, sliced ready with any juice*
*2 finely chopped chillies or peppers*
*1 teasp caraway seeds*
*seasoning*

In a heavy pan melt butter and add the mangoes, the juice if any, the chillies and the caraway. Allow all to melt together but not to brown. Season. Serve hot.

To make Mango Mousse whip together equal quantities of ripe mango and whipped cream. Sugar to taste and add a squeeze of lemon. Blend for a few seconds until light and fluffy. Chill before serving.

PRESERVING  Recipes for Mango Chutney are numerous. Here is a simple one, but good, from Yamba in Australia.

### Mango chutney

*6–8 green mangoes, cut into small pieces*
*2 cups under-ripe tomatoes, sliced*
*4 cups sliced onions*
*4 cups raisins*
*4 cups brown sugar*
*3 cups vinegar*
*1 or 2 chillies*
*½ cup salt*
*curry powder to taste*

Mix all the ingredients together and boil for 1 hour. Pour into jars and seal.

Mangoes can be dried and they can be crystallised, when they are nicely chewy and not too sweet.

# MANGOSTEEN
*Garcinia mangostana*

## Origin

A member of a genus of about 180 species of evergreen trees, natives of tropical Africa, Asia and Polynesia. Some of them produce good timber, others yield resin and gamboge, many of them produce delicious and refreshing fruit. The Sapodilla, or St Domingo Apricot, belongs to the same family, Guttifereae. The generic name is in honour of Laurent Garcin (1683–1751), a French botanist who travelled widely in India and was the author of botanical books. The mangosteen itself is a native of the Malayan Peninsula, the East Indies and the Philippines.

The fruits of the mangosteen are not yet well known, but are held in high esteem by those familiar with them. It figures among the list of plants estimated to have a commercial potential for tropical Australia. It is grown commercially on a small scale in Java and the West Indies.

Among the species known locally for their fruits are *G. dulcis,* from the Moluccas, *G. livingstonei,* or Imbe, from tropical Africa and grown in Florida, and *G. xanthochymus,* syn. *Xanthochymus pictorius,* Cochin-goraka, an Indian species which also yields gamboge.

## The fruit

The globose fruit is slightly flattened and some 6–8 cm (2½–3 in) in diameter. It has a thick rind which is smooth and somewhat leathery, becoming deep purple when mature. Juice for the rind stains skin and fabric. The rind encloses 5–7 segments arranged in the same way as those of an orange, each with a seed surrounded by white, pink-veined, jelly-like flesh, the aril, described by some as having a similar texture to a ripe plum.

Imbe, *G. livingstonei,* has smaller fruits. Those of *G. xanthochymus* are borne in clusters and are bright glossy green when young, and an attractive golden yellow when ripe. They are roughly the same size as the mangosteen. The flavour of the flesh is more acid and distinctive.

## The plant

The mangosteen is a small, slow-growing tree which ultimately reaches a height of about 6 m (20 ft). The slender, elliptic-oblong, pointed leaves, 13–15 cm (7–8 in) long, which are deep green and leathery and glabrous on both sides, grow in pairs. The attractive red flowers resemble a single rose with 4 round petals. These grow solitary at the ends of branches.

Imbe, *G. livingstonei,* is a smaller tree than the above. It has blunt-ended leaves which have undulated margins. The 5-petalled flowers which grow solitary or in clusters of 2–5 are produced in the leaf axils. They are pale green and vanilla-scented.

*G. xanthochymus* is much taller than the others and will grow as high as 12 m (40 ft), with a tall trunk and a conical habit. Its branches grow almost parallel to the ground. The leaves are long, 23–46 cm (9–18 in), and are glossy and pendulous. The male and hermaphrodite flowers are small and white and are produced in clusters in the leaf axils.

## Cultivation

The mangosteen needs the tropics and a plentiful rainfall. It does not grow so well in sub-tropical districts. Temperatures which fall below 5°C (41°F) can kill the plant. When the temperature drops below 20°C (68°F), growth is slowed down, and consequently flowering and fruiting are affected. It is a challenge to a gardener who lives in a suitable climate, because it is considered to be a difficult plant to grow.

Soils should be fertile and high in organic matter. They must also be well drained.

Seedlings produce trees true to type. They need care because many seedlings are weak. For this reason they should be grown in the shade. They are easily damaged by wind and drought, so they must be given some protection. Seeds are best sown individually in fairly large pots which should be plunged in a medium which can be kept moist. Plants sometimes take from 8 to 20 years to produce fruit. So far only grafting has been found to be a suitable method of propagation outdoors and this is said to be difficult. Plants grown in glasshouses under stove conditions can be propagated from cuttings or ripe shoots rooted in sand under glass with heat, or in an electric propagating case.

Where young trees are acquired, these should be container-grown, not lifted from the ground. They should be planted in well-prepared soil during the rainy season.

## Culinary uses

This fruit should not be picked until it is quite ripe and then it should be eaten soon after. Inside the tough rind, the soft treacly flesh is divided into segments which can be separated. The fruit can be eaten raw, by itself or with others in a fruit salad.

Mangosteen is used in Indonesia to make vinegar, which indicates that it can first be made into wine.

# MEDLAR
*Mespilus germanica*

## Origin

In spite of its specific name, this plant, a member of the rose family, is a native of south-east Europe and lands beyond as far as Iran. It is the single member of its genus. It has become naturalised in central Europe and it is found growing wild in most countries to the west including England. However, there is some doubt that the medlar is a true native in England. The plant was once much more widely grown than it is today, in both gardens and orchards, and deserves to be better known now.

Mespilus is an old name for the plant and is made up from 'mesos' a half, and 'pilos', a ball, a reference to the characteristic shape of the fruits.

Cultivated medlars tend to differ in several aspects from the species in their habit of growth. There is a variety, *M. g. gigantea,* which as might be expected is a much larger plant generally than

the type and which bears very large fruits. There is also a variegated form.

## The fruit

Botanically a pome, the medlar is distinguished from its related fruits, such as apples and pears, by the fact that it is wide open at the top, revealing the ends of the carpels, hidden or enclosed in the others. The persistent calyces give each fruit a little crown.

## The plant

A deciduous, sometimes spiny tree, growing up to about 7–8 m (25 ft), a medlar makes an individual, interesting and unusual specimen tree for the garden, often assuming a contorted shape. It tends, like the apple, to be shaped by the prevailing wind. The spreading branches often make a right-angled turn when they produce new growth. The wide, solitary, white, sometimes pink-flushed flowers are produced at the tips of the main and side shoots in summer. Individually, these are quietly beautiful, framed with leaves; 5-petalled, they have centres of 30–40 stamens with red anthers. The leaves are quite large and handsome, being oblong to elliptical and 5–13 cm (2–5 in) long, downy and dull green. They turn colour attractively in autumn.

The species is thorny, but cultivars are thornless.

## Cultivation

Although medlars will grow in almost any type of soil, a well-drained warm loam in a sunny situation suits them best. They do not thrive in cold soils and they will not tolerate waterlogged conditions, although it is possible to grow them in moist places. In this case, medlars grafted on to a quince stock seem to do best.

The fruit is usually grown as a standard tree, with the varieties propagated by cleft grafting or shield budding onto species medlar, pear, quince, azarole or hawthorn stocks.

Medlars can also be raised from seed. These should be stratified and they are slow to germinate. This method is not really recommended, for the plants are too likely to return to type and give small fruits produced on very spiny growth.

The chief varieties in cultivation are: Dutch, which has large fruit and is a tree of spreading habit with very crooked branches; Nottingham, a tidier, more erect tree, with small, well-flavoured fruit; and Royal, which crops heavily with small fruits and makes a moderately sized, spreading tree.

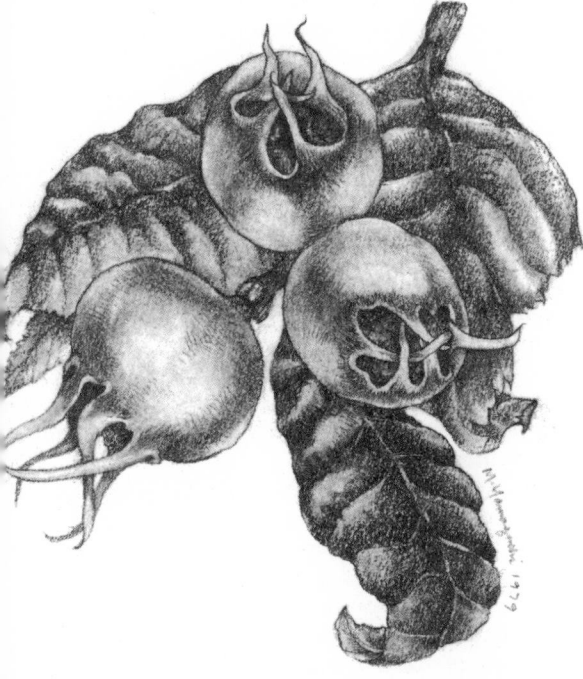

When ripe, in the late autumn, the fruits are brown, apple-shaped and hard. No doubt their original value, in the days before year-round fruit was on sale, lay in the fact that this is a winter fruit. Often harvesting is delayed until the first frost. This is thought to hasten the rotting period known as 'bletting', when some of their compounds are converted into sugars; medlars are not palatable until they are half rotten and melting in the mouth. They are bletted by laying them on a bed of hay in a well-ventilated place for some three weeks to two months, and are brought out to eat or cook as they are ready.

## Culinary uses

In some countries where the season is long, the fruits ripen on the tree and so can be gathered and eaten right away. Elsewhere the fruits have to be bletted (see above). They become a little like sleepy pears. Their flesh is then soft, brown and buttery, slightly fragrant, and although unattractive to look at, delicious to eat. (It helps the fruits to last longer in store if the stalk is dipped in brine.)

The medlar has long been valued for its therapeutic value, for it is said to be both diuretric and astringent. It is less versatile than most fruits, with a character very much of its own, but if you have a tree it is possible to make the most of a crop. The fruits are mainly eaten raw. To serve, wash and drain the fruit well. Place on a dish with a spoon to take out the flesh. No sugar should be needed.

One can make an excellent cold sweet by mixing this spooned flesh into which a little lemon juice is also blended with cream. Test for taste and add sugar if necessary.

PRESERVING   With the seeds removed medlars can be used for jams and with lemon for marmalade. For jelly, boil the fruits with sufficient water to cover them, mashing them as they boil. When the fruits are well mixed with the water, strain. Use about 1½ cups of sugar to every 2 cups of juice. The jelly can be flavoured with cinnamon or cloves. Boil one lemon, rind and juice, with every 6 cups of fruit. This jelly can be boiled down to make a cheese or a paste, as with quince.

DRINKS   It is possible to make a medlar wine (indeed, it is possible to make a wine from any organic material) in the same way that all other country wines are made (see basic recipe, p. 34), except that because of the mildness or blandness of its flavour a little outside tannin is advised. However, the resulting drink has none of the characteristic medlar flavour, so one questions the purpose of the exercise.

# MELON
*Cucumis melo*

## Origin

Believed to be native to Asia, but some say tropical Africa – the subject is controversial. The family itself, Cucurbitaceae, which contains the cucumber, gourds, marrow and pumpkin, a genus of about 30 species, has representatives in tropical Africa, Asia, America and Australia.

Cultivated since ancient times, in the Nile Valley for certain and perhaps further afield, the melon appears not to have been introduced into Europe until some time at the beginning of the fifteenth century. The French claim that Charles VIII brought it to their country from Naples after his Italian campaign in 1495. It is said that the new fruit was received with such enthusiasm by gourmands that some people, among them Pope Paul II, died from having eaten too much of it. Now it is grown on a grand scale in many regions of France, where as one travels through them, the scent of melon hangs deliciously on the air; regions such as the Vaucluse, the Bouches-du-Rhone, the Gard and along the Garonne, where they are cultivated outdoors from May until the end of November, being given cloche protection early and late in the season. Melons of some variety or another are also widely grown in almost all parts of the world.

The melon is a variable species. It is often difficult to define the many varieties, which seem to grow in number each year. However, there are some distinctive types into which all can be roughly grouped. These, of course, are also being interbred.

The cantaloupe, *C. m. cantaloupensis,* syn. *C. m. chate,* sometimes called the Rock melon, is said to have been first grown in Europe at the castle of Cantalupo in Italy. It is believed to be a fairly recent name, dating back to the mid eighteenth century. One belonging to this group, or thought to do so, is the Israel Ogen melon, now exported in quantity and highly popular in those countries to which it is sent. This is said to have taken its name from a kibbutz in Israel where it was bred. This variety is so easily recognisable and distinctive that some consider it to be a new type. Some of the new garden varieties such as Sweetheart much resemble this type.

*C. m. reticulata* is the Musk, Netted or Nutmeg melon. In cold countries, where melons are usually hothouse grown, these are the most popular type for this purpose. *C. m. inodorus,* or Cassaba, is the variety from which the winter melons have been bred. Best known of these is probably Honeydew. These melons have very hard skins and they can be stored for a month or more, unlike the other types of melons which ripen

quickly. Obviously this makes them excellent fruits for the export market. These are widely grown in Spain and the Canary Islands. The melon has given rise to so many forms that it should be possible to find varieties to suit the different climatic conditions which prevail in widely separated countries. The water melon is not a member of the *Cucumis* genus and is dealt with separately later under its own heading.

## The fruit

Botanically, a 3–6-celled, many-seeded berry. The different types of melon vary in size and appearance as well as in the colour of their flesh and the thickness of their rind. The cantaloupes have hard rind which is somewhat warty or scaly. These melons are often deeply grooved and seem to offer 8–12 sections into which the fruit can be cut for serving. Cantaloupes usually have orange-coloured flesh, although sometimes, but more rarely as in Fordhook Gem, this can be a lovely green. The ripe flesh is not firm but juicy and a little mealy.

The Ogen melon, even though it is believed to have come from the cantaloupe, is much smaller. Often one melon is served to one person. Instead of the deep grooves it has green markings or ribs on the yellow-orange skin. Some Musk melons are also segmented by broad ribs and grooves, yet others have a smooth skin. The green or yellow-green skin is netted, that is to say, it is covered with a slightly raised network pattern lighter in colour than the skin. The juicy flesh, usually highly scented, varies in colour according to variety, some being green, orange or even pink-orange. Fruits are rounded or oval. Winter melons, or Cassabas, are quite different in appearance from these already mentioned. They are usually oval, sometimes twice as long as they are wide. Their skins can be smooth, but more usually are shallowly corrugated. These are green or yellow. The flesh is pale, sweet when ripe, and crisper than the other melons, although it lacks their perfume.

Melon seeds are edible.

## The plant

A half hardy trailing herbaceous annual, considered by some to be vegetable rather than fruit. The leaves are large and rough to the touch, usually palmate lobed. The flowers are monoecious. The yellow, bell-shaped male blooms often grow in clusters, while the females, easily detectable by the tiny fruit below the flower, are usually solitary. In some varieties hermaphrodite flowers are produced.

## Cultivation

Almost everything depends upon the climate. One has to consider that the plants take about four months from sowing seed to ripening their fruits. There are some 'hardy' varieties which can be grown in cold frames, but on the whole melons cannot tolerate conditions under which the night temperature falls below about 18°C (65°F). It is important to select the varieties which will suit the mode of cultivation to be followed.

In some warm countries the melons can be grown out of doors in just the same way as pumpkins, usually on low circular mounds of specially prepared soil, some 1.2–1.8 m (4–6 ft) apart. Sometimes they are allowed to trail along level ground as marrows do. In other regions they may be grown in pits. They are not easy to grow in moist, tropical areas, mainly because they are very susceptible to fungus attack under these conditions.

In countries with late winters and cold springs, in Britain for instance, frosts can be expected until the last week in May or even early June, melons can be grown successfully only under glass, except in unusual summers, and then obviously success is more a matter of chance than planning. However, in sunny districts they can be grown the year round under glass.

In northern countries, where plants are to be grown in heat, it is important to sow seed early. Seed can be sown in November for fruits in April, and so on in succession, the last seed being sown in August for November and December fruit.

For frames and cold greenhouses, for which a different variety should be used than that for a hothouse, the seeds are usually sown in early May. The cantaloupe is best for frame production, as are some of the new varieties offered by garden seedsmen. Frame production is not easy and calls for skill and close attention to the plants.

When plants are set out it is the practice to raise them slightly on mounds of specially prepared compost. This is done to prevent stem rot, a disease which affects the cucumber family generally. Some gardeners plant the seedling in its bed, its root ball half in and half out of the soil. When the plants have rooted, the soil is washed away from the upper section of the root ball. These roots become tough and hard, more resistant to fungus attack. The plants in greenhouses are trained on a trellis of vertical and horizontal wires, so that each shoot can be tied in place and well spread out. Usually the main shoots are tied to the vertical wires and stopped when the plant is some 1.2–1.5 m (4–5 ft) tall. The side shoots, tied to the horizontals, are also stopped when they are no more than some 30 cm (12 in) in length. Gardeners try to keep the fruits on the side stems and do not allow them to form on the main stems. Usually fruits are restricted to four to a plant.

It is usually necessary, certainly advisable in most countries, to hand-pollinate the flowers, outside as well as indoors. This is best done at noon on bright, sunny days, using a soft camel-hair brush to take the pollen from the male to the female flowers. An alternative method is to pick off a male flower, turn back the petals to expose the stamen, and simply insert it in a female flower and leave it there for a day. One can tell which flowers have been pollinated, because the small fruits soon begin swelling. It is then that the rest are pinched off.

Both watering and ventilation are critical. Young seedlings need a temperature of about 18–21°C (65–70°F) and a moist atmosphere. Once they are away and growing sturdily, the temperature should not be allowed to fall below 16°C (60°F) at night, although the day temperature may safely rise. Once it reaches 27°C (80°F) the house should be ventilated.

Rich composts should not be used because these encourage too lush a growth. Any one of the proprietary potting mixtures will suffice, although nurserymen tend to use clean soil which has been manured for some previous crop, so that while it is rich in humus, this has been well broken down. They prefer heavy loam to a light soil, and this is improved by mixing in a little clean sand to keep it open. Fertilisers mixed with loam in the preparation of a soil mixture include hoof and horn and bonemeal in equal parts.

After a while white rootlets may appear on the

soil surface. This is an indication that a top dressing is needed. Apply well-rotted manure or home-made compost. Take care to keep this away from the base of the stem and not to cover it.

In all cases water must be given sparingly as the fruits ripen, otherwise they tend to split.

It is also important to isolate the fruit in some way so that air can flow freely around it. Large fruits are usually supported by slipping them inside special melon nets hung from the structure. In frames, or when the plants grow on the ground, a simple method is to use upturned flower pots and to rest the melon on their bases. Alternatively, make small platforms of conveniently slatted wood.

Few melons sweeten after harvesting, although they do soften. If melons are to be really sweet and full flavoured they must be allowed to ripen fully on the plant. Most melons accumulate the greater part of their sugars in the last few days of maturity. Many varieties, cantaloupes or Rock melons particularly, on reaching full maturity develop a crack around the edge of the stem or button, the enlarged section of stem which joins the fruit. If one applies gentle pressure to this area with the thumb or forefinger and the fruit is fully ripe, the button will come away easily from the fruit. One should never have to tug the stem off.

Winter melons are sometimes treated differently. These can be picked when unripe and stored for weeks in a cool but dry and airy place, where they will soften. Obviously these will be better if left to ripen on the plant, but this is not always convenient.

## Culinary uses

Melons are another of those lovely, refreshing fruits that are almost like a solid drink. It is said that one can carry this further and make an air hole in the top of a melon, plug it again and then in a few days find that the whole of the interior has turned to liquid, delicious to drink. Well, perhaps. We haven't tried it.

Ripe melons can be refrigerated for a day or two. Ideally they should be served chilled but not icy or they will have little flavour. If the fruit is to be placed near other foods, it is best to put it in a plastic bag so that it keeps its flavour to itself. Melon flesh contains about 94 per cent water

and only 5 per cent sugar, which as one authority points out is only half the sugar content of an apple or pear. The fruit is rich in vitamins and mineral salts. Taken with lemon, melon is said to help eliminate uric acid from the body.

For the cook, the fruit is an inspiration to the imagination, for it can be prepared in so many ways. One can begin the day simply with a slice of the raw fruit, which is absolutely refreshing on its own, and is also good with cereals, providing fruit sugar instead of the refined kind.

It is delicious at the beginning of a meal, when it can be served alone with a little lemon juice or ginger, or as an accompaniment to raw smoked meat or fish. In Italy and elsewhere it is often served with thinly sliced prosciutto. It makes an excellent hors d'oeuvre. Melon cubes or balls can be mixed with shrimps or prawns and served in a sauce made with cream and curry powder. This looks good served in individual glasses with a little mint as a garnish. A bowl of diced melon, or a filled fruit shell, can be smothered with a piquant sauce made from:

### Melon piquant sauce

*1 destsp curry powder*
*1 teasp ginger*
*1 small glass port*
*1 destsp kirsch*
*4 tabsp whipped cream*
*1 tabsp apricot purée*
*honey*

Blend curry powder, ginger, port and kirsch. Add the cream, purée and honey to taste.

For a soup, use very ripe fruit. Peel and cube the melon and reserve a few nicely shaped cubes for garnish. Blend or rub the remainder through a sieve. To every 2 cups (and this should be enough for 4, but it's not a bad idea to make a batch so that you can refrigerate or chill it for another day) add 1 cup of orange juice, 1 tablespoon lemon or lime juice and a generous pinch of cinnamon or ginger, according to taste. Chill for at least an hour before serving. Pour into chilled soup cups, garnish with the cubes and mint sprigs and hand round ginger as a condiment.

The melon shell with the flesh scooped out makes an excellent vessel for a special dish. Individual salads, chicken or tuna for instance, into which a little of the flesh has been incorporated, can be heaped into small shells. The flesh can be cut out and diced, or it can be scooped out with a special melon baller. Melon à la Parisienne, for example, is simply a shell filled with fruit salad, into which some of the melon flesh has been introduced and moistened with kirsch or maraschino.

Melon with Wine makes a sociable party dish. You need a ripe melon (a honeydew is especially good for this) and a bottle of a sweet white wine. Cut a small triangular piece off the stem end of the fruit to act as a plug. Stand the fruit in a bowl so that it stays upright. Scoop out the seeds. Incidentally, always strain these to get extra juice and remember that the seeds can be eaten; some people roast them first. Fill the cavity with wine and replace the plug. Chill for 6 hours or so. Before serving, pour the wine into a glass jug or decanter. Leave the melon in the bowl and cut it down in slices. Serve a glass of wine with each slice of fruit.

Small melons with the seeds scooped out can be filled with a water ice or sherbert; lemon and lime are good for this.

PRESERVING  Melons make delicious jams, jellies and conserves. Small, unripe melons left on the plants at the end of the season can be pickled like any small cucumber. The inner rind of any melon need not be wasted. Remove the tough, outer skin with a parer and dice the rind. To make jam use 3 lemons with every 2 cups of flesh and 1½ cups of sugar.

Melon and Mandarin Marmalade is unusual, a good gift preserve.

### Melon and mandarin marmalade

*3 mandarins*
*6 cups melon flesh*
*4 cups boiling water*
*6 cups sugar*
*1 teasp lemon juice*

Slice the mandarins, cover them with the boiling water and allow to stand overnight. Cover the cubed melon with half of the sugar and allow that to stand also. The next day, boil the mandarins in the water until the skin is tender. Drain in a colander. Add the fruit to the melon and sugar and put all into a preserving pan. Bring to the boil, add the rest of the sugar, boil briskly with the

lemon juice until the mixture sets. Pour into hot jars.

# MONSTERA
*Monstera deliciosa,* syn. *Philodendron pertusum*

## Origin

From Mexico and Guatemala, one of a genus of about 30 tropical evergreen climbers belonging to the arum family, Araceae, and the only one of them, so far as is known, which produces a delicious fruit. Originally a jungle climber, it is now frequently seen in gardens in tropical and sub-tropical regions. The large pinnate leaves are perforated with oblong or oval holes which remind some people of Emmental cheese, hence one of the common names. In some countries the monstera is popular as a house plant. It seldom fruits in the home, but will do so in a greenhouse if conditions are right.

*M. d. borsigiana,* from Cordoba and Mexico, has smaller, glossy leaves, with few if any holes, and a leafstalk wrinkled where it joins the leaf. This variety does not fruit so well as the type.

*M. d. variegata,* sometimes known as *Philodendron pertusum variegatum,* is a mutant with handsomely coloured leaves, with cream and green-yellow splashes and streaks and sometimes an entire leaf coloured, although new growth sometimes turns back to green unless it is removed. Once thought to be a different plant, *Philodendron pertusum* is now known to be no more than the juvenile form of the monstera. Once it reaches a certain stage in its development, the leaves change their character and become large and perforated.

## The fruit

Botanically, a composite fruit. It is long, about 23 cm (9 in) in length, and is a dull, deep green, cone-like in appearance or, as some think, like a narrow ear of green maize. This develops from the spadix of the flower and takes just a little longer than a year to mature.

The fruit is covered with a rind consisting of hexagonal plates or scales, which protect the individual fruits. The little fruitlets ripen from the base of the cone upwards. The rind then slowly disintegrates, the little plates falling away to reveal the scented white pulp. It can be inconvenient to have, or to eat, partially ripe whole fruits. In fact, unripe fruitlets if eaten cause irritation to mouth and throat, so it follows that the whole fruit must be properly matured. It is possible to induce the fruit to ripen evenly by picking it at the point when the base of the rind is beginning to wrinkle and then wrapping the whole fruit in paper and keeping it for a few days. When unwrapped, all the little plates should fall away.

## The plant

Although often seen in a fairly compact state when grown as a house plant, the monstera will, in fact, climb 15 m (50 ft) or more. It is a stout, woody-stemmed, close-jointed tree climber. It attaches itself by means of adventitious roots, meanwhile producing long cord-like roots which dangle in and draw moisture from the moist air

in which the plant normally grows. These same roots will grow into or on almost any obstruction they meet. The large, thick, glossy green leaves will grow as long as 1 m (3 ft) and almost as wide, on the ends of long stems. Small leaves, and entire leaves without holes, when appearing on mature plants, indicate a starvation diet.

The inflorescence looks like a thick, slightly yellow arum. It consists of a bisexual spadix enclosed in a creamy-white, boat-shaped spathe. The flowers are borne in the leaf axils singly or in clusters.

A monstera begins to bear fruit after its second or third year from planting. It will continue fruiting indefinitely, providing that the soil is fertile and the conditions kind.

If grown indoors as a decorative plant, the monstera is most unlikely to flower or fruit. To encourage good leaves with plenty of dramatic holes, go contrary to normal practice with house plants and use a pot or other container larger than necessary. The sometimes unsightly aerial roots can be led down into this or they can in fact be

Top: Ripening Mangoes *(G. R. Roberts)*
Bottom: Papaw *(M. Withers)*

Top: Passion Fruit "Purple Gold" *(L. Johns)*
Bottom: Beura Bosc Pears *(M. Withers)*

cut off completely without doing more than delay the development of the plant.

## Cultivation

This plant is not only handsome and distinctive, it is also vigorous. It will grow in tropical or sub-tropical regions. It revels in a warm, moist atmosphere and a rich soil. It dislikes too windy a situation, where it fails to grow quickly, or characteristically it may hug the ground and even become bush-like instead of climbing. Given adequate support it will climb high, even to the top of a very tall palm, but one should keep in mind that fruit from any tall plant is difficult to harvest. It is therefore best used around a porch, to cloak, grace or render profitable a shed, fence, tree stump or even to cover a mound or bank.

The roots will securely fix themselves to any support. Where none exists, even a plank of wood will suffice, for the roots will soon grow into this, but whatever is used should be strong and well anchored.

It is not often possible to grow monstera from seeds, mainly because these are not often produced, and anyway it takes a long time for a plant to fruit from seeds. Fortunately the plant is easily enough propagated by cuttings, stem sections of the mature wood, each bearing a leaf or two. Shoots can also be air layered and shoot tips will root in water.

In a greenhouse the plant will need a moist, warm atmosphere and plenty of food if it is to fruit. It should be repotted as soon as the roots fill its present home. It needs to be supported early in life. One of the best supports is a stout stake well covered with moss into which the roots can grow and from which they can draw extra moisture. Some people use a cylinder of wire netting to keep the moss in place, but it can also be simply bound to the stake with string.

## Culinary uses

Some find that the fruit leaves an unpleasant aftertaste, others declare it to be delicious, a blend of bananas and pineapple. The pulp is used, well strained, as a summer drink, as an ice-cream flavouring and for other creamy desserts.

# MULBERRY
*Morus nigra*

## Origin

One of a dozen species of deciduous trees and shrubs grown mainly for the beauty of their foliage, and belonging to the Moraceae, a family to which the fig and breadfruit also belong. It has been grown in Asia and parts of Europe since ancient times, not only for its fruit, but also in some regions for its leaves, on which the silkworm feeds. It seems probable that the mulberry originated in Persia, although some say in the southern parts of the Caucasus, or in the Nepal mountain area, and because of its thirst-quenching, juicy fruits the plant spread to other countries. Those who once used it for silkworms found that another species, *M. alba,* from the eastern and central areas of China where it had long been cultivated for its part in the silk trade, has leaves which when converted by the grub made silk of a superior quality, and so in time the black mulberry became cultivated for its fruits alone. So widespread has been its cultivation, whether for fruit or silk, that in those European countries blessed with a warm climate the tree has become naturalised in some places. The Greeks are believed to have introduced it into Europe from its homelands. The Romans praised its fruit. Indians grow and dry it. Back in Iran and Turkestan the tree has been exploited properly, and there are now seedless varieties cultivated in those countries. In Australia we saw many inferior mulberries, referred to as 'English' mulberries, with small, hard fruit. These are nothing like the mulberries which deserve to be cultivated and were probably growing in too dry and arid a soil in too hot a climate. These were probably *M. alba,* popular in home gardens and capable of producing acceptable fruit if well grown.

The mulberry came to Britain in the 1500s. King James I had an idea that he could enliven the country's economy by producing silk, and for this purpose he ordered mulberry trees to be planted in gardens about the country, some 100,000 in all, it is said. Planting continued until the beginning of the seventeenth century. The trees flourished, but not the silk trade. Some of the same trees can be found today in old gardens, for the mulberry is long-lived.

## The fruit

Botanically, not a berry but a collective fruit, in appearance like a swollen loganberry. To describe the fruit one must first describe the flowers, which are small and unisexual, the two sexes on short, green, pendulous catkins of no beauty, strictly utilitarian. The flowers which produce the fruits are made up of clusters of individuals consisting of four leaf-like structures which are grouped into two pairs. These enclose the pistil. When this has been pollinated and the seed begins to mature, these green growths do not fall away, as do for instance the petals of a bramble blossom, but they and their fleshy bases begin to swell. Ultimately they become completely altered in texture and colour, being succulent, fat and full of juice, and finally a purple-red in colour. In appearance, each tiny swollen flower roughly resembles the individual drupe of a blackberry, except that you can trace the shape of the perianth. The fruit is first green, then pink, finally becoming a crimson or purple-red. It is very juicy when ripe, and has a pleasant, slightly musty acid flavour.

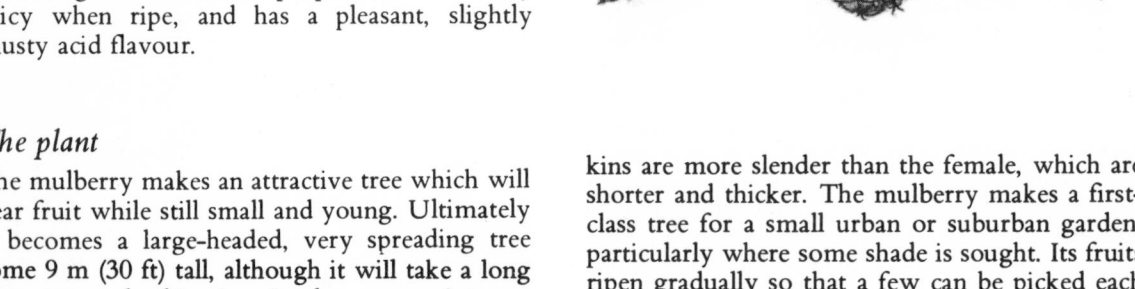

## The plant

The mulberry makes an attractive tree which will bear fruit while still small and young. Ultimately it becomes a large-headed, very spreading tree some 9 m (30 ft) tall, although it will take a long time to reach this size. It also grows into an attractive, informal shape with a short, rugged trunk. Some of the centuries-old trees still to be seen are often supported with struts under their branches, leaning, gnarled and dignified, but still beautiful and fecund.

In northern climates the mulberry is one of the latest of trees to break its buds, later sometimes than the walnut. It does not resist the early autumn frosts either, so that it is bare for a great part of the year.

The young shoots are downy. The leaves, broad and somewhat heart-shaped, 2–5-lobed, with coarsely toothed margins, are 8–23 cm (3–9 in) long, the difference in size depending on whether they grow on the fruiting or on barren shoots. They are a dark green, rough-textured on the upper sides, downy beneath. The flowers appear soon after the buds break. The male cat-

kins are more slender than the female, which are shorter and thicker. The mulberry makes a first-class tree for a small urban or suburban garden, particularly where some shade is sought. Its fruits ripen gradually so that a few can be picked each day for several weeks.

## Cultivation

The mulberry makes a good town tree which will grow well in a tub. Although it does not enjoy tropical conditions, it is a sun lover. It likes a warm, well-drained soil, preferably a deep loam.

In temperate regions this is one of the few trees that need to be watered in dry seasons. If the roots become too dry during drought, the fruit is likely to drop before it has fully ripened. For this reason shallow soils such as those frequently found on chalk or gravel are not recommended.

In cold countries the best time to plant a mulberry is in the spring when the ground is becoming warm, since this encourages root action. Take care not to damage roots, which should go about 15 cm (6 in) below the soil surface.

It is not advisable to prune the trees heavily since the plant is inclined to bleed at the cuts. Obviously dead wood should be cut away as should any damaged or crossing branches. If pruning is carried out while the tree is dormant, bleeding will be kept to a minimum, and in any case pruning is always easier when there are no leaves to obstruct the view. Old trees tend to lean, so where an elderly tree exists it is prudent to begin shoring up any branches which look as though they might need it one day. Try to keep the tree well balanced and attractively shaped.

The mulberry can be grown in the usual fruit tree forms, i.e. standard, half-standard, bush or pyramid, depending largely upon what the nurseryman has to offer. It can also be fan-trained, a good shape to choose if the tree is to be grown in a cold garden, for it can then be given the protection of a warm wall.

Obviously, if the tree is to be trained as a pyramid, it will require a certain amount of pruning. One should cut back laterals, the side shoots, to about six leaves in summer, but the leaders ought not to be cut, or if this seems advisable because they are very strong growing, nip out only the tips. Plants trained against a wall should be inspected, and those shoots growing out at right angles to the wall should be shortened, again to about six leaves. Trees grown in pots, usually 25 cm (10 in) size, should be repotted annually before growth starts. Those in larger containers are best top-dressed.

Plants can be raised from seed, but unfortunately the seedlings take many years to produce fruit. Cuttings and layers are quicker. Take cuttings in the early autumn, selecting 20 cm (8 in) shoots of the strong new growth. Strike them in moist sand in a cold frame. They should root in early spring. Transplant to the open ground in a sheltered spot, and move them to their permanent positions the following spring.

Another method is to take short cuttings, just 3–5 cm (1–2 in) long, with a heel of old wood attached. This should be about 8 cm (3 in) long. Insert these firmly in the open ground in a shaded, sheltered position, with just two or three buds or eyes remaining above soil level. Roots should be well formed by the following autumn, but keep the plants in this place until the follow-ing spring, unless it is more convenient that they should be planted in the autumn. This is a good way to provide pot plants. Layering should be done in autumn.

Under certain conditions, i.e. in cold, wet situations, or after or during periods of drought, the fruit may drop from the tree before it is fully ripe. It can be collected and allowed to ripen and then used for jellies or preserves. The ripe fruits fall easily, and if the tree is growing in grass they come to little harm and do not become soiled. One should keep watch, however, for birds, which love the fruits. It is possible gently to go over the lower branches of the tree each day and gather the ripest fruits. Unwashed, they will keep several days in a refrigerator in a covered container.

## Culinary uses

The ripe fruits contain about 9 per cent sugar, with malic and citric acid, which means that they are sweet yet tart. We think that they are at their best when eaten straight from the tree with cream. Although one should handle the fruits as little as possible because they are so juicy and quickly stain the fingers, we like to wash them, especially as we have to collect so many from the ground. This is best done by dunking a colander holding just a few fruits into cold water, letting it drain well before emptying it and then washing another batch. Fruit for freezing is washed and allowed to dry in the air for a while.

The refreshing tart taste, in some ways reminiscent of grapefruit, means that these fruits can be enjoyed in salads and mixed with most of the foods that go so well with grapefruit – cream cheese, sour cream and yoghurt, for example. They also go well with meats – try a mulberry sauce with roast lamb.

They blend well with other fruits, especially ripe pears and apples. Garnish a compote with the berries at the last moment so that the juice does not get a chance to run.

The mulberries can be used in any way that other berries are used, in pies, tarts, puddings, sieved and raw, made into a fool by being stirred into a custard or cream, or sweetened and puréed as a sauce for ice-cream or a plain pudding. To make a compote pour boiling syrup, or better still mulberry juice syrup, on the raw fruits. We find that mulberry ice-cream is quite delicious; simply follow the basic recipe given on page 33.

The fruits really do stain, so take care. The juice is sometimes used to colour certain wines or cordials.

PRESERVING   Although these fruits are excellent pulped and put through a straining bag for jellies, which incidentally can also be boiled down to a paste, a preserve in which the fruits are kept whole is more unusual. For this a quantity of the juice is needed as well as the fruit. Use inferior fruits to render down for the juice.

### Mulberry preserve

*2 cups juice*
*4 cups ripe, selected mulberries*
*5 cups preserving sugar*

Boil the sugar with the fruit juice and skim if necessary. Add the mulberries and turn off the heat. Leave the mulberries to warm through slowly in the syrup and then bring the mixture slowly to the boil and simmer it for 10 minutes. Pour it out carefully into a large bowl. The following day re-boil, again slowly, then simmer the mixture until it becomes thick and sets when tested. Ladle carefully into pots. This is a good preserve to serve with scones or home made bread. It is also very good served with vanilla ice-cream, especially if you pour on a little liqueur.

There is nothing like having a mulberry tree of one's own to discover how best to use the fruits. Since our own little tree came into bearing, our fruit menus have been greatly enriched. A surprising quantity can be gathered from a comparatively small and young tree.

DRINKS   There is an ancient drink still to be found in odd corners of France which was made from mulberry juice sweetened with honey, or some say mead. We have never tasted it, but it certainly sounds better than the somewhat wasteful country wine made from mulberries. Much preferable, we say, is mulberry gin, made from equal parts of mulberries and gin, sweetened with about 1 cup of sugar to every 2 cups of liquid and with the addition of a few drops of almond essence. Leave the gin on the berries for several months and then strain off without crushing the berries, which will largely have disintegrated by this time. These gin-flavoured fruits can make an unusual and appetising sauce for a rich meat dish.

# MYROBALAN PLUM
*Prunus cerasifera*

## Origin

The plant is believed to have come from western Asia and the Caucasus, but it has been so long in cultivation that it is now to be found in most countries. It has been used so long and so intensively as a farm hedge and as a rootstock for plums that as one might expect it has escaped in some areas and sometimes appears to be a wild plant. It makes an excellent windbreak hedge and it was thought at one time that it might supplant the thorn, although experience has indicated that it is slightly more expensive to raise on a large scale.

*P. cerasifera* has given rise to many beautiful varieties which have become important decorative garden plants in many parts of the world. One with purple leaves and rose-coloured blossom is perhaps the best known and most greatly appreciated. This is *P. c. atropurpurea,* which was introduced from Persia in 1880 and is sometimes known and listed in catalogues as *Prunus pissardi.* More lovely forms have been derived from this.

## The fruit

Botanically, a one-seeded drupe, brightly coloured, orange-red and yellow, the fruits about 4 cm (1½ in) in diameter, round but with a tiny point on the end. The stalk is well indented. The flesh is yellow, soft and quite juicy, though perhaps not fully flavoured until cooked. In some climates the ornamental varieties fruit well. The skins of the fruits of *Prunus pissardi* are of similar hue to the plant's foliage, with the flesh also dark and sweet, rounder than the type and a little larger.

## The plant

Probably the best use for this section of the prunus family is as garden hedges or screens. This precludes very largely the gathering of a rop of fruit, simply because of the constant trimming that is required. Nevertheless, the attraction of the flowers and the foliage and the efficacy of the screen or hedge thus made amply justifies its use in this way. There are many lovely forms of *P. c. atropurpurea,* including Trail Blazer, which has dark foliage, white blossom and crimson cherry plums. Like all other blossoms, cherry plum branches can be used in flower arrangement.

Left to grow naturally, *Prunus cerasifera* makes a neat, round-headed tree of some 8 m (30 ft). Its leaves are much shinier than those of other plums, about 4–6 cm (1½–2½ in) long, toothed and slightly downy on the veins on the undersides. The white flowers, almost 3 cm (1 in) across, grow in clusters of two or three from buds made on the previous year's shoots. The bark is brown.

## Cultivation

Myrobalan plum will grow on most soils so long as this is not too dry, although it also likes the sun. It is usually planted as a hedge in two rows some 23 cm (9 in) apart with 30 cm (12 in) intervals between the plants. Trimming should be carried out in summer. It will grow on lime and usually succeeds near the coast.

## Culinary uses

Use as for plum (q.v.).

# NATAL PLUM
*Carissa grandiflora,* syn. *Arduina grandiflora*

## Origin

A genus of evergreen, spiny shrubs or small trees, natives of Africa, Asia and Australia. It was introduced into Florida in 1886 by T. L. Meade, and again in 1903 by Dr David Fairchild.

## The fruit

An ovoid berry about 5 cm (2 in) long, scarlet and plum-like.

## The plant

This is a handsome shrub growing 2–4.5 m

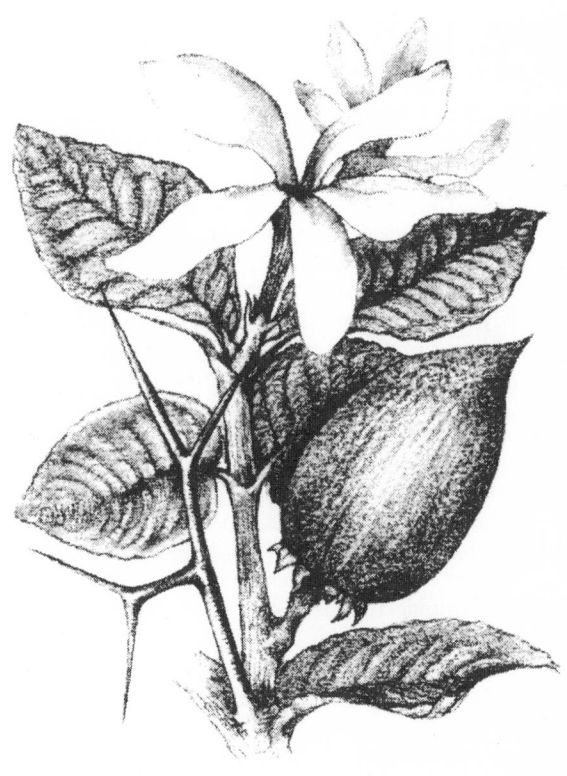

(6–15 ft) tall, with long spines and leathery leaves 2.5–8 cm (1–3 in) long. The attractive white, orange-blossom-like flowers appear for most of the year, sometimes simultaneously with the fruits.

## Cultivation

It grows in ordinary, well-drained soil, equally well in coastal and inland areas. It makes a good hedge plant.

## Culinary uses

The fruit can be eaten raw, in which case it should be fully ripe. It need not be fully ripe for cooking. It looks attractive when served in halves, either raw in fruit salads or in compotes. It is excellent used in pies, flans and tarts.

PRESERVING   A fine jelly is best made with slightly unripe fruits.

FREEZING AND BOTTLING   It can be frozen and/or bottled and canned like plums.

# NECTARINE
*Prunus persica* var. *nectarina*

## Origin

See the section on Peach. As its botanical name indicates, the nectarine is a variety of the same species as the peach. It is likely to have begun life as a 'sport' of some peach tree somewhere, a long time ago, probably in the Far East, and was fortunately nurtured and propagated by gardeners there for centuries. However, this was not likely to have been the only chance, since peaches seem to have a tendency to be sportive and will often bear nectarine fruit, just as a nectarine tree will sometimes sport a peach. Stones taken from a nectarine and sown may develop into a peach tree, and those taken from a peach may develop into a nectarine. There have also been records of fruits which were half nectarine, half peach.

The popular name is supposed to have been derived from 'nectar', the drink of the gods, because of the delicious and unusual flavour of the fruit, which differs slightly from that of the peach.

Possibly because of its smooth, plum-like skin, there is an old belief, still held by some people, that the nectarine is the result of a cross between a peach and a plum, which is another prunus, but every scientific evidence rejects this theory in favour of the above explanation.

The history of the nectarine is thus inevitably linked with that of the peach, which is believed to have originated in China, in spite of its specific name *persica*. However, it seems certain that the nectarine was introduced into Europe from Persia and thence into Britain some time in the sixteenth century. Here it was grown only by those wealthy enough to maintain expensively heated houses for the fruit, or to be able to heat walls on which the fruit was trained, since it is not quite so hardy as the peach, which can be grown out of doors in many districts in Britain. Inevitably, its cultivation spread to the New World, where now more than 50 varieties of nectarines are grown outdoors in those regions favourable to them. These include many of the eastern states and along the Pacific coast.

In spite of its close relationship with the peach, in this book we have treated it separately because it is 'sufficiently distinct both in flavour and general appearance to be considered as a separate fruit for dessert and exhibition purposes' to quote the Royal Horticultural Society *Dictionary of Gardening*.

## The fruit

Botanically, a one-seeded drupe. The nectarine is generally smaller than the peach and is instantly recognisable by its smooth skin and brighter colour. It looks more like a round plum than a peach. The flesh varies according to the variety – white, yellow or red. Some nectarines have flesh which clings to the stone, some are freestone. Some have a pleasant and strong perfume. Some commercial growers are finding that the new yellow-fleshed nectarines of the 'Nectared' type are becoming popular. These are not so likely to bruise with handling and transport as the white-fleshed kinds.

## The plant

In all respects like a peach tree.

## Cultivation

Nectarines can be cultivated in the same way as the peach (q.v.), bearing in mind that they are not quite so hardy, and need more water at the roots while the fruit is swelling.

## Culinary uses

Use in the same way as peaches.

# OLIVE
*Olea europea*

## Origin

The name comes from an old Latin word, probably used for the oil extracted from the fruit of the tree. The plant is one of a genus of about 50 species of evergreen shrubs and trees in the family Oleaceae, which also includes the ash, privet, jasmine and lilac.

*O. europea* has the varieties *oleaster*, found growing wild, a spiny form with inedible fruits, and *O. e. sativa,* syn. *communis,* the cultivated, oil-yielding form with larger leaves and fruits.

As is inevitable, with a plant so widely cultivated and for centuries of such value to mankind, the origins of the olive are somewhat obscure. There are some who believe that its original home is probably Asia Minor and Greece, while others say that it first grew wild in a region limited by the Caucasus, Iran and the coasts of Syria and Palestine, and that from these regions it spread into Egypt, Asia Minor, North Africa, Greece and Western Europe and so to other countries much further afield. Yet others say that the species still found growing wild in Egypt is the ancestor of this important fruit. Whatever its origin, there is no doubt that the plant can now be found growing in a great many places and countries throughout the world, and has become naturalised in many warm places. In the Mediterranean lands it forms a characteristic feature of the landscape.

The olive will grow in the mildest areas of the British Isles and can be found thence right across the world to Australia and New Zealand. To these 'new' lands it travelled in the wake of immigrants from Spain and Italy.

Since the fruits are inedible until they are processed, it was not for their flesh that they were originally cultivated, but for the oil which can be expressed from them. This was first used for purposes other than food. For centuries and in many lands and to serve many religions, olive oil was venerated. It was used in religious ceremonies, for burning and for anointing. For the latter purpose it was used also in the secular world as a base for perfumes. Today the oil still plays a great part in world economy, used for food and also in the manufacture of soap, for pharmacy and for dressing wool, to give but a few examples. It is estimated that at least 1 million tonnes of oil is produced each year, 90 per cent of it from Spain and Italy.

Once processed or pickled, the fruits are palatable. They form an important part of the diet of Mediterranean peoples. They are also exported to many other countries where they are ranked as luxury foods. Greece produces 72 per cent of the world's pickled olives. The plant is also grown commercially in Australia, California, China, the south of France and to a lesser degree in several other Mediterranean countries.

Obviously, after such a long domesticated life, there must be many cultivars of the olive. It is estimated that there are more than 700 named varieties. Many of these are local favourites. Some varieties suit some areas and conditions better than others. Some provide olives best for pickling green, others for ripe pickle and yet more for the Black Greek pickle. Those grown for oil extraction may differ. Some, such as Mission, are suitable for pickling and for oil. The fruits of 'table' olives are usually larger than those grown for oil.

## The fruit

Botanically, an oval, oily, fleshy drupe with one hard seed. Fruits vary in size considerably, according to the variety. The fruit of the species is about 2 cm ($\frac{3}{4}$ in) in length, and there are others which vary from as little as 1.3 cm ($\frac{1}{2}$ in) to 4 cm ($1\frac{1}{2}$ in). The fruits, maturing in autumn through winter, are green at first, gradually changing colour until they assume a dark blue or purple hue when ripe. Bitter and inedible until processed, the fruits bruise easily.

## The plant

A small, round-headed, much branching evergreen tree, which grows slowly, reaching 3–12 m (10–40 ft) according to its age and environment.

It is very long-lived; some trees in Jerusalem are believed to be more than a thousand years old. The bark is grey and sinuous. The trunk is often picturesquely twisted, and much divided near the base. Its numerous branches bend downwards, adding to the bushy appearance of the plant. The leathery leaves are narrowly obovate or oval, 4–8 cm (1½–3 in) long, grey-green on the upperside, glaucous white below. These and the bark give the tree its characteristic appearance.

The white, fragrant flowers, 2.5–5 cm (1–2 in) long and narrow and unisexual, are borne in small, erect clusters in the axils of the leaves. They bloom in late spring. The short inflorescence carries 20–30 flowers on the stem. Often only the first two of these mature. Sometimes a cluster forms, 'hen and chickens' to the commercial grower. If all of them mature, the fruits will be inferior. The plant is tolerant of drought conditions, but it will not then crop well, since flowers or fruit or both will drop. Most varieties crop biennially.

## Cultivation

Olives need a climate which can provide a long, hot summer and a cool to cold winter. Some chilling in winter is essential to initiate the formation of the flower buds; no chilling means no blossoming. On the other hand, it must be realised that the climate can be too cold. If the temperature falls below −9°C (15°F) the tree will be killed. Frosts of −2°C (28°F) or below will injure both flowers and fruit, according to season. If the fruit is to be large and of a good quality, the tree must enjoy a long and relatively hot summer. If there is a lack of moisture, in particular in the critical early spring period, the tree will lose some of its leaves. This loss is known to affect the blossom, increasing the number of deformed flowers. This fault also occurs if the tree is overcrowded; pruning and thinning can redress this situation.

It is important to realise that the production of blossom and fruit occupies the tree for a lengthy period. During all of this time, the tree should not become dry at the roots. The olive is shallow rooting – even old trees have been found to have roots no deeper than 1 m (3 ft), which means that they are not difficult to keep watered. This should not be understood to mean that the plant will grow in moist or wet soil which becomes waterlogged. Drainage must be good. While the soil should be fertile and of a good texture, it should not be too rich in nitrogen for this will result in an over-generous supply of leaves and little fruit.

When bought from a nurseryman, the small tree should already be pruned so that it will grow as required. Otherwise, cut the seedling main stem back when it is some 60 cm (2 ft) tall, leaving just three or four shoots to develop as limbs or main arms. Shorten these so that they are each about 15 cm (6 in) long, making the cut just above an outward pointing bud.

It is not wise to allow a tree to grow too tall, otherwise it will be difficult to harvest. Fruit must be carefully picked. A height that you can reach with a 2.5 m (8 ft) ladder is the safest.

Varieties differ in their habit of growth: some grow tall and others droop a little like a willow and may be spreading as well, so it is prudent to enquire about the habit of an olive before it is bought, so that a suitable place can be found for it. Incidentally, olive trees make excellent windbreaks.

If the plants are left unpruned they tend to become too tall and unmanageable. For this reason, upright shoots growing away strongly from the centre of the tree should be cut back, as should any others which seem too vigorous in comparison to the remainder of the branches. By cutting back developing upright growths to outward growing laterals, the tree can be made to grow lower, though broader.

Where there is little garden space to spare, as many as five varieties can be grafted on to one stock to make a family tree. One can be sure this way that the flowers are pollinated. It is always best to plant more than one olive in one location for reasons of pollination. Plants can be raised from seed, but this is a long business since the seeds may lie dormant for a year before germination takes place. The seeds have a very hard shell, and some gardeners very carefully crack this before sowing. Others stratify the hard stones. Even then, germination is still slow. It is best to sow the seeds individually in pots, especially for plants which are to be greenhouse grown. The seedling can then be kept in its pot until it is 13–15 cm (5–6 in) tall, when it can be moved to a larger pot or transplanted outdoors if the climate is suitable. Remember, though, that seedlings do not necessarily grow into plants which resemble the parent in every way.

While most plants are grafted onto seedling stock, it is possible to strike cuttings in sandy soil with bottom heat in a greenhouse. Use strong shoots taken in summer, 10–15 cm (4–6 in) long. The leaves from at least half the stem length should be removed and the bare portion inserted into the soil. The cuttings should then be enclosed.

In most northern countries the olive needs greenhouse conditions, at least in winter. Generally speaking, one should aim to give the plant a temperature that does not fall below 4–10°C (40–50°F). The olive can be container-grown and given protection until all fear of frost is past. The plant can then be stood outdoors for the summer. It should be watered only moderately during winter but freely in summer when growth is at its peak and the plant is in blossom. From late spring until early autumn the plant should be sprayed daily with clean water.

Details of harvesting can be found in the Culinary section.

## Culinary uses

It is important that olives be handled carefully because they bruise so easily. If they are to remain as green olives, in most cases the fruit should be harvested when their deep green colour begins to change to a lighter, straw-yellow hue, but this depends also upon varieties. Some become too soft at this stage and should be gathered earlier. Firm-fleshed varieties, Manzanillo for example, can be left until a tinge of the purple coloration can be seen. Obviously, when buying an olive plant, one should enquire about its season of maturity. If the fruits are harvested too soon, both their flavour and their texture is impaired. For the simplified method used in home pickling, it is important that the fruits are firm.

The fruits should be sorted and graded so that those of similar size can be processed together. Because at this time the fruit should be handled with care, some people prefer to delay the operation until after they have been given the lye treatment (see below) and washed, by which time they should be harder.

Fruit should be processed immediately after harvesting, but it can be held for a while in a 3 per cent brine solution.

Olives contain a natural, unpalatable bitterness most of which has to be removed before they can be eaten with pleasure. This is done by soaking the fruits in a solution of caustic soda. Commercially this is done in large vats. At home earthenware vessels or jars can be used, but if the jars are glass they should be kept out of the light.

It is doubtless unnecessary to point out that the solutions should be carefully mixed or the fruit may be spoiled. The usual strength of the lye is between 1.25 and 2 per cent, i.e. $\frac{1}{4}$–$\frac{1}{3}$ cup of caustic soda to 16 cups (5 1/8 pts) of water. A weaker strength is the safer, for the stronger solution can cause fruit to soften and blister. A small quantity of salt, $\frac{1}{4}$–$\frac{1}{3}$ cup to 16 cups, slightly counteracts the softening properties of the lye.

Green olives which are to remain green should be kept completely submerged in the lye. Exposure to air darkens the flesh. If ripe olives are to be pickled in lye in this manner, it is customary to expose them to the air two or three times and for varying periods during the lye processing. Some say that this impairs both flavour and texture and that it is best to keep the ripe olives submerged, when they retain their brown or purple-black hue instead of becoming jet black.

It is not desirable that the lye should penetrate the entire fruit, otherwise all the characteristic flavour will be lost. While the fruits are soaking they should be examined from time to time and cut open and the yellow stained flesh examined. In this method the penetration should reach only halfway to the stones or pits. The period required can vary from 8 to 24 hours or even longer, so constant and careful inspection is necessary. If after 12 to 15 hours the solution seems to have been taken in very little, it is advisable to change it and start afresh.

The next step in the processing is to remove all excess caustic soda. This is done by washing the olives in fresh clean water. Change the water frequently, but do not aerate it too much by rapidly running the water into the vessel. Keep the olives out of the air as much as possible. If this washing is too prolonged, the olives will not have such good texture, colour or flavour. This means that very slight traces of the lye should remain in the fruits.

From this point the fruit is passed through a

series of brine baths as follows:

| no. of days in salt solution | amounts of salt per 16 cups of water |
|---|---|
| 1 | ½ cup |
| 3 | ¾ cup |
| 7 | 1 cup |
| 7 | 1½ cups |
| 7 | 2 cups |

This makes a 25-day processing routine.

The olives are then placed in fresh brine containing 3 cups of salt to every 16 cups of water. This should be changed each month as the olives are kept in store. Remove what fruits are required two or three days before use. Keep them in a cool place. Wash them in cold water several times until the salt is all leached out. The olives are then ready to eat. They are improved if they are covered in olive oil into which chopped herbs are mixed. These green olives can also be pitted and stuffed.

Black olives to be pickled by the Greek process should be gathered when they are fully ripe. They should be washed and graded and packed into wine jars with alternate layers of coarse salt. The purpose of using the wine jars is that surplus juices can easily be drained off. The olives are left in the salt until they are palatable. Taste them to test from two months onwards. When they are ready, wash them, put into jars and cover with olive oil. This can be with or without herbs. The best herbs are those from the shrubby plants – rosemary, marjoram or oregano, thyme and bay.

Another method for ripe-picked black olives is to wash them in several waters, put them into boiling brine, then dry and pickle in oil.

# ORANGE
*Citrus* species

## Origin

Oranges appear to have come from Asia, including the tropical regions, depending on the species. To most people, the orange is typified by the sweet fruit one can take in the hand, peel easily and eat raw, but there are other sorts. The common fruit is *Citrus sinensis*, syn. *C. aurantium sinensis*, which is believed to have originated somewhere in India, Siam or southern China. The other important oranges are as follows.

*C. aurantium*, syn. *C. bigaradia*, the Bitter or Seville orange, is a native of tropical Asia and was introduced into Spain by the Arabs. Here there still exists a thriving commercial production. This is the orange largely used for making the conserve known mainly to the English-speaking world as marmalade, and not to be confused with the French *marmelade*, the Italian *marmalata* or the Portuguese *marmalada*, none of which need have any citrus content.

*C. a. bergamia*, the Bergamot orange, a subspecies, has never been found growing wild and it is believed to have arisen in Calabria in Italy, where it is now widely cultivated. This orange is not valued for its taste, but for its fragrance, its peel being used in the manufacture of eau-de-Cologne and other toilet waters and perfumes.

The Blood orange is a variety, *C. a. melitensis*. The Tangerine or Mandarin is *C. reticulata*, syn. *C. nobilis deliciosa*, and this is dealt with separately under its own heading.

The sweet orange, which some believe to have derived from the bitter orange, appears to have been known to the Romans, but was cultivated more widely about the Mediterranean during the period of the Arab empire. It does particularly well in Mediterranean regions, particularly on flat coastal valleys or on hillsides in sight of the sea below 500 m (1,500 ft) altitude, and in those countries which enjoy a similar climate (no. 1 on the world chart, p. 18). So it is no surprise that it is now to be found throughout the world, growing in the smallest gardens and in vast orchards in warm countries such as Australia, Brazil, California, Florida, Israel, North Africa, Sicily, South Africa and Spain, to mention only some of the most important.

The Citranges are hybrids between *Citrus sinensis* and the hardy *Poncirus trifoliata* and are described under Citrange.

## The fruit

Botanically, a berry of a special type known as a hesperidium. The fruit of *C. sinensis* varies in size, even in the species, but it is generally nearly globose, though sometimes oval, with a rind of varying thickness, a solid pith and a sweet flesh. The Navel orange has a somewhat smaller fruit, almost or entirely enclosed at the tip of the main fruit.

Fruits of *C. aurantium* are usually about 7–9 cm (2¾–3½ in) across, globose or sometimes flattened at the tip or at both ends, the core of the fruit hollow when ripe and the flesh acid.

*C. a. bergamia* produces large – 8–10 cm (3–4 in) – pale yellow, pear-shaped fruits, with a thin rind and an acid but fragrant flesh.

One should perhaps mention that in the tropics fruits often fail to develop the true 'orange' colour, although in fact the flesh may be ripe under the green skin. Commercially such oranges are treated and coloured by means of gas storage.

## The plant

The orange is an evergreen, rounded tree with regular branches, attractive in its own right. *C. sinensis* has few or no spines and those it does bear are slender, flexible and blunt. It grows some 5–10 m (15–30 ft) tall after 20–25 years. The leaves are handsome, waxy, dark green when mature, with pale green new growth, of medium size, ovate-oblong, their stalks narrowly winged. The flowers are white, small but fragrant.

*C. aurantium*, the hardiest of the species, is a smaller tree with regular branches and a neat, rounded top. The leaves are slightly wedge-shaped at the base and pointed at the tip, pale green, with the leaf-stalk broadly winged. The Bergamot orange is a small tree with very small but fragrant flowers. The leaves are oblong-oval, with long winged stalks.

## Cultivation

Outdoors the best climate seems to be one where there are definite winter and summer seasons, although of course the winters must not be too cold. Oranges, mandarins, tangerines and the like are generally less successful in urban gardens than lemons and grapefruit, but where the atmosphere is cleaner, the sun clearer and the soil richer, Washington Navels and Valencias are said to be the best oranges for small gardens.

It is best to buy one-year-old trees, grown from the bud, preferably with balled roots wrapped in hessian or some similar material. The chosen site should be protected against strong winds, open to the sun and preferably away from the competition of established trees or areas of the decorative garden. Careful preparation of the planting hole will ensure that the young tree gets away quickly and establishes a root system that will support and sustain prolific fruit production for many years. Dig the hole about 75 cm (2½ ft) deep and wide, break up the soil at the base and mix into this two generous handfuls of a good general granular fertiliser. On the top of this place a good layer of farmyard manure or home-made compost mixed with soil from the hole and plant the young tree on this after the roots have been well soaked in water for a couple of hours. Place the whole root ball in the planting hole and cut away the hessian while it is in position. Make sure that the bud union, clearly defined at the base of the main stem, is well above ground level as you fill in the hole and scatter soil over the roots. Firm this soil into position, making a shallow saucer around the base of the plant. Water the plant in well, using several buckets of water or a sprinkler system for at least two hours.

When the tree has been planted go over it carefully with a pair of sharp secateurs and trim it back to leave only three or four well-balanced branches some 15–20 cm (6–8 in) long. Failure to prune off most of the foliage at this stage is a common cause of leaf drop and poor development.

Where the sun is likely to be strong, protect the trunk of the young tree for its first few months. Merely wrap it in newspaper or some similar material, tying top and bottom.

In the first and subsequent summers ensure that the plant gets plenty of moisture not just occasional surface waterings but sufficient to ensure that the lower roots are kept moist. Heavy mulches of peat or grass mowings will help keep the roots cool and moist.

Citrus trees require a great deal of nitrogen to enable them to bear fruitfully and it is advisable to apply a good nitrogenous fertiliser once every 6–8 weeks during the first summer. Examples are 40–50 g (1½–2 oz) of ammonium nitrate, half this quantity of urea or a third as much again of sulphate of ammonia. Water this in well. After the first year use a general fertiliser according to directions and apply heavy mulches of organic matter in order to encourage earthworms and bacterial activity.

Little pruning of established citrus trees is necessary. Merely remove any shoots which develop on the trunk of a young tree and cut back any growth that is so strong that it unbalances the symmetry of the tree. Older trees should be examined from time to time and any dead or damaged growth removed.

Fortunately for urban gardeners most citrus trees make excellent pot plants, either to stand outdoors or to grow in a heated greenhouse where the climate is unsuitable for cultivation in the open ground. Under glass a temperature no lower than 7–8°C (45–50°F) must be maintained.

The urban gardener in northern lands in particular will surely draw comfort from the fact that in the past oranges were usually grown in large pots or tubs in the open in summer and removed to an orangery in winter. The trees were grown mainly as ornaments and for the sweet scent of their blossom rather than for their fruits. Grown this way in a greenhouse the plants need no more than protection from frosts. They can be greenhouse-grown for the whole year or they can be moved outside for the warmest months. Grown this way in the northern hemisphere they should come into new growth in March or early April, flower late, usually about midsummer, and the fruits when formed will hang green throughout the winter to ripen the following summer. If the plants are given warmer conditions, the fruits will ripen the same season that they were produced.

It is important, whatever manner of cultivation is adopted, that a moist atmosphere is provided during the peak growing season, otherwise the plants will be stunted and will not fruit satisfactorily. This means that when grown in pots under glass, the pots, the plants and the air around them should be kept moist. The roots in the pots should never at any time be allowed to dry out completely.

If the plants are to be grown in pots, they should be given a moderately heavy soil mixture containing a good proportion of well-rotted animal manure or home-produced compost. Sand mixed in will ensure that the mixture is kept open and well drained. It is important also to pot

firmly, otherwise growth will be soft and sappy, and without well-ripened, hard wood no fruit can be expected.

When the plants are growing well they can be fed with liquid manure, but this should be gradually withheld as growth slows down. If the plants are kept under glass they should receive good ventilation during summer and it is better if they can be stood outside at this season.

## Culinary uses

Oranges are rich in vitamins, especially C. 'One fresh orange 2⅝ inches (6.5 cm) in diameter," says the United States Department of Agriculture, "contains 66 mg of ascorbic acid, or a little more than the minimum daily adult requirement of vitamin C." The juice of the fruit is rich in sugars and acids, one reason why it is so delicious.

This fruit can be used in a hundred ways, on its own or with other fruits. Generally speaking, oranges, i.e. all sweet oranges such as tangerines and clementines, can be used in most recipes given for lemons, except that as a rule less sugar will be needed.

Orange juice is used almost as much as the flesh of the orange. A glass is a good way to begin, or end, the day.

Orange is also associated with meat in many dishes, either in the sauce, or sometimes, as with veal, cooked with the meat. Pork, ham, especially baked hams, and chicken go well with orange. Bigarade sauce, which is served with duck and game, is made from Seville oranges. Often, marmalade instead of fresh orange is used in a sauce for meat, frequently with redcurrant jelly.

Orange Rice is a good dish for a buffet meal. Although you may require more, work to these proportions.

### Orange rice

½ cup finely chopped celery
3 tabsp chopped onion
¼ cup butter
1 cup orange juice
1 tabsp grated orange rind
1 cup long grain rice
salt, pepper
1½ cups water

In a heavy saucepan sauté the celery and onion in the melted butter until tender, but do not brown.

Stir in the water, orange juice, grated rind, salt and pepper. Bring to the boil and then sprinkle in the rice. Cover closely and cook on a low heat for approximately 20 minutes by which time all the liquid should have been absorbed. Fluff with a fork and add chopped chervil or parsley. Failing these use the finely chopped blanched leaves of the celery.

Oranges are not often served with fish, yet orange slices make a good substitute when lemons are scarce, and Orange Butter is good with sole. Into a ¼ cup of butter work the finely chopped peel of 1 orange, ½ teaspoon paprika, 2 teaspoons orange juice and ½ teaspoon finely chopped shallot.

The peel as well as the flesh and juice is often used to flavour puddings, cakes, breads, biscuits and a great number of desserts. It is as well to have a store of orange peel ready to hand. Pare it finely, let it dry and then grind or chop finely. For cakes and desserts this can be mixed with sugar – ½ cup of peel to 2 cups of sugar – and stored in airtight jars for use in cooking.

The flowers and leaves of orange trees can be used in a tisane. Those of the bitter orange are considered to be the best for this purpose since they are the more strongly scented. The essential oil of oranges is known as neroli. That of the bitter orange is called *essence de petit grain* and is used for scenting creams, custards and batters. Scented orange-blossom water, manufactured commercially, is used in patisserie and confectionery.

Orange-flower sugar is used, as are all flavoured sugars, to make petits fours, and if the tree blossoms, why not take advantage? Dry the flower petals by spreading them out on kitchen paper in a dry place. Add to them twice their weight in sugar. Pound the two together until they are amalgamated, and store in an airtight jar.

To make Iced Oranges, first wash the fruit and carefully cut a slice from the top so that the flesh can be taken out and the fruit skin kept intact in the two sections. It is easiest to run a sharp knife right round and then the top will lift off like a little cap. Make an ice-cream mixture. Shortly before serving, spoon out the cream into the fruits, cover and serve.

## Orange soufflé

2 large oranges
⅛ cup butter
1 tabsp Grand Marnier
2 eggs
1 tabsp cream
⅛ cup sugar, possibly more
1 rounded teasp arrowroot

Slice the tops from the oranges. See that they stand firm, and if not, take a sliver of peel from the base, taking care not to puncture the fruit. Scoop out all the flesh (a soup spoon is good for this). Dry and butter the insides, best done by melting a little butter and brushing it on. Blend or sieve the flesh and strain it to get all the juice. Boil it with the sugar to make a good syrup. Mix the arrowroot with 2 tablespoons cold water and add to the syrup to make a sauce, stirring as it thickens. Allow the sauce to cool. Pour in the Grand Marnier. Beat in first the egg yolks and then the cream. Taste and adjust the sweetening if necessary. Beat the egg whites until they are stiff, and fold them into the orange mixture. Fill the orange skins two-thirds full with the mixture and bake in the oven at 190°C (375°F, gasmark 5) for 35 minutes. Serve at once. These can be prepared in advance, leaving the whipping and mixing in of the egg whites until the last minute before placing the dish in the oven.

PRESERVING    This is a good recipe for making the ever-popular Seville Orange Marmalade.

## Seville orange marmalade

6 oranges
2 lemons
8 cups water
2 cups sugar to each 2 cups fruit

Cut up the fruit and peel as required, very finely or chunky. Some people prefer to mince this. Save the seeds and put them all together in a piece of muslin and tie. Put all together in a bowl. Boil the water and add it to the fruit and pips. Let it stand for 24 hours. Cook until the fruit is soft then let it stand again for another 24 hours. Weigh the pulp, reheat and then boil rapidly for 10 minutes. Add the sugar. Simmer until it sets when tested.

FREEZING AND BOTTLING   The freezing and the bottling of oranges is just the same as for grapefruit (q.v.).

DRINKS   Orange juice features in many recipes for delicious drinks, but an equal number have as their main ingredient not the juice but the skin. The dried peel of the local green orange is used to make curaçao. Orange skin is also used to make Van der Hum, Triple Sec, Cointreau, Grand Marnier and several others. An 'Archbishop' is a winter drink made with hot, sweetened red wine in which floats a clove-studded orange.

You can make your own wonderful orange liqueur flavoured according to your personal taste, if you follow and adapt this recipe.

### Orange liqueur

6 oranges, depending on size
4 cups brandy or white spirit
2 cups sugar
1 teasp cinnamon
½ teasp coriander

Remove the peel of the oranges with a potato parer so that no pith is included and chop it finely. Squeeze the oranges. Blend the juice with the sugar, spices and peel. Put all into a large jar, pour on the spirit and mix. Cover and leave to infuse for 2 months, then filter and bottle.

Orangeade made from pure orange juice and water is improved by the addition of just a little brandy, rum or curaçao. It should then be served iced.

The orange drink that is more popular than any others is undoubtedly Orange Squash, which can of course be made any way you like, according to your own tastes and those of your family. We have found a good recipe to be made up from:

### Orange squash

2 cups orange juice
5 cups sugar
3 cups water
1 tabsp citric acid

Prepare the drink in exactly the same way as for Lemon Squash (p. 154).

# PAPAW
*Carica papaya*, syn. *Papaya carica*

## Origin

The plant gives its name to a family, Caricaceae, of which there are only two genera. *Carica* is a genus of about 20 species of unbranched, evergreen trees which are natives of tropical America. They all produce an acrid, milky juice. *Carica papaya* is said never to have been found growing wild, but it is widely cultivated throughout the tropics and can be seen in many gardens, including those of town houses. A number of cultivars are known, many, as might be expected, being local. Although described as a tree, the plant is in fact a large herb, or softwood tree, like the banana. It is distinctive enough for it to be regarded with interest by horticulturists. In Europe young papaw plants are often used in outdoor formal bedding schemes in summer. Elsewhere it is cultivated for its fruits. In some areas it is known only as pawpaw, in others as papaya. Some people believe them to be different fruits, but it is only the varieties which differ from each other, or the sex.

It was probably taken home first by the Portuguese from America, and from there its cultivation spread through the hot countries of the Old World. Later, other visitors must have helped disperse it. Now it is to be found in most tropical and sub-tropical regions. It is grown in latitudes within 32° north and south of the Equator. It is grown commercially in many of them, including Malaya, Australia, the West Indies, Hawaii and Florida. It has some commercial importance apart from its fruit. *Carica papaya* contains an enzyme known as papain, present in fruit, stem and leaves. The milky juice is extracted, dried and used in chewing gum, medicine (it is an aid to digestion), toothpaste and meat tenderisers. Meat can be wrapped in a bruised papaw leaf before it is cooked to make it more tender. Another species, *C. quercifolia*, contains more papain than *C. papaya*.

## The fruit

Botanically, a large berry, often many-seeded and very variable. Papaws measure 10–50 cm (4–20 in) in diameter and weigh an average of nearly 1 kg (2 lb), sometimes much more. Fruits weighing 9 kg (20 lb) are not rare. Those from hermaphrodite plants are usually less in weight and are long and narrow, somewhat cucumber-shaped in appearance, with a rib down one side. In Queensland, elongated fruits are known as Long Toms. Fruits from female plants vary in shape from globular to oval. However, in some strains variations in shape occur and a plant may produce a beaked fruit or one which tapers at the stem end. Fruits on female plants are carried on short stalks and grow close to the stem of the plant. When a so-called male tree produces hermaphrodite flowers, as some frequently do, the fruits which develop on the ends of the branches are very long and misshapen. Fruits on male trees grow on very long stems which hang far below the leaves.

As all the flowers are axillary, papaw fruits grow at the bases of the leaves.

The skin of the young papaw is smooth and green. Some varieties remain green when ripe, but most begin to turn colour when they ripen, becoming deeper in tone, yellow and orange, after harvesting. The dwarf Philippine variety, Zamboanga, has red fruits.

Papaw flesh is abundant, soft and juicy, orange-yellow or salmon-pink in colour, surrounding a central cavity containing numerous brown-black, pea-sized seeds. These can be used as a spice. Some people chew them. Unripe papaws can be cooked as a vegetable. In some equatorial countries, papaws are in season the year round, but elsewhere the fruiting season is more limited.

## The plant

A large herbaceous plant, sometimes called a softwood tree, usually unbranched, although some plants tend to branch more than others. Branching trees usually produce small fruit and the branches are not sturdy, often breaking under the weight of the fruit. Trees will grow 2–10 m (6–32 ft) high, but they are seldom allowed to grow too tall when cultivated, because the trunk tends to break and of course there are problems in harvesting the fruit. Furthermore, the fruit diminishes in size as the tree grows taller. As one might expect, the stem or trunk is soft and not woody. The papaw has large, handsome, palmate leaves which are usually 7-lobed. These leaves are

very fragile and are easily broken or damaged by wind, hail or sand blast. The last also damages ripening fruit.

There are three kinds of papaw flowers, male, female and hermaphrodite, produced on separate plants. Thus they fall into two groups according to varieties, monosexual and bisexual.

Plants of the bisexual type are more suitable for tropical regions, while the monosexual plants thrive better in cooler areas. The true male flowers should produce pollen only, but sometimes a so-called male tree produces fruit. This is because under certain conditions, during cool spring and autumn months, for instance, male trees often produce bisexual flowers. The flowers of the male tree are white, fragrant, and produced in large numbers on many-branched stalks up to 1.5 m (5 ft) long. The female flowers are larger than the male and grow on single or simply branched stalks. These range from 2 cm ($\frac{3}{4}$ in) upwards, according to variety.

The bisexual or hermaphrodite flowers resemble those found on female trees except that their petals are joined at the base, and of course they have pollen-producing stamens. These are usually at the terminals of the stems, with the so-called subsidiary pollen-producing flowers near the base of the stalk. Plants have been known to slowly change their sex during their lifetime.

The papaw grows and matures quickly. In some areas fruit is produced after the first year from seed, in others within 18 months from planting out, but the plant does not remain prolific for more than a brief period of some three to four years. The flowering period is often prolonged, some fruit ripening throughout most of the year. This may coincide with two main flowering periods. Much depends on the region concerned.

## Cultivation

Where bananas will grow, papaws also will grow. It is important to realise that the papaw is susceptible to low temperature. Light frosts and cold winds will injure the plant in some way or another. As is often the case, young trees cannot tolerate adverse conditions which might prove only a slight setback for older plants. Prolonged frost can kill even well-established plants.

The plants often do very well in a garden, especially one which is well protected by a wall or a fence. They need sun, but one should take care that the ripening fruits are not subjected to sun scorch. The plant can be grown successfully in dry areas; high humidity is not required either for pollination or fruit setting.

Most soils are suitable so long as they are well drained and rich in humus and plant foods. Papaws do not like acid soils and a pH of 6.0 to 6.5 is best.

Since the plant grows so easily from seed so long as proper care is taken, this is the best method of propagation, although where one wishes to increase the stock of a particular variety, soft stem tip cuttings can be taken. These root readily enough, but the ensuing plant is not really vigorous. Seed loses its viability quickly after it has been taken from the fruit. If necessary, dry seed can be kept in an airtight container at a cool temperature. The seeds should be washed clean of pulp and membranes. This is best done by holding them in a rough cloth under running water and rubbing them in the cloth.

Several methods are followed for seed sowing. Seedlings grown from seed sown *in situ* are not so likely to suffer a check when transplanted. Make a depression in the soil, fill it with organic material, space three or four seeds about 30 cm (1 ft) apart, cover to about twice their depth and then water the area. Trickle irrigation is very effective for papaws. Shade the young seedlings if the weather is hot or dry. A leafy branch pushed into the ground and sloped over them is quite effective. Allow the plants to flower so that their sex can be determined and then thin out. Cut off unwanted plants at ground level to avoid disturbing the roots of the others. One male to nine females is considered sufficient, but obviously if only one female is required, one male must also be grown. Alternatively, sow the seed in small containers, three to each. See that they do not become dry and are kept in the shade. Transplant when conditions are favourable and when the seedlings are 10–15 cm (4–6 in) high. Be sure to plant them at the same depth as they were previously and try to disturb the root ball as little as possible. Keep them in a group for thinning later. In their final stations they can grow as closely as 1 m (3 ft), but are better at twice this distance. Where the soil is poor be sure to prepare the sites

beforehand and add a complete fertiliser. Commercial growers apply a dressing of 55 g (2 oz) of sulphate of ammonia to each group two weeks after planting. The plants become very tall after a few years and it is prudent to keep a steady supply of seedlings going and to practise successional cropping wherever this is convenient.

The papaw is a greedy nitrogen feeder. A liquid plant food in which this element is present will prove beneficial, especially if the plant's leaves are pale and its growth slow.

If a tree has branched it may be necessary to prop any particularly heavy limbs to prevent them breaking. Branching sometimes takes place when the main growing point is injured. Old trees can be rejuvenated so long as they are healthy, and made useful for a few more years. Cut them back to about 60 cm (2 ft) from the ground at a point where the stem is solid. Do this in early spring. Cover the cut surface with an upturned tin can or a piece of black polythene sheeting tied into place to prevent it from cracking. When the stem shoots, allow only two or three strong growths to develop.

It is important that the female flowers are well pollinated. Commercial growers wisely plant the male trees where the pollen can be blown by the prevailing wind on the female plants. Hand-pollination should be carried out every three or four days. Female flowers which have been pollinated can be identified by the brown and withering stigma. Male flowers usually bloom before the female so the last of their flowers have to be saved for the females.

After the fruit has set, it is best to thin it to about two fruits per node.

For greenhouse culture the seedlings should be moved to large pots or planted in a greenhouse border in the spring. Here they should be watered freely during the growing season, sparingly at other times. Temperatures should be 13–18°C (55–65°F) in winter and about 18–30°C (65–85°F) in summer.

Seeds should be taken from the fruit and washed and then sown in individual pots under enclosed conditions. Germination takes place quickly, in about two to six weeks. Remove the covers as soon as the seedlings are growing well and keep them warm to prevent them damping off. Once germinated, the seedlings grow quickly. They can be grown in an ordinary seed

Peach Peregrine *(L. Johns)*

Top: Pineapple on plant *(G. R. Roberts)*
Bottom: Pomegranate *(G. R. Roberts)*

sowing mixture to begin with, but should then be moved to a good potting soil. Good drainage is essential. Plants can be fed with liquid fertiliser, either a balanced solution or one high in nitrogen.

As it draws near to ripening, the papaw develops yellow streaks. These eventually merge and deepen in colour, giving the whole fruit a yellow–orange skin. When fully ripe the fruit is soft to the touch. It is easily cut, even with a blunt knife. It is best in summer to pick the fruit when it is showing only some yellow and then to hold it until it becomes ripe. Take care not to damage the skins of the fruit as it is being gathered or the sap flowing from the wound will stain and spoil the fruit.

It is important that the fruit stalk is cut and not pulled from the tree. It is also important that this stalk be cut close to the stem, otherwise the portion remaining may damage the immature fruits as they grow. Sometimes, especially when fruits are crowded close to each other so that it is difficult to get a knife among them, the fruit may have to be gathered by giving it a sharp twist. Wear gloves and protect the eyes and skin when gathering, because the sap of the plant is acrid.

## Culinary uses

Papaws contain useful amounts of calcium and vitamins A and C. Remember that the juices from the unripe fruit, as well as the bruised leaves and stalks, contain papain, a meat tenderiser. You can wrap meat in partially bruised leaves before roasting it. Alternatively marinate the meat in some papaw juice or under cover of sliced, unripe papaw. You can also rub the flesh and seeds into the surface of the meat. Remove before cooking.

Papaw is a delicious breakfast fruit. Try it blended with yoghurt and a little honey. It can be eaten raw in many ways. It is often served as a first course and is then good with ginger and salt and pepper. We were once served papaw with smoked beef and realised how good it would be with prosciutto, too.

For a dessert, serve with sugar, lemon juice, ice-cream, what you will. Fruit cubes can be added to fruit salads. You can treat the papaw shell like a melon and scoop out the flesh and seeds to refill with a fruit mixture. This can also be embedded in a fruit jelly. Allow the jelly to cool and pour it over the fruit. Papaws make good sherbets and water ices; treat as melon.

Green papaws can be served as a vegetable, hot with butter and garnished with chopped mint, or cold in a vinaigrette sauce. Treat as squash and steam.

PRESERVING    Papaws can be made into jam, add lime or lemon juice to help them set. They also make good pickles and chutney. Try this Green Papaw Chutney.

### Green papaw chutney

1 large almost ripe papaw, diced
6 cups brown sugar
4 cups vinegar
¼ cup garlic, chopped very finely
1 cup chopped onion
1 cup preserved or crystallised ginger, sliced
¼ cup salt
1 teasp ground cloves
2 lemons, juice only
1 cup sultanas
½ cup raisins, halved
1 tabsp whole peppercorns, tied in a piece of
   muslin
1 chopped red pepper

Boil sugar and vinegar together and simmer well for half an hour. Put all the ingredients in a pan and add the syrup. Bring to the boil and simmer for about 1½ hours or until the chutney is thick. Pour into hot jars and seal immediately.

DRINKS    A drink which can be as delicate or as strong as you care to make it is Papaw Rum. The basic ingredients are:

### Papaw rum

4 cups papaw pulp
1 cup rum
2 cups sugar
1 cup lemon juice

Beat the papaw pulp with the sugar and lemon juice and allow the mixture to stand for a day or two. Place into a jelly bag and allow to drip. Add the rum, more according to taste.

# PASSION FRUIT
*Passiflora* species

## Origin

The genus belongs to a family named after it, Passifloraceae, consisting of mainly climbing plants with some shrubs and herbs, found in the warmer regions of the world, in particular Africa and America. The striking flowers of the plant have given the fruit its name. Found growing around them, they were used by the colonising Spanish priests to explain the story of the Passion or Crucifixion to those they had come to convert. They showed how the three styles represent the nails, the ovary the sponge soaked in vinegar, the stamens Christ's wounds, the filaments the crown and the petals and stamens the apostles. The plant became known as the Passion flower and its fruit, the Passion fruit. With such an association it is not surprising that some of the species have travelled the world, one might almost say evangelically, and are cultivated in any country with a climate warm enough.

Passiflora's history is strangely undocumented. The distinctive *P. edulis*, for instance, appears not to have been introduced into Britain until the early years of the 1800s, but judging by its popularity on the other side of the world, it cannot have been introduced to Australia much later.

There are more than 350 species of passiflora, many of them with the characteristic flower, but the fruits of only eleven of these, as far as can be discovered, are of any significance here. The most important is *P. edulis*, a native of Brazil, and its variety, *P. e. flavicarpa*, the Golden or Hawaiian Passion fruit. This fruit and its cultivars are now grown commercially in Australia, Kenya, New Zealand and South Africa, on a smaller scale in some other countries, and in gardens in many countries. Other species are *P. incarnata*, known as May Pops and May Apple, a native of the south eastern United States; *P. laurifolia*, the Jamaican honeysuckle, Water lemon or Bell apple, indigenous to Brazil and the West Indies. It is common in Malaya and is sometimes called the Singapore Passion flower. It was introduced from Malaya into Australia. There are also *P. ligularis*, syn. *P. loweii*, the Sweet Granadilla from Peru. This fruit is highly esteemed by those living in the mountainous regions of Mexico and Central America. *P. quadrangularis*, the Granadilla, with its variety *P. q. macrocarpa*, the Giant Granadilla and *P. maliformis*, the Hardshelled Passion flower, sometimes called the Sweet Calabash, both from tropical America; and *P. mollissima*, once known as *Tasconia mollissima*, the Banana Passion fruit, from tropical South America. Some of these are hardly known outside their own country or even locality, but all of them offer a source of delicious and refreshing fruit for those who garden in suitable climes.

## The fruit

Botanically, a berry, usually covered with a hard, tough, even leathery shell or skin. In the full range of species, the fruits vary in size from that of a pea to a small melon. However, those under consideration are of average, useful dimensions.

Passion fruits are valued for their juicy, seed-filled pulp, often delightfully fragrant, pleasantly sweet, refreshingly acid, with a certain character all of their own. As is to be expected, the fruit flavour of some species is superior to others.

Of them all *P. edulis* is the best and possibly the best known. Its fruits are usually egg-shaped although some of its cultivars are a little more rounded. Before ripening they are a soft, almond green. When the fruits are ripe the tough skin is a dull purple and no longer plump, but often dimpled or indented. The flesh is a light orange and surrounds many small dark seeds. The fruits of *P. e. flavicarpa* are yellow. These contain a greater amount of seed pulp than does the fruit of the type. This is considered by some to be more aromatic and more acid. There are hybrids between the type and its variety. The best of these have large, egg-shaped fruits with a wine-coloured skin. The pulp has a little of the character of both parents. This variety is important commercially. Hybrids are grafted on to its stock in order that they may escape fusarium wilt.

Good varieties are Purple Gold, a heavy cropper with a golden pulp, and Lacey Special, a seasonal cropper. The fruit of the Water lemon or Bell apple, *P. laurifolia*, is large, up to 8 cm (3 in) long and egg-shaped, orange-yellow. It is partly enveloped in three long persistent sepals. The skin is soft and somewhat spongy. The pulp is thin, white and fragrant, pear-scented to some.

*P. ligularis*, the Sweet Granadilla, has orange to orange-brown fruits, sometimes with purple coloration, 8 cm (3 in) long, with a thicker skin than most. The perfumed pulp is more liquid than that of the others and acid; it is said to have the best flavour of any of the passion fruits.

The largest of the fruits comes from *P. quadrangularis macrocarpa*, the Giant Granadilla, which can grow as long as 30 cm (12 in). The fruit resembles a small water melon, light green at first, becoming yellow. It has a thick, purple, well-flavoured pulp; its seeds are similar in size to those of a cantaloupe. The fruit of *P. quadrangularis*, though smaller (about 20 cm/8 in), contains proportionately more pulp than its larger fellow, but this is not so well flavoured.

The Hardshelled Passion fruit, *P. maliformis*, has round fruits 4.5 cm (1¾ in) in diameter, with a hard, yellow shell covered by three large, cream-coloured persistent sepals. The pulp does not have the characteristic passion fruit aroma and flavour, but is more grape-like in taste. The fruit of *P. mollissima* is yellow-green, slightly downy and about 8 cm (3 in) in length. It is called Banana Passion fruit because of its colour and because of the texture of its pulp.

*P. incarnata* has oval, yellow fruits, with a juicy pulp.

## The plant

All the plants under consideration are perennial climbers furnished with tendrils by which they climb. Many have angular stems. Most of the flowers are strikingly beautiful and distinguished by a crown or corolla of filaments which often covers the petals and stretches as far as the sepals which are thick and often coloured. *P. edulis* has angular stems which are slightly downy or glabrous. The leaves, which are 10–15 cm (4–6 in) across, are deeply divided or lobed in three parts. The flowers are 6 cm (2½ in) wide and white banded with purple.

The flowers of May Pops, *P. incarnata*, are a little larger, 8 cm (3 in), and the petals are white or pale lavender, with pale lavender sepals behind them. The leaves are long, 8–15 cm (3–6 in), also three-lobed.

As its name suggests, the leaves of *P. laurifolia* are laurel-like, 8–13 cm (3–5 in) long and glabrous. They grow closely on the stem, densely furnishing the vine. The attractive flowers are fragrant, 5–8 cm (2–3 in) wide, with red, white and violet coloration in petals and sepals. The latter are large and persist on the fruit. This plant is described as being strictly tropical. It grows readily from seed and cuttings.

*P. ligularis* is a strong climber. Its leaves give it distinction – they are 10–23 cm (4–9 in) long, heart-shaped and glaucous on the undersides. The pale green flowers are 8–10 cm (3–4 in) across, the corona white and barred with purple.

The Granadilla and its variety display how these passifloras came to be called quadrangularis. They have stout, four-angled stems. The leaves are large, ovate, 10–20 cm (4–8 in) long and the flowers 11 cm (4½ in) across. These are particularly striking, because of the crown or corona which spreads across the very pale pink petals and is made up of filaments of banded blue and purple. This is essentially a tropical plant calling for both high temperatures and high humidity. The flowers produce little or no pollen under dry conditions, consequently little fruit is set.

*P. maliformis*, the Hardshelled Passion fruit, will climb 6 m (20 ft) or more. Like the Granadilla, its leaves are not lobed or divided but are long, cordate and pointed. The flowers are fragrant, 7–8 cm (2½–3 in) across, with green-white, purple spotted petals and a fantastically beautiful corona, red-violet barred with white in the inner circle, violet and white in the shorter outer ring.

The tall stems of the Banana Passion fruit, *P. mollissima*, are rounded and distinguished by a soft down, as the name suggests. The leaves are deeply lobed, 7–13 cm (2½–5 in) long, toothed, and covered with the same soft down. Flowers on this plant do not have the handsome corolla of the other species, but they are 8 cm (3 in) across and pink. They are enveloped in a long calyx tube of three large sepals which persist on the fruit as it grows and ripens.

Bisexual flowers are produced by *P. edulis* and hybrid varieties. These are self-pollinating. However, *P. edulis flavicarpa* is not self-pollinating and needs other vines of the same variety near it. Hand-pollination is always helpful.

Passion fruit vines need not be formally grown in a garden. They can be used to cover an old tree stump very effectively and with the bonus of fruit. We have seen the vines used as a ground cover under banana plants on sloping ground in Queensland. They can also be used to sprawl over a bank, wall or shed, even to weave through a hedge. It is important, though, that at least once a year the plant should be cleared of dead leaves and other growth.

Both the flowers and the fruits, young or mature, bring a special atmosphere to arrangements of mixed flowers or to flowers and fruits. When these are assembled, stems of some of the divided leaves and tendrils add to the general effect. These may need hot water treatment before they will take water well.

## Cultivation

The most important factor is that the passion vine should be given a sunny site in a place where it is sheltered from cold winds and free from frost. However, although sun is important, a newly planted young vine may need protection by shading until its roots are well established.

Most soils suit passion fruits, but these should not be heavy or the plant will not grow well. Soils must be well drained or they will stay wet and this is a condition which is likely to induce disease attack. All the same, it is important that the roots of the vine do not become dry in the early days after planting. During the first year all possible care should be taken to see that the plant grows well. Prepare the soil and enrich it a little but not too generously. Apply a little more fertiliser in a month's time and then roughly every four weeks. Keep this well away from the stem base.

Passion fruit vines tend to become deficient in manganese. Symptoms are a yellowing between the veins of the leaves. Foliage sprays of 5 g of manganese sulphate per litre of water (1 saltspoon to 1¾ pt) give a seasonal control. If the vine is not planted against a wall or existing trellis, it will need support. Commercial growers simply strand wires between two posts so that these are about 2 m (6 ft) above ground and at the distance apart necessary or required. Two wires are then fixed, one about 7 cm (2¾ in) from the top of the post and the other 50 cm (20 in) below this. Strainer posts and heavy wires are recommended because of the subsequent weight of the crop. Some growers extend the vine a little more by fixing a cross piece to the top of each post. This is about

40 cm (16 in) long. An extra wire is attached to each arm end. More air circulates around the plants this way. The vine should be planted at the centre of this trellis.

Once the vine is established it will begin to send up several shoots from ground level. Select the best one or two pairs of these and remove the remainder. Fix a cane behind each vine, long enough to go into the ground and then to reach the wire above, to which it should be secured. Tie a shoot to each cane. Pinch out any laterals which form but be careful not to remove the leaves which the plant needs for growth. Once the shoot reaches the bottom wire allow two laterals to develop and train them along the wire in opposite directions. Allow the main shoot to grow up to the top wire. A cane or stout twine can be fixed from one wire to the other to support it. When it reaches the top wire its tip or growing point should be pinched out, and once again two laterals should be trained on each side of it. The laterals can be allowed to grow the full length of the wire before they are pinched out, should this be necessary. These will themselves produce laterals and it is on these that the flowers and fruit grow.

Where two shoots and not one are originally left on the young plant, keep one to furnish the bottom wire, which means pinching out its tip or growing point when it reaches this extremity, and let the other reach to the top wire. When the plant is in fruit it is important to make sure that it does not suffer from lack of water. Trickle irrigation is helpful, but it is wise to inspect the soil should the weather be very hot, just to make sure that the irrigation is providing sufficient moisture.

The purpose of pruning this plant is to remove dead and diseased tissue, to cut back any stems which are lying too low, to thin out spent fruiting wood should this be necessary so that more light and air can reach all stems, and generally to clean up the plant. For instance, dead leaves can be shaken off and removed both from hanging stems and from the ground. The fruits are produced on shoots which grow from the previous season's growth; when these become too long, they should be shortened back to a healthy young side growth. In some areas the vines can be pruned after harvesting, provided that there then remains a spell long enough for new growth to be made before cooler weather sets in. When vines are semi-dormant they do not respond to pruning. Where vines have been established for some time, and the stems have become very intertwined, it is quite in order simply to clip the mass with shears. The most practical means is to shear off all the hanging stems to within about 1 m (3 ft) from ground level. In a few days return to the plant and remove the dead stems and leaves.

Plants can be raised from seed, but one should always make certain that the fruit has come from a healthy vine. Hybrids do not come true to seed. Seed is best sown in late summer or spring. It does not remain viable for long. Commercial growers hold ripe fruit for two weeks, remove the pulp, allow the seed to ferment for three to nine days, wash it to remove the pulp, and then sow it in a suitable medium.

For greenhouse cultivation in a cold climate, a warm house is required. The minimum temperature should be 13°C (55°F) and the maximum in summer about 29°C (85°F). The plant can be grown in a greenhouse border, but it is particularly adaptable to container gardening. Often the root restriction exercised on a plant in a large pot or tub helps to promote a good crop of flowers. The passion fruit vine should only be grown in a greenhouse which can be kept humid, so it is not suitable for the average garden room.

When ripe, a passion fruit will fall from the vine. It is important to pick it up as soon as possible because if it lies in the sun and heat it will deteriorate in quality. At the same time, any well-coloured fruits still on the vine can be picked, taking care that the stem is taken with the fruit to avoid damage to the fruit skin.

## Culinary uses

Only when you have lived in passion fruit country do you come to realise the haunting quality of this unusual fruit. It seems that only the smallest amount of the succulent, soft-pippy pulp is needed to bring a very special taste and fragrance to a fruit salad, ice-cream or some other dish or drink.

Recipes for this fruit are not very plentiful – possibly, one assumes, because it is so good in taste and texture just as it is, prepacked and ready for use. However, it offers a challenge to the adventurous cook. The Australians say that you can always tell a Pommie, or Englishman, because he spits out the seeds from the passion fruit. These are plentiful but they are not in any way intimidating: simply swallow them down with the juice. When passion fruit juice and drinks are made the pulp is normally sieved or strained. This juice is extremely refreshing and it may be mixed with other juices or blended in a milk shake. The flesh is particularly refreshing mixed with orange juice and a little sugar.

When the fruit is ripe the skin becomes translucent. At this stage there is a layer of juicy green pulp beneath the skin. In the centre of the fruit are a number of seeds enclosed in a pulpy sac. Both the outer flesh and the seeds should be scooped out. Some people seem only to use the centre pulp, but this is uneconomical. Granadillas can be used in the same way as the other passion fruit. The smaller granadilla fruits are not so juicy and need orange or pineapple juice with them to bring out their flavour.

The fruit can be served raw at table, the flesh being spooned out, but this is not the most convenient way. We suggest that the pulp can be treated in the same way as that described for ripe gooseberries. Once this is squeezed out it can be used in the same way as any superior sweet fruit sauce. The classic Australian passion fruit dish is Pavlova, which is a meringue pie case, crisp outside, gooey within, filled with passion fruit, topped with pale pink ice-cream or whipped cream and suitably decorated with cherries and angelica. It follows then that the passion fruit pulp is just the thing to serve with small meringues, accompanied if you wish with pale pink ice-cream. Better still, we would suggest, make passion fruit ice-cream, following the basic recipe on page 33.

PRESERVING   Passion fruit can be introduced into jam made with other, lesser fruits, e.g. apple or pear. Use about 2 dozen passion fruits to 8 cups of diced other fruit, 7 cups of sugar and a little water, about ½ cup.

The following recipe for Passion Fruit Skins Jam may appeal to those who like to use every bit of a fruit where possible. To every 12 skins (these can be collected and stored in the refrigerator or even the freezer if the waiting time is less than one month) use the juice of 1 lemon and 6 cups of water. Measure the pulp later and add 1 cup of sugar to every cup. Boil the skins just covered with water, with the lemon juice for about 20 minutes, or until the skins become puffy and the interior soft enough to be spooned out. Drain all in a colander and save the water which drains away. Mix the pulp and water and measure. Return to the saucepan and add the sugar. Bring to the boil and let it continue to boil briskly for about ¼ hour, by which time begin to test it. When the liquid jells, pour it into hot jars.

### Passion fruit curd

6 passion fruit
4 tabsp butter
1 cup sugar
2 eggs

Place butter and sugar in a saucepan over slow heat and melt slowly. Beat eggs, then add the pulp of passion fruit and add to the butter and sugar. Simmer slowly until it reaches the consistency of honey. Pour into small jars.

FREEZING    To freeze passion fruit, simply remove the soft centre and pulp and pack it, unsweetened, in a suitable container. This is best done in small convenient quantities of the size normally required.

DRINKS    Many of the passion fruit drinks sold are made from synthetic flavourings and contain no actual passion fruit at all. A pleasant and non-alcoholic drink containing real passion fruit, which can be used as a kind of cordial or base for the addition of whisky, gin or vodka, is known as a Passion Fruit Painkiller.

### Passion fruit painkiller

10 passion fruit, pulp only
2 cups water
1 cup sugar
2 tabsp citric acid

Make a syrup of the sugar and water and pour this over the passion fruit pulp. Add the citric acid, stir and leave overnight. Stir again and then strain. Chill. Serve with ice cubes alone or with spirits.

From Queensland in Australia comes a delicious drink called an Attorney; it is made from equal parts of passion fruit and pineapple, well chilled and heavily laced with rum.

# PEACH
*Prunus persica,* syn. *Amygdalus persica, Persica vulgaris*

## Origin

The peach is a member of the rose family and closely related to the almond. As its specific name suggests, it was for a very long time considered to have originated in Persia, now Iran. However, it is now apparent that it came from China, where it has been cultivated for thousands of years, for there is mention of it in Chinese literature as far back as 551 BC. One fact that confirms this research is that the wild peach does not occur in Iran, but it has been found in many parts of China. There also are to be found all the main types in cultivation about the rest of the world: the round type to which most of our cultivars belong, the pointed type once popular but now little grown, and the flat peach which is grown there and in the warmer climates.

It is believed that the ancient Persians carried the peach into their country along the old silk routes. It seems to have been known in Europe before the first century BC. Alexander the Great may have brought it into the Graeco-Roman world. It is interesting that judging by the fruits pictured on ancient frescoes, the varieties of peach grown and enjoyed by the Romans were as large as they are today. Most ancient fruits are smaller than modern cultivars.

Peaches must have come early to Britain, since the Anglo-Saxons had a name for the fruit, *perseoc-treou*. By the time of Queen Elizabeth I, nectarines and peaches, mainly of French origin, were in cultivation. British gardeners began raising splendid peaches. An example is Pitmaston Orange, raised by Mr Edwards of Pitmaston in 1815, a variety which has not yet been surpassed in flavour. Another famous name is Thomas Rivers of Sawbridgeworth, and after him his son and grandson carried on his work with great success. Famous varieties raised by this firm are the early-maturing, white-fleshed, Duke of York; mid-season Peregrine with yellow flesh; and Pineapple, a late, white-fleshed variety.

The Spanish took the peach to Latin America during the sixteenth century. In the following century it was being grown in California. By the nineteenth century the fruit was being produced in Australia and a century later in South Africa.

Today, with the apple and the orange, the peach is probably the most widely cultivated fruit in the world.

As one would expect, since the plant has been in cultivation for such a long time, there are thousands of varieties or cultivars. Some have disappeared after a few years but others are constantly appearing. The important feature in some of the new peaches is their early ripening. This applies particularly to those varieties raised in America. The classification of the peach is based on the ripening of the fruit as well as upon certain characteristics of a plant such as the shape of the leaves, the colour, size and shape of the flowers, and the type of fruit – its colour, texture and whether or not the flesh clings to the stone.

Some peaches are grown entirely for the beauty of their early blossom. These do not produce fruits, or do not produce fruits of sufficient numbers or quality to be included here.

Peaches need mainly a warm climate to ripen properly and they are grown widely in temperate regions. On the other hand, low temperatures play an important role. Both peaches and the closely related nectarines need a certain amount of chilling during the trees' period of winter rest or dormancy in order for the normal development of buds to take place the following spring. The amount of chilling necessary varies. It is measured in the number of hours at or below 7°C (44°F). In some varieties the leaf buds need more chilling than the flower buds. Much research has been carried out on this factor and it is possible to select a variety, or several varieties, to suit a particular climate. However, there are several peach varieties developed locally to suit particular local needs that appear not to need chilling 'to break dormancy'. Leaf fall, followed by a short but not chilled rest, seems to suffice. It is well worth making enquiries before making a final selection for one's garden. Obviously, it is important when one lives in a warm climate to plant only those varieties that need a fairly low chilling period.

Italy and the United States produce the greatest amount of fruit; crops are also raised commercially in Canada, China, Japan, Australia, Israel and New Zealand, as well as smaller and more localised crops in Spain, France, Greece and Yugoslavia. Peaches will grow outdoors in cooler countries such as Britain, but not on a commercial scale, although in the past many were greenhouse-grown. Gardens in many parts of the world contain a peach tree or two, since these can often be easily protected where this is necessary. The peach is a fine urban garden plant, although in built-up areas some gardeners need to beware of what has been called the 'finger-blight' applied by small boys!

The greatest disadvantage of the peach is that it blossoms early, but where means can be found to prevent the flowers from becoming frosted, the plants produce well. We have successfully grown peaches outdoors on the edge of the Cotswold escarpment in England, overlooking the river Severn, in a none too well sheltered garden. Yet, generally speaking, this is not a hot climate crop. Both the quality and size of many varieties of the fruit decreases as the tropics are approached, warns one authority on growing fruit in warm climates. All the same, it is possible to find certain kinds which will crop heavily. One of these is the China Flat peach, *P. p. compressa*, sometimes known as *P. p. var. patycarpa*, as well as varieties from the southern China race of peaches which have oval, pointed fruits with a deep groove situated at the base.

## The fruit

Botanically, a drupe, usually of a spheroid shape, with a longitudinal groove, the pedicel being attached to the fruit at the bottom of a deep cavity. Depending upon the variety of the peach and also upon the soil, the fruit varies in colour. The velvety skin may be pale green, white or yellow. Usually one cheek, on the sunny side, is well coloured, but sometimes the flush covers the whole of the fruit. In some varieties this red colouring is deeper than in others. The colour of the flesh also varies. This also may be a very pale green, a white or a yellow. The white flesh is generally considered to be of the finest flavour. Plants bearing white-fleshed fruits are the hardiest for cold climates. Most yellow-fleshed varieties need warmer environments. Many of these varieties are American; an example is Hale's Early, which has an apricot-like skin, flushed and mottled with carmine red.

The stone of peaches is pitted and hard. In some the flesh clings to the stone, in others it parts freely. The varieties are classified into freestones and clingstones.

## The plant

A neat small, deciduous tree, often short-lived (20–25 years), but highly productive and early maturing. Peaches from a budded tree should crop well in five years. Its flowers vary a little, some being small and a deep rose-pink, others being larger and pale, almost white, produced in pairs or solitary. The leaves are slender, lanceolate, 8–15 cm (3–6 in) long and finely toothed.

## Cultivation

The selection of a suitable site for peaches and nectarines is most important. Spring frosts are likely to do most harm. In cold climates be sure that the site is frost free. Peaches should be grown where they can be protected without too much difficulty, and also in places where the early morning sun cannot play on the blossom after a frosty night. Low-lying land is particularly dangerous. Peaches should also be protected against cold winds.

In warm areas, the Chinese Flat peach, of which there are many varieties, is recommended because it flowers very early, before most other peaches, and by so doing often misses the frosts which are apt to occur at the more normal flowering times.

Many kinds of soil prove suitable. Peaches generally prefer light, warm, sandy or loamy soil which is well drained. They can be grown in heavier soils so long as these are well cultivated and well drained. A certain amount of lime in the soil is beneficial as with all stone fruit, but excessive lime content can be detrimental. Although soils should be fertile, they should not be too rich nor recently manured. Areas on high water tables are not suitable.

In an equable climate a peach tree can be grown in the open like any other tree, but in a cold climate it is usually grown in such a way that one's attention is inevitably focused more closely upon it, as it would be, for example, if it were growing trained against a warm wall. This is just as well, since a peach tree more than any other demands pruning and training throughout its life. Having said this, the mental picture of a peach tree in a Sydney garden, laden down with fruit, comes vividly to mind, since it was a tree which by most standards had been long and sadly neglected!

However, the first need is to decide in what way the plant should be grown, as a free-standing tree or bush, as a fan-trained specimen against the wall or an espalier growing on wires. The forms that can be produced by pruning are extremely varied. The greatest fruiting area on a tree is produced by a natural goblet, or the vase or inverted cone, such as one sees in commercial orchards in Australia, America and France. The French gardeners have even more elaborate goblets, *l'Y de la vallée de l'Eyrieux* and the *gobelet fleur de Liseron*, and for those gardeners who like the idea of an espalier to conserve space, they have the *U double*, the *palmette Verrier à quatre branches* and above all the *palmette à la diable*.

The greatest skill in the cultivation of the peach, however, lies in the way the plant is pruned so that it will continue to bear fruit. Pruning needs studying. The shoots produced by the peach are of four types and each of these needs a different treatment. There is the growth shoot, the flowering shoot bearing both growth and flower buds, spurs bearing a cluster of flower buds and usually a central growth bud and coarse growth shoots which spring from near the base of the tree. The main aim is to encourage the tree to continue to produce fruit and to promote and make space for new shoots, so that the old, non-fruiting shoots can be removed.

Bush trees are the easiest of all to grow in the open and this form can be used for peaches grown in containers. Once the plant is formed, little pruning is required and should consist mainly of the cutting away of infertile, badly placed or crossing branches.

Fruits of the peach and nectarine are naturally produced on long shoots made in the previous year, and also sometimes on short shoots or spurs. Of these two, the former is the more important. This fruiting wood does not fruit again. If left to grow naturally, the shoot will make new growth at its tips, which means that as it lengthens, the fruit is produced further and further away from the main stem. The object of pruning is to change the future zones of fruit production. Briefly, shoots which have borne fruit should be cut back each year to encourage new growth. Where a fan-trained plant is being grown, those shoots growing out to the front and back of the branches have to be removed to keep the tree on one plane. This is best done in spring and early summer by simply rubbing the young shoots off their stems. When the required growth is some 7–15 cm (3–6 in) long, it can be tied to the wires and kept within the fan pattern. Try to have the growth for the new fruit about 5–8 cm (2–3 in) apart all over the plant.

As frost is such a determining factor in the success of a peach crop, it is well worth protecting wall plants by covering them at night during periods when frost can be expected. The covering should be removed as soon as it is safe, so that early foraging insects can pollinate the blossoms. Yet even so some artificial aid is helpful. When the blossoms are open, pollinate them with a soft brush or the traditional rabbit's tail or paw, brushing one flower's stamens and passing on to the next and so on. Do this each day for ten days or so, or until all the blossom has opened, largely because some of the flowers are sure to be missed.

When the fruit is about the size of a hazel nut, thin out to 7–10 cm (3–4 in) apart, and repeat when the size of a walnut to about 20–25 cm (9 in). Some varieties thin themselves by dropping small fruits. On the other hand thinning frequently reduces this action, cutting the strain on a tree. So much of plant food goes into making the peach stone and kernel that by removing surplus fruits more food is available for those that remain. Work from the larger fruit, leaving these. Separate twins and remove all misshapen fruits.

When the tree is fruiting well, encourage it by feeding it a dose of ¼ cup of sulphate of ammonia per square m (square yd). In spring apply a good, deep mulch of well-rotted manure or garden compost right around the base of the tree.

Almost all peaches suffer at some time from peach leaf curl, and this can be prevented by spraying with Bordeaux mixture or a proprietary preparation as soon as the buds begin to swell in early spring. Evidence of the disease is the appearance of discoloured, distorted and swollen leaves.

## Culinary uses

There are several recipes for peach drinks, mainly liqueurs though some wines. None of them give a product anything like as delicious, delicate or characteristic as the raw fruit itself, so without any equivocation, we say that if you would like to drink a peach, eat one raw, in the peak of condition, and you cannot do better.

Immediately before they become ripe these fruits increase in size as well as improve in colour, so if you pick unripe fruit you are likely to be losing both quantity and quality. Even so, the fruit will continue to ripen and gain in flavour after it is picked, but it should be watched so that it does not become over-ripe.

The sugar content of a peach is about 9 per cent and the vitamins, especially of A and C, are greater than in most other fruits. Peaches contain a considerable amount of minerals and are lower in calories than either apples or pears. They are highly versatile fruits. When truly ripe they are among the most delicious in the world, as succulent and sweet eaten raw as cooked.

They are mainly eaten as desserts. They are excellent in compotes, mousses and ice-creams and in many types of pies, puddings and other sweets. They can be served in jellies, *bavarois*, stewed, baked, grilled or flambéed. They can be put, again fresh or cooked, into fritters, pancakes, dumplings and sweet batters of various types. Their juice is so good that it is often known as nectar. Any recipe given for nectarines or apricots can be used also for peaches.

Peaches have an affinity with almonds. One Italian sweet calls for halved peaches stuffed with a macaroon mixture, the biscuits being pounded with a little of the peach pulp, egg, butter and sugar. The peaches are then baked for 30 minutes.

The fruits can also be used in savoury dishes, baked with meats, spiced, or made into pickles. They can be served raw, bottled or canned, with cream cheese, nuts, lettuce or watercress and a vinaigrette sauce, as a side or a main salad. Try wrapping very thin slices of ham around peach halves filled with cream cheese and chives, or salami smeared with the merest hint of an aromatic mustard around a peach slice.

To make a Peach Sauce for ham, bacon and poultry, including a replacement for the ubiquitous orange sauce with duck, try the following.

### Peach sauce

*1 cup thick peach juice*
*3 teasp cornflour*
*3 teasp prepared English mustard*
*1½ tabsp white vinegar*

Simmer the peach juice and combine the other

ingredients and mix them until smooth. Add them to the peach juice, and stir continuously until the mixture thickens. Serve hot. This same sauce can be poured over peaches baked with the meat and handled separately.

The tips of young peach tree shoots flavour a milk pudding or ice-cream much as a vanilla pod would, but with its own characteristic almond scent. This is a use for any prunings.

PRESERVING Peach and Orange Jam can be made from:

### Peach and orange jam

12 cups yellow peaches
3 oranges
9 cups sugar

Peel, stone and cut up peaches. Grate orange rind and squeeze juice. Cook for 30 minutes. Add sugar and cook quickly for ½–¾ hour. Bottle and seal.

One of the most luxurious ways of preserving peaches is to bottle them in brandy. They are then ready to serve with cold meats on special occasions. Peaches can also be made into jams, the yellow-fleshed varieties being considered the best for this purpose. Use 6 cups fruit with 4½ cups sugar. In marmalades they can be used with lemon, oranges, limes or with melon. Conserves, preserves and butters can be made from them. Any of these can be incorporated into sweet sauces for pancakes and ice creams as well as for fillings for layer cakes.

FREEZING To freeze peaches, one method is to take fully ripe fruit, blanch them for ½–1 minute and remove the skin. The peaches can then be left whole or halved and stoned. They should then be packed in a heavy syrup with ascorbic acid.

One disadvantage of this method is that some fruits are liable to turn brown and to soften. To eliminate this possibility, peel the fruit under a little cold running water. Once they are peeled, brush them with lemon juice.

BOTTLING To bottle peaches prepare the fruits as for freezing. Process as for apricots.

And finally an unusual recipe for a sweetmeat, Peach and Apricot Leather.

### Peach and apricot leather

2 cups dried apricots
1 cup dried peaches
caster sugar

Mince the fruit finely, two or three times, mixing them well in the process. Using a pastry board and rolling pin, roll out the mixture. This is best done a little at a time. Dust the board and the pin generously with the sugar and keep dusting the pin. When the leather is about 3 mm (⅛ in) thick, cut it into strips and slice these into pieces about 5 cm (2 in) by 2.5 cm (1 in). Roll the strips lengthwise into tight rolls.

DRYING Peaches can be dried like apricots (q.v.) and used in the same ways.

# PEAR
*Pyrus communis* and other species

## Origin

The plant is a member of the rose family, Rosaceae. The genus contains more than 30 species from widely differing climatic areas. Its name is derived from *pyrus,* the Latin for pear tree. The European pear, or wild pear, is a native of temperate Europe, including Britain and western Asia, reaching in fact to the Himalayas. It has been cultivated in Europe since ancient times. Obviously always highly esteemed, it has been uncovered in palaeolithic sites where it is believed to have been known some 40 centuries ago. We read of it from Pliny, who listed 39 varieties known to the Romans of his time. Authorities believe some of these to have been very similar to William's Bon Chretien, known as the Bartlett pear in America, after the man who took it there. This pear continued through the centuries to be grown in Italy. A list exists which shows that 232 varieties were known in the sixteenth century.

In Europe the most important pear growing areas appear always to have been in France, Belgium and west Germany, mainly because the climate is so suited to the cultivation of this fruit which needs warm summers and sufficient moisture at its roots; but another factor which contributed to this situation was that there were many rich amateurs living in these countries who were able to spend money on producing fine varieties. Dr Van Mons in Louvain and Major Esperen of Belgium are two names recorded. Many of these varieties are unsurpassed and are still grown, not only in their homelands but in many other countries about the world. The famous Doyenne du Comice pear first appeared in France in 1849.

From the early days onwards, many of the French varieties were grown in British gardens and are still being grown there and elsewhere, wherever Britons have settled. Jargonelle, known in 1600, still figures in today's lists, as does the early maturing Doyenne d'Ete which was raised in 1700, and many, many more. In the eighteenth and nineteenth centuries British nurserymen and gardeners alike, amateur and professional, bred many fine varieties, some of which are still grown or remembered, but perhaps the only two really outstanding varieties are John William's Bon Chretien and Thomas Rivers' Conference, the variety which is the most widely grown in Britain today.

The American pear, Seckle, said by some to be the most highly flavoured of all, was a true gift from the gods. It was discovered some time around 1765 by a trapper who had bought a piece of woodland and found the seedling growing there.

William's Bon Chretien comes into the picture again with some of the North American varieties which are thought to be hybrids between this and the Japanese sand pear, sometimes called the Chinese or Asian pear, *P. pyrifolia,* with synonyms *P. serotina* and *P. sinensis.* This pear and its varieties have long been cultivated in China and Japan. It is now also grown in Australia and central America and recommended for tropical highlands generally, along with cultivars from *P. koehnei,* an evergreen pear indigenous to south China, and *P. calleryana.* These are pears which can tolerate warmer conditions than the European pear, though the species themselves are inedible.

There are said to be more than 3,000 varieties of pears, but only a very few of these are known to and cultivated by the general public. Pears have not always been grown for dessert. They were once widely grown for perry. Perry pears have to contain a high percentage of tannin, and most varieties still grown for this purpose are very old.

## The fruit

Botanically, a pome. The fruits vary considerably in the species as does skin colour. All have flesh which contains many grit cells, a characteristic of the genus. Sand pears are grittier than most, and their flesh is harder. Some pears are pear-shaped, others are sub-globose and apple-shaped. As may be expected, their cultivars also vary a great deal one from another. The fruits are classified according to the main shape patterns, which are:
1.  Round or flattened, rough-skinned and russetted, mainly old varieties.
2.  Bergamot or top-shaped, also rough-skinned and russetted, or green when ripe.
3.  Conical, pears which taper but are not waisted, usually russetted, yellow or red flushed.
4.  Pyriform, pear-shaped with a distinct waist, usually yellow when ripe. Among these are the choicest varieties.
5.  Oval, mainly russetted and without any red colouring.
6.  Calebasse or Long pears, brown or golden russet, although a few are smooth green, mainly cooking pears.

## The plant

The tree is often of a pyramidal shape, growing to some 12–15 m (40–50 ft) in the wild, sometimes spiny. It has a rugged, rough, grey-brown bark. The wood is firm and hard and greatly valued by cabinet makers. The leaves can vary from oval to almost round or heart-shaped. They are 3–9 cm (1–3½ in) long. The flowers are the typical five-petalled blossom, each flower 3–4 cm (1–1½ in) wide, clustered in corymbs some 5–8 cm (2–3 in) across, with numerous stamens, often wine red. Not all of the cultivars make such robust plants as the species. Doyenne d'Été, for example, is a very small and weak tree. On the other hand, Jaronelle is a large and spreading tree. We have an old Pitmaston Duchess which is believed to be well over a hundred years old, very tall and pyramidal. It bears every year, but has never borne so prolifically, nor produced such excellent fruit as the crop of the drought year, 1976, which incidentally followed the hot summer of 1975. The following year, 1977, it produced no fruit at all.

Pears are very beautiful when in flower. Some take on beautiful colours in the autumn.

## Cultivation

Generally speaking, pears are grown in much the same way as apples. However, they are more adaptable to humid and misty areas than are apples, which means that they can be grown more successfully in tropical regions provided suitable varieties are selected. Some pears, especially those derived from the European varieties, need a certain amount of chilling during their resting period. There are some varieties which will tolerate wet conditions better than apples, but even these will not grow where the soil is permanently wet. Those pears grafted on to quince stocks are said to tolerate moist conditions best. Pears need adequate moisture at their roots throughout the growing season. The plants like full sunshine.

Soils should be deep. Pears will not grow well in shallow soils or in poor, sandy ones. Clay soils need to be well prepared and well drained. Pears blossom fairly early, and where frosts occur the blossom can become damaged. Winds also can cause damage, usually to the fruit and especially just before harvesting. This suggests that where possible protected sites should be chosen.

It is possible to grow just one pear tree which is self-pollinating, but most pear trees crop best when another variety is grown nearby, even if this is in a neighbour's garden, although it goes without saying that the two must blossom at the same time. A pear described as Triploid has no good pollen and two other varieties are needed to make it crop. It is possible to have several varieties of pears grafted on one family tree.

Pears may also be trained in the same way as apples.

Unlike many other fruits, pears usually continue to ripen off the tree. After a period in storage they reach their finest flavour and quality. They should be picked when hard, but also when fully developed. Should you pick fruit too early it will shrivel. Shrivelled pears can be cooked, but they do not become good dessert fruit.

They need careful storing. Unlike apples, they should not be stored in layers, one above the other, for they tend to rot very quickly this way. Instead they should be open to the light. Only the late maturing varieties are suitable for long storing, the best examples including Catillac, Glou Morceau, Josephine de Malines and Winter Nelis.

## Culinary uses

Pears are a nutritional food, containing vitamins A, B and C, carbohydrates and, among the minerals, iodine. They contain a very small amount of sodium. Like the apple, there are cooking, dessert and perry or drink pears. Cooking pears are hard. They can be divided into summer, autumn and winter varieties. Many of the summer ripening kinds do not keep once they are mature, but soon go 'sleepy'. Unripe dessert pears can be cooked if desired.

Cooking pear flesh is usually granular and sometimes tart, although not especially so, and although they ripen in the technical sense of the word, most of them are not good to eat raw. There are a few exceptions and we are happy to say that our Pitmaston Duchess pear matures to a delicious sweet-sour flavour. Cooking pears are useful because they can be stored for use in winter. Most of them need long cooking and as a rule the cooked pears turn a dusky pink and their texture differs from that of the softer dessert pears. One of the best ways is to cover them with syrup and bake them slowly in a covered jar. These pears can be spiced, using mainly cinnamon and cloves.

Dessert pears are among the most delicious of all fruits and it is generally accepted that they are best eaten raw. However, they usually crop so abundantly that one has to find many ways to cook and preserve them. Fortunately they bottle splendidly and most varieties freeze well. Usually the more delicious the pear is raw, the better it is cooked.

One should make the most, though, of the ripe, raw fruit. They can be treated in much the same way as melons. Serve them as a starter to a meal and hand round ginger and/or lemon just as one would for a melon. If you are in a party mood, pour a little port into the centre from which the core should have been scooped out. If you brush the cut surface with lemon juice the flesh will stay white. Alternatively, as nuts go so well with pears, try chopping walnuts finely and pressing the cut surface into the nuts to give it a coating. Pear halves or slices are as good as melon with Parma or other ham and with cold cooked bacon. Serve them with smoked mackerel and other raw or cooked smoked fish.

Generally speaking, pears can be cooked as apples, merely altering the name of the fruit in he recipe. Try, for instance, Pear Fritters, Baked Pear Dumplings, Pear Charlotte. Quince and pear go together also. Bake a pear pie, like an apple pie, and add a tablespoon of ground almonds to the pastry mix, and sprinkle a little more, mixed with sugar, on the top before baking. Add a piece of cinnamon stick, if you like the flavour, or dust the top with mixed cinnamon powder and sugar before serving. Poached pears cooked in a vanilla syrup can be drained and used in many lovely desserts and flans. Cardinal Pears are poached pears covered with raspberry purée sprinkled with chopped almonds – quite delicious. But try also this variation: use bramble purée and hazelnuts, browned a little in the oven before they are chopped.

Baked Pears in Wine need:

### Baked pears in wine

*4 almost ripe pears, peeled but with the stems left on*
*4 cloves*
*2 cups red wine*
*½ cup sugar*
*½ cup water*

Push a clove into the bottom end of each pear. Stand them in a deep casserole on to which a lid can be fitted. If you haven't one deep enough, lay the pears on their sides. Mix the wine, sugar and water together and pour the mixture into the casserole. Bake at 200°C (400°F, gasmark 6) for 30 minutes. Test, and if almost tender, uncover and cook for another 15 minutes, otherwise baste the pears and leave them covered and cooking a little longer. Serve hot or cold with cream or ice-cream.

PRESERVING   An Italian speciality, Mostarda Cremonese, is a relish made with semi-candied fruits in a sugary syrup flavoured with a mild European mustard. It demands pears of a small size, whole and coloured red or green.

Dessert pears can be crystallised like any other fruit, whole or quartered. In France they are then partly dried in the oven and flattened on one side. They can be found in the shops under the name *poires tapées*.

Many kinds of preserves can be made from pears. In addition to sweet kinds, they make good chutney and they are good spiced.

Our own Pear Marmalade is so good that we always make a large batch for gift jars. We use:

### Pear marmalade

*8 cups (about 12) ripe but not mushy pears,*
*    weighed after peeling and coring*
*6 cups sugar*
*juice of 4 lemons*

Dice the pears, place in a basin with the sugar and lemon juice and leave to stand overnight. Put into a preserving pan, bring to the boil slowly and then boil quickly until the jam sets on test.

This is the basic recipe. It can be lifted from the ordinary by adding ½ cup stem ginger, which should be put into the mixture a little while before it reaches setting point. Another variation is to use ¼ cup ginger and ¼ cup candied citrus peel.

Frozen pears can be used for this recipe. Put them in with their juice and let this boil down.

Our Pitmaston Duchess pears are also used for Honey Pickled Pears which we make each harvest. Any other firm but ripe pear can be used and the recipe also suits non-fluffy apples.

### Honey pickled pears

*2 cups honey*
*1 cup good vinegar, cider for instance*
*5 cm (2 in) cinnamon stick*
*6 cloves*
*12 cups (about 15) peeled, cored and quartered*
*    pears*

This pickle is made in stages. Put the honey, vinegar, cinnamon and cloves into a pan and bring to the boil. Cook about half the fruit in the syrup, or less if this is more convenient. Move the pears about from time to time but do not squash them. Let them simmer until they are transparent. Lift out with a draining spoon and put into a bowl. Repeat with more fruit. When all has been cooked, divide the fruit into sterilised jars, cover with the syrup and seal.

FREEZING   Pears for freezing should not be over-ripe or they will be mushy and of a generally unpleasant texture when they are thawed. They are best frozen in a thin syrup in which they have been poached for about 1½ minutes. As a rule the pears are peeled, cored and quartered, but we often freeze whole pears, leaving the stems on but removing the cores. These can then be used in recipes calling for whole pears, or simply thawed and served with kirsch and cream.

Pears should be prepared and frozen quickly. We find it best to have a pan of simmering, vanilla-flavoured syrup at the side and to deal with a few pears, enough to fill one container, at a time. This way they never become discoloured. Drain the pears, allow them to cool and pour the cool syrup over them. When the pears are to be served with a chocolate sauce, or some other kind, the syrup may be used in this.

BOTTLING   Cooking pears are not really suitable for bottling, unless the pear is a type which becomes mellow and like a dessert variety. They should be peeled, cored and halved. One of the best methods of coring is first to cut the fruit in half downwards, and then, using a pointed teaspoon, scoop out the central fibrous portion. Save skins and cores to make pear wine or perry. While preparing the fruit have ready a bowl of water into which ½ teasp and 1 teasp respectively of salt and citric acid per 4 cups has been added. Put the peeled fruit into this to avoid discoloration. Rinse the pears quickly in cold water, pack them into jars, core sides downwards and cover with syrup.

DRYING   Pears can be dried in the same way as apples. They should first be cut into quarters or eighths.

DRINKS   Pear juice can be made into a number of excellent drinks, few of which seem to be properly exploited. Perry, for example, a pear cider, is made in exactly the same way as apple cider and can be either sparkling or still. The French make an appetising perry which is widely accepted and drunk, but the English seem to turn most of theirs into a rather sickly-sweet imitation champagne, and in other parts of the world there is almost no utilisation of this fruit for the making of drinks. As liqueurs there appear to be only Birnengeist or Birnenwein or the better known Williamine. Pears are used in the basic wine recipe on p. 34.

To make Pear Wine you will need really ripe pears, even sleepy fruits. Use also peel and cores left from any other cooking. Soak the pears in the water. Cover, opening only to stir daily for two weeks. Strain and measure. Add 6 cups sugar to every 16 cups liquid. Add the prepared yeast, stir and cover. When fermentation takes place, about

2 days, pour into a jar and insert airlock. Bottle when fermentation has completely stopped.

# PERSIMMON
*Diospyros* species

## Origin

Members of a large genus of both deciduous and evergreen trees and shrubs, to which the Ebony tree also belongs, in the family Ebenaceae, distinguished for their delicious yet astringent fruits. The plants under discussion originate from China, Japan, western Asia, the Himalayas and North America. *D. virginiana* is the American persimmon, *D. kaki* the kakee or Chinese persimmon and *D. lotus* the date plum.

Along with a few other fruits mentioned in this book, which although well known and esteemed in their own countries are comparatively unknown outside, persimmons seem to be on the threshold of universal popularity. More and more are being cultivated commercially in more and more countries. The plant is also a delightful garden tree.

The fruits of the American persimmon are often gathered wild in that country. It is hardy and fruits as far north as the Great Lakes. The fruits of the kakee or Chinese persimmon are large, about 8 cm (3 in) in diameter, sometimes larger, and with flattened ends. This persimmon has been popular for centuries in the East. There are, for instance, some 1,000 known varieties in Japan alone. It is also grown in many warm and tropical countries, especially in the Midi and the olive-producing zones of southern France, Italy, Spain, many other Mediterranean countries and onwards into the sun. It is a familiar sight in gardens, where its highly ornamental foliage clothes it handsomely and paints it bright in autumn. Even when the leaves fall, the ripening orange fruit hangs on and ornaments the bare branches. Recently persimmons have become increasingly popular in some regions of Australia as more people from Mediterranean areas settle in that country and look for the fruits with which they are familiar and at home.

*D. kaki* has many cultivars. It is the most widely grown of the three species. The species itself has given rise to varieties: *D. k. aurantium,*

*D. k. costata, D. k. elliptica* and *D. k. mazelii.*

In some countries these are sometimes given popular or trivial names, such as the ribbed persimmon, the mandarin persimmon and the lycopersicum, the last confusing because this is the generic name for tomato, which the fruits resemble.

## The fruit

Botanically, a berry with a persistent calyx. Some fruits contain seeds and some are seedless as explained below. Pollinated fruits contain one to eight black seeds. Unripe persimmons are unpalatable, being exceedingly astringent; they contain tannic acid. Fruits have to be allowed to ripen fully so that they become soft and almost watery.

The fruits of the date plum are quite small, 1–2 cm ($\frac{1}{2}$–$\frac{3}{4}$ in) in diameter, yellow at first, becoming purple-black. The flesh is firm, sweet and date-like. The fruits of the American persimmon are smaller than the kakee, 3–4 cm (1–1$\frac{1}{2}$ in) in diameter. Usually they are yellow with a red cheek, but they can also be dark red or purple-red and not unlike a plum in appearance.

The fruit of the kakee, is a wide, depressed globe, some 7–8 cm (3 in) or more in diameter. The fruits of the varieties differ from the type as do some of the cultivars. *D. k. aurantium* has apple-shaped orange-yellow fruit; *D. k. costata* has large, orange-yellow fruit furrowed so that it appears to be in sections; *D. k. elliptica* has oval fruit, orange-yellow; and *D. k. mazelii* has round, orange-yellow fruit with eight sections. The flesh of the type is orange, fleshy, and sweet when ripe, but it differs again with some cultivars. Fuyu, for instance, a large, flattened fruit, has very dark flesh which is beautifully firm when ripe, so that it can be eaten in the hand like an apple. The fairly thin skin is firm and does not peel easily. It is softly shining and slightly waxy. Unripe fruits sometimes have a bloom on them.

## The plant

Like many trees, the date plum does not grow so vigorously in cultivation. In the wild it will reach 20 m (60 ft), but in a garden rarely more than 6 m (20 ft). It is a deciduous, round-headed tree. The oval, dark green, glossy leaves, downy on the undersides, are 5–13 cm (2–5 in) long and 3–5 cm (1–2 in) wide. Flowers are small, and white with a red coloration.

The American persimmon is a taller tree with a very rugged bark. The leaves are similar to those of the date plum. The male flowers, small and green, grow one to three in the leaf axils. Female flowers are both larger and solitary. Both are more or less bell-shaped.

The leaves of the kakee are much larger than either of these, 8–20 cm (3–8 in) long and half as wide, shining green above, with paler, pubescent undersides in which the veins can be clearly seen. The flowers are more conspicuous, being yellow-white, 4 cm (1$\frac{1}{2}$ in) wide, with a four-lobed calyx which is persistent and remains attached to the fruits at the stem end.

Diospyros are mainly unisexual, but the kakee is of a more complicated nature. The plant is dioecious, but sometimes there are separate males and females on the same plant. The female flowers do not have to be pollinated by the male in order to produce fruits, but as one might expect, such fruits tend to be seedless. Seedless fruits ripen differently from those containing seeds. The main difference is that when finally coloured they are not ripe, and where the climate is favourable these are best left on the tree to mature. Otherwise, give them a longer period of post-harvest ripening.

The fruits are borne singly on the branches. The diospyros has a tendency under certain conditions, possibly climatic, to fruit biennially. In some regions the plant assumes delightful colours in winter.

## Cultivation

Persimmons prefer a medium loam, but they will grow well in most ordinary soils. They will not tolerate acid soils. The plant does not thrive in dry situations, but seems to be quite happy in heavy, clay loams. The kakee is also one of the few fruiting plants which can be said to tolerate a certain amount of waterlogging, though obviously the more that can be done to improve such soils the better. The site should be well prepared and enriched before planting.

In Britain and countries with a similar climate, it is prudent to treat the kakee as a half hardy plant and to give it greenhouse conditions. It should there be planted in a soil border.

Where conditions are kinder, any of these three species are agreeable trees to grow in a garden, although a kakee will probably be the most profitable. This can be trained as a fan or an espalier if space is limited. Plants can be raised from seed, which is best stratified, but the seedlings are very variable and do not come true to type. Furthermore, trees grown from seed become very large. Budded trees are smaller because of the dwarfing effect of the rootstocks. However, these are not always very vigorous, and for this reason it is recommended that they should be headed back when the young plant is about 60 cm (2 ft) tall. Four or five buds should be left to grow into branches. The same method should be used for seedlings. After this, pruning is not important unless the plant is being fan- or espalier-trained. One simply keeps the dead or unwanted branches cut away and the centre open to allow air to circulate and light to penetrate.

Grafted plants soon become established, often bearing a good crop in their second or third year.

Do not disturb the soil too much around the base of the tree as this may encourage suckering.

It is best to mulch to keep weeds down and to keep the roots moist. Persimmons need plenty of water during their growing period. Give them fertiliser in early spring and a smaller dose in summer.

Because of the intricacies of pollination some trees are likely to drop flowers. This seems to happen more if they have been grown from seed. Often this fault can be corrected by planting a suitable pollinator nearby. Self-fertile varieties can be obtained. Examples are Tanensahi, an early, conical, seedless variety with red fruit and a bright red hue when mature; Dai Dai Maru, seedless, with orange mature fruit; and Haichiya, a lovely red-orange when ripe, with large fruits some 10 cm (4 in) in diameter, a very sweet flesh and of fine quality. Triumph is reputed to bear a generous crop.

Anyone who has ever eaten persimmons will know that the fruits must be ripe, otherwise they are quite unbearably astringent, almost caustic in the mouth. One of the simplest techniques of ripening the fruit is to place an apple among them. The apple emits a vapour, ethylene gas, which triggers and hastens ripening. Enclose the fruit, 1 apple to each 6–8 persimmons, inside a plastic box, dome or bag. The fruit will ripen in 3–7 days at room temperature. Remove from the container when the persimmons appear to soften. Refrigerate them if they become jelly-like.

## Culinary uses

The persimmon is a nutritious food fruit with a high percentage of protein and glucose; the tannic acid content disappears only when the persimmon is fully ripe. The dark-fleshed varieties are less astringent and can be eaten in the hand like an apple as soon as they are ripe and sweet enough.

Eat fresh, puréed, cooked, iced or candied. Use for desserts, tarts, cakes, ices, sorbets, compotes, jams and other preserves. Some varieties can be candied or otherwise made into sweetmeats.

Persimmons can be used in recipes in place of apple sauce. Try them in an apple sauce cake, and with pork, goose or any meat with which apple is normally served in some way. Try them in fritters with bacon. They are easily made into a purée. Wash, stem and quarter the fruit, scoop out the pulp from the skins and blend or sieve.

Top: Hips of *Rosa moyesii* 'Geranium' *(L. Johns)*
Bottom: Strawberries *(K. Muir)*

Sour Sop *(G. R. Roberts)*

The fruits are so refreshing that they can be served for breakfast or as a starter for another meal.

To eat them raw, the easiest way is to take a sharp knife and slit the skin downwards so that it can be pulled back exposing the mass of pulpy sweet inside. This can then be eaten in the hand or spooned out.

Those persimmons with tough skins can be stuffed in various ways, mixed with grapefruit or pineapple for a first course for instance, or instead of another fruit, with cooked rice and a little salad dressing.

FREEZING Persimmons freeze surprisingly well. We were given some by a friend who grows the fruit and who maintains that they can go into the freezer not quite ripe, unskinned and whole, and that the freezing process breaks down the tannic acid into sugars. How scientifically correct this is we are not sure, but we do know that the fruits when thawed were fresh in appearance and sweet in flavour and we enjoyed them immensely. The usual method is to freeze them the same way as for passion fruit, or to put them in a dry sugar pack.

DRYING We are told that the Japanese dry certain varieties of persimmon. The skin is removed and the fruits, suspended by their stems on strings, are then exposed to the sun. After a time they lose their form, and also become quite dark. They become covered with sugar crystals as the juice dries out. These dried fruits are said to be delicious and a little like dried figs in texture.

DRINKS We have never tasted nor even heard of a persimmon drink, and in our percipient lives we have never had access to sufficient supplies of this delectable fruit to experiment for ourselves and so fill an obvious gap in the possibilities of man's enjoyment of his environment.

# PINEAPPLE
*Ananas comosus*

## Origin

A native of Brazil, the pineapple has been given a South American name for its generic term. 'Comosus' refers to its tufted growth. It is one of the most delicious and deservedly popular of all tropical fruits. As one would expect, once discovered it was soon distributed and since it is one of the easiest of all plants to grow, given the right conditions, it is now to be found in all tropical regions. In some, such as certain areas of Asia and Africa, it has become naturalised.

Christopher Columbus is said to have brought the pineapple to Spain, although this may be a legend. The Portuguese are said to have introduced it into India in 1583. It was brought to Britain at the end of the seventeenth century and was for many years grown widely in hothouses both in private gardens and commercial nurseries until fruits began to be imported from the Azores in about 1860. One variety then grown, the Queen, a small plant with small (1–1½ kg/2–3 lb), golden yellow fruits, less juicy though sweeter than many varieties, is still grown extensively in South Africa. Another variety, Cayenne or Kew Giant, introduced for greenhouse culture about 1841, with large (2.7 kg/6 lb) fruits, yellow green with pale yellow flesh, has become the most widely grown variety. Like the other pineapples it has sharp, spiny leaves which make cultivation difficult, for apart from damage to the person, clothes also become torn as workers pass down the rows. A cultivar, Smooth Cayenne, has smooth leaves and is gradually superseding some of the older varieties for obvious reasons, even though its fruit is not of such a good flavour. It is a dual purpose variety, being grown both for canning and as fresh fruit.

Now these two old-established fruits form, with the Spanish type, the three main groups into which commercially grown pineapples are divided. The Smooth Cayenne is the variety principally grown for canning. Others in its group are the Hilo of Hawaii and St Michel of South Africa. From the Queen group, grown exclusively for the fresh fruit, several local selections have been made in different regions of the world. In Queensland the rough-leaved or Common Rough lost popularity because of the plant's tendencies towards producing suckers, but the MacGregor, a local selection, proved more to the growers' taste. Ripley Queen and Alexandra are others. The Spanish group is characterised by the Red Spanish, grown in Cuba and Puerto Rico for the US fresh fruit trade. Another group, Abacaxi, contains those varieties mainly grown in gardens in the tropics. The fruit is excellent, but not tough enough to withstand the rigours of transport.

Today, pineapples are produced on a commercial scale in Australia, the Azores, Brazil, the Canary Islands, Cuba, Formosa, Hawaii, Malaysia, Mexico, South Africa and in small pockets elsewhere, such as the Bahamas, where the Sugarloaf pineapple is produced and enjoyed locally. The most important producing area, however, is Hawaii.

The species has given rise to varieties, and *A. c. sativus* has many forms. There are also *debilis, lucidus, porteanus* and the lovely *variegatus,* in addition to the many cultivars.

### The fruit

Botanically, a multiple fruit, known in this case as an infructescence. As the individual flowers are fertilised they fuse together and join, with the bracts around them, to form a fleshy structure. The stem on which the flowers were attached continues to grow above the fruit and forms a tuft or crown of leaf-like bracts. This stem forms the hard core which runs through the centre of a pineapple.

When mature the fruit differs according to variety, beginning to colour at the base and spreading up to the 'shoulders'. Smooth Cayenne, for instance, is a deep to copper yellow, Ripley Queen is red rather than orange or yellow, Spanish Red is a deep tone, and so it goes on, ranging from white-yellow, green-yellow, olive green, brown-yellow, orange and red-orange. The colour of the flesh also varies. Those varieties with pale flesh are often sour. The yellow and golden flesh varieties have the best flavour.

### The plant

Pineapples are monocotyledonous herbaceous perennials belonging to the Bromeliaceae, a family which includes such plants as aechmea, cryptanthus and neoregelia, often grown as house plants. Variegated forms of the pineapple are often grown for decorative purposes because of the beautiful green, cream and pink coloration.

The height of a pineapple plant depends upon the variety as well as the conditions under which it is grown. It ranges from about 60 to 120 cm (2–4 ft). Characteristically, the leaves are rigid and grooved. They have sharp spines along the margins and pointed, sometimes dangerous, tips, although there are forms which have smooth leaves. These leaves, long, fleshy and trough-like, are arranged spirally around the stem. The flowers, which grow sessile on the flowering stem, are produced from the centre of the rosette of leaves. Only one inflorescence, and subsequently fruit, is produced on each stem. The little flowers are borne in a dense spike of about a hundred (often more according to variety) individual flowers, their colours varying somewhat between the varieties, Smooth Cayenne having light purple flowers with red bracts, others having lavender-coloured, yet more with purple flowers.

As the fruit matures, sometimes shoots with what appear to be tiny pineapples at their bases will appear around its base. These are known as slips, gill sprouts, buttons or robbers. They are usually produced on vigorous plants. These are considered by some to be the best material for propagation, and usually produce their own crop of fruits in a year or so when grown on. Another kind of shoot, usually longer than a slip and known as a sucker or a ratoon, arises in the leaf axil of a stem. This type can be left to form a fruit, or it can be used for propagation. A follow-on crop is known in some countries as a ratoon crop, there being first and second ratoon crops. Sometimes in certain varieties they sprout from below the soil and, as might be expected, these readily produce roots. Sometimes they begin to make their own roots while they are still attached to the parent plant.

Under some conditions a pineapple plant will flower within 12–18 months of planting, depending upon the quality of the plant, the soil and the season. From this point summer fruit takes about five months to mature, winter fruit another two months or so. One can expect one fruit from the initial sucker, two from a plant if really well grown, and more, depending on how many ratoons are allowed to develop.

There is no need to grow pineapple plants in rows. They fill a round bed handsomely. Often this is an ideal way to grow them in a small garden. They also look well seen growing against the sunny side of a white wall.

## Cultivation

A frost-free climate is required for pineapples. Cold nights do more harm than anything else. They like warm, wet districts best, but they can be grown where the rainfall is not great so long as they are watered freely. Take care though, for we were told that the average home gardener is likely to over-water. They need full sunlight, and a rich, well-drained soil. They prefer a sandy loam but will grow in clay, even in rocky soils. They like a low pH, about 4.5 to 5. Actually, land prepared for vegetables is usually in the right condition for these plants. It should be enriched and deeply dug. The soil around the plants should be kept well mulched.

If there is space to spare it is a good plan to propagate pineapples in succession so that as one plant is cropped another is producing fruit to take its place. Plants need to be about 30–75 cm (12–30 in) apart, and if they are in a row, leave a space of 45–90 cm (1½–3 ft) between the rows. Some varieties make bigger plants than others. Plant food is best applied just as the plants begin to produce their flower stalks.

It is possible to buy pineapple plants, but even the most amateur gardener should find no difficulty in raising his own. Although slips are favoured by the commercial grower, their propagation presupposes that one has access to a growing plant. If there is an opportunity to take them, the slips should be pulled from the base of the fruit stalk. The little pinelet at the base has to be removed; this should be done cleanly by snapping or cutting. The slips should then be allowed to dry in the air for a day or two. The basal leaves should be stripped away and the cuttings planted close together under dry conditions in a sunken nursery bed which has been made up from a good rooting medium, and well watered. Once they have rooted they can be planted in their permanent positions, preferably during a rainy spell. Incidentally, plants grown from slips are usually more uniform than those grown from suckers.

When pineapple tops are used for cuttings, these also should have their small lower leaves removed, leaving a little of the base exposed. This is easiest done when the top has been freshly cut. Allow the cutting to dry for a least 24 hours before planting.

Depending upon conditions, and assuming that these are favourable, slips mature faster than tops.

As was stated earlier, suckers often root while they are still attached to the parent plant. If these roots are allowed to develop too far, the sucker will receive a check when it is taken from its plant. This has the effect of inducing the plant to fruit prematurely. Unfortunately, the early fruit thus produced is small and of poor quality.

Pineapples make good house plants and these can be raised from tops, slips or suckers. The attractively coloured variegated pineapple is often to be found on sale as a decorative plant. Like the plain green form, this can be expected to fruit indoors given reasonable care. As with outdoor grown plants, the shoot, from whatever part it is taken, should be trimmed of its lower leaves to leave about 2.5 cm (1 in) of clear stem base. It should then be exposed to the air so that the cut portion dries well. This prevents rotting later. A rooting powder can be used. The stem end should then be inserted into moist sand, sandy loam, or a proprietary cuttings compost and made quite firm. It sometimes helps to anchor it in place by wedging two or three canes upright around the shoot. If possible the pot should then be placed over bottom heat. In countries where central heating is necessary, it is possible to use a shelf over a night heater or radiator for this purpose, but one must take care that the soil does not dry out. The entire pot and cutting can be enclosed in a plastic bag to increase humidity.

Once the plant has rooted it should be potted in good soil, and here a word of warning. Being (or so it sometimes seems) surrounded by pot pineapples in our home, we know only too well how heavy a thriving pineapple can become and how easily it will topple over unless weighted or wedged in some way. Wherever possible use clay pots because they are heavier, and put into them at least half their depth of some heavy drainage material such as shingle or pea gravel. When potted, stand the pot inside yet another heavy container and in this place plenty of plunge material such as peat to give humidity. One other tip: the pointed leaves can sometimes be most aggressive, so when placing a plant in a room, make sure that no leaf tip is at eye level.

Pot-grown pineapples need plenty of water if they are to fruit well. They must also have good light. Water should be poured into the leaf funnel as well as over the roots. It helps also to spray the plant with clean water daily.

It is important that a pineapple be ripe before use. The ripest fruits have the strongest aroma. Colour is not really a good guide since this can vary with the variety, although if you grow the fruits yourself you will get to understand them. Some people test ripeness by pulling at one of the 'leaves' in the top tuft and if this comes away easily the fruit is said to be ripe. Others say that this is not a good guide. Some tap the fruit to see if it gives back a dull, thumping sound, which indicates ripeness.

## Culinary uses

Pineapples have a high water content, 15 per cent sugar and malic and citric acids. Like fresh papaw, the fresh pineapple contains an enzyme, in this case bromeline, which possesses digestive properties. This means that contrary to the most widespread custom, pineapple is really best served at the end of a high protein meal. This enzyme also prevents gelatine from setting, so raw pineapple cannot be used in dishes that call for gelatine. When the fruit is cooked, the enzyme is destroyed and it can then be used in any way. Pineapples can be boiled whole to maintain flavour and then peeled and prepared.

The best way of cutting a pineapple is to use a sharp knife and make slanting cuts downwards between the 'eyes', which can then be removed with the skin. Use a stainless steel knife. The fruit should have the core removed.

Because it is such an excellent neutraliser, pineapple is a welcome accompaniment to richly prepared meats such as a glazed baked ham. Slices spread over a ham or mutton roast, and the juice used to baste these meats, will give them extra succulence. Bacon slices can be wrapped around pineapple and grilled for hors d'oeuvres. Kebabs can be made from bacon, chicken livers, pineapples and mushroom and served with rice. When it is to be served with any food with a rich sauce, rice is often improved if it contains some small pineapple portions. Pineapple slices can be grilled with meats or pan-fried. They go well with sausages. Pineapple and cheese are good companions, too.

Probably its great value lies in the fact that it is such a splendid sweet-sour food, a quality that lends it to successful inclusion in almost every type of dish, fresh or cooked, hot or cold. If you like Chinese cooking, pineapples will stand you in good stead.

We have already mentioned pineapples many times in describing ways of cooking other fruits, for it is a good mixer. On the other hand, it should not be limited to fruits alone, for it goes well with many vegetables, especially those used in salads. Not only slices of the fruit, or pieces of the whole flesh, but also the pulped or crushed flesh and the juice can be used. The latter makes a refreshing drink as well as an excellent table jelly.

Pineapples are popular additions to cakes, pies, breads, biscuits, fritters and many other puddings. They are often used with sweetened rice in moulds. Sections of raw pineapple can be used as garnishes and for cake fillings and decorations. Glazed and preserved pineapple can be used this way also. Pieces of these are often used in a rich fruit cake.

PRESERVING Pineapple makes excellent jams and other preserves. A good marmalade can be made from equal weights of pineapple, grapefruit and lemon. Allow 6 cups of water to every 2 cups of fruit, and later 2 cups of sugar to every 2 cups of boiled pulp.

To make Preserved Pineapple Slices with Brandy, allow the following to each pineapple:

### Pineapple slices in brandy

1 clove
1 teasp brown sugar
2 cups granulated sugar
1 tabsp brandy to every pineapple

Scrub the fruit well and remove the top leaves only. Put into a large enamel or porcelain pan with the cloves and brown sugar and just enough water to cover the fruit. Boil until tender. Test with a skewer. Drain, cool and remove the peel. Slice the fruit into rings about 6 mm ($\frac{1}{4}$ in) thick. Remove a central, 2.5 cm (1 in) core. Reserve 4 tablespoons of the water in which the fruit was boiled for each fruit. In a deep bowl lay the rings in layers, sprinkling each with the granulated sugar and finishing with a sugar layer. Allow to stand overnight in a cool place. Next day drain off the syrup and mix it with the water reserved from the boiling. Boil this and skim it until it is clear. Add the brandy. Meanwhile, pack the pineapple rings into wide-mouthed jars. Pour the hot syrup onto them so that they are covered. Seal the jars while they are still warm.

### Glazed pineapple

*8 pineapple rings, cooked*
*1 cup cooked pineapple juice*
*2 cups sugar*
*3 tabsp white corn syrup or clear honey*

Using a wide-based pan, bring juice, sugar and syrup to the boil. Add the fruit. Simmer until it is translucent or clear. Lift the rings and place them on a sieve to dry.

FREEZING  To freeze pineapple, use only mature fruit. Peel and core. Cut as you will, into slices, cubes, wedges or sticks, and put into bags with sugar.

BOTTLING  To bottle, do exactly the same but with syrup instead of sugar.

DRINKS  Rather surprisingly, there appear to be very few pineapple drinks. There is, almost inevitably, a French *crème d'Ananas,* a sweet liqueur, and pineapple juice is used in conjunction with other fruit juices for other mixtures such as the Australian Attorney, a blend of pineapple and passion fruit juices.

# PLUM
*Prunus* species

## Origin

A member of the rose family, the prunus is a large genus of some 200 species of trees and shrubs, many of which are grown in gardens, mainly for their beautiful spring blossom. Also in the genus are the apricot, cherry, nectarine and peach. Plums can be found growing wild in the northern hemisphere all the way from the Pacific coast in America going east right to Japan. So although there must always have been wild crops which could be gathered, it is not possible to say when plums were first cultivated, but this prac-

tice must reach back down the centuries to ancient times. Many of the best known varieties of plums appear to have been originally discovered in woods and hedges as wildings. At the present day we find that the family has been so hybridised that it is very difficult to trace clearly the ancestry of many of the most popular varieties. For instance, *Prunus domestica,* the garden or European plum, for a long time listed as a separate species originating in Europe and western Asia and long cultivated, is now considered to be a hybrid between *P. spinosa,* the sloe or blackthorn, and *P. cerasifera,* the cherry or myrobalan plum, so called because the fruit is cherry-like. It seems that these two species which grow together in Asia Minor have interbred in nature for thousands of years. Cherry plum varieties are grown commercially, mainly because the fruit matures early. Damsons are often classified under *P. domestica,* but they have now been given a specific status and are *P. damascena. Prunus institia,* a European species which is closely allied to *P. domestica,* contains those plums popularly known as Bullace, Mirabelle plums and Greengages, which are derived from a variety *P. i. italica,* sometimes called *P. italica.* The plums derived from the *P. domestica* group are the hardiest of all stone fruits, and although these may not be the finest dessert varieties, they are highly prized all the same for preserving and conserving. The plums are widely cultivated in the east European countries and in Britain and her near neighbours. In Britain plums are said to be the most important cultivated hardy fruits after the apple.

The Japanese plum, *P. salicina,* syn. *P. triflora,* actually originated in China, but earns its sobriquet, like many other cultivated plants, by the fact that it has long been cultivated for its fruit in Japan, where it was introduced somewhere about 1500. In 1870 it began to be cultivated in America, where it is now grown extensively in some parts. It reached South Africa at the beginning of the twentieth century and it probably reached Australia somewhat earlier. There are now many cultivars. Japanese plums are grown extensively in Australia, particularly in the Murrumbidgee Irrigation Area and in the Young and Camden districts. Both the Japanese and the Cherry plum have been gaining in popularity in Australia, and the cultivation of the European varieties has been declining in consequence. One of the most widely planted varieties of plum in NSW is Narrabeen, a Japanese type, but a chance seedling of local origin. It is considered a good variety for all districts. Another chance seedling is Donsworth, found growing in a Sydney garden and believed to have originated from a tree brought from Syria. There appear to be many hybrids between Japanese and Cherry plums.

Some people find the difference between gages and plums confusing. The typical greengage is found in what appears to be a wild state growing in Asia Minor, and, as we have seen, it is a variety of *P. institia*. The fruit of the species variety, *italica,* is small, but sweet to the taste and deliciously scented. These latter two qualities are what distinguish a gage from a plum. The greengage we know today may have been in cultivation for centuries, but unfortunately no records have been kept, or at least none appear to have been found. We know, though, that it was brought to England in about 1725 by Sir Thomas Gage from France, where it was known as Reine Claude. This variety is known as Green Gage, and is still listed by nurserymen. Some gages which are believed to have had plums as parents are still classed as gages because they retain more characteristics of the green fruit than the coloured. The delectable Transparent Gage is a very old French variety, and is perhaps the best flavoured of all. It is still grown. Famous seedlings taken from this variety are Early Transparent Gage and Late Transparent Gage, which while outstanding in flavour appear to crop only moderately.

Widely grown in Europe is the pretty little Mirabelle plum, not unlike an apricot in appearance, very highly perfumed and known as a 'golden gage'. There are many cultivars of this kind. There are also fruits which are not quite plums, not quite gages, which are gage-like in flavour but plum-like in size and colouring, all of which are golden-fruited sorts.

Generally, plums are divided into cooking and dessert varieties. While the latter are varied in nature, the former have an acid and very firm flesh and, although this does not appear to be significant, most of them have blue-black skins, although there are some notable exceptions to this rule. Just a few, such as Grand Duke, a late variety, and the early Victoria, can be used for either cooking or dessert.

Prunes are dried plums. Not all plums will dry well – some ferment instead. It is important also that the stone or the pit of the plum is small, otherwise the dried fruit would appear to be almost all stone instead of dried flesh. The plum also needs to have a high sugar content. Most of the world's prunes are produced in California, although there are small pockets of production in other countries such as Algeria, Iraq, Jordan and Spain. Prune production is one of Australia's smallest horticultural industries although plums have been grown in that country since the end of the nineteenth century and one variety reigns supreme everywhere. This is the self-fertile d'Agen, first grown in France in 1756.

## The fruit

Botanically, a one-seeded fleshy drupe, grooved on one side. *P. domestica,* or garden plums, have both round and oblong fruits, according to variety, which vary in size from about 2.5 cm (1 in) in length upwards. Their skins are often black. The flesh is yellow and scented and it either clings to or is free from the stone it surrounds. The fruits of the sloe, *P. spinosa,* are very much smaller than the others, only about 12 mm (½ in) in diameter. These are round and blue-black, often with a powdery bloom like some grapes. The flesh is yellow-green and bitter. Their stones are round.

*P. cerasifera,* the cherry or myrobalan plum, has red- or yellow-skinned, glabrous, round fruits 2.5–4 cm (1–1½ in) across, with yellow, juicy flesh. They have a deep indentation at the stem end.

*P. damascena,* the damson, has oval fruits as a general rule, although there are some which seem to be intermediate between damsons and bullaces. The skin is blue-black or red-black, often with an attractive bloom on the surface. The flesh is firm and green-yellow. There exists an old 'white' damson which has fruits with yellow-white skins sparsely dotted with red. The flesh is pale yellow. The bullace, of the *P. institia* group, unlike the damson for which it is often mistaken, and in whose place it is sometimes sold, is round. However, the old Black Bullace has slightly oval fruits. Like the damson it is small, very much like a sloe in appearance but larger and shinier. The fruits usually grow in pairs, as do most of this group. When it is ripe the flesh is yellow and does not have the green colouring of the damson, but it is acid and so, like the sloe, the fruit is often left on the tree until it has been frosted, when it is then less acid. Shepherd's Bullace has large, rounded-oval, green-yellow fruits with yellow flesh. White Bullace has small, flattened fruits, with the groove or suture inconspicuous, clouded yellow skin with a thick, white bloom, the sunny side being mottled with red. The flesh is pale yellow and sweeter than most bullaces. The stone is rather large for the size of the fruit. The stalk is in a deep cavity. Bullaces ripen later than damsons or plums.

Fruits of the Japanese plums, *P. salicina,* are slightly different in shape, being cordate, about 5–8 cm (2–3 in) long with a deep depression at the stalk end, often pointed at the apex. Some are round. The colour differs according to the variety, often yellow, sometimes red. Not all of these are good to eat raw. Many have a very sharp flavour but are excellent for processing.

Some varieties are known as Blood Plums. Examples are Cycasmomo, or Upright Blood, which has dark, ruby-coloured flesh. Donsworth has firm, blood-red flesh, well flavoured. Mariposa, an American cultivar, is considered one of the best of the blood plums. Its well-flavoured flesh is also blood-red.

## The plant

Most plums are slender, often graceful, deciduous trees which blossom early. They have brown bark. Their leaves are coarsely toothed, thick in texture, with downy undersides. Their white flowers are carried singly or in pairs, rarely in threes.

Botanists have grouped the plants in the *Prunus* genus into seven classifications, details of which do not concern us here, except to note that the plum, with a few other species, is in group 1, the Prunophora, and is distinguished from the rest because it has its leaves rolled in the bud. Peaches, for instance, in group 2, have their leaves folded in the bud.

*Prunus spinosa,* the sloe or blackthorn, makes a densely branched, spiny bush, although it can be trained into a standard if the lower shoots and suckers are removed and the main stem encouraged to make a trunk. It grows to some 2.5–3 m (8–10 ft). The leaves are small and open after the flowers, which although small themselves often smother the tree with blossom. The foliage often turns a bright golden yellow before it drops. The plant is seldom seen in urban gardens, yet it grows easily from seed and also makes a splendid and impenetrable farm hedge.

*P. cerasifera,* the cherry or myrobalan plum (q.v.), makes a round-headed tree and will grow up to about 9 m (30 ft). Its leaves, some 4–6 cm (1½–2½ in) long and sometimes oval, ovate or oblong, are shining and attractive. The tree bark is a lovely brown. The blossom opens with the leaves. The flowers, about 2 cm (¾ in) across, are white. There are also purple-leaved ornamental forms of this species, including an ornamental fruiting kind, Trailblazer, which is very handsome when the white flowers contrast with the bright young growth. Later, the fruits are crimson. There is a well-known variety, *P. c. atropurpurea,* with pale rose blossom changing to ruby-red, which was imported from Persia in 1880 and which most people know by its synonym of *P. c. pissardi.* Fruits from any ornamental variety are edible.

The damson is usually grown as a half-standard, otherwise it can be inconveniently tall when it comes to gathering the crop. There is a compact, pyramidal damson known as Farleigh Damson and also as Crittenden's and Cluster Damson, which is often planted closely to make a windbreak, for which purpose this plant is most suited. The tree much resembles a plum in appearance. However, the damson can be somewhat temperamental, and will flourish in some districts and fail in others.

The bullace makes a large bush or a small tree. In most, the young shoots are downy. The tree has some spines, but less than are on the sloe. It resembles a sloe more than a plum when it is growing.

The Japanese plum, *P. salicina,* characterised by its early flowering habit, has smooth, dark shoots, with long smooth leaves, finely and evenly serrated, 8–11 cm (3–4½ in) long, which are downy in the axils of the veins beneath. The flowers, usually growing in threes, are white and about 2 cm (¾ in) across, in clusters. The tree is often grown for its decorative value.

## Cultivation

The various sorts of plums are excellent fruit trees for the small garden. There are many, like the bullace, which deserve to be better known and which grow into an attractively shaped tree. Where the climate is suitable, the Japanese plums make neat, comely plants. It is worth bearing in mind that plums do best in cultivated ground rather than in grass. It is possible to keep plums somewhat restricted in their growth by using semi-dwarfing rootstocks. Nurserymen should be able to supply these, and to give advice on the most suitable for a particular locality. It is possible to train trees into pyramid and fan shapes as well as to have them as bush and half standards. Fan training is particularly recommended for gages. It is generally found that plums trained against a warm wall in northern latitudes have the finest flavour.

All the same, the garden or European plum has a high chilling requirement and does not do well in areas where the winter is too mild. In these the Japanese plum does best. Cherry plums, because of their early flowering habit, need a warm site. Coastal districts in some areas are best for them.

Plums are best grown on a well-cultivated soil, although they will grow on all kinds except those which are badly drained and waterlogged; nevertheless they must have sufficient moisture. They do not like a very acid soil, so any with this tendency should be dressed with lime.

The trees need good light. They will not grow well in the shade of tall trees or high buildings. Since they blossom early, the site must be relatively free from spring frosts. Plums can become starved. The plants respond to generous dressings of compost and farmyard manure and other organics. Soil should be enriched before planting, when artificial fertilisers can be incorporated.

Many plums are self-sterile, which means that they must be pollinated by another cultivar. This should be in the same group, i.e. European, Japanese or Cherry plum as the case may be. It appears that most of the last are self-fertile, but even these crop better with a pollinator. Local expert guidance should be sought on this matter. Yields are not the same for all varieties or kinds of plums. Gages and some other cultivars, for instance, never produce such heavy crops as some others. Plum trees from the nurseryman should be already trained to grow into their required

shapes and it is up to the gardener to guide the young tree to keep its form. One should keep an eye on the trunk also, and remove any buds which may appear. Any suckers which are produced should also be removed. Since the tree needs to be well balanced, pinch back any of the leaders which appear to be racing ahead of the others. In most countries it is usually advisable only to cut the tree during the growing season, when the risk of infection by the silver leaf disease is at its lowest.

Among varieties of Japanese plums are some which have a very upright habit of growth. Santa Rosa is an example. It is the practice of commercial growers to open out trees of this shape. Conversely some are too spreading, Narrabeen for instance, and these are trained in such a way that they take on a more upright form. Generally speaking, however, the amateur need only confine himself to the removal of dead, broken, rubbing and crossing branches and preventing the head of the tree from becoming overcrowded. In temperate countries it is prudent to carry out the pruning only in spring after growth has commenced, when wounds will heal quickly, or immediately after the fruit has been gathered, or when trees are dormant.

It is not wise to remove large branches, certainly not in winter. However, should removal be unavoidable, carry it out during the growing season. The cut, and indeed all but very small cuts, should be neatened, i.e. pared and smoothed, and then coated with bitumen paint, soft grafting wax, or best of all with a proprietary disinfectant protector such as Arbrex.

Plums are best not picked until they are really well developed, although they do continue to ripen after they have been gathered. But the longer they are on the tree the better their flavour will be. Try to pick the fruits with their stems on, unless they are to be processed immediately. Pulled stems rupture the skins and plums are thinskinned, highly perishable fruits which should be given as much care as possible. Some varieties, especially the late ones, can be stored, sometimes for weeks. They should be wrapped individually in paper and stored in single layers. It is worth trying a few of your own plums to test their storage life.

## Culinary uses

Plums are rich in vitamin A, especially the purple ones. They also contain many mineral salts.

As we have seen, there are a great many different plums and recipes can be found for all of them, even the bitter sloe, which apart from sloe gin is sometimes used in country wines and with other fruits to make jams and jellies. The little mirabelle plum can be used in any recipe given for the apricot.

Plums can be roughly divided into cookers and eaters, the dessert plums having a richer flavour and a higher sugar content. It is said that usually these are found to have a green or golden gage as a parent. The original gage, the transparent gage, is probably the most delicious of all. Plums used for cooking, and many of those sought after for jam, are acid and have a dry, almost juiceless flesh when raw. Most of them have blue-black skins, although some are green-yellow or even purple-red. Split them open and taste them and you will need have no doubt.

A really ripe dessert plum is delicious raw. Many dessert plums are cooked, which is a pity since they can be skinned, stoned and served this way with a little cream just as though they were a cooked compote. Try them heaped on ice-cream or used as a filling in a layer cake. Plums make excellent desserts raw or cooked. Their juice makes a good table jelly.

A little lemon peel is often added to plums when they are being cooked. Mrs Beeton tells us that 'A little allspice stewed with the fruit is by many persons considered an improvement.'

There are occasions when plums can be used in savoury dishes. When they are in season we like to flavour a lamb roast with them. Three split in half, but with the stone left in, are placed on the joint when it is put into the oven. The juices which then come ready flavoured from the meat make a delicious gravy. It is not surprising that the plum should go so well with this meat, which traditionally has sharp condiments, mint sauce and redcurrant jelly for example. Try slicing firm but ripe plums very finely and adding them to a salad to eat with cold lamb.

Plums also go well with pork. A Danish dish *svinemörbrad*, consists of spare ribs of pork which have been well flattened, made into a sandwich with well-soaked dried plums and apple between. The two ribs are tied together and roasted for half an hour, being basted with little milk.

We suggest that fresh plums with a little chopped sage added to them can be used in much the same way. Most stone fruits suit pork and bacon.

PRESERVING Plums make excellent jams, preserves, chutneys and pickles. They can be spiced and put into brandy. Greengage jam makes a delicious and unusual sauce for dessert. Heat it, sieve it and flavour it with a little kirsch or benedictine.

Sloe and Apple Jelly to serve with meats is a simply made condiment. Cook equal parts of ripe sloes and green apples, unpeeled, unskinned, uncored and unstoned, in water which barely covers the fruit until all is soft. Strain all through a jelly bag. To each pint of juice add 2 cups of sugar. Boil fast until the liquid jells.

Sloe and Apple Cheese is made in just the same way, except that the fruit is put through a sieve so that the resulting liquid is thicker. Add $1\frac{1}{4}$ cups of sugar to every 2 cups of this.

Firm cooking plums can be pickled whole, an example of which is these Pickled Plums.

### Pickled plums

*8 cups plums*
*4 cups brown sugar*
*2 cups spiced vinegar*

Remove the stalks from the plums and wash them. Prick them all over with a fork. Boil vinegar and sugar for 5 minutes, add the plums and simmer until they are tender, about 10 minutes (not so long that they are broken). Lift out the plums with a draining spoon. Put them into hot, sterilised jars. Reboil the vinegar mixture, pour it over the fruit and then cover the jars.

FREEZING Plums can be frozen whole or they can be halved. Often, if they are stored for a long period, the stones tend to flavour the fruit. Before freezing, the plums should be washed in ice water and then dried. They can be packed in plastic bags with no further treatment, or they can be packed in a syrup in rigid containers. Our own method for freestones is as follows. First wash, then skin and halve the ripe plums, placing them cut side downwards in rigid containers. When one layer has been made, sprinkle brown sugar over it and then make another layer. Cover this with the sugar and continue until the container is almost full, leaving about 1.5 cm (½ in) headroom. When the plums are removed from the freezer slip the contents of the container, still in layers, into a dish and allow them to thaw. Let them stand for a few hours before serving them with cream. We like to pour a little brandy or slivovitz over them and add a few blanched almonds.

BOTTLING   Plums can be bottled whole or, should they be freestone varieties, halved. Obviously, more of the halved fruits can be packed in a jar. They should all have stems removed and be well rinsed in water. Those dark varieties with a pronounced bloom should be wiped.

DRYING–PRUNES   If you wish to dry plums, the dark-skinned, fleshy varieties are best if you have no special prune plums. In some countries plums will dry on the tree. Select good, unblemished fruits and first wash them. Stand them on or in trays and put them in a temperature not higher than 65°C (150°F). It is recommended that they are best started about 50°C (120°F) until the skins begin to shrivel, when a little more heat can be applied. Test for drying by gently squeezing the fruit. The skin should not break, neither should any juice be exuded. A cooling oven, a shelf over a stove, or a greenhouse make good drying locations. When the fruits appear to have been sufficiently dried, let them stand in a dry atmosphere for a further day and then pack them into jars and store.

Prunes, while being low in sodium, are high in vitamins A and B as well as in iron – in fact prune juice contains more iron than orange juice. Prunes are often soaked before cooking, but this is really not necessary. They should always be simmered rather than boiled, and in just enough water barely to cover them, in a lidded pan. They should be left in the liquid to cool and they will then end up quite plump.

Ginger Stuffed Prunes are made from cooked prunes, having made sure that they are not too soft. Carefully stone each fruit and replace each stone with a piece of crystallised ginger. Heat the juice, with the addition of a little port wine, and pour it over the prunes. Cover and allow to cool, then chill the fruit for a few hours. Serve with whipped cream.

An unusual and effective dish for a special occasion is Prune Fritters.

### Prune fritters

*20 good plump prunes*
*5 cm (2 in) cinnamon stick*
*1 glass red wine*
*5 cm (2 in) lemon peel*
*20 blanched almonds*
*20 small pieces candied orange or any citrus peel*
*fritter batter*
*grated, plain chocolate*

Simmer the prunes in the wine with cinnamon and peel until tender. Drain and stone, replacing the stones with an almond and a piece of candied peel. Have ready the fritter batter and the chocolate. Dip each prune into the batter and fry in deep fat. Drain well on kitchen paper and roll in the chocolate. Have ready a cold dish on which chocolate has been spread. Arrange the prunes on this.

Prunes can make an attractive as well as a tasty and nourishing ingredient in a salad. The prunes themselves can be stuffed in various ways – excellent with cream cheese and walnuts. Small slices of bacon wrapped around the prunes and grilled can be served cold with apple slices on a bed of lettuce or finely sliced cabbage.

DRINKS   We find it a little surprising that members of the plum family do not, as a general rule, make very good wines, sometimes needing a little body, such as barley, to give the fermentation some strength. But on the other hand plums seem to make excellent liqueurs of several kinds and with many names.

Perhaps the best simple recipe for Plum Wine is:

### Plum wine

*12 cups plums*
*7 cups sugar*
*16 cups water*
*yeast and nutrient as required*

Cut the plums as small as is convenient and squeeze them to extract the juice. Boil half the water and pour it over the mash, adding the other half in a couple of hours, together with any nutrient you consider necessary. Leave, covered, for two days, stirring occasionally, and then strain off the liquid. Boil this and pour it over the sugar, stirring to dissolve. When the solution cools to blood heat add the yeast and pour into a fermenting vessel and fit a fermentation lock. When all fermentation has finished siphon it off into clean bottles and cork.

We have had considerable success in the past with Plum Port, which can be made with any kind or variety of plum. The recipe does not require the addition of yeast as it uses the natural yeasts on the plum skins.

### Plum port

9 cups plums
9 cups sugar
16 cups (1 gal) water

Pour the boiling water over the plums and then leave for about a week, stirring and squeezing twice a day. Strain through a jelly bag, add the sugar, stirring until dissolved, and then pour in a large cupful of boiling water. Leave to ferment in a bucket or similar vessel for another week, then strain again and bottle.

Whether you call it Mirabelle, Pruna, Quetsch, Racky, Tuica or Slivovitz makes no difference, for they are all basically the same thing: Plum Brandy. Usually the commercial brands are made by distillation, but this is impossible by law for amateurs in most countries, so instead one can make excellent Plum Brandies by soaking pricked plums in brandy or white spirit, adding sugar to taste, and then straining off the result into bottles. The drink it makes can be delicious and it is not cheap, but one has the consolation that the discarded plums or plum pulp are heavenly! This is also the same process for the making of sloe gin, the only difference being that gin is used instead of the brandy or the white spirit.

# POMEGRANATE
*Punica granatum*

### Origin

Pliny called the pomegranate the 'Apple of Carthage', *Malum punicum*. Centuries later botanists adopted his specific term for the generic name. The word means 'grain apple', an allusion to the numerous grain-like seeds within. The pomegranate is classified by botanists in a family of its own, the Punicaceae, a genus of just two species.

The plant occurs, both cultivated and naturalised, over the whole of the Mediterranean region, and eastwards to northwest India. It is widely cultivated in India where there are many cultivars. Granada in Spain is thought to have been named after the fruit. The Moors planted an avenue of pomegranates there. It was also included in the city's coat of arms, split to show the 'grains'.

It seems always to have captured the imagination. For centuries it has been connected with religious ceremonies and with religious buildings. The pomegranate motif is often to be found on temple carvings and in Chinese paintings as well as those of Egypt, Persia and Rhodes. It has been a symbol of fertility since the earliest times. It is supposed to have been the fruit given by Venus to Paris. There are many references to the fruit in the Bible: the wandering Israelites yearned for its refreshment; Moses promised them 'a land of wheat and barley and vines and fig trees and pomegranates'; Solomon had a pomegranate orchard. The prophet Mohammed is said to have advised that to eat the fruit was to purge the spirit of envy. In spite of this mystic connection, the pomegranate has had and continues to have a utilitarian importance. It is used by herbalists for many disorders. The cooling juice of the fruit has long been esteemed, since Solomon's time, if not before, not only for a raw fruit drink, but for wines, sherbets and conserves. In France, the pomegranate was once used for Sirop de Grenadine (*grenade* is its French name), Gagin being a favourite variety for this purpose; and for a Vin de Grenade, for which the variety Cherabani is favoured. The rind of the unripe fruits yields a red dye which is used in the production of morocco leather. A dye is also made from the flowers. The rind, with the flowers, is also a powerful astringent.

The species has given rise to many varieties. There is *P. g. albescens* with dull white flowers, *albo-plena* with double white blooms, *flore-pleno* with double red flowers, *legrellii* with double flowers striped in red and yellow-white, and *nana*, a shrub with narrower leaves and with slightly more hardiness than the type.

There are many cultivars, but named varieties do not come true from seed. Among the varieties are Rabbab, Granada, Early Red, Spanish Sweet, Wonderful and Travernicht, a semi-dwarf.

The fruit is now widely cultivated in the tropics and sub-tropics. It has become naturalised in South America and elsewhere. In colder climes where the plant usually blooms but fails to fruit, it is grown simply as an ornamental garden plant. It sometimes fruits in a greenhouse.

## The fruit

Botanically, a berry with a leathery pericarp and pulpy flesh formed by the fleshy outer seed coats of the numerous seeds. The fruit, 6–9 cm (2½–3½ in) in diameter, is sometimes deep yellow, or coloured to a red-purple, sometimes on one cheek only, the sunny side. The calyx is persistent and crowns the fruit. The rind or the skin is hard and thick, the flesh surrounding the individual seeds a beautiful carmine pink. It has a sweetly acid flavour. The inside of the fruit is divided by septa, or walls of bitter tasting pith, into small, irregular cells which contain the seeds. Once the fruit is ripe it splits or 'laughs'.

## The plant

The pomegranate is a neat, small, rounded, bushy tree of about 4–5 m (12–16 ft), with stiff, angular but slender branches, which in the species are likely to be spiny. It has glossy, leathery, narrow, lance-shaped leaves and an erect trunk which is covered by a red-brown bark which later becomes grey. It is sometimes deciduous, but in certain areas the leaves will persist on the tree. The flowers are beautiful, scarlet, more than 2.5 cm (1 in) across, with five to eight crumpled petals and a red, fleshy, tubular calyx which persists on the fruit. In their centres are some twenty stamens. The flowers may be solitary or grouped in twos and threes at the ends of the branches.

The blossom time is often prolonged from spring into summer. Under suitable conditions the fruit should mature some five to seven months later. High temperatures are essential during the fruiting period to get the best flavour. The tree seems to enjoy long, hot summers, although it sets most fruit after a cold winter. Although long-lived, the vigour of a pomegra-nate tree declines after about fifteen years, so it is as well to keep a succession going.

It does well in a shrub border and we have seen a row in NSW planted along the driveway to a house. We have also seen it grown as a pair, one on each side of a front door. It would look good this way tub-grown.

As one might expect, such decorative fruits look splendid in many kinds of flower decorations and in groups of fruits and foliage. Small, slightly immature fruits will dry on the stem and can be used this way in ensembles of perpetuelles.

## Cultivation

Urban gardeners should find this compact and beautiful little tree ideal for their purposes. As an extra bonus it is perfectly at home as a contained plant. Any of the commercial varieties make excellent ornamental plants, and where there is space available the pomegranate makes a superb hedge plant.

The pomegranate enjoys hot and dry conditions and is moderate in its demands for water. A humid climate adversely affects the formation of fruit. Low temperatures affect its quality. If temperatures fall below freezing the plant suffers significant damage although it is unlikely to be killed except under heavy or prolonged frosts. It can be container-grown in a greenhouse during the winter only, in which case it will be standing outside during its prettiest period.

The plant does best in well-drained ordinary soil, which should be well mulched annually with rotted farmyard manure or home-made compost. Outdoors the plant will withstand drought, but it will give a better performance if watered from time to time.

The pomegranate can be raised from seed, but one cannot be sure that it will come true if propagated this way. Cuttings root easily and plants from them will bear fruit after about three years. They should be taken from mature, one-year-old wood, 26–30 cm (10–12 in) long, in winter. The leaves should be removed from the stalks and the cuttings inserted for about two-thirds their length into the soil or into some other warm rooting medium in a shady place. Plants can also be propagated by layers or by grafting. Little pruning is required, but it is helpful to train the plant from the beginning if this has not been done by the

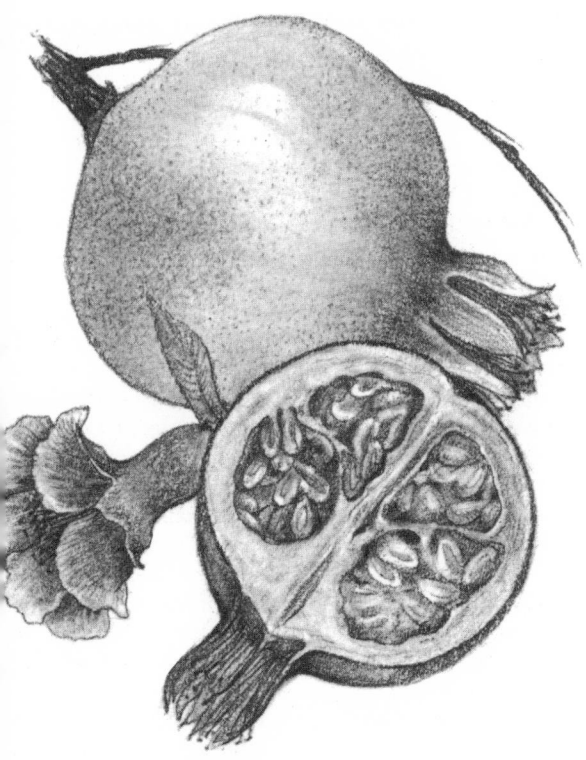

not bruised or smashed, because these too are sometimes bitter.

These seeds can be eaten with sugar or salt, which gives us a clue that they can be used in both sweet and savoury dishes. They make a most attractive garnish and look highly appetising when sprinkled on any rich dish, especially when black olives are also used. An interesting looking salad dish can be made by mixing chopped walnuts, a little finely chopped shallot and cream cheese together and moulding them into balls or rolls, which are then pressed into the red seeds so that they are pleasantly coated.

The one disadvantage of using these seeds is that the kernels are not eaten and have to be spat out. They are not inedible, simply numerous, and to some people unpalatable. Because of this the pomegranate juice alone is most often used.

The best means of peeling a pomegranate is to cut a slice from the crown end. Do this with the stem end towards you so as not to be stained by the spurting juice. Then incise the skin from the cut downwards in two or three places. It should then be possible to peel it back and the seeds should be well exposed. In order to draw out the juice easily without pressing the seeds, warm the fruit slightly and then roll it between the hands to soften the seeds inside. Make a hole in the base of the fruit opposite the flower end. Stand it on a glass and let the juice drain into it. Squeeze it anew from time to time until it appears that all the juice has been drained.

This juice can be used in many ways, in soups served like cherry and redcurrant soup at the end of a meal, in cold or hot sauces, sweet or savoury, for sorbets, ices, for fruit salads and for table jellies. You can turn the last into an unusual dish by using the fruit shells as dishes. Remove the top to use as a lid. Remove all seeds and every trace of skin. Make a jelly with the juice, let it half set and then pour it into the skin or shell. When it has set, decorate the surface with unpressed pips or cover with a little cream. Replace the top.

A pomegranate syrup can be used as a sauce with other fruits. Using a measure of volume, not weight, put sugar to equal half the bulk of seeds – i.e. 1 cup of sugar to 2 cups of seeds – with the seeds in a bowl. Bruise very lightly to get some of the juices flowing. Cover and allow to stand for 24 hours. Put all in a heavy saucepan, bring to the boil quickly, remove from heat and

nurseryman. Plants grown by the gardener should be stopped when they are about 60 cm (2 ft) high. From this point allow four or five shoots to develop. These should be evenly distributed around the stem to keep the plant well balanced. These will probably start from about 30 cm (1 ft) from the ground, which will give a short but well-defined trunk. Any shoots which appear above or below the main branches should be removed, as should any suckers. Meanwhile the main branches should have their laterals cut back a little the following year to encourage the tree to become bushy. Fruiting spurs develop on mature shoots.

## Culinary uses

The pomegranate is really a most versatile fruit, although it is unfamiliar to so many people. It is the shining red seeds which fill the skin that are used. It is important to remove every piece of the skin which surrounds them since this is bitter. It is also important that when the juice is being extracted the kernels inside the fleshy seeds are press or strain through a muslin or fine sieve but do not bruise the kernels. The syrup can then be poured into jars or bottles. Try using it with baked apples. Peel and core the apples and arrange them in a baking dish. Pour the syrup in the core holes and over them. Cover the dish and bake for 45 minutes at 160°C (325°F, gasmark 3). Cool and chill. Serve with cream or vanilla ice-cream.

The following sweet-sour Pomegranate Sauce can be used in a casserole, the meat or chicken pieces being browned in one pan while the sauce is prepared in another. Finally the two can be blended and simmered together for a further 20 minutes.

### Pomegranate sauce

½ cup butter
1 cup pomegranate seeds, or the same bulk in
   purée or juice
½ cup dried apricots, quartered but not soaked,
   sautéed in half the butter for 5 minutes
2 tabsp lemon juice
½ cup sugar
½ cup finely chopped onion
stock for thinning sauce

Put onion with butter in a covered pan to soften and turn golden but not brown. Add pomegranate and cook for a further 5 minutes. Combine the cooked apricots with the onions and pomegranate. Add sugar and lemon juice, stir well. Pour in the stock until the sauce is at the right strength. Add the sauce to the meat. Serve with rice.

PRESERVING  Pomegranate juice makes a good jelly. Extract the juice and follow the general directions for jelly, but use commercial pectin and lemon juice.

DRINKS  So far as we are aware there is no alcoholic drink made from pomegranates. Grenadine, a sweet, pink syrup, was once made from pomegranates but is now almost universally made from substitutes, sometimes with a little alcohol added. It is used as a sweetening agent.

A refreshing non-alcoholic pomegranate drink can be made as follows. Mix the juice from the pips of 6 pomegranates, the juice of 2 lemons and 2 oranges, the zest of 1 lemon and 1 orange. Add twice as much water as there is juice, strain through a fine sieve and chill. The drink is much improved by the addition at the last moment of a sprig of mint and borage and perhaps lemon balm.

# QUINCE
*Cydonia oblonga*, syn. *C. vulgaris*

## Origin

A member of the rose family, the quince is of doubtful origin, a situation common to plants which have been cultivated for centuries. It seems most likely that it came from a region stretching from Iran to the Caspian Sea, because a wild form with edible fruit of a slightly sweet flavour can be found growing there. Certainly it eventually appeared in the ancient Graeco-Roman world, where it was much esteemed and was dedicated to both Venus and Aphrodite as a symbol of love, fertility and happiness. Eating the fruit was a part of the nuptial ceremony at one time.

It is today widely grown in all Mediterranean countries both privately and as a commercial crop. Italy has a special quince marmalade, *cotognate*. The Spanish name for the quince is *marmelo*, and as this fruit is made into conserves in Spain, this is possibly the origin of the term 'marmalade' in English, used now mainly in relation to conserves of citrus fruits (see also Orange). Other countries growing the quince commercially include Australia, Ecuador, Guatemala, Israel, Rhodesia, Syria, Turkey, Tunisia and the USA. For some reason production is declining in Australia although the fruit is still to be seen in gardens.

The genus was once classified with chaenomeles, but it has now been reduced to this one species, cydonia. Other plants named cydonia belong, in fact, to the first species. However, cydonia does have varieties and cultivars. Of the first there are *C. o. lusitanica*, with deeper coloured flowers and larger fruit than the type, and *malformis*, with apple-shaped fruits. Serbian quinces are much sought after as garden plants. The Vranja quince, from Vranje, now in Yugoslavia, is thought to be the most handsome of all, its fruits being large, 1½–2 kg (3½–4½ lb) in weight, pale gold in colour and very fragrant.

Another lovely cultivar is Bereczki, also from Yugoslavia, which is highly ornamental when in flower, and a very similar form, Portugal, said to be the finest variety of all. French gardeners grow Géant de Leskovats.

## The fruit

Botanically a pome, and closely related to the apple and pear, it differs from these fruits in that it has many ovules in each carpel or section, sometimes as many as twenty, instead of two. The fruit of the type is pear-shaped or oblong and is from 6–10 cm (2½–4 in) long, but cultivars vary from this in a few ways.

Cultivars can be divided into two groups, one including those producing round fruits, grown mainly commercially, the other producing oblong or pear-shaped fruits. The fruits are hard, with a yellow skin almost downy, which in some suggests the bloom on a grape. The golden yellow flesh is also hard and acid. It has a pleasant aroma and is often cooked with apples and pears, to which it passes on its characteristic and slightly pungent scent.

## The plant

A small, usually spreading, deciduous tree, some 4.5–7.5 m (15–25 ft) tall, often thickly branched and becoming twisted by the weight of the branches, or sometimes sculpted by the wind. Yet where the conditions are kind, and depending also upon the individual tree, a quince can sometimes be upright and strong. It will live to a great age. The young shoots are woolly and the woolliness persists on the undersides of the leaves which are broad and ovate, 5–11 cm (2–4½ in) long. The solitary flowers are wide, about 5 cm (2 in), five-petalled, with an attractive centre of twenty stamens, either white or pink, but often a deeper rose in cultivars. These are produced on the ends of short twigs.

The trees are shallow rooting, and are often used as stocks for pears and some other fruits.

## Cultivation

The quince is a very adaptable plant. It will tolerate most soils, except those which are very light or shallow or likely to become very dry. It particularly likes heavy, moist soils. Gardeners in the past maintained, as some do today, that the quince grows best in a wet soil, which is why in older gardens it is often to be found at the side of a pond or stream. In NSW we learned that wild trees producing well-grown fruits are often to be found growing near creek banks. That this is true we do not dispute, but it would be a pity if a gardener dismissed this fruit simply because no water was nearby. We have to report two 25-year-old quince trees we saw growing, heavily fruited, in a garden near Trundle in the Central Western Plains of NSW, where it becomes very hot and dry indeed. These trees were watered from time to time, but when we saw them, they were rising from hard, sun-baked earth. It seems generally agreed that the plant will grow from areas which have cool, temperate conditions such as Britain, to the cooler parts of sub-tropical regions. Before leaving the subject of water, one should point out, especially to northern gardeners, that water is often associated with a frost pocket. One should make sure that the site is frost-free before planting. Quinces are not as exacting as apples and pears as to their winter chilling requirements. They do not require much chilling in dormancy.

Not only should protection be provided from frost, but also from wind. All quinces have sensitive skins and exposure to strong winds can cause blemishes on the fruits. These are not necessarily injurious, but obviously the less damaged a fruit is, the better it will keep.

In cold areas the quince is sometimes grown as an espalier or as a fan-trained tree against a warm wall or fence, but generally this plant does not respond well to pruning. It is often best to let it go its own attractive way. However, this does depend a little on varieties and not a little upon the region in which it is grown. The trees we saw at Trundle, for instance, are pruned back hard each year. Commercial growers in NSW develop their quinces as vase or open centre trees, as they do other deciduous fruits, and of course they have to consider certain factors such as mechanical aids. The thing to keep in mind is that the quince, unlike most other deciduous fruits, produces its flowers and fruit on fairly short shoots which are produced during the same season. For this reason young wood should not be cut back hard.

It is important where conditions are dry to water sufficiently to keep the plants growing steadily. Mulches with moisture-holding humus will prove to be highly beneficial, and these should be applied at least annually.

Quinces appear to be self-fertile, since many single trees have been seen to produce good crops, but here as with other fruit cross-pollination proves advantageous.

Trained trees can be bought from nurserymen.

The best method of propagation appears to be grafting, with seedlings used as rootstocks. These have an advantage in that plants grown from them do not produce suckers. Unfortunately, trees grown from cuttings tend to make these suckers which then have to be removed. When seeds are used they should be stratified or vernalised. Trees on seedling stock should produce some fruit in five years. Quinces can also be propagated by layering.

Apart from those already mentioned, cultivars include Champion, a mild-flavoured, pear-shaped fruit; Ispahan, a vigorous variety collected in Persia; Pineapple, also pear-shaped and medium-sized; Orange Quince, a large, golden fleshed, irregularly shaped fruit with a fine flavour; Portugal, large, pear-shaped and tapering at each end;

and Rea's Mammoth, resembling Orange Quince but much larger.

The harvesting of quinces is perhaps not quite so casual a matter as with some fruits. As the fruit ripens, and this refers to most varieties, the skin colour gradually lightens in hue and changes from its green to a yellow. Do not be deceived by the apparent hardness of the quince skin, for this becomes easily marked if roughly handled and the fruit also becomes bruised. To prevent damage it is prudent to shorten any long stems in the vicinity so that they do not stick into or whip against the fruits. Quinces can be stored in the same way as apples, but it is wise to keep them apart from other fruits in case their aroma affects the others. Inspect them frequently.

## Culinary uses

Quinces contain a great deal of pectin. The quince-like fruits of the ornamental chaenomeles, sometimes called japonica, have a tarter flavour than the true quince. Because of its tartness, one often uses half and half with apples. Actually, almost any apple recipe can be used for quinces, but because of the tartness of the fruits, the apples are brought in. A little quince cooked with apples or pears enchances their flavour. Quince can be cooked alone as a compote, poached in a vanilla syrup in the usual way. When cooked, the colour of the quince changes to a dull pink or dusky rose. The fruits were once used much more widely than they are today, obviously because they were more widely grown. Like apples and pears, the fruit need not be limited to sweet dishes. There is a Persian dish which calls for quinces stuffed with mutton, similar in concept to the Arabian dish for apples stuffed with chicken. Keen cooks might enjoy making experiments in this field. Try serving a quince-apple sauce with meat for a change. Quince jelly is good with roast lamb in place of redcurrant jelly.

Apart from the usual apple-quince pie filling, the following is good, all combined together.

Tamarinds *(T. Rodd)*

Tree Tomato *(Thompson & Morgan)*

## Quince pie filling

2 cups diced quince
1 cup diced apples
½ cup raisins, chopped if very large
1 cup brown sugar
½ teasp cinnamon
¼ teasp mixed spice

**PRESERVING**  As one would expect from its affinity with the apple, quince can be used in jams, jellies, various other preserves and chutneys. It can be mixed with other fruits for jams and preserves, e.g. quince and blackberry, quince and cranberry, quince and pumpkin, quince and pear. Quince marmalade is made in the same way as apple marmalade.

The following recipe for Quince Marmalade has been taken complete from a copy of *The Floral World and Garden Guide* of 1861.

'Let the crop hang on the tree till one falls on the ground; then gather the crop. Pare, quarter and core them; but scrupulously save every pip. The pips of quinces abound in mucilage, as may be perceived by taking one in the mouth and chewing it, when it will make the lips stick together as a piece of gum-arabic would. Put the quinces with the pips into a stew-pan, with a sufficiency of lump sugar, and just enough water at the bottom to keep them from burning. As the sugar dissolves and the liquor boils, continue stirring the whole mass. When the fruit becomes tender, break and mash it well with a spoon. In about an hour from the commencement of the operation, it will be enough. It may then be turned out into preserve jars; a portion should be put into shapes to be used as dessert in the same way as bullace and damson cheese. The next morning it ought to be perfectly stiff and gelatinous, from the strong mucilage of the pips having been thoroughly incorporated with the whole mass. The quantity of sugar used may be rather less than is necessary for other preserves. If tied down the usual way it will keep good for a long time.'

Quince Paste, or Contignac, is often served as a sweetmeat at the end of a meal in some countries. These candies make good gifts. There are several recipes. In one, quince jam or marmalade is boiled down until it is really thick and is then spread over a shallow baking dish and dried slowly in a warm oven. It is then cut into shapes

and dusted with caster sugar. It must then be stored in wooden boxes between layers of waxed paper.

Another recipe is as follows:

## Quince paste

5 cups peeled and cored quinces, cut small
1 cup water
finely chopped or grated rind of ½ lemon and juice
preserving sugar, equal quantities with pulp
caster sugar

Cook the quinces in the water until they are very tender. Put in blender or through a sieve. Weigh the pulp and add an equal weight of sugar. Return to the pan adding the lemon juice and peel. Cook slowly, stirring frequently until the mixture is very thick. Allow it to cool and then pour it into shallow baking tins which have been lined with greasproof paper. The paste must now be dried. The trays can go into a cool oven or in an airing cupboard, or can be left in warm dry air elsewhere but not in the sun. Test from time to time to see if a piece of cut paste can be handled. When it is quite dry cut into shapes and dust with caster sugar. Nut meats can be added to this just before the mixture is ready to pour out.

**FREEZING AND BOTTLING**  Freeze quinces as pears. To bottle quinces prepare as for pears, but bear in mind that quince is often needed in small quantities only, so use small containers.

**DRINKS**  The name ratafia is given to an infusion of quinces in white spirit or brandy just as it has been adopted for almost any other fruit treated the same way.

More of a quince liqueur is made thus. Quarter and core but do not peel the quinces and then grate into a bowl. Cover and allow to stand for three days, then squeeze through fine mesh or muslin. Measure the quantity of the juice obtained and mix this with an equal quantity of white spirit or brandy. To every 4 cups of this mixture add 1¼ cups sugar, 1 clove and a 2.5 cm (1 in) cinnamon stick. Infuse in a covered jar for at least two months, then strain and bottle.

# RASPBERRY
*Rubus idaeus*

## Origin

A member of the rose family, *rubus* is the old Latin name for the plant. The wild raspberry is a native of most European countries, including Scandinavia and Great Britain, its area of coverage stretching through Italy and Greece to north and east Asia. It is found growing mainly in hilly country, on lower mountain slopes, and on acid soils. A cool climate and a neutral to acid soil are said to be the two main factors which contribute to the productivity of this fruit.

Like the strawberry, the wild raspberry was gradually brought into gardens and cultivated, no doubt when someone found a plant superior to its fellows. Gradually, good forms were selected and more propagated from these. The raspberry, called the hindberry in those days, is known to have been cultivated in England in the mid sixteenth century. However, it seems that in many other countries people remained satisfied with the wild fruits and continued to search for these rather than grow them in their own plots. To this day in Italy and Greece the raspberry is little cultivated, although in France it is highly esteemed and home-grown.

The raspberry was taken to America, but there it was found that the European type failed to do well in the warmer, dryer climate. The same situation, in reverse, was the case later when American varieties were sent to Britain. Modern American varieties are derived from *R. occidentalis,* a native of North Ameria which has black or yellow fruits, and *R. strigosus,* so closely related to the European *R. idaeus* that some believe it to be a variety of that type. Its synonym is *R. idaeus strigosus.* This variety has light red, or occasionally white or yellow fruits. There are now British hybrids between the red and black fruiting varieties, raised by the East Malling Research Station, a body responsible for the majority of modern varieties such as Malling Jewel, Malling Promise and Malling Admiral.

On the American continent purple, black and yellow raspberries are grown as well as the red. The first three are not as hardy as the red, so they are most suitable for the milder areas. The black raspberry, known as blackcap, is a native of North America and is found growing wild along the margins of woodlands from the north, in Ontario, down to the Carolinas. It has been cultivated since the beginning of the nineteenth century, and by 1832 there were named cultivars. Unfortunately all varieties are susceptible to the disease verticillium wilt. Black raspberry cultivars include Bristol, Black Hawk, Jewel and Huron. Purple raspberries are hybrids of the black and red. Sodus and Columbian are examples.

The raspberry is particularly subject to virus diseases and this has led to the disappearance of many fine old varieties. During the Second World War, virus-free stocks were discovered in New Zealand, and Norfolk Giant, a vigorous, popular, all-round garden variety, which was thought to have completely disappeared because of the inroads of the disease, was re-introduced into Britain from the other side of the world.

The yellow raspberry, *Rubus ellipticus,* has long been cultivated by those who appreciate its fine and delicate flavour and soft, almost velvety texture. Modern hybridists are also turning their attention to this strain and there are now some good, strong varieties as well as a few old favourites, such as the new American Fallgold, an autumn fruiting variety, and Golden Everest.

Golden Mayberry is a cross between *R. palmatus* and Red Raspberry.

A new breakthrough has come with the introduction of Zeva, described as a perpetual fruiting raspberry, a Swiss cultivar. Fruits are produced from mid-summer to late autumn and these are very large, 2.5 cm (1 in) or so in length and of a fine flavour. Not only will this variety do well in the open ground, it can be contained and thus used on patios or even on roof gardens.

## The fruit

Botanically, these are one-seeded drupes, many grouped on a cone-shaped receptacle. In raspberries the fruits come away from the receptacle in a rounded or helmet-shaped cluster. The fruits of *Rubus idaeus* are deep red, sweetly perfumed and of a fine flavour. They differ in size according to variety, most modern cultivars producing fruits about 2 cm ($\frac{3}{4}$ in) long, while, with the wild species, fruits measure only about 6 mm ($\frac{1}{4}$ in).

The many different varieties can be divided into two groups. There are those which fruit once a year in summer, the fruits being produced on growths made the previous year. The other group consists of those which fruit twice a year, in summer and in autumn, the latter on the current season's growth.

## The plant

A small, deciduous perennial with erect or arched biennial stems or canes which make their growth in the first year and produce lateral shoots from their buds which then produce fruit in the second year. The stems are from 1.2–1.8 m (4–6 ft) high in the species, sometimes taller in cultivars and are sometimes slightly prickly. The leaves are compound, 3–5 leaflets, ovate, coarsely and double-toothed, white felted on the undersides. The small white flowers are borne in racemes on the ends of the laterals. European raspberry plants are of a more open habit than the American and are generally easier to gather.

## Cultivation

The most suitable soil for raspberries is one which is a deep, well-drained, light or medium loam. Heavy soils are not suitable, and light and sandy soils only if they have been well charged with organic moisture-holding matter since it is essential that the plants do not dry out in times of drought. Waterlogged soil is not suitable. The plants grow best in an open, sunny situation, although this fruit will tolerate some shade, but not the shade cast by overhanging trees, which also may drip heavily during rain.

Whatever the kind of soil it should be well enriched before the canes are planted. Planting should be shallow, with the roots covered with no more than 7.5 cm (3 in) of soil, which should be well firmed by gentle treading. Once planted, one should take care not to dig around the roots. Instead, maintain a good, but not too deep, mulch over them.

Grass mowings can be used, and if these are kept clear of the actual area at the base of the canes, they will also help to inhibit the production of suckers beyond the area of the plant row.

Raspberries need moisture, 2.5–4 cm (1–1½ in) of water a week from the time they bloom until all the fruit is gathered. In dry seasons this means that water must be applied artificially.

If possible, plant raspberries so that the rows run from north to south. Plant the canes singly, about 45 cm (18 in) apart and some 1.5 m (5 ft) between the rows. The canes soon send up new growths and the row becomes both filled and wider. As the canes grow they are best tied to parallel wires. If growth is very vigorous it helps to make two lines of wires, one on each side of the row, so that the canes are not too crowded. Light and air are necessary to all growth.

Quite often, plants produce an abundance of canes and if these are allowed to mature the quality of the fruit may suffer. Remove all weak canes in early spring, leaving a space of 10–15 cm (4–6 in) for each cane. Keep the thickness of the rows well defined, 38–45 cm (15–18 in) in width, removing any suckers which arise beyond this distance in spring. Although very tall varieties are best kept cut back to maintain them at an easy picking height, say 1.2–1.5 m (4–5 ft), one should not cut or pinch back the canes in summer or winter or they will make too many side branches. The exception is for the autumn fruiting varieties, and here all the fruited canes should be cut right back in early spring.

Fruiting canes should be cut right back to soil level once they have been harvested. The plants should bear well for seven to eight years and it is advisable to begin establishing a new row when the existing plants are in their fifth or sixth year, according to their productivity.

Keep them well fed. Apply sulphate of potash each autumn, about 20 g per square m (¾ oz per square yd). This will make all the difference to the size of the berries and the total weight of the crop.

The black and purple raspberries have a more ungainly mode of growth than the red raspberries, and should be trained and pruned accordingly. They can be tied to supports or trellis in the same way as the red and they can also be grown without supports in deep rows. If the latter method is followed they should be treated thus: the new shoots arise from buds at the base of the old canes, unlike the red raspberries, whose shoots or suckers come from the roots, so these young shoots should be limited in number. Any of them which are less than about 1.5 cm (½ in) in diameter should be cut out in early spring, leaving from five to eight strong canes to each plant, spaced if possible from 15–20 cm (6–8 in) apart, with the width of the row some 30 cm (12 in) through.

The tips of the unfruited shoots should be pinched out in early summer, which operation induces the canes to form laterals or side branches. If this is not done, the main shoots grow very long and are difficult to manage. Tipping involves taking black raspberries back to 60–75 cm (2–2½ ft) and purple raspberries back to 75–90 cm (2½–3 ft). As a rule this cannot all be done at one time, and instead one has to go over the plant several times, cutting off the shoots just after they reach the required height. If the main stems are allowed to grow too tall before tipping, growth is dissipated and the stems are weakened.

The laterals which are encouraged as a result of tipping sometimes grow to 1 m (3 ft) or more, and most of their buds are fruit buds. It would not do to allow all of these to mature, because then the fruits would be small and of poor quality. For this reason the tips of the laterals themselves should also be cut back to 8–10 buds for black raspberries and a little less for the purple varieties. At the same time cut off any growth injured during the winter.

Propagation is from young, healthy canes, taken from near the base of existing plants. Those selected should be of medium size. Reject any obviously weak canes, as well as those which have grown vigorously, and see that each has a good mass of fibrous roots. It is a good plan to water them well in the days immediately before lifting, for then more roots will come easily away from the soil. As soon as these new canes are planted, cut them back as directed.

## Culinary uses

Raspberries are one of the most delectable of fruits. They can be eaten raw, as dessert, compote, table jelly, as a *bavarois,* in many different kinds of desserts, in flans, charlottes, pancakes, in jams and jellies. A good way to use up inferior or broken fruits is to purée them and add them to cream, custard, or arrowroot or cornflour sauces to make various desserts. One of the nicest ways is to hand guests the purée to pour over sweet, plain meringues.

Two cups of fruit make 1 cup of purée. Simply rub the fruit through a non-metal sieve with a wooden spoon to separate the flesh from the seeds – easier to do if you blend it first.

Raspberries go especially well with a few other fruits: witness the success of Peach Melba. Cut a peach for each person and put it into a glass topped with raspberries and just a sprinkling of sugar to bring out the flavour. Use raspberries to fill ripe melon halves, either simply seeded, with a core of raspberries, or scooped out and the melon flesh mixed with the raspberries and returned to the shell. A little white dessert wine poured on this is worth while.

Raspberry Cream is easily made, and few things are better.

### Raspberry cream

*1 cup single or light cream*
*1 cup white wine*
*1 cup raspberry purée*

Blend them all together, pour into chilled glasses and garnish with a few fruits. It is a good plan always to freeze a few small quantities of choice fruits for out of season garnishes. Many of the recipes given elsewhere can be used for raspberries or their purée. The best compote is made by making a syrup and pouring it, boiling, on the fruit rather than poaching the fruit in it.

PRESERVING   For Raspberry Conserve allow equal quantities of sugar and fruit by weight. Put each separately into oven dishes, the sugar in a deeper dish, cover with foil and bake in a warm oven until they are really hot but not discoloured. Have the jars warming also. Take out the raspberries and mash them with a wooden spoon so that there are no whole fruits. Add them to the hot sugar, stirring really well so that both are perfectly blended. Spoon into the hot jars and tie down. This conserve will not keep as long as jam unless you freeze some, but it has the advantage that its seeds are not so hard and woody as they tend to be when the fruit is boiled.

Raspberry Jelly is simply made by adding 1½ cups of sugar to 2 cups of strained juice.

FREEZING   Perfect, unbroken fruits are best frozen by the dry freeze method and then packed dry in bags. The alternative is to mix the berries with sugar. Freeze purée in rigid containers, leaving just a centimetre or two (½ in) of headroom.

Raspberries are very delicate fruits and they look so much better if they are unbroken and unmarked, so watch points here. Instead of leaving the fruit unwashed, we find that washing is best done by putting a few fruits into a colander, lowering this into the water, briefly, then tipping them out gently on to a large dish. If the dish is tilted slightly by putting the handle of a wooden spoon under one end, the surplus water will run down to the other end. This can be tipped out, or more safely drawn out by using a piece of kitchen paper as a wick. If a few fruits are done at a time, so that there is no great pressure on any, they do not become damaged.

BOTTLING   Select the largest, firmest fruits for bottling. The others can be made into jam or purée. Enthusiasts, who like to see well-packed jars and who sometimes put them in for competition, sometimes plug each raspberry with a single redcurrant, tedious to do but beautiful.

DRINKS   The following recipe for raspberry ratafia or liqueur is simple enough, but unfortunately wildly expensive today. To each 1 kg (2 lb) of fruit allow 4 litres (8 pt) of white spirits or brandy. Cover the fruit with the spirits, cork the jar and allow it to infuse for at least two months, putting it in the sun whenever possible. Finally strain the liquid and add 450 g (1 lb) sugar and stir to dissolve. When this has settled, filter and bottle. It will continue to soften and mature for many months.

Raspberry vinegar was once widely used to soothe sore throats.

### Raspberry vinegar

*2 cups ripe raspberries*
*2 cups white vinegar*
*1 cup sugar*

Cover raspberries with vinegar and allow to stand for up to a week, stirring occasionally. Then strain off the liquid into a pan with sugar and boil for about 10 minutes. Bottle and seal.

# REDCURRANT
*Ribes* species

## Origin

Closely related to the blackcurrant and akin to the gooseberry, red and white currants appear to have derived mainly from a type of *Ribes sativum,* a European species, and then to have been crossed and inter-crossed. Confusingly, this species is often called *R. rubrum,* the northern redcurrant, a completely different species and a plant which is still grown, or its varieties, in some Scandinavian gardens. *R. rubrum* has been cultivated for a long time and it is believed that it was used as a parent in some early crosses of this fruit, redcurrant variety Raby Castle, for example. *R. sativum* was originally listed as *R. sativum rubrum,* which may account for the confusion.

*Ribes sativum, rubrum* and *petraeum* are found growing wild in several countries of the northern hemisphere, from Europe through Asia to Manchuria and Siberia in specific regions. The plants appear to have been taken into cultivation in the fifteenth century, although from evidence of contemporary illustrations, it would appear that the cultivated fruits were no larger than those of the wild. Inevitably, selection soon began to take place and larger fruits appeared. All of the three species listed above were used for crossing in one country or another. In the early 1800s named varieties began to be more commonly cultivated. These, naturally, were transported across the world as people moved to other countries, and they are now widely cultivated. Two points are in their favour: red and white currants withstand drought and will tolerate poorer soil conditions far better than will blackcurrants.

Whitecurrants are a variety of the red. They have a distinct flavour and are not so acid as the redcurrants.

## The fruit

Botanically, a juicy, many-seeded berry, red or white according to variety, borne in pendant racemes.

## The plant

A small, deciduous bush or shrub, growing up to about 1.5–1.8 m (5–6 ft) tall, but because of pruning usually seen shorter than this. The leaves are simply, 3- or 5-lobed, with a currant scent, although with nothing like so strong a scent as the blackcurrant. The small flowers are green or green-white and grow in little racemes.

## Cultivation

Ordinary soil is suitable if is well drained and the potash content is sufficient or can be adjusted. The plants respond to an annual boost of some 25 g (1 oz) per square m (square yd) of sulphate of ammonia in the spring and the same quantity of sulphate of potash in the winter. It is important when selecting a site to bear in mind that the plants flower early, and for this reason should be placed where frost cannot damage the blossom. Red and white currants are pruned differently from blackcurrants. Their fruit is produced on the old wood. This means that they should be pruned hard in the winter and again, not so severely, in the summer. In the first case shorten the main or leading shoots by one-third and cut the side shoots back to two or three buds. In summer shorten the side shoots so they carry only five leaves. Leave the main shoots until winter.

These are plants, unlike the blackcurrants, which respond to training. They can be grown as cordons with one, two or three stems, or as fans against walls, fences or wires. In the northern hemisphere they will grow on a north-facing wall or fence. They can also be grown as standards. In a small space you can conveniently grow two tiers, standard fruits at a higher level with bush fruits below.

## Culinary uses

These two kinds of currants can be mixed. Green (i.e. unripe) fruits are delicious when cooked, and surprisingly do not need so much sugar as the riper fruits. Currants are good sweetened with honey. The juice can be used in many kinds of dishes. It makes good, refreshing sherbet.

Rödgröd med Flöde is a Danish sweet which can be adapted for other kinds of fruit. In Scandinavia it is sometimes served for supper.

### Rödgröd med flöde

2 cups redcurrants
1 cup raspberries
¼ cup blackcurrants
¼ cup sago

Stew the fruit in just enough water to cover the bottom of the pan, until it is soft. Strain it through a sieve. Set a little of the juice aside to mix with the sago, about 4–6 tablespoons, and boil the rest. Sweeten to taste. Add the moistened sago and simmer, stirring the mixture well for about 2 minutes. Remove the pan from the heat and continue to stir until it is cool. Pour into individual dishes. Serve with cream and sugar.

Currants can be crystallised or frosted in the same way as grapes, using egg white and sugar.

PRESERVING  Bar de luc is a redcurrant jam made in the French town of that name. In jams, redcurrants can be mixed with black, with cherries, raspberries, loganberries and strawberries.

Red and white currants can be mixed to make Redcurrant Jelly.

### Redcurrant jelly

12 cups currants
2½ cups sugar
2 cups of juice

Currant jelly differs from most in that there is so much pectin in the fruit that the jelly tends to set in the preserving pan before it can be ladled out, so work quickly. This makes about 6 cups of jelly.

An alternative recipe in which the fruit goes further calls for 4–6 cups of water to be added to the fruits before they are strained. Strain once and then return the pulp to the pan, cover with water and strain again. Allow 2 cups of sugar to each 2 cups of water.

For immediate use it is possible to make an uncooked redcurrant jelly. The fruits should be squeezed through muslin to extract all the juice. To each 2 cups add 2 cups of caster sugar which should be warmed in the oven until it is hot to the touch. Mix the juice and sugar until the latter is quite dissolved. Stand it in the refrigerator. The jelly should set in a day.

Redcurrant jelly is used by confectioners as a glaze for red fruits used in pastries and open flans and similar dishes. Melt but do not boil the jelly before brushing it on the fruits.

FREEZING  To freeze the fruits, wash them, remove them from their stems and dry. They can then be frozen as whole berries in syrup, as a dry sugar pack or unsweetened. They can be crushed, using the dry sugar pack and mixing the fruits and sugar together.

The strained juice can be frozen, sweetened or

unsweetened. Warm it before sieving, but do not boil.

BOTTLING   Bottled redcurrants are best processed as juice.

# RHUBARB
*Rheum* species

## Origin

We should first point out that botanically rhubarb is not a fruit but a leaf stem or stalk. However, it is used as a substitute for fruit and is cooked as a fruit or with other fruits in tarts, pies, desserts of many kinds, preserves, pickles and wines. Therefore it deserves recognition in a book of this nature. Nurserymen and seedsmen usually list it under Vegetables.

Rhubarb is a member of the Polygonaceae family and is closely related to the wild dock and garden sorrel. Its name is believed to be a corruption of the old name *Rheon barbarum*. *Rha* is its ancient Greek name.

The rhubarbs, to include all, are species of some 20 distinctive herbaceous plants, all with thick, even woody rhizomes, natives of Siberia, the Himalayas and east Asia. Many are extremely handsome garden plants. Some type of rhubarb or another has been cultivated for centuries. There are records going back to more than 2,000 years BC. Most of these plants were not grown for food, but for the astringent and purgative qualities of their roots. *R. palmatum,* the Turkish or Chinese rhubarb, is still grown and used pharmaceutically, and so is *R. officinale.* Turkey rhubarb is thought to have followed the old spice routes. It seems to have reached Europe via Constantinople, hence its common name. Later it was exported from its native China through Shanghai. In France rhubarb was known in the thirteenth century, but the first species known to have been introduced into Britain, some time before 1573, the year in which it was recorded, was the Siberian or Common rhubarb, *R. rhaponticum.*

The common rhubarb was obviously grown to be used, but it would probably never have become the favourite it is today had it not been that the plant became hybridised and consequently revealed that it possessed latent possibilities for use in the kitchen rather than the pharmacy. It is believed that *R. rhaponticum* was crossed with another species, possibly *R. palmatum,* though some botanists say that it was more likely to have been *R. undulatum* and *R. hybridum,* the latter being a name given to more than one hybrid of different species. So obviously the 'fruit' rhubarb's ancestry is by no means clear.

One can understand the speed with which the new varieties sprouted in gardens everywhere, for rhubarb is easily grown from seed and can be tasted and tested within a year or two, unlike a new fruit which may take years to crop from seed.

It is interesting to note that it was not until the eighteenth century that in Britain and in some other European countries the stem of the plant was used for culinary purposes. It seems to have reached the USA by way of Italy around 1800 and by the mid century it had become accepted there as a pie fruit. One reason for the rhubarb's success, once a good strain had been raised and once it had been discovered that it could be forced to grow out of season, was that it offered an attractive substitute for fruit at a time of year when real fruit was scarce. It could also be forced indoors, a great convenience in winter in places where snow could be deep. In America it seems to have caught on first in New England.

Once the possibilities of rhubarb were appreciated, many varieties were raised, particularly in English gardens. Evidence of this exists in such names as Mitchell's Royal Albert, Randall's Early Prolific, Lyatt's Linnaeus and The Elford, raised by Mr W. Buck. Once the rhubarb became a commercial crop and early forcing an important part of its culture, exclusive varieties were raised by certain specialist growers. These were selected for their earliness, their amenability to forcing, their thin skins and their fine colour.

Rhubarb was quite an important source of home-made wines, which were given such names as Hawke's Champagne and Champagne Early.

As they became known, many rheums were grown for their decorative qualities. Gardeners were fascinated by the enormous leaves and handsome towering spikes of flowers, although some plants of course were strictly utilitarian. In the *Gardener's Assistant,* 1859, Robert Thompson states that 'Rhubarb is cultivated for its leaf stalks', goes on to describe how it is used, and then says, 'For these purposes several species and varieties of Rheum are cultivated.' Among the best, he says, is the Tobolsk rhubarb. After describing other varieties, he tells us that 'The leaf stalks of *R. australe* (syn. *R. emodi*) attain an immense size, but they are unfit for use in consequence of their strongly purgative properties, but the leaves, which are frequently a yard in diameter, are very useful for covering baskets containing vegetables or fruit, and it is only on this account that the species is mentioned here.'

## The 'fruit'

The long, fleshy leaf stalks of *R. rhaponticum* are channelled on the upper side and rounded at the edges. Appearance differs a little according to variety. The skin of the stem is easily peeled off from the base upwards.

## The plant

Rhubarb usually grows to about 1.2 m (4 ft) if the plant is in good condition and on good soil, with large, rounded leaves, deeply cordate at the base, undulate and five-veined. They are deep green, glabrous above and sometimes slightly downy on the underside and on the veins.

Forced rhubarb stems are beautifully coloured, a bright magenta pink, and the blanched leaves are lemon yellow. The leaves of rhubarb are inedible. They have a very high oxalic acid content and can poison some people. The root, known as the crown, is a thick, woody rhizome, and the stems rise individually from this. The flower stems do not rise in their axils but are produced independently. The flowers grow in a tall, dense, leafy, fastigiate panicle, creamy-white or yellow-green, some 1.8–3 m (6–10 ft) high. They should be cut off and prevented from developing so as to keep the strength of the plant in the leaves. The young leaf stalks can be induced to develop rapidly by growing the plant in the dark.

Not only the stems of forced rhubarb are differently coloured from those grown naturally in the open: their leaves also differ. These seldom open very wide and are a bright acid yellow, crinkly and in some ways coral-like. Since these have to be removed when the rhubarb is prepared for cooking, and as they are so very attractive, it seems a waste not to use them in some way.

They look delightful in flower arrangements, especially, for instance, grouped at the base of the bare stems of daffodils and other early spring flowers which are likely also to be forced and so will last just about as long as the rhubarb leaves in a flower arrangement.

## Cultivation

Almost any type of soil will suit rhubarb. It does best in light, rich soil into which plenty of humus has been incorporated. It needs an open and sunny site.

One of the easiest ways of growing rhubarb is from seed. One variety, Glaskin's Perpetual, can be pulled during the same year as sowing, distinct from the others which are best left for another year. Simply sow the seeds outdoors in shallow drills, or indoors in boxes, in spring. Thin or transplant them to 15 cm (6 in) apart, and when they touch transplant them to their final positions about 1 m (3 ft) apart.

Alternatively, well-grown crowns can be bought from the nurseryman or garden centre. In each case you should wait for a year at least after planting before pulling the stalks. Once the plant has become well established it bears prolifically, so give it an opportunity to do so. It is worth while to plant several crowns if you have space and to pull half the plants or alternate ones while leaving the others untouched. This means that when these are really prolific the plants first pulled can rest for a year and then the process can be repeated.

Plant rhubarb with the crowns at soil level. Top dress the soil with well-rotted manure or home-made compost each winter. Lightly fork this into the surface. After four years, lift the crowns, divide them into smaller pieces and replant.

Do not allow the plants to flower. Cut off the flowering stems as soon as they appear. Pull no stems after about mid-summer.

Rhubarb growing in the open ground can be forced in mid-winter by covering the plant in some way, with an upturned bucket or box or a special rhubarb pot. All daylight must be shut out. After this cover has been put in place, cover this in turn with fallen leaves and fresh stable manure, or failing this with home-made compost, anything to add warmth and keep out the cold. The stalks should be ready in about three weeks. The plant can be re-covered to force more stalks, but once used this way the plant should be discarded, for it will take a long time to regain its vigour.

Roots for forcing indoors are best lifted at the beginning of winter and onwards and left on the ground for a few days to be exposed to the frost. Then place the roots close together in deep boxes or plastic bags with a little soil or peat between them under the staging in a warm greenhouse, where they can be kept dark, or in a cellar, even in a spare room, somewhere in a temperature of about 13–24°C (55–75°F). Water a little to begin with so that the soil is just moist, but as growth accelerates give water more freely. Slip the boxes inside waterproof plastic bags if you do not wish the floor to become wet.

Harvest rhubarb by pulling or tugging the stem off the crown; do not break it or cut it off.

## Culinary uses

Rhubarb is a most versatile fruit, used in many kinds of desserts, in puddings, pies and tarts, conserves, jams, pickles, sorbets and wines. Serve it at breakfast, stewed slowly in a light syrup so that the 2.5 cm (1 in) slices are intact and beautifully coloured. It goes well with all kinds of cereals and with milk puddings, including rice. It cooks well in a batter. It can be used in desserts or jams to eke out other fruits for it blends well with most. When made into a compote it can be variously flavoured with lemon, orange, candied peel or ginger. Try unskinned raw rhubarb cut into wafer thin slices and mixed in a salad if you are looking for a sharp and refreshing flavour.

Try Rhubarb with Ginger made like this.

### Rhubarb with ginger

*3 cups rhubarb*
*¾ cup sugar*
*1 cup water*
*level teasp ground ginger*
*¼ cup thinly sliced, preserved, stem ginger*

Prepare the rhubarb, remove the stem bases, cut well below the leaves, wipe the stems and with a clean knife cut into 2.5–5 cm (1–2 in) lengths. Boil the sugar and water together. Mix the ginger with a little of the syrup until it becomes a paste and then add it to the syrup. Take off the heat

and add the rhubarb. Cover the pan and return to heat, allowing it to simmer for some 5 minutes or until the stems are tender but still firm. Lift out the rhubarb and place in a serving dish. Pour on the juice and garnish with ginger. This goes well with cream or vanilla ice-cream.

### Rhubarb crisp

*2 cups prepared rhubarb*
*¼ cup quick cooking oatmeal*
*1 cup plain flour*
*¾ cup brown sugar*
*pinch salt*
*¼ cup butter*
*generous pinch cinnamon*
*½ cup mixed nut meats*

Well butter a baking dish and spread the rhubarb in it. Mix together the other ingredients except the nuts and cover the rhubarb. Sprinkle the nuts on top separately and then bake for 30–45 minutes at 180°C (350°F, gasmark 4). Serve warm, topped with whipped cream.

PRESERVING  To make Rhubarb Sauce, take:

### Rhubarb sauce

*10 cups rhubarb, cut but not peeled*
*10 cups onions, peeled and roughly chopped*
*6 cups brown sugar*
*1 teasp salt*
*2 teasp peppercorns*
*1 teasp chillies*
*1 heaped teasp dry mustard*
*1 heaped teasp curry powder*
*1 tabspn bruised root ginger*
*6 cups brown vinegar*

Simmer all but the sugar together for 1½–2 hours until well amalgamated. Sieve or blend, but if the blender is used tie the spices in muslin before cooking. Stir in the sugar. Boil all together until the liquid is of a creamy consistency. Pour into jars or bottles and seal securely.

FREEZING  For freezing you can pack rhubarb raw, or to help keep it a good colour it can be blanched for 1 minute. It can also be syrup soaked. Purée or the strained juice can be frozen. Thaw the pieces before baking them in pies or tarts.

BOTTLING Rhubarb can be bottled in two ways, soaked or unsoaked in syrup. For the former, remove the stem bases and cut well below the leaves, clean the stems and cut them into even lengths of 2.5–5 cm (1–2 in), using a sharp knife. Pour on hot syrup and let this stand for 8–12 hours. This drives out the air from the stems and the pieces can then be packed more economically. Reduce the syrup to its original volume, for it will have been increased by juice from the fruit, and then pour it into the jars and over the fruit.

It might be worth noting by some that rhubarb reacts with hard water, which means that you may find a slight white deposit in the jars. This is not harmful, nor can it be tasted, but it can be prevented by using water which has been previously boiled.

DRINKS Rhubarb contains rather more oxalic acid than is sometimes palatable and although this can be disguised in cooking it sometimes shows in rhubarb wine. There are two ways of dealing with this problem: either add about 30 g (1 oz) of precipitated chalk, which will fizz or effervesce the acid out, or blend the wine with almost any other, for we all know that one of the virtues of rhubarb as a fruit is that it will submerge its own flavour with that of any other fruit.

**Rhubarb wine**

10 cups rhubarb
16 cups water
7 cups sugar
thinly peeled rind and juice of 1 lemon
1 cup chopped raisins
sherry or sauterne yeast

Clean the stalks but do not peel. Slice thinly. Pour the cold water over the rhubarb and allow it to stand for 5–7 days, stirring daily. Strain and squeeze the pulp as dry as possible. At this stage add the precipitated chalk if considered necessary. Otherwise add the sugar, the chopped raisins, the thin lemon peel and its juice to the liquid. Put all in a pan and heat gently, stirring all the time until it is warm but not hot. Cool to lukewarm and add the activated yeast. Cover and stand in a warm place for 24 hours. Pour into the jar and fix an airlock. Bottle when all fermentation has ceased.

# ROSE HIPS
*Rosa* species

## Origin

The horticulturally important rose family, Rosaceae, a genus of some 125 species, contains 95 which are of Asian origin, 18 American and others from Europe and north-west Africa. The rose occurs throughout the northern hemisphere and is not indigenous to the southern at all, although as one might expect, many roses are now cultivated in countries in this half of the world. Roses grow wild from Alaska and Siberia south to Mexico, south India, the Philippines and Ethiopia.

The wild dog rose, *R. canina* – the term 'dog' comes from the Anglo-Saxon word *dagge* meaning dagger and not dog, and may be an allusion to the spines, or perhaps to the hard wood of the wild rose which was used for dagger handles – produces fruits or hips which are particularly rich in vitamin C. These, even at a time when the value of vitamins was not appreciated, have been collected by country people and used fresh or dried in many ways.

There are varieties: *andegavensis* found wild in Europe, Turkey and Syria and sometimes called *R. andegavensis; blondaeana* found in Sweden and south through Europe and again sometimes known as *R. blondaeana; leucochroa*, growing from southern England to the Alps and Pyrenees, with the synonyms *R. circulosa* and *tomentella*. These all vary from the type by slight botanical differences.

Other species, in many ways perhaps more suitable as garden plants than *R. canina,* also bear suitable fruits. These include the Ramanas rose, or *R. rugosa,* from northern China, Korea and Japan, sometimes called the Japanese rose. It is the parent of many splendid garden roses. There are varieties such as *R. r. alba*, with white flowers; *alba-plena,* with double white flowers; *fimbriata,* with pretty white fringed petals and *plena* which has double purple flowers. *R. villosa*, the Apple rose, grows from northern Europe to Asiatic Turkey. It was once named *R. pomifera.* The variety *duplex,* with semi-double rosy-purple flowers, is also known as the Double Apple rose and as Wolley Dod's rose.

Many varieties of roses bear hips, some very large indeed. All rose hips are edible, but some are richer in flavour and vitamins than others. The reader must experiment and judge for himself.

## The fruit

Botanically, a fleshy receptacle, almost closed at the mouth, enclosing a few to many hard or bony seeds or achenes often covered with tiny yet persistent bristles. The rose hips are attractively coloured in almost all species and varieties. Those of the dog rose are very variable, usually bright scarlet. They can be slightly bottle-shaped, ovoid or globose. They vary from about 1–2.5 cm (½–1 in) long. When the calyx falls off there remains a conspicuous disc on the tip of the fruits.

The fruits of R. rugosa are orange red, although its varieties may have different colours, some being a very dark red. They are about 2.5 cm (1 in) wide, round in shape with flattened poles. The calyx is retained and is very conspicuous, adding to the general attractiveness of the fruits.

R. villosa, the Apple rose, has very bristly dark red fruits, 2–2.5 cm (¾–1 in) wide, which in appearance are not unlike a dark red gooseberry. These are globose and hidden by large bracts. They contain many seeds.

## The plant

R. canina grows to 1.8–2.4 m (6–8 ft), with long, arching branches or briars bearing compound leaves with 5–7 oval to elliptic leaflets. These are glabrous, sometimes very thinly hairy, with pointed ends and sharply toothed margins. The fragrant flowers are white, pale rose to a deep rose pink, sometimes borne in attractive clusters, sometimes solitary, with five heart-shaped petals. The sepals, which can best be seen when they are protecting the buds, are also usually glabrous and feathered or pinnate. These become reflex as the flowers open.

The rugosa species grows to 1.5–2.4 m (5–8 ft) and has stout, bristly branches on which prickles are mixed with the bristles. The leaves give an impression of width and tough texture. There are 5–9 leaflets, each 3–5 cm (1–2 in) long,

M. yamaguchi 1979

wrinkled, shining above but hairy and reticulated on the undersides. The ends are acute and the margins are toothed. These turn a rich golden yellow in autumn. The flowers are large, 7–8 cm (2½–3 in) across, usually solitary, white, rose red, or in varieties variously coloured, and fragrant. The hairy calyx becomes reflexed and is persistent on the fruit. This is the parent of many good garden roses.

*Rosa villosa* grows upright and stiffly for some 1–2 m (3–6 ft) and often sends out many suckers. These and the young growths are often attractively red- or plum-coloured. The branches carry some scattered, straight prickles. The leaves are variable in size, having 5–9 elliptic leaflets, some of which may be as large as 5 cm (2 in). These are attractively resin-scented, grey-green with downy stalks with large stipules at their bases. The flowers are usually only slightly scented. They are 2.5–6 cm (1–2½ in) across, growing sometimes in a few flowered clusters, sometimes solitary. The persistent calyx becomes reflexed.

Hips are delightful in flower arrangements, especially when they can be used with cut roses, even if these are not of the same species or variety. They also look well with all kinds of seasonal flowers, fruits, seed heads and foliage. After use in arrangements the fruits can be washed and used or dried, although they do not remain plump. If they are kept in a vase for a long period they will usually begin to dry naturally, but they should be washed to remove any dust they may have collected. Pat them dry on kitchen paper and allow them to finish drying naturally.

## Cultivation

In small gardens the roses described above can be grown as specimens. *Rosa rugosa* and its varieties make good and attractive hedges. The dog rose will make a formidable barrier, but is greedy of space and so is not suitable for very small gardens.

In whatever way the roses are to be grown, the soil should be well prepared. They need a deep soil which has been well enriched with rotted manure and/or garden compost. Where soils are light, heavy manures need to be incorporated, just as heavy clay soils need to be lightened. It is necessary also to mulch the soil annually with compost or manure. This is best applied during the dormant season, and very lightly forked into the surface in spring.

The roses described above need little pruning – only the removal of old or unproductive wood. Where they are to be kept closely under control, cut almost down to ground level. New growth will be promoted in time by this action. Plants can be raised from seed, but this should be vernalised. *R. rugosa* varieties will not come true to seed. Take cuttings in late autumn to early winter.

## Culinary uses

Rose hips are so full of vitamin C that they deserve to be used by all who grow roses. There are many ways of using them, but it really is important that the seeds are removed from the fruits if they are not to be sieved or strained, because these seeds are covered with tiny but highly throat-irritating hairs. Split the hips and nick out the seeds with a pointed knife and then finally rinse them.

Use the hips in tarts (especially the large and luscious fruits), for compotes and puddings and almost all other desserts, including fools, creams and table jellies, like any other fresh fruit. They are more economically used by being mixed with other fruits, especially apples, pears and rhubarb, or any that seems of the right nature. Dried fruits can also be used for this purpose.

PRESERVING  They can be made into jams, jellies and other preserves used in the following quantities.

### Rose hip preserve base

*4 cups rose hip purée*
*12 cups sugar*
*12 cups water*
*peel and juice of 2 lemons*

In this case again they can be combined with other fruits, rose hip and apple jelly for instance has a fine colour and excellent flavour. Rose hip and rhubarb jam can be made at a time of year when jam stocks might be getting low. Use 1 cup of chopped, seeded hips to 4 cups diced rhubarb, 1 cup water, 2 cups sugar, a pinch of salt and a tablespoon of lemon peel.

Probably more people know of rose hip syrup

than of any other rose hip product because it is fed to babies and infants in many parts of the world. Apart from this, the syrup is also an excellent aid to the cook. For instance, it is a good basis from which to make a fruit salad when fruits are scarce, in winter or between seasons. Apples, pears and oranges combine well, so do prunes, apricots and other dried fruits. Frozen fruits are given a really fresh flavour by being sprinkled with it. Use it also to enrich an apple sauce. Combine it with dried fruits and nut meats to stuff apples, pears and others. Use it in sherbets, alone or combined, half and half with some other fruit juice, even that of a dried fruit.

To make this vitamin-rich Rose Hip Syrup, then, you will need:

### Rose hip syrup

*4 cups rose hips, coarsely minced*
*2 cups sugar*
*9 cups water*

Have 6 cups of the water ready boiling and put the rose hips into it. Bring it to the boil once more, then remove from the heat and allow to rest for a ¼ hour. Pour into a jelly bag and let most of the juice come through. Return the rose hips to the saucepan and add the rest of the water. Bring this to the boil, remove from heat, let it rest for 10 minutes and then strain.

Pour all the juice into a clean saucepan. Let it boil until it is reduced to 3 cups. Add the sugar. Let it boil for another 15 minutes. Pour the hot syrup into clean jars or bottles (small ones are best because the syrup does not keep long once it is opened). Process by boiling for 5 minutes, then remove and seal.

FREEZING  You can freeze rose hips if you first remove the seeds, wash the hips, dry them and contain them in bags. The purée can also be frozen.

BOTTLING  One would imagine that it is hardly necessary to bottle rose hips since the dried fruit take so little trouble or room to store, but they can be bottled in a light syrup.

DRYING  The hips will dry with little trouble. Use them like any other dried fruit.

# ROSELLA
*Hibiscus sabdariffa*

## Origin

A tropical member of a genus of some 150 herbs, shrubs and trees of the mallow family, Malvaceae, this is now widely cultivated in the Far East, Hawaii, the West Indies and Australia for its fruits.

## The fruit

Botanically, not a fruit at all, but the fleshy calyx and bracts which surround the petals of the flower.

## The plant

A rapidly growing annual shrub 1.5–2 m (5–7 ft) tall, attractively ornamental, with red coloration on stems and leaves. The latter are glabrous and lobed and are carried on long stems. The flowers are solitary and almost sessile in the leaf axils. They have yellow petals with which the fleshy calyx and bracts contrast attractively.

## Cultivation

The plant will tolerate most soils so long as they are well drained. A long summer growing period is needed if the plant is to be fully productive. Seed should be sown in the spring. When the seedlings are 15 cm (6 in) high they should be planted 90–120 cm (3–4 ft) apart. If they are in rows, allow 90 cm (3 ft) between the rows. The plants should flower some 6–7 weeks after planting and the first fruits should be ready for harvesting about 3 weeks later.

## Culinary uses

Rosellas should be harvested before the calyces become tough. The fruits can be stewed or used for tarts and other desserts and for drinks. They make excellent jellies, which in turn can be used for various cream desserts, including ice-cream.

To prepare, separate the calyces or husks from the seed pods.

Use in the same way as cranberries to make sauces.

Flowers and young stems can also be used and the leaves are often taken to use as a savoury herb.

PRESERVING  To make Rosella Jam, shell the fruits, putting the fleshy pulp into one saucepan and the seeds into another. Cover the fruit with water and boil until soft. Cover the seeds with water and boil for 10 minutes. Cook and mash one green apple. Strain the liquid from the seeds into the fruit and then add sugar, cup for cup, and bring to the boil. Add the apple and cook until the jam jells.

# ROWAN
*Scorbus aucuparia edulis*

## Origin

Closely related to Chequers, or Service berry, the tree is a native of Europe, including Britain, and western Asia.

## The fruit

The fruits are little pomes, bright red and attractive (birds are very fond of them).

## The plant

The attractive rowan is widely cultivated as an ornamental plant. It has white, almond-scented blossom, and in autumn the heavy clusters of fruit bear down its slender branches. The rowan has a number of varieties: *asplenifolia, integerrima, lanuginosa, moravica, edulis* (this one being grown especially to produce fruit for preserves, and which in turn has its own variety, *laciniata*, with deeply lobed leaflets), *pendula*, and *xanthocarpa* with yellow fruit.

## Cultivation

The plant is hardy and will grow well in most soils, including chalky and limestone types, as long as these are well drained. It needs a sunny position if it is to flower and fruit well.

## Culinary uses

Rowan fruit is rich in pectin and for this reason is used mainly in jellies. Its own flavour is a little bitter for some palates, although there are others who think that the jelly is just the thing with rich meats such as mutton and venison. It is probably more useful when combined in jams with other fruits, particularly apples. It is also used with peaches and pears.

An unusual ketchup can be made by mixing:

### Rowan ketchup

*2 cups of the purée*
*1 cup vinegar*
*2 cups brown sugar*
*2 tabsp mixed pickle spices, tied in muslin*

(Simmer the berries in a little water before sieving them to make the purée.) Bring all to the boil and simmer for 45 minutes to 1 hour. Put into small pots and seal well.

DRINKS   There is a recipe for a rowan liqueur which makes use of nothing but the berries, some white spirit or brandy and a little sugar. It sounds wonderful. The berries, about 1 litre or nearly 2 pt, should be heated in the oven after washing and stemming. Leave them there for half an hour at about 140°C (275°F, gasmark 1), then pour over them about the same volume of white spirit, vodka or brandy and leave for several months. Then strain off the liquid, taste and flavour as you like it with a plain sugar syrup.

# SAPODILLA

*Achras sapota,* syn. *Sapota achras*

## Origin

With just one genus consisting of one species in the Sapotaceae family, the sapodilla's generic name comes from 'achras' which means a kind of pear. The tree is a native of the West Indies and Central America. It has become commercially important because of the milky latex or chicle gum which can be obtained by tapping the bark. This is then coagulated by heating and is used as a basis for chewing gum. For this purpose the plant is cultivated in Mexico, British Honduras and other countries in Central America.

It is also widely cultivated in tropical countries for its fruit, which some say tastes like brown sugar. It has been described as 'melting' with 'the sweet perfumes of honey, jasmine and lily-of-

the-valley'. Many say that it is one of the best native fruits of tropical America. The plant was introduced into Europe in the early 1700s. It is widely cultivated for its fruits throughout tropical countries. One authority suggests that sapodilla has promise for fruit growers in Australia.

Sapodilla is sometimes confused with *A. zapota,* popularly known in America as sapote or mamey sapote, both of which terms closely resemble the common name of sapota. Both the fruits belong to the family Sapotaceae.

In India the sapodilla is the only kind that is of any importance grown solely for its fruits. Sapote (q.v.) has a single seed in each fruit, elliptical in shape, brown, hard, smooth and shiny, but the fruits of the sapodilla have several shining black smooth seeds.

There is still another fruit which bears a similarity in name to the sapodilla, designated in California as the White Sapote, *Casimiroa* (q.v.), and grown extensively in Mexico and perhaps to a lesser extent in Southern California. It belongs to the family Rutaceae. The fruit resembles a quince in shape and has a soft and very sweet pulp, tinged with a slight bitterness. The skin of the fruit is smooth, green to yellowish-green, sometimes with a dash of bright orange or yellow. The leaves are palmate and dark green. Unlike the White Sapote, the sapodilla is grown both for its fruit and for its latex.

The Green Sapote, *Lucuma viride,* and the Yellow Sapote, *L. salicifolia,* are other plants which are likely to be confused with the sapodilla.

There appear to be a number of Indian cultivars of the sapodilla, including a Pot Sapota, said to be especially good for container cultivation.

There is one more in this confused list. It is known only as Sapote, *Calocarpum ammosum* (q.v.), again native to central America.

## The fruit

The sapodilla fruit, usually produced in pairs, varies from round to oval according to the variety, 5–8 cm (2–3½ in) across. Green at first, the skins finally turn a russet brown, thin but rough and corky. The fruit cannot be enjoyed until it is perfectly ripe because the immature fruits contain both tannin and a milky, inedible juice. When fully ripe, the honey-coloured pulp is juicy and translucent, tender and very sweet, with a pleasant flavour and an appetising fragrance. The seeds in the centre of the flesh are hard and shining black.

## The plant

This makes an attractive, large, slow-growing, evergreen tree about 5–18 m (15–60 ft) in height and very beautifully shaped. It has many tough, often horizontal branches which will withstand strong winds and evidently a certain amount of salt spume. The dark green, glabrous leaves are some 5–13 cm (2–5 in) long, with pointed ends and thick midribs borne on slender stalks. The little flowers are inconspicuous, green and slightly brown, much like the main stems in hue. They are carried in clusters in leaf axils near the tips of the shoots. The tree crops when it is about five years old.

## Cultivation

The sapodilla grows best in a well-drained soil which has plenty of organic matter incorporated,

yet it is an adaptable plant and will also grow well in poor soils. It does not object to lime in the soil. Ideally it needs a warm climate with a winter temperature not falling below 18°C (65°F) and in summer not below 24°C (75°F). Young trees can be killed by frosts. It will tolerate very high temperatures by day and, although a tropical plant, it does not need a great deal of humidity. It tolerates dry conditions and will resist strong winds. For this reason it can be used as a windbreak.

Plants can be propagated from seed, but these do not come true to type. They can, however, be used as stocks for grafts when they are a year old. When this is done the latex should be allowed to bleed from the cut before the graft is introduced.

## Culinary uses

The fruit should be gathered and eaten when fully ripe. It is important that the seeds are removed and not swallowed. They are hooked and have been known to lodge painfully in the throat.

To prepare, scoop the flesh from the skins and remove the seeds. This flesh can then be mashed, chopped or blended and used in various creamed dishes. It can also be cut into sections and used in fruit salads, or with mayonnaise or lime juice. The mashed flesh is added to breads and pancakes. In some countries the crushed fruit and juice are boiled to make a syrup or 'honey'.

Sapodilla goes well with coconut.

# SAPOTE
*Calocarpum mammosum*

## Origin

Indigenous to Central America, this is said to have been the fruit that kept Cortés and his army alive on their historic march from Mexico City to Honduras.

## The fruit

This is egg-shaped, 8–15 cm (3–6 in) long, with a brown, scruffy surface. A thick woody ring encloses the pulp and one large seed. The flesh is fine and reddish and its flavour varies from very sweet and rich to flat and insipid.

## The plant

A very large deciduous tree which will grow to 20 m (65 ft) high. It has a thick trunk and limbs and oval leaves up to about 40 cm (16 in) long. Large numbers of flowers are produced from the leaf axils. The fruit takes about eight months to reach maturity from flower. See also Black sapote, Green sapote.

## Cultivation

Its roots appear to enjoy growing in heavy clay soils. It prefers tropical lowlands although it has been known to fruit elsewhere. Cold weather causes damage, but it is said to have withstood a temperature of 2°C (35°F) in Florida.

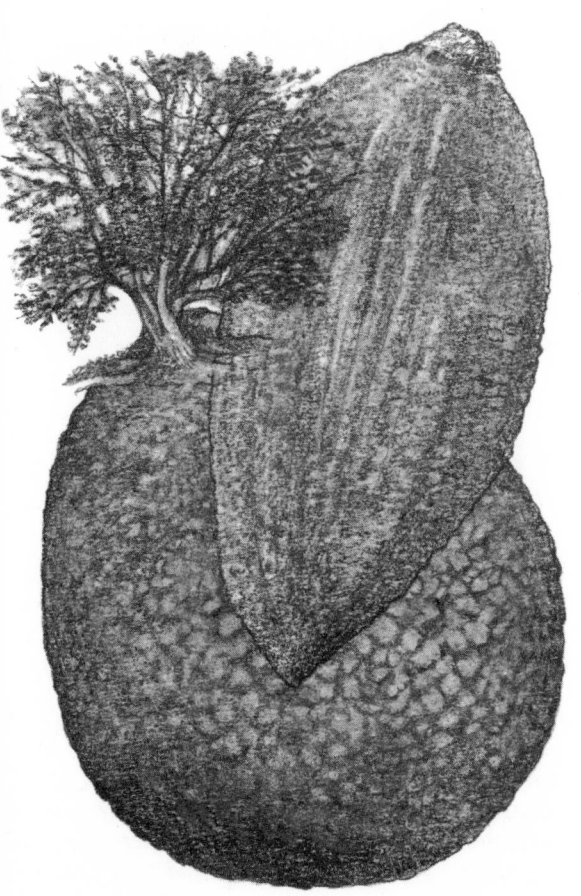

## Culinary uses

The fruit can be eaten fresh and is sweet but lacks acid. However, drinks made from the pulp are popular. It is also used in sherbets, desserts and jams. Unripened fruits can be used as a vegetable.

# SEA BUCKTHORN
*Hippophae rhamnoides*

## Origin

The name is ancient Greek for a prickly spurge. One of only two species of hardy, deciduous trees or shrubs from temperate areas of Europe and Asia, it is a member of the family Elaeagnaceae.

## The fruit

Attractive clusters of bright orange berries, round and about 5–10 mm ($\frac{1}{4}$–$\frac{1}{2}$ in) in diameter, drupe-like, with a hard central nut-like stone. They last well on trees because they are unpalatable to birds.

## The plant

A tall shrub or small tree 3–6 m (10–20 ft) tall, much branched and bearing many spines. Leaves are small, narrow, silvery. The plant is tough and is one of the few that grow well in coastal areas.

## Cultivation

Plants are generally grown from root cuttings or by layering, although suckers will frequently appear in spring and these can be separated and planted up. The plant is dioecious, which means that a male must be provided to 6–8 females in order to produce berries. Generally males produce their flowers before their leaves and females simultaneously.

## Culinary uses

The fruit possesses most of the properties of rose hips and is very rich in vitamin C. It is not pleasant eaten raw, but its juice is good and well worth extracting and preserving. It can be used to make jams, jellies, marmalade and most other dishes for which fruit juices can be employed.

# SOUR SOP
*Annona muricata*

## Origin

See also Cherimoya. The sour sop's native home is tropical America. Its popular name is an allusion to its skin, which has a sour and unpleasing scent. The specific name relates to the rough spines on the skin.

## The fruit

This is very large, 15–23 cm (6–9 in) long, heart-shaped and green, with rows of soft spines running down the skin. It is the largest of the annonaceous fruits, often weighing some 3.5 kg (8 lb). Varieties include Bays and Booth (late ripening), Carter, which sets without pollination, Chaffey and White.

## The plant

Although so far this annona bears the largest fruits of this group, the plant is a small, upright and compact tree, reaching 4.5 m (15 ft) when grown in the open. Its leaves are leathery, glossy dark green on the upperside and rusty beneath. The large flowers are fragrant, with fleshy outer petals, green outside and yellow spotted within.

## Cultivation

As for Cherimoya.

Pick the fruit from the tree while it is still firm. Keep it at room temperature. When it is slightly soft to the touch it is ready to eat. Although the skin is leathery in appearance, it is in fact thin and tender and easily broken, so handle with care.

## Culinary uses

This fruit is more acid than the other annonaceous fruits. The less acid fruit can be cut melonstyle and served raw. The acid fruits are excellent stewed with a little sugar, garnished with sliced banana and served with cream. This is also a good way to use those fruits with a fibrous or cottony pulp.

The texture can be unattractive – someone once described it as 'like slimy cotton wool'. However, its juice is abundant and sweet-acid, and makes good drinks with water or milk. The purée can be used as ice-cream or blended with

vanilla ice-cream to make a fool, in various cream desserts including those in which gelatine is incorporated (as in a cold soufflé for instance), and in sherbets. It can be used to make jellies and other preserves.

# STAR APPLE
*Chrysophyllum cainito*

## Origin

The name comes from 'chrysos', gold, and 'phyllon', a leaf, a reference to the golden undersides of the leaves of this handsome plant. It belongs to the same family as the sapodilla, Sapotaceae, and is one of a genus of about 60 species of tropical evergreen trees, mainly from the American continent, although a few come from Africa, Asia, Australia and the Sandwich Isles. *C. cainito* is from the West Indies and Central America. It was introduced into Britain in 1727 and was immediately popular as a stove plant because of its handsome appearance. It is grown in Cuba, Jamaica, Sri Lanka, Hawaii and Florida, often as an ornamental tree.

## The fruit

The star apple gets its name from its appearance when viewed from the top, where the pattern of the calyx is seen to be star-shaped. The fruit, 5–10 cm (2–4 in) across, is rounded but flattened at the top and base. The skin varies, sometimes green with perhaps a yellow and rose coloration, sometimes a dark purple-brown, according to type. Under the skin, between it and the white translucent flesh, which is divided into eight segments, is a layer of drier flesh. Both this and the inner pulp are edible. The flesh is soft and sweet, the seeds black when ripe.

## The plant

A large tree reaching 9–15 m (30–50 ft), spreading eventually to about 7–8 (25 ft) in an open situation. The branches are covered with silky, rust-coloured down. The long, handsome, compound leaves, 7–12 cm (3–5 in) long, are copper-coloured on the undersides, which gives the tree an attractive appearance when stirred by a breeze. The flowers are small, white and inconspicuous. The plant will fruit in about seven years after being raised from seed, gradually bearing

larger crops until after about ten years it can be expected to produce a crop of several hundred fruits a year.

## Cultivation

The star apple is a tropical plant, which means that it can be grown outdoors only in the warmest of climates. It needs a humid atmosphere and a high temperature for the whole of the year. It will grow on poor soils, but ideally they should be deep, moist and well drained.

The plant is commonly grown from seed. Seedlings also can be used for stock plants for grafting when they are a year old. The seed remains viable for several months, but takes about six weeks or more to germinate.

Do not allow the fruits to become ripe on the tree. As they ripen they lose their glossiness and become slightly wrinkled and soft. It is best to gather them when they reach maturity, when the skin has turned a deep purple, and allow them to ripen indoors.

## Culinary uses

This is not a fully flavoured fruit, but it can be greatly improved if it is mixed with citrus fruits, particularly with orange. It can be blended with orange to make a tasty drink.

It is important not to bite into the skin, as this contains unpalatable gummy latex. Instead, break open the fruit and spoon out the sweet, white, jelly-like flesh. Alternatively, prepare the fruit this way: remove half of the skin by cutting around the equator of the fruit with a sharp knife, incising the rind but not cutting into the flesh below. Then, holding the fruit with its stem end downwards, move the top section about gently so that the rind frees itself from the flesh. The lower section of the rind will eventually come away, taking most of the core with it. The fruit can then be stood on its rind end and served.

# STRAWBERRY
### Fragaria species

## Origin

A member of the rose family, the strawberry gets its generic name from 'fragra', the old Latin name, which itself is derived from 'fragrans', an allusion to the perfume of the fruit. The popular name is also known to be very old and is derived from the Anglo-Saxon *streawberige,* which does not allude in any way to the laying of straw around the plants as some believe, but which means instead that the plant is inclined to stray, by means of layers or runners.

Except for the so-called 'alpine' strawberries, the plants which are grown for fruit today differ greatly from the species. The history of the strawberry is not only quite recent, it is also quite involved and is botanically extremely interesting.

For many centuries in Europe the wild or wood strawberries have been held in high esteem because of their delicious flavour, even though the fruits are tiny, little more than 1 cm ($\frac{1}{2}$ in) across, which obviously means that to gather a useful quantity of them involves long and tedious labour. It appears that it was not until some time in the Middle Ages that they were taken into gardens, where it was discovered that they could be cultivated to produce larger fruit, perhaps twice as large as those growing in the wild.

*F. vesca,* the wild strawberry, the most common of the European species, was planted on a grand scale for King Charles V of France (1364–80) in the royal gardens at the Louvre in Paris. A variety of this species, *F. vesca semperflorens,* which has a larger fruit and, as its name indicates, a longer season of fruiting, became a garden plant in northern European gardens some time in the eighteenth century and joined two others already in cultivation, the musky-scented *F. moschata,* syn. *F. elatior,* known as the Hautboy or Haut bois, and *F. viridis,* a species found growing wild in Europe and northern Asia. Although the occasional plant produces 'large' fruits, it has never been possible to hybridise these species in order to produce significantly larger fruiting sorts. This is because the chromosome count is not compatible within the different species, and one will not pollinate the other.

However, while the wild European species were being cultivated in European gardens, species from the New World were also being sent back. The North American *F. virginiana,* or Scarlet strawberry, still with fairly small but aromatic fruits, was introduced into France in 1624 and five years later into England. It is still grown under the name Little Scarlet and is used in the manufacture of 'alpine' strawberry jams and other conserves. There is a variety, *grandiflora,* known as the Pine strawberry on account of its pineapple flavour.

But the great breakthrough came in 1714, when a French naval officer, Lt Col Amedée François Frézier, engaged in studying (or rather spying on) the fortifications of Chile and Peru, disguised as a merchant and, obviously with a very human passion for strawberries of whatever size, found a large-flowered, large-fruited species growing in Chile and sent or brought some plants back home to Plougastel in Brittany, still, incidentally, one of the most important centres of strawberry cultivation in France. Only five of the plants survived the six-month journey. These were *F. chiloensis,* a species which also grows in other countries along the Pacific seaboard of North and South America, sometimes even in the sand itself. Although these five plants apparently flowered well enough, they did not set fruit. Fortunately it so happened that they were grown among some other species, in particular *F. virginiana,* the North American Scarlet strawberry, a species from which, in their homelands, it would have been separated by geographical barriers. Cross-pollination resulted in fruit and, naturally, in seed, which when sown gave very exciting results. The most celebrated progeny of this marriage was the Fraisier-ananas, the Pineapple strawberry. From this point the development of the modern, large-fruited strawberry can be traced. The memory of the strawberry-loving sailor-spy is perpetuated in the French name for the fruit, *fraisier,* or so goes the legend.

Later, hybridists in England produced many outstanding varieties, but since so little was known about strawberry diseases in the early days, many of these have now died out, although excellent modern varieties abound. Thomas Laxton's Royal Sovereign, bred in 1892, and still thought to be the best ever, has fortunately been retained. Because the strawberry is so universally popular, hybridists in all countries are continually searching for the perfect variety, one which will be highly productive and will easily and quickly become adapted to local conditions and climates. The demand for commercially grown strawberries is so great that apart from the considerable quantities imported, growers in all countries try to prolong or to advance the fruiting season.

There is a group of strawberries known as the Perpetuals or Remontants, and these flower all through summer and produce fruit from late summer until autumn, depending upon the season. Some summer-fruiting strawberries will produce a second crop.

In spite of modern varieties with large fruits, the tiny-fruiting sorts are still extremely popular, probably because of the delicacy of their flavour. In France these are known as *les fraisiers des quatre saisons* and they are divided into two groups, those which produce runners and those which do not. Among these are the popular Baron Solemacher and Alexandria, both without runners, and the prolific and rampant Reine des quatre saisons.

## The fruit

Botanically, a false or accessory fruit, an enlarged fleshy receptacle covered with numerous very small, partly or wholly embedded achenes or seeds. (Technically achenes are not seeds, but are instead one-seeded fruits.) In some sorts of strawberries, the achenes are grouped more closely at one end of the fruit. Achenes tend to drop off alpine strawberries when they are ripe. The alpine strawberries have a different texture from those of the large fruited varieties. Some, Cambridge Favourite for example, resemble the flesh of a ripe banana more than they do the firm flesh of some large varieties. Most also come away from their hulls more easily and they are therefore gathered without the stem and calyx which adhere to the larger strawberries.

The colour, perfume and flavour of the fruits vary according to the species or the variety. The fruits of *F. chiloensis,* pendulous on slender stems, are rosy or white, with white flesh and faint but unmistakable pineapple scent and flavour. The fruits of the variety, the Pine strawberry, *F. c. grandiflora,* are red, with a stronger scent and flavour. *F. moschata*'s fruits, as the name suggests, are musk-scented. They are pink-red, with their achenes grouped more densely towards the tips of the fruits, and these tend to adhere a little more to their calyces than do the others. *F. vesca* has pendulous, small, round, sweet fruits. Its variety, *F. v. semperflorens,* has larger fruit than the type, sometimes oblong, sometimes rounder, sometimes red, sometimes white. The flesh is yellow-white. *F. virginiana* has pendulous, deep red fruit which is tumid or swollen.

The famous variety Royal Sovereign has large, even, conical to wedge-shaped fruits, which are a shining bright scarlet, with paler firm flesh, juicy and full of flavour. It matures early. All varieties differ a little in some way or another.

## The plant

The strawberry is a herbaceous perennial, in which it differs from the other fruits which are produced on bushes and trees. The plant, with rhizomatic roots, has a leafy crown with three-foliate leaves, deep green on the upper side, often lighter coloured, even hairy on the underside, with toothed margins. From the crown also radiate runners, prostrate stems which develop leaf clusters and roots and eventually grow into new plants. The flower stem rises from the plant centre and bears the flowers at its tip.

*F. chiloensis* grows about 30 cm (12 in) high, has leathery wrinkled leaves with silky undersides and white flowers. *F. moschata,* similar in appearance to the above, makes few runners. It has a curious form, long known but uncommon, called the Plymouth strawberry, in which the carpels are replaced by small leafy growths.

*F. vesca,* the wild strawberry, grows only 15–30 cm (6–12 in) high and is generally less robust than the previous types in shape and form. Its variety *semperflorens* is more vigorous, up to 25 cm (10 in) in height. *F. virginiana* spreads quickly and can be used as a ground cover, especially on a sunny bank. It grows about 30 cm (12 in) tall.

Alpine strawberries make attractive edgings to paths and borders, but they should not be planted in dry, sunny places – semi-shade is best. Like other strawberries, the alpines can also be grown in special terracotta strawberry pots or in barrels pierced with holes. In many ways they are better than the large fruiting kinds when grown this way simply because they have a longer season. The so-called 'climbing' strawberries are also good for this purpose, but the runners should be allowed to hang down and root in the holes instead of being supported so that they appear to be climbing.

Strawberries which have been allowed to become thoroughly ripe are far superior in flavour to those which have been picked prematurely. A really ripe fruit has a shine on it, as though its skin was stretched to bursting point. It is also fully coloured in most varieties.

More important than flavour even, is the fact that it has been proved that the quantity of vitamin C in the ripe fruits is increased in relation to the length of time in which the plant has been in the sun during the last few days before the fruit was picked. The vitamin C content is lowered when fruits are cut or damaged.

Pick the fruits with their stems and calyces on. Wash them before you hull them.

## Cultivation

The soil for strawberries should be rich and slightly acid, with plenty of humus to make it moisture-retentive. It should be firm, or if freshly dug should be left to settle for at least a month before planting. It is not advisable to follow these crops with strawberries: strawberries, raspberries, potatoes, tomatoes, peppers, aubergines. This will help to keep them free of certain serious root diseases. Strawberries do best on a sunny site, but alpine varieties prefer partial shade.

The best planting time for strawberries varies from country to country depending upon the severity of the winters and the type of strawberry. Where winters are very cold, planting is best postponed until the spring. Otherwise the recommended practice is that when summer-fruiting strawberries are planted in late summer or autumn they can be allowed to fruit in the following year. When they are planted in spring, any flowers which form should be picked off so that the plant can build up strength for the following year. The yield is then likely to be much heavier than it would have been had the flowers been allowed to spend their energies on forming fruit that same year. The number of runners produced by the plant is also greater.

Perpetual varieties can be planted in autumn or early spring. However, in the year following planting, flowers formed in late spring are best picked off. There should then be a good crop from late summer onwards. After this the flowers should be left on the plant at whatever season they bloom. Fruits are often formed in late autumn. Some of the perpetual fruiting varieties fruit very late and are improved by a cloche cover

if the weather turns cold. Here they are also safer on a warm, raised bed.

If plants are bought by mail order, unpack them as soon as they arrive so they are in good light. Stand the plants in water for ten minutes and if they cannot be planted at once, heel them into moist peat. Place them close together in a small trench with their roots well covered and, as soon as the weather allows, plant them out 30–45 cm (12–18 in) apart, with rows 60 cm (2 ft) apart. See that the roots are not cramped and that the crown of the plant rests at soil level and is not buried. Firm the soil around the plants. In winter the frosts sometimes lift the plants from the soil, so in spring go along the rows firming it on each side of the plants with the feet.

Like raspberries, strawberries benefit from a good watering when the fruits have formed. Try to give a good soaking once a week, or even more if the climate warrants. The only other time to water is after planting, should the weather be so dry that the plants wilt. Usually at or about the same time that the plant fruits, sometimes later, stolons or runners are formed. The stems of these are best cut off close to the parent plant unless you wish to increase your stock, i.e. produce new plants, in which case leave just one or two runners from each plant. These will root into the ground, but it helps considerably to induce them to root instead into pots of good soil from which they can be transplanted when these are filled with roots. Perfectionists take runners only from stock plants which have not been allowed to fruit.

Of the perpetual varieties few produce runners. However, those that do quickly bear flowers and fruit. The best method here is to keep the runners in line with the main plants. The young plants can be lifted and replanted in new soil every third or fourth year to keep the stock rejuvenated.

In most countries it is usually convenient to grow summer strawberries in rows across the garden or alongside a path. It is also a good plan to grow them on a three-year system, which means that each year there is a young, freshly planted row, one that is two years old and one that is three. When the last has finished fruiting, it is dug out and some other crop put in its place, while the new row is made on fresh soil. New or maiden plants are used for this purpose.

Plants in cold countries that have been given winter protection fruit earlier and are usually of a better quality than those which have had to struggle against the elements. Low winter temperatures harm the roots and the crowns and injure the flower buds. Where winters are severe straw can be used to protect the plants and this is usually applied after there have been one or two light frosts, but before the temperature falls as low as, say, −7°C (20°F). If the straw covers the plants before they have become dormant they are likely to rot.

In many countries cloches of various types are used to cover the plants when the cold weather sets in. When the berries have formed is the time to lay down some protective covering over the soil to prevent the fruits becoming splashed and muddy with rain. Traditionally straw is used for this purpose, but make sure that it has not been treated with herbicide at any time. Alternatively black polythene sheeting can be used. Remove the ground cover when the fruit is all harvested. To keep the plants free from pests and diseases it is recommended that immediately after fruiting all the leaves should be cut off each summer-fruiting plant and burned. One of the quickest ways to do this is with a pair of garden shears. With the perpetual fruiting and alpine kinds, cut off the leaves when all fruiting is done, usually in late autumn or early winter.

If you have any doubts about the health of the plants it is best to lift and burn them and begin anew. Strawberries sometimes suffer from virus diseases and one should always buy plants which have been certified virus-free by the Department or Ministry of Agriculture or some similar official body. Symptoms of virus attack are discoloured, misshapen, curly and crinkled leaves. Aphis also can be troublesome but are easily cleared.

## Culinary uses

The fruit is rich in vitamins, particularly C, with $B_1$ and $B_2$ as well as sugars and various minerals. It will not last for long and after two or three days the nutritional value lessens. Should berries become muddied by rain, they can be very lightly scrubbed. The raw fruits can be used a thousand ways – in desserts, jams, ices, drinks, in fact in almost any way one can devise. The purée made from raw fruit is good in ice-creams, mousses and similar dishes. Tart and flan sweets can be filled with the strawberries and then topped with a glaze or with cream.

To gild the lily, as one might say, serve Cardinal Strawberries. Place the hulled strawberries in a dish. Cover them with a purée of ripe raspberries sweetened to taste. Sprinkle with finely chopped, unpeeled almonds.

For Strawberries à la Creole you will need a large pineapple. Wash and clean this and cut off the top to the shoulder. Remove the flesh of top and bottom (best to remove the core first). Avoid damaging the shell. Cut the flesh into pieces and mix it with the strawberries. Together they should provide sufficient to fill the shell. Sprinkle with sugar and kirsch or some other liqueur. Two hours before serving fill the pineapple and put the top back on. To prevent the juice oozing out, seal the joint with butter. Stand the pineapple on ice and keep in a cool place until serving.

Less ambitious are Maltese Strawberry Baskets, a good dish in which to use up some of the smaller berries. Allow a half orange to each person and make each into a basket. Squeeze the juice and pour it over the strawberries, adding a little sugar and a dash of curaçao. Chill. Before serving pile the fruits into the orange skins. Serve on ice.

PRESERVING  Choose the very best specimens of your crop to make Glazed Strawberries. Make a syrup by boiling together in a heavy saucepan:

### Glazed strawberries

*1 cup sugar*
*4 tabsp water*
*½ teasp liquid glucose*

Bring the syrup to the boil without stirring. Brush sides of pan with brush dipped in boiling water to remove any sugar crystals which may form. Boil to hard crack stage. Tilt pan gently so that the bubbles subside. Holding the strawberry by its stalk, dip it and swirl it around in the syrup until it is coated, a matter of moments. Have ready an oiled slab or dish and place fruit on this to set, which usually takes about 5 minutes. Do not serve inside 2 hours. If the glazed berries are to be kept, store between waxed papers.

FREEZING   Some strawberries collapse when they are frozen, which is why they are often halved or sliced, although this affects the vitamin content. Some varieties behave better than others, but freeze any strawberries as quickly as possible after picking. Wash them, but do not pull out the hulls until they have been drained and are ready to go into the freezer. They are best open frozen before being packed in bags. We tend to freeze the smaller samples of a long-fruited crop, a few whole in limited lots for garnishing and the mass as a purée.

We find that our little alpine strawberries freeze the best of all; we freeze them in small lots, of 1 cup or less, quite enough for a sweet for four. These are taken from the freezer, thawed, mashed and added to cream whipped with a little vanilla-flavoured icing sugar and a dash of kirsch. The cream is then put into individual glasses and chilled. If we want it to go just a little further, we crumble a small macaroon or ratafia cake in the base of the glass, soak it with the liqueur and top it with the 'ambrosia'.

BOTTLING   Bottled strawberries are not really very satisfactory. Not only do they shrink considerably when the air is driven out of them, but they also lose colour and no longer look appetising, although it is possible to use food colouring in the syrup. Some varieties are a little better than others, so it is worth experimenting on a small scale to see how yours behave.

DRINKS   The flavour of strawberries appears to be too delicate to be captured in drinks of any kinds except those that make use of the artificial concentrates or essences. There is the German *Erdbeerlikor* and there are the French *Fraise* and *Fraisia*, none of which are particularly strawberry-like and all of which are expensive.

On this basis then, let us first go the whole way and suggest a Strawberry Wine Cup.

### Strawberry wine cup

*2 cups strawberries*
*2 cups brandy*
*1 bottle white wine*
*1 bottle champagne*
*sugar optional*

Steep the strawberries in the wine and brandy for two hours. At the end of this time pour into a punch bowl or a claret jug, add ice and the champagne, even sugar if required. Although this may appear to be a somewhat extravagant recipe, may we point out that it is possible with it to make use of small, late season, and even damaged strawberries!

For those readers who are less than millionaires, try adding equal parts of water to strawberries, mixing and mashing well and leaving overnight. Then strain, add again an equal part of sugar, stir until dissolved and let stand for four days. Put in a suitable jar or barrel and keep for six months or so before bottling.

A fermented Strawberry wine is made from:

### Strawberry wine

*16 cups strawberries*
*7 cups sugar*
*1 cup raisins*
*16 cups boiling water*
*yeast*

Place strawberries and water in a preserving pan, bring to the boil and simmer quietly for about 15 minutes. Strain onto the sugar and raisins, stir, and when lukewarm add the yeast. Leave for 24 hours, then pour into a fermenting jar with an airlock. When fermentation finishes, siphon off into clean bottles.

# SUGAR APPLE
*Annona squamosa*

## Origin

See Cherimoya. Many people believe this to be the true custard apple. The pale yellow, sweet, pleasantly flavoured flesh or pulp from which sherbets have long been made adds credence to this belief. It was introduced into Europe from tropical America in 1739. It has long been grown in northern countries as a stove plant, where it has fruited and been enjoyed by a select few. It is grown as a garden tree in Central America and in some parts of the near east and in Queensland. It is a popular fruit in India.

## The fruit

The sugar apple is conical or heart-shaped like

The fruit is borne on both old and new wood. After the leaf fall the tree is dormant for about two months.

### Cultivation

Outdoors it thrives in a fairly hot, dry temperature and in a sandy to medium loam, needing much the same cultivation as cherimoya.

### Culinary uses

The fruit can be eaten raw in fruit salads and used to flavour various desserts, including ice-cream. A refreshing drink can be made by mixing the pulped or blended flesh with five times its volume of water and chilling the mixture.

# TAMARIND TREE
*Tamarindus indica*

### Origin

The plant is believed to be a native of Asia and Africa. Its name is a combination of the Arabic *tamr* and the Indian *hind*. The plant is a tropical member of the pea family, Leguminoceae, and is the only member of its genus. It was once listed as *T. officinalis,* and it certainly has been of service to man, for most parts of the plant are economically useful – the bark, wood, leaves, flowers, seed pods and seeds. It is believed that it was the Arabs who brought the plant from India into Europe. The date of its introduction into tropical America is uncertain. It is now widely cultivated, mainly for its fruit, which is used as a flavouring. In some countries the leaves and flowers are also eaten. It is a familiar tree in the West Indies and the Bahamas.

### The fruit

A strap-shaped pod, 8–15 cm (3–6 in) long and about 2.5 cm (1 in) wide, containing 3–10 black seeds. These contain an acid pulp with a high concentration of citric, malic, oxalic and tartaric acids, of fructose, glucose and sucrose and of potash and pectin. When mature, the pods are a dark chocolate brown, and sweet.

most of the fruits of this genus, and is 5–8 cm (2–3 in) in diameter. While it is young and still yellow-green it appears to be scaly. This is due to the loosely adhering carpels which later drop off as the fruit ripens. The fruit also has a bloom on the skin. The firm flesh is pale yellow, sometimes white and custard-like and very sweet, hence the name. It contains a greater number of seeds than the custard apple.

### The plant

A bushy, deciduous tree of about 4.5–6 m (15–20 ft), slow-growing. The young growth is downy at first and the leaf stalks remain downy, but the leaves become a pale green with tiny dots on both surfaces. These are shed immediately after the fruit has ripened. The flowers, in terminal clusters of two or four, are very similar to those of the custard apple, *A. reticulata*. They grow on nodding stalks and are fleshy, olive green to yellow without and sometimes purple hued with a darker blotch within.

## The plant

This makes a tree reaching 12–18 m (40–60 ft), with attractive pinnate leaves consisting of 20–40 opposite leaflets. Unlike many others of this family it has no spines. The little flowers, 12 mm (½ in) in length, are yellow striped with red and they grow in racemes in which only the upper three are developed.

## Culinary uses

The fruit or pod is used in many ways. When it is young and tender it is acid and is then used in some countries as a seasoning in meat and fish dishes and with rice. When the pod is fully grown, the pulp is described as being like a very acid apple butter, both in appearance and taste. At this stage the pods are shelled and the pulp is eaten out of hand. When the pods are fully grown but not ripe, it is said that local children, who call them 'swells', bake the fruits by covering them with hot coals until the shells burst and the pulp is bubbling and foaming. The skin is then easily peeled off (though no doubt with some burned finger tips), and the popped tamarinds are dipped in seasoning – one authority says salt mixed with wood ashes! – and eaten hot.

Some of the pods are allowed to dry on the tree. They can then be shelled and the ripe pulp cooked in various ways, usually in sugar or in a syrup.

Tamarind juice is widely used to make a drink much like lemonade. Indeed, where in a recipe tamarind juice is prescribed, lemon may be substituted. It has not quite the same distinctive flavour, but it is a good substitute. The simplest way to obtain the juice is to blend the tamarinds and sieve the pulp.

Tamarind Syrup is simply made by boiling together and then simmering for 45 minutes:

### Tamarind syrup

½ cup juice
1 cup sugar
2 cups water

Strain and cool. Use as a cordial, best served with ice.

The juice is often used in curry dishes and the dried pods are infused in water for making curry sauce. It is also used for marinating fish.

PRESERVING  Tamarind Chutney is made with mature but green fruits.

### Tamarind chutney

1 cup tamarinds, sliced
1 tabspn English mustard powder
¼ cup green ginger
½ cup chilli
½ teasp salt
½ cup garlic
1 cup sugar

Pound all the ingredients together until they form a paste. Put into small jars.

# TANGERINE
*Citrus reticulata,* syn. *C. nobilis deliciosa*

## Origin

As one of its popular names hints, this fruit is from the Far East, probably originating in China or Indo-China. It is found also in the Philippines. There is often confusion over the various names these small, loose-skinned oranges have been given. There appears to be no fundamental difference between tangerines and mandarins, as there is thought to be by some people, merely that one is a variety. Generally speaking, the term Tangerine is applied to varieties which produce deep orange or scarlet fruits. Mandarin is the older name. Clementine, another variety, is also known as the Algerian Tangerine. King Orange and Satsuma are also names originally given to varieties which have become accepted, although they describe quite different fruits. The Calamondin is another variety. This is often used as a rootstock because of its resistance to certain diseases. It is listed separately. There is a variety, *C. r. austera,* which produces the Sour Mandarin. Like many of its kind, the Mandarin crosses easily, thus we have Tangelo, which is a cross between *C. reticulata* and *C. paradisi,* a fruit which is widely grown in New Zealand. San Jacinta tangelos are pear-shaped. Yuza, cultivated mainly in China and Japan, with acid fruits, is from a cross between *C. reticulata,* var. *austera* and *C. ichangensis,* a wild species native to China. The Ugli is a tangerine-grapefruit hybrid.

The tangerine is grown extensively in some

regions. The plant has more resistance to cold than the orange, which means that tangerines can be grown a little further to the north in some countries – Spain, China and Japan, for example. The most important areas of commercial production are the USA, South Africa, parts of France and Algeria and southern Europe.

## The fruit

Botanically, a berry. Tangerines are generally smaller than oranges. Their skins are a deeper colour and they are more easily detached from the segmented flesh inside, which is usually well coloured, very sweet and juicy, with the characteristic flavour of tangerine. The seeds are smaller and pointed at one end. Satsuma varieties tend either to be seedless or almost so.

## The plant

A small, spiny, evergreen tree, somewhat variable in its habit, but generally small, with slender branches which become very pendulous with the weight of fruit. The leaves are a glossy green and when crushed they have the same scent as the fruit. The perfumed flowers are borne singly or in clusters in the leaf axils of the preceding growth. Under ideal conditions these open at more than one time of year, elsewhere only once.

## Cultivation

As for citrus generally (see the section on Orange). The plant is more resistant to the cold than the sweet orange, mainly because when the weather chills it stops growing and becomes dormant. It can be grown in pots.

## Culinary uses

Tangerines can be used in any way as an orange. They lend themselves more agreeably to certain sweets because of their distinctive flavour, and are particularly good in or with drinks. The tiny segments make good crystallised fruits.

Ortanique, a Jamaican tangerine-orange hybrid, contains more juice but has a tougher skin.

Ugli can be used as grapefruit. These fruits are good when baked whole in the coals of a barbecue, cut open when roasted and sprinkled with sugar or a liqueur. They can also be oven-baked.

# TREE TOMATO
*Cyphomandra betacea*

## Origin

The plant belongs to the same family as the tomato and the physalis, the Solanaceae. It is a fairly new fruit on the world scene. Actually the genus has about 30 species, but this seems to be the only one well known. Tamarillo is a native of South America (southern Brazil), and was first classified as *Solanum fragrans*. It is now grown in many tropical and sub-tropical countries for its fruits. New Zealand growers are producing small crops which are sold as fresh fruit and also processed. It has been sugested as a potential crop for Australia. It is ideally suited to small gardens in tropical and sub-tropical climates, being neat, convenient and easily tended.

## The fruit

Botanically, a many-seeded berry. The fruits are egg-shaped, two-celled like tomatoes and about 5 cm (2 in) long. There appear to be three types, with yellow, red and dark red fruits when ripe. Of these the yellow fruits are the most palatable, being sweet and pleasantly sub-acid. The red fruits have a harsher flavour. The flesh is firm and lighter in colour than the skin. The seeds are dark and although the peel or rind is tough, it can easily be peeled away.

## The plant

An erect, branching, shrubby, soft-wooded, fast-growing evergreen, reaching up to about 4 m (13 ft). It has fleshy, cordate-ovate leaves, similar to those of the physalis, which are softly hairy. These have an unpleasant scent when bruised. They are 15–20 cm (6–8 in) in length. The fragrant flowers grow clustered, or sometimes in long, pendulous racemes. These are continuously produced, with their peak blossoming times in spring and autumn. The individual flowers, of characteristic solanum shape, are purple in bud, opening to green-pink, with a purple stripe on the back of each segment.

## Cultivation

Tamarillo needs a rich, moist, well-drained soil. The plant will tolerate neither waterlogging nor drought. Being shallow-growing, the roots are easily damaged if the soil is disturbed. For this reason, and to keep adequate moisture at the plant's roots, heavy mulching is recommended. If the roots become too dry or are damaged in some way the fruit will not mature but will drop. It is advisable to water regularly and to give extra water during very dry periods. Plant foods are also helpful. When climates are a little below the sub-tropical, the plants can be given protection and extra warmth by planting them against a wall or fence.

The tree tomato can be propagated from seed and the seedlings usually come true to type. They grow quite fast and unbranched, reaching as high as some 2 m (6 ft) before branching. Plants raised from cuttings produce lower, bushier plants. Cuttings should be taken in spring or autumn, 60–90 cm (2–3 ft) long.

Where plants are grown in rows they should be set about 3 m (10 ft) apart.

Plants grown in a greenhouse will need warm conditions in winter. At this season it is better not to water the plant too freely but to allow it to rest for a while. This will keep it a little warmer and help prevent any form of root rot. In summer, however, it will need abundant water. Where a warm and protected place can be found for it, the potted tree tomato can be taken out of the greenhouse in the summer. It should be brought indoors, however, before the evenings become too cold.

Seeds should be sown in a high temperature of some 24–29°C (75–85°F) in spring. Cuttings need enclosed conditions and bottom heat to take well.

### Culinary uses

The flavour of this fruit is reminiscent of both the tomato and the Cape gooseberry and it can be used in any way adopted for these two. It can be eaten raw, and is good in fruit salads, compotes or preserved as jam.

PRESERVING Tree Tomato Jam can be made using the following: 6 cups tree tomatoes, 6 cups sugar, 5 cups boiling water, 2 lemons using both cut flesh and finely shredded peel. Pour the water on the tomatoes and let it stand for 5 minutes, then pour the water back into the pan. Skin the fruit and cut it up. Discard the peel and return the flesh to the pan. Add the lemon flesh and peel to the tomatoes. Boil until the fruit is tender, about

30 minutes. Add the sugar and boil until the jam sets when tested. Remove from heat and skim if necessary. Allow the jam to cool for 5 minutes or so and then pour into jars. This recipe can also be used for Cape gooseberries.

# WATER MELON
*Citrullus vulgaris*, syn. *Cucumis citrullus*, *Cucurbita citrullus*

### Origin

The generic name for this plant does not seem well chosen, since it comes from citrus and is believed to be an allusion to the orange-like fruits, obviously from some other species and not the one under discussion. The water melon, though of another genus, is of the same family as the other kinds of melons mentioned earlier, the Cucurbitaceae. In its genus there are only four species, all tendril-climbing herbaceous plants which are natives of Africa, Asia and Mediterranean regions. There is some controversy over which is the homeland of *C. vulgaris,* some saying tropical Africa and perhaps India, while others, including the great Linnaeus, believe that it originated in southern Italy. Whatever the case, the fact is that this delicious and refreshing fruit is now cultivated in many regions of the world, in warm, temperate, sub-tropical and tropical countries.

*Citrullus vulgaris* has two very different varieties. *C. v. amarus* is also known as the bitter apple of South Africa and the sweet water melon under discussion is var. *caffer*. From this second have been derived many cultivars. The fruit is particularly popular in hot countries because of its refreshing, thirst-quenching, juicy flesh and, just as with all fruits which enjoy a wide popularity, there has been a great deal of plant breeding in order to produce suitable commercial varieties. Today's water melons differ greatly from those grown and marketed only a few decades ago.

Some of the new $F_1$ hybrids have few or no seeds. These may not be so popular in regions where water melon seeds, oily and nutritious, are eaten and enjoyed. Modern cultivars can be roughly divided into groups according to their characteristics, although it is likely that before long even different ones will come along to join them. There are those with relatively small, round fruits, weighing 2.7–4.5 kg (6–10 lb) such as Sugar Baby, grown in Israel and exported to Europe, and the American New Hampshire Midget. Those with larger fruits – twice, three times or even four times the weight of the first group – though still round, include such varieties as Black Diamond and Florida Giant. Charleston Grey and Klondike Striped have very large ovoid or oblong fruits. There is now also a small ovoid fruit, with few seeds and a fragrant flesh known as Sweetmeat.

## The fruit

Botanically, a polymorphic berry, usually almost globular, with a smooth, hard, green or yellow rind. The fruit of the species is often about 25 cm (10 in) in diameter. The flesh is sometimes red, sometimes yellow or paler. Cultivars differ from this and from each other, as we have seen. Sugar Baby, for instance, has a dark green rind which is pruinose or powdered. Others have variegated, patterned rinds, some with longitudinal dark green markings on a light green background, others faintly mottled in dark green. The flesh also varies from a soft magenta pink through to a deep, rich red. There is a light-coloured zone below the rind, and this is edible.

## The plant

An annual, herbaceous, tendril-climbing, tender plant with shoots reaching 1.8–3 m (6–10 ft). The glabrous, or somewhat hairy bright green leaves are deeply lobed in three or five parts, with the lobes themselves often subdivided. The solitary, five-partite flowers, 4 cm (1½ in) across, are unisexual, like those of other members of this family. They grow in the leaf axils. Usually three to five fruits are produced on a plant.

## Cultivation

Generally speaking, the cultivation of the water melon is much the same as for other melons, but with one great difference: it cannot be grown outdoors except where the climate is equable and the summers long and hot. It cannot be grown in frames and under cloches. It can be grown in a greenhouse, but in this case it is not so successful as the other melon types. In northern latitudes water melon production begins in the south of France and goes on into Italy and the Mediterranean countries and thence eastwards and southwards.

In warm climates where there is also a very heavy rainfall, cultivation is not always successful, mainly because the plants are inclined to suffer from fungoid diseases in too moist an environment. Some growers recommend that under these circumstances less compost and more fertiliser such as superphosphate and sulphate of potash be used, since these tend to promote a tougher, less lush growth than the first.

Another difference in the method of cultivation is that the shoots of the water melon are not pinched out as directed for the other melon types.

The plants are usually allowed to trail over the ground in the manner of marrows. However, their fruits should not be left on the soil surface but should be raised. Commercial growers use a small platform of slatted wood for this purpose. This enables the air to flow freely around the fruits.

Where predators are a nuisance, the female flowers can be enveloped inside muslin bags after they have been hand-pollinated. The bag should be large enough to remain on until the fruit ripens.

## Culinary uses

This is an ideal fruit for slimmers, for its calorific value is low. It contains about 92 per cent water and 3 or 4 per cent carbohydrates, but it has a good vitamin content. It also has diuretic properties.

It is no wonder that it is so much esteemed in hot countries as a refreshing fruit, for a slice is as good as a drink. Although it is not quite so substantial, the water melon can be served in most ways that the other melons are presented. One great advantage is its colour, an appetising rosy red. Water melon dice or balls bring beauty to a fruit salad.

Nothing of a water melon need be wasted – even the seeds are oily and nutritious. The white or pale green rind immediately under the skin and hard compared with the rosy flesh, can be saved and cooked in various ways. Like the unripe melons, this rind can be cooked in the same way as any squash, i.e. steamed and served with butter, seasoning or nutmeg. It is this rind also which is used for jams, pickles and for crystallising.

Before the rind is used, the entire shell of the melon can be employed as a vessel in the manner described earlier for other types of melon. It is possible to cut it in such a way that a basket is formed.

Water Melon and Onion Slices makes an unusual salad dish. Use a melon baller to make water melon rounds. Mix with thin onion rings, and serve with French dressing or lemon juice.

PRESERVING   To make Water Melon Pickle with Ginger, cut the rind into strips or circles. Soak overnight in cold water and then drain. Put the rind in a saucepan and boil it rapidly for about 10 minutes, until it is tender but not soft. Drain, but keep the water.

### Water melon pickle with ginger

*to every 2 cups of rind use:*
*2 cups of sugar*
*2 cups water melon water*
*1 tabspn root ginger, preserved or chopped ginger*
*1 large lemon, thinly sliced and seeded*

Boil the water and sugar together until they make heavy syrup. Add the ginger and lemon towards the end of the boiling, after 10 minutes. Add the water melon. Bring again to boiling point and then simmer for 5 minutes. Have ready hot jars. Lift out the water melon and fill these. Reboil the syrup and let it go on until it is thick. Cover the rind in the jars with it while it is hot. Seal immediately.

To make Water Melon Jam, peel the melon thinly, carefully separating the pink flesh from the white and saving the pink for dessert. Cut the white into small cubes and soak in salted water for about 5 hours. Drain and wash in cold water. Weigh and place in a greased pan with the shredded slices of 3 oranges and 3 lemons. Bring to the boil and simmer slowly until tender. Add one cup of sugar to each cup of pulp. Boil rapidly until it jells.

Water melon rind can be crystallised like other fruits. Boil it twice, draining the rind as it comes to the boil. The third time boil until it is tender, about 20 minutes and then crystallise.

# INDEX

# INDEX